RUSSIA IN THE WORKS OF
Rainer Maria Rilke

RUSSIA IN THE WORKS OF

Rainer Maria Rilke

Patricia Pollock Brodsky

WAYNE STATE UNIVERSITY PRESS
DETROIT 1984

COPYRIGHT © 1984 BY WAYNE STATE UNIVERSITY PRESS,
DETROIT, MICHIGAN 48202.
All rights are reserved.
No part of this book may be reproduced without formal permission.

•

Library of Congress Cataloging in Publication Data
Brodsky, Patricia Pollock, 1941–
   Russia in the works of Rainer Maria Rilke.
   Bibliography: p.
   Includes index.
   1. Rilke, Rainer Maria, 1875–1926—Knowledge—Soviet Union. 2. Soviet Union in literature. 3. Literature, Comparative—German and Russian. 4. Literature, Comparative—Russian and German. I. Title.
PT2635.I65Z6288   1984   831'.912   84-7557
ISBN 0-8143-1757-X

•

Grateful acknowledgment is made to the following for permission to use the following copyrighted material:
   Comparative Literature, for excerpts from Patricia Pollock Brodsky, "Russia in Rilke's *Das Buch der Bilder,*" Vol. 29 (1977), pp. 313–27.
   The Germanic Review, for excerpts from Patricia Pollock Brodsky, "The Russian Source of Rilke's 'Wie der Verrat nach Russland kam,' " Vol. 54, No. 2 (Spring 1979), pp. 72–77.
   Germano-Slavica, for excerpts from Patricia Pollock Brodsky, "Rilke and Russian Art," Vol. 2, No. 6 (Fall 1978), pp. 411–26.
   Insel Verlag, for excerpts from Rainer Maria Rilke, *Briefe an einen jungen Dichter,* Insel Bücherei No. 406; *Briefe aus den Jahren 1904 bis 1907,* 1939, Vol. II of *Gesammelte Briefe,* edited by Ruth Sieber-Rilke and Carl Sieber, 6 vols., 1936–40; *Briefe aus den Jahren 1906 bis 1907,* 1930; *Rainer Maria Rilke—Lou Andreas-Salomé. Briefwechsel,* edited by Ernst Pfeiffer, 1952; and *Sämtliche Werke,* edited by Ruth Sieber-Rilke and Ernst Zinn, 6 vols., 1955–66.
   Innsbrucker Beiträge zur Kulturwissenschaft, for excerpts from Patricia Pollock Brodsky, "Rilke's Relation to Russian Painting," Sonderheft 51, 1981.
   Nauka Publishing House, for excerpts from A. S. Pushkin, "Skupoj rytsar," in *Polnoe sobranie sočinenij v desjati tomax,* Vol. 5, 1964, p. 342.
   Penguin Books, Ltd., for excerpts from Fedor Tyutchev, "Silentium," in *The Penguin Book of Russian Verse,* edited by Dimitri Obolensky (The Penguin Poets, rev. ed., 1965), pp. 132–33. Copyright © Dimitri Obolensky, 1962, 1965. Reprinted by permission of Penguin Books, Ltd.

He was under the strong influence of the Russian people as Dostoevsky portrayed them. . . . Many of the impressions were reflected in his art, as polished Bohemian glass renders the image of reality in abundant transformations, enriching it in its color and form.
    Heinrich Vogeler on Rilke

•

It is becoming clearer and clearer to me that Russia is my homeland, and everything else is—alien.
    Rainer Maria Rilke
    Letter to N. A. Tolstoy, 1902

•

What do I owe Russia—it made me what I am, I emerge internally from there, the whole homeland of my instinct, all my inner resources are there!
    Rainer Maria Rilke
    Letter to Leopold von Schlözer, 1920

Contents

Preface		9
Note on the Text		11
Acknowledgments		13
1.	Teachers and Models	15
2.	First Fruits: Russia in the Dramas, Translations, and Early Scattered Works	25
3.	The Aesthetic Religion: *Das Stunden-Buch* and the Essays on Art	59
4.	Russia as a Source of Imagery: *Das Buch der Bilder*	84
5.	God as Artist and Prodigal Son: *Die Geschichten vom lieben Gott*	96
6.	The Search for Self: *Die Aufzeichnungen des Malte Laurids Brigge*	132
7.	Death and Authenticity: *Malte Laurids Brigge*	153
8.	Subtle Echoes: The Middle and Late Poems	177
Abbreviations		210
Notes		212
Selected Bibliography		232
Index		256

Preface

In the spring of 1899 and again in 1900 Rainer Maria Rilke made extensive trips to Russia, each time in the company of the Russian-born writer Lou Andreas-Salomé. In preparation for these trips he began studying Russian and made rapid progress. His Russian was far from perfect, but it was sufficient to enable him to read widely in Russian literature and to write letters and a few marred but recognizably Rilkean poems in the language. Rilke's biographers and critics duly note these facts and typically devote a brief chapter to them. Many of these accounts are anecdotal, concentrating on his travels and his meetings with Russian contemporaries. Others accord Russia a greater significance in Rilke's life, but focus only on its supposed religious importance for him. But in general his Russian experience is treated as a somewhat quaint excursion into the exotic, which captured the young poet's imagination for a time, but then faded and was replaced by other and, by implication, more important concerns. Very few critics have seriously pursued the theme of Russia through Rilke's oeuvre. Fewer still recognize that this theme plays an important role in all his major works from 1899 onward; indeed, there exists a certain amount of resistance to this idea. No study to date attempts to discover the literary products of Rilke's intense involvement with Russia.

The present study reevaluates Rilke's writings in the light of this involvement. To do so it poses the question: where in Rilke's works have Russian literature, art, history, folklore, or Russian reality as he perceived it borne fruit as allusion, motif, metaphor, or philosophical attitude? The search for answers includes every one of Rilke's major works written after the autumn of 1899, as well as a number of scattered and lesser-known works. The reader is asked to keep several things in mind. First, the concern of this book is primarily with what Rilke wrote. Naturally a certain amount of biographical and historical material will be required to provide a convincing context, but the emphasis here will be on the literary texts and on the poetic transformation of experience into literature. Second, my intention is not to provide a complete analysis of each work discussed. Rather, I offer a reinterpretation of some works, and add to the possibilities for understanding others, by providing new information, making new connections, and in general challenging the limitations of traditional readings. Finally, readers will perceive the transmutations which Russia and its culture have undergone in Rilke's hands. Rilke was a poet, not a historian. The Russia that appears in his works is not the real, historical entity, nor was it intended to be. It is the fictional product of a poetic transformation, at times merely the suggestive echo of a perceived reality; and it is precisely this transformation that interests us here.

Note on the Text

This study focuses on a twenty-three-year segment of Rilke's creative life, from 1899 until 1922. The works written during this period are examined in roughly chronological order. The chapters overlap to a certain extent, since the works themselves overlap. Rilke would often begin a new set of poems or stories while still working on, refining, or revising an old one. For example, the *Geschichten* were written in 1899 and revised in 1904; the poems of the *Stunden-Buch* were written over a period extending from 1899 to 1905; the *Buch der Bilder* contains poems from 1898 to 1906; the *Neue Gedichte* stretch from 1903 to 1908; and *Malte Laurids Brigge* was written between 1904 and 1910. Since the *Neue Gedichte* and the poems written after them, including the last great cycles, the *Duineser Elegien* and the *Sonette an Orpheus,* show the fewest Russian influences, I have grouped them together in the final chapter. But though they overlap, each work represents a discrete whole, with its own peculiar approach and mood. In almost all cases the texts used are those from the excellent standard edition, the Insel Verlag's six-volume *Sämtliche Werke* (*Complete Works*), published between 1955 and 1966 under the direction of Ruth Sieber-Rilke and Ernst Zinn. Works contained in the *Sämtliche Werke* are cited in the text in parentheses by volume and page number only.

I have also utilized some of the many thousands of letters Rilke wrote. Two problems were involved here. Rilke's correspondence ranks among the greatest in modern German literature, both in volume and in intrinsic interest. His letters, particularly those to Lou, to his wife, Clara Westhoff, and to his long-time friends Nanny Wunderly-Volkart and Marie von Thurn und Taxis, are profoundly personal. But they also often served as rough drafts or variants of his literary works, as well as a sort of podium for his public persona. The reader of Rilke's letters must keep this dual function in mind. The editions of the letters present another problem. The letters were first edited, and often expurgated, by Rilke's daughter, Ruth Sieber-Rilke, and her husband, Carl Sieber. They published both a six-volume *Gesammelte Briefe* (*Collected Letters*) and numerous individual volumes which often, but not always, overlap with the contents of the *Gesammelte Briefe*. For example, a given letter might be found in the *Gesammelte Briefe* only, in an individual volume only, or in both. There have been, in addition, numerous editions of Rilke's correspondence edited by persons other than the Siebers. The Abbreviations list gives the titles of the volumes and the abbreviations used for them; for further clarity, letters cited are identified by both volume and date.

Research for this study has involved the use of sources in a number of languages besides German and English. The following conventions have been observed concerning translation and transliteration: quotations from Rilke's poetry are given in both German and English; quotations from his prose, including fiction, essays, letters, and diary entries, are given in English only, except where attention is specifically drawn to the language or style of the original; quotations from other sources are given in English. All translations are my own, unless otherwise noted. Titles of Russian works are given in English in the text and in transliteration in the Notes and Selected Bibliography.

For the systems of Russian transliteration used in the text, see J. Thomas Shaw, *The Transliteration of Modern Russian for English-Language Publications* (Madison, 1967). All Russian personal and place names have been transliterated according to Shaw's System I (e.g., Yasnaya Polyana, Fyodor Dostoevsky, Alyosha). All bibliographical information as well as Russian words as words conform to Shaw's System III, the international scholarly system (e.g., Jasnaja Poljana, Fedor Dostoevskij, Aljoša). Russian names used by Rilke for characters in his works are left in the German transliteration (e.g., Aljoscha).

The Selected Bibliography is divided into a number of sections: Bibliographies and Collections; Archives; Editions of Rilke's Works, including German, Russian, and English editions, letters, and diaries; Rilke's Translations from Russian; and Secondary Sources, including works focusing on the topic of Rilke and Russia and other works consulted. To aid readers who wish to use the pre-Revolutionary Russian texts, I have included publishers' names when it would be useful in locating these items. The Selected Bibliography is a large and varied one, and obviously not every work listed is cited in the text. However, I feel it can be of use to readers as an extensive overview of works which illuminate my central thesis and which have aided me in arriving at my conclusions. I present it as a starting point for further research.

Acknowledgments

I would like to express my appreciation to the following persons and institutions for their help in the preparation of this study: the staff of the Slavic Reference Service of the University of Illinois Library, Urbana-Champaign; the Center for Russian and East European Studies, Urbana-Champaign; Dr. Rätus Luck of the Rilke-Archiv, Schweizerische Landesbibliothek, Bern; the staff of the Deutsches Literaturarchiv, Marbach; Frau Hella Sieber-Rilke of the Rilke-Archiv, Gernsbach; the staff of the Spencer Rare Book Library, Lawrence, Kansas; the Research Council of the University of Missouri-Kansas City for numerous travel and research grants; Dr. Andrij Hornjatkevyč of Edmonton, Alberta, for his help with Ukrainian matters; and my husband, David, for his critical eye, his erudition, and his faith and his sense of humor through it all.

· ONE ·

TEACHERS AND MODELS

One sometimes gets the impression when reading of Rilke's enthusiastic reaction to everything Russian that Russia in 1899 was still terra incognita for the Westerner. But while the country was huge, distant, and in many ways alien, its literature had nonetheless already made an impact on Western intellectual circles. Still little known in the 1870s despite forty years of translations into German, Russian writers had suddenly achieved popularity in the West in the 1880s. This was due largely to the welcome given them by the rising naturalist school in Germany.[1] The Naturalists were rebelling against a period of stagnation in German letters and indifference to social questions; they found in Tolstoy and Dostoevsky representatives of a new voice, outspokenly critical of the status quo, concerned about the common man. Besides these two, the writer most congenial to the needs of the Naturalists was Gorky; also widely read were Garshin, Korolenko, and Gogol. Major Western critics such as Georg Brandes, Paul Ernst, and Michael Georg Conrad began to write approvingly of Russian writers.

In addition to the Naturalists, Neoromantics such as Ricarda Huch and A. Moeller van den Bruck would soon turn their attention to Russia, thanks in large part to the appearance in 1886 of E. M. de Vogüé's book *Le roman russe,* which propounded a vision of Russia as the cradle of future humanity. Along with other works of a similar persuasion—for example, Nina Hoffmann's *Th. M. Dostojewsky. Eine biographische Studie,* which appeared in 1899—Vogüé helped to create the myth of a "Russian soul" which was broad, humane, simple, and thirsting for God. The Neoromantics, in their belief that modern man was hopelessly at odds with himself and his fellows, and in their search for a world of "whole" persons, discovered Russia, "not so much the real capitalist Russia, as an idealized Russia, a country which had no past but only a future. In the Russian people they found a youthful powerful tribe, slowly awakening from a thousand-year sleep!"[2] Suddenly the German reading public was faced almost daily with new translations, book reviews, editorials, and essays dealing with Russian subjects. The era of Russomania had arrived, and it would flourish until 1905, when the first Russian Revolution turned many bourgeois proponents against their Russian contemporaries.

Thus by the mid-1890s, when young Rilke moved from Prague to Munich, met Lou Andreas-Salomé, and began his education in things Russian, there existed a very sympathetic context for such studies. He was not the first of his generation to discover Russia, but his discovery was of a profoundly personal and creative nature. It is important to note that what Rilke found in Russia was precisely what he sought. His perceptions were acute but highly selective, and he skillfully avoided dealing with those aspects of Russia that didn't fit his needs. Just as the Naturalists saw in the Russian Realists only those elements that corresponded to their own beliefs—social protest, moral outcry—so, as we shall see, Rilke chose to define Russia and its culture in his own terms.

This supportive atmosphere would not in itself have been enough to turn Rilke so strongly toward Slavic culture; there were other factors at work. Born into the German-speaking minority in Prague in 1875, he developed an interest in the problems of the Czechs and wrote several works relating to them (the *Prager Geschichten* [*Prague Stories*] and some early poems). Thus he began early to cultivate a natural affinity for Slavic peoples. And indeed throughout his life he was at some pains to prove that he himself had Slavic—probably Carinthian—blood in his veins. In 1896, Rilke went to Munich to study and in May of 1897 he met Lou. By that summer they were lovers, living in a rented rustic cottage in Wolfratshausen near Munich.[3] It was there that they first began their joint study of Russian culture. They were joined in early June by a Russian literary critic, Akim Volynsky, who stayed until the middle of July.[4] During his stay, Volynsky and Lou devoted much time to discussions of Russian literature and criticism. He provided raw material, and Lou wrote it up in a series of essays, which she published in various German periodicals. Rilke sat in on the discussions and wrote out the fair copies for Lou's articles.[5] It was through these essays that she established her reputation as an expert on Russian literature and thought;[6] she was already well known—indeed, infamous in some circles—as a critic, having published works on Ibsen, Strindberg, Nietzsche, German literature, religious questions, and women's rights, as well as her first novel, all before 1897.

16

Like most men who met Lou, Rilke had fallen under her spell almost immediately. She apparently found in the intense, rather naive young poet, fourteen years her junior, something which fulfilled an emotional and physical need of her own—something which had not been touched or satisfied by her previous complicated relations with men, from the philosopher Paul Rée to Nietzsche, from the great Naturalist Gerhart Hauptmann to Frank Wedekind, from her official husband Karl F. Andreas to her unofficial one, Dr. Friedrich Piniles.[7] In any case, she and Rilke were practically inseparable from May 1897 until April 1898. Then Lou sent Rilke off to Italy for several months to experience the art there (his nominal occupation at this time was student of art history at the University in Berlin), to acquire some independence, maturity, and order, and to give Lou herself breathing space to do her own writing. During the second half of 1898, they lived near one another in Berlin, seeing each other almost every day. In preparation for their trip to Russia, Lou began to instruct Rilke in many aspects of Russian culture, including language, history, literature, and art. Then, along with Lou's husband, they spent the weeks from 25 April to the end of June 1899 in Moscow and St. Petersburg.

On their return they immediately plunged once more into the study of Russian culture, to the extent that their hostess for the summer, Frieda von Bülow, complained that she rarely saw her guests and that, when she did, they were too exhausted to keep up a conversation. In the spring of 1900, Lou and Rilke once more traveled to Russia, this time without Andreas. They covered a much greater territory, allowing Rilke a glimpse of rural Russian life. Their trip took them to Moscow, Yasnaya Polyana, and Kiev, then up the Dnieper and the Volga to Kazan, Nizhny Novgorod, and Yaroslavl, and finally back to Moscow and St. Petersburg. They were gone from 7 May to 22 August. During both trips Rilke spent a great deal of his time visiting museums and galleries. He also developed a special love for the remains of medieval Russia—churches, monasteries, and icons. The vast rural landscape with its exotic villages made an equally deep and lasting impression.

However, by midsummer of 1900 it was evident that his relationship with Lou was under a severe strain. Lou, a serious writer herself, always very independent, and by her own admission incapable of long remaining true to any one individual, was chafing under Rilke's extreme dependence on her for companionship, love, emotional support, and psychological reassurance. In addition, Lou's response to Russia, the homeland she had left in 1880 at the age of nineteen, was a sort of epiphany. She felt she had rediscovered her roots and her identity, had become young for the first time in her life. Rilke may have seemed to her a reminder of her other, unhappy life in the West—the life which revolved around an unreal and inescapable marriage and a series of secretive relationships with more or less worshipful men of letters. In any case, the autumn of 1900 saw the actual end of their intimacy; it was terminated symbolically in a letter from Lou to Rilke in early 1901. But in spite of the break, their friendship, based on a great spiritual affinity, was to last until Rilke's death in 1926, carried on in letters and in rare visits.

Lou was central to Rilke's experience of Russia. She introduced him to the latest in critical thought on Russian literature, taught him an enormous amount about Russian history, and literally was his guide and mentor on his journeys to the heart of Russia. As his "Russian education" occurred entirely under her tutelage and supervision, during the most intense period of their relationship, it is inevitable that the young man should have absorbed, perhaps unconsciously, the biases of his beloved teacher.[8]

Lou was born into a German-speaking family of Huguenots in St. Petersburg in 1861. Her father was a general in the Tsarist army, and she spent her childhood in the upper reaches of Russian society. Thus her knowledge of Russia was shaped by her class origins and the strong Germanic element in her family. One biographer remarks, "Like a little princess, Lou lived in an enchanted world. She didn't know that behind the glistening facade of life in St. Petersburg lurked the specters of poverty, sickness, ignorance, superstition, and the distant muttering of revolution."[9] Whether her delusion was as total as this implies is debatable, for she did like to slip away from the safety of the General Staff Building and wander the streets, talking to the ordinary people she met. But it is true that her Russia was primarily that of the upper classes and the intelligentsia, not that of peasants, village priests, and petty clerks. From her earliest days, her outstanding characteristics were an independent spirit, a passion for knowledge, and an almost total disregard for convention. She lost her traditional religious faith at an early age, and the vacuum thus created crucially affected her thinking. Ever after, the search for faith and the problems of the individual's relation to the totality of creation were of central importance to her, whether she was debating with Nietzsche or studying under Freud. These problems inevitably colored her attitudes toward Russia as well.

Lou was well-read in her native literature and brought powerful critical faculties to bear on it, as well as on German literature. In the early '90s, before she met Rilke, she became friendly with a number of the Naturalists in Berlin, even collaborating with them in their theater, the Freie Bühne.[10] But she was not herself a Naturalist; from the beginning her writing tended more to the philosophical and the psychological than to the sociological or the political, and she continued to search for "a new belief which affirmed the glory and sensual joy of life."[11] Given her in-between role as a Russian writing in German, Lou was in a particularly good position to act as interpreter of Russia to the West. She was aware of the most likely Western reactions, and could support or counteract them with her own insights into the Russian character. In the article "Russische Dichtung und Kultur, I" ("Russian Writing and Culture, I"), she contrasts the formally sophisticated literature of the aging, decadent West with the young, rather formless, but vital writing of Russia. It is precisely in this that she finds the attraction of Russia for Westerners, who, as representatives of a worn-out culture, are naturally drawn to the sensitivity, vitality, and profundity of the East. She shared with the German Naturalists a preference for the realistic writers. She has little to say about the new generation of Russian writers, the Symbolists and Decadents who were active from the '90s until after the October Revolution, and who numbered among their ranks thinkers and poets like Solovyov and Merezhkovsky, Sologub, Bryusov, and Balmont. In "Russische Dichtung und Kultur, II," she does mention several of the younger writers briefly, but sees them as mere transitional figures, "in whom the modern poetic spirit still burns, while it waits for a Great One," someone closer to the character of the Russian people, "simpler and more naive, more inward and profound."[12]

Like Volynsky, whose book *Russian Critics* she cites,[13] Lou is skeptical about the traditional social school of Russian criticism based on the ideas of Belinsky, Chernyshevsky, and Dobrolyubov, who were interested in literature purely in its rational, didactic, and melioristic role. There is a strong nationalistic feeling in the opinions Lou expresses—an essentially Slavophile faith in the Russian people as the ultimate source of cultural strength. In an 1899 review of an anthology of Russian short stories, she maintains, "I am convinced that the most intimate attraction of Russian writing lies precisely in the . . . relationship between poet and people: it lies in the peculiar directness by means of which the finest, spiritually most sublimated sensitivities of the artist merge into one with the primitive realism of the as yet unrefined Russian personality." She concludes this essay, "Scratch a Russian and you'll find a poet."[14]

In an essay on Tolstoy she focuses on what she, like many writers before her, considered the basic conflict in Russian development: the imposition of Western culture on that of Russia and the subsequent cultural schizophrenia in Russian ambitions, ideals, and self-image.[15] Once again she emphasizes the importance of the people for literature. She sees Tolstoy's extreme rejection of art and his radical embracing of the peasant life as merely the logical consequences of a trend begun by Pushkin, when he first paid serious attention to the fairy tales of his old nurse—that is, when the subterranean voice of the folk found its way into "high" liter-

19

ature. Lou emphasizes the passivity and patience of the Russian people, which she sees as the source of its peculiar kind of religiosity. She finds the Russian folk in a state of expectation, as if the nation were awaiting its moment of fruition, as if "in the depths of Russianness, their own personal individual culture lay buried, which only awaits its hour and its masters."[16] She characterizes the Russian God as a figure of goodness, simplicity, and endearing fallibility, "not a particularly great ruler, for he can also be forgetful, and quite a bit escapes his notice."[17] As for Tolstoy himself, Lou defends his writing of the polemical "What Is Art?" even while admitting that it may appear absurd and incomprehensible to a Western reader. She sees in Tolstoy a living example of the profoundly Russian struggle between artist and man—between form and culture, on the one hand, and an obsession with the bare truths of life and death, on the other. Elsewhere she describes Tolstoy as a typically Russian phenomenon, only one with gigantic dimensions, the Russian character manifested in a genius.[18]

These conceptions of Russia are strongly similar to those Rilke held, as can be shown in dozens of passages from his works and letters. Throughout the *Buch der Bilder* (*Book of Images*) and *Das Stunden-Buch* (*The Book of Hours*), for example, we find repeated Lou's vision of the Russian people as patient, humble, and religious, facing a great unknown future. In one letter Rilke declares:

> Russia became for me reality, and at the same time the profound, daily insight: that reality is something distant, which comes with inexpressible slowness to him who has patience. Russia—that is the land where people are lonely, each with a world within him, each full of darkness, like a mountain; each deep in his humility, without fear of humbling himself, and therefore pious. People full of distance, uncertainty and hopes: people who are *becoming*.[19]

In the *Geschichten vom lieben Gott* (*Stories about God*), the *Stunden-Buch,* and the essays on Russian art, Rilke gives to the dichotomy of East versus West an ethical and even an aesthetic value, as Lou had done. He leaned heavily on Lou's tastes in literature, reading widely but ultimately preferring Dostoevsky and Tolstoy, and remaining cool toward the Modernists. Even in more specific matters Rilke echoes Lou's personal biases. For example, in "Russische Dichtung, I," she had declared that for Tolstoy, "from the beginning, death stood at the center of his observations and spiritual impressions—death, that nestled into everything."[20] In the novel *Die Aufzeichnungen des Malte Laurids Brigge* (*The Notebooks of Malte Laurids Brigge*), Rilke devoted several pages, later deleted, to Tolstoy's obsession with death; and death, "that nestles into everything," was to remain one of the dominating motifs of Rilke's own writing.

In addition to the importance of Lou's ideas for Rilke, there were other, more general, influences which helped form his views of Russia; these included his reading about Russian culture. It has been noted that Rilke spent a great deal of time preparing for the two trips. Aside from studying the language, primarily in the summer and fall of 1899, Rilke pored over art books and histories.[21] In the works of Vogüé and Hoffmann appear attitudes and ideas, similar to those of Lou, concerning the East-West dichotomy or the creative potential of the Russian folk which are echoed often in Rilke's writing, sometimes even to the borrowing of stylistic elements or images. For example, both Hoffmann and Vogüé emphasize Russia's vastness and relative emptiness, a theme which seems to have powerfully grasped the imagination of Westerners, with their spatially more narrow experience. Vogüé's description of the plains of the Ukraine, in his discussion of Gogol, contains the following images:

> The habit of looking creates that of thinking. That distant emptiness attracts it, thought seeks itself in space, without losing itself; it is the flight of a bird departing into the brightness, which one accompanies mechanically as it diminishes in the shadow, which one searches for once more, vanished in the ether. Thence comes, for the man of the steppe, the inclination to dream, the falling back on himself, the flight inward, to the imagination.[22]

In a diary entry of 2 December 1899, Rilke notes that he has recently read the *roman russe* "with great inner success."[23] In a story written in late 1899 as one of the *Geschichten,* "Das Lied von der Gerechtigkeit," Rilke presents a description of the Ukrainian steppe:

> And in this land where graves are mountains, the people are abysses. Deep, dark, taciturn are the inhabitants, and their words are but weak, wobbly bridges over their real existence. Sometimes dark birds rise from the kurgans.[24] Sometimes wild songs plunge into the dim people and disappear deep inside them, while the birds are lost in the sky. In all directions everything seems boundless.
>
> (VI, 330)

While Rilke embellishes the scene, the basic perception is nevertheless the same.

Hoffmann focuses on another aspect of Russia which was to become central to Rilke's vision: the humility and patience of its people. As a biographer she is permeated with the attitudes of her subject, and seems to accept completely many of Dostoevsky's ideas about Russia. Among the things she lists as typical of the Russians are: "a capacity for suffering and sympathy . . . the humility of the Russian which is bound up with a profound religiousness."[25] She notes that Westerners tend to misinterpret Russian behavior as "an image of cowardly self-abasement . . . undependability, unpunctuality, lack of discipline."[26] These things which offend superficially more disciplined sensibilities stem, however, from what Hoffmann sees as a broadness of nature, a love of flexibility and need for it, and an emphasis on living each minute as it comes. What Westerners perceive as abjectness comes, in reality, from the Russian's essential humility before God, his fellow man, and himself. Rilke connects this essential humility with the vastness of Russia and, like Hoffmann, juxtaposes this humility to Western incomprehension. The narrator of the *Geschichten* relates that in Russia people behave the same way to God and the Tsar.

> They throw themselves down before both, feel the ground with their brows, weep, and say "I am sinful, forgive me, Father." The Germans who see this maintain: a quite unworthy slavery. I have a different opinion about it. What is this kneeling supposed to mean? It is supposed to express: I am respectful. For that it's enough to bow one's head, thinks the German. Well, yes, the greeting, the bow, to a certain extent they too are expressions of this, abbreviations which arose in countries where there wasn't so much space that each man could lie down on the earth.
>
> (IV, 311)

Like Lou, Vogüé and Hoffmann also stressed the divergences between East and West in Russian history and consciousness, a theme which was to become central to Rilke's image of Russia, particularly in the *Stunden-Buch*. Hoffmann presents Dostoevsky's view of a messianic, nationalistic Russia which must be freed from the imposition of Western philosophies and systems. This idea, by the time Rilke concerned himself with it, had indeed become a commonplace of Russian Slavophilism. Another mutual emphasis of both Lou and Hoffmann concerns the importance of the relationship between Russian writers and the folk, which "demands from its poets above all, collaboration in its difficult process of becoming."[27] This idea of becoming is also, as we shall see, crucial to Rilke's view of Russia. Further, his views on the rhythm of Russian history echo Hoffmann's. She says of the Russian people, "This people . . . experiencing slowly its process of development, stands today in its childhood and is ambling toward its middle age."[28] Like Dostoevsky, she sees a vital role for the Russian people in the distant future: "Sometime, in centuries, perhaps, . . . after following a cultural path which lies beyond our calculation (for it is highly intelligent, tenacious, indeed even stubborn), [the folk] will make its own revolution . . . within its faith, and throw something new, earth-fresh, as a fruit of its culture into the lap of an astonished Europe. . . . Then it will probably enter the life of nations in a natural manner and speak along with others in deciding its own fate."[29]

Rilke too saw the future of Russia as a patient development toward a late but inevitable flowering, a movement leading toward the realization of the Russian essence. In a letter to Lou dated 15 August 1903, he suggests:

Perhaps the Russian is created to allow human history to pass by, in order later to fall into the harmony of things with his singing heart. He has only to endure, to hold out, and like the violinist who as yet receives no signal, to sit in the orchestra holding his instrument carefully so that nothing happens to it. . . . Ever more and with ever deeper approval do I feel an attraction to this wise, holy land.[30]

The concept of a slow becoming, of a fate based on humility and patience, is also central to Rilke's image of the Russian God, who is so important for the *Stunden-Buch*. There God, a dark, protean, essentially Russian deity, is envisioned as an unfinished work of art, the ever-growing, not yet completed product of man. The ideas of Hoffmann, Vogüé, and writers like them, and especially those of Lou, found fertile soil in the young poet. They helped form the basis for a vast panorama of feelings and attitudes which eventually were given concrete expression in a multitude of literary forms.

Rilke's meetings and friendships with a variety of Russians during and after his travels had a much slighter effect on his writing. They did, however, contribute to his knowledge of Russia, help cement his personal affections for that country, and keep open channels to its people. Of the Russians he met, artists especially attracted his interest. He met Repin and Trubetskoy, and became friends with Alexander Benois and Leonid Pasternak. The latter visited him in Rome in 1904, and their correspondence continued until Rilke's death. Through Pasternak, Rilke also became acquainted with his son, Boris. Among writers, Rilke met minor figures like Drozhzhin and Yantshevetsky, both of whom he translated into German, and the giant among living Russian authors, Leo Tolstoy, who was to play a major role in the formation of Rilke's image of Russia. Other acquaintances included Princess Tenisheva, a social reformer and well-known patroness of the arts; Pavel Ettinger, an art historian; and Sophia Nikolaevna Schill, a journalist who wrote under the name of Grigory Orlov, and who was instrumental in arranging many meetings and excursions for Rilke and Lou during their travels. Rilke's attraction to Russia and Russians continued after his return to Germany, and an examination of his correspondence shows repeated reference to Russian writers and artists.[31]

The sources, then, which exercised the greatest influence on Rilke's views of Russia, particularly in the early years of his interest, were above all the personal contact with Lou Andreas-Salomé, but also his travels in Russia, his wide and varied reading, his informed interest in Russian art, and his acquaintance with Russians both during and after his journeys. All of these had their effect partially because of the congenial intellectual atmosphere of the time but, more importantly, because there was something in his nature which was drawn to what he found in Russia. Russia was, for Rilke, primarily the patient peasant and the vast slumbering countryside, the magnificent but bloody history, the splendid rituals of the Orthodox church, and the slow, silent, omnipresent Russian God. As any reading of his diaries and letters, as well as his literary works, will show, Russia was a land that for Rilke would yield a spiritual and an artistic experience of the greatest magnitude.

· TWO ·

FIRST FRUITS:
RUSSIA IN THE DRAMAS, TRANSLATIONS,
AND EARLY SCATTERED WORKS

As one might expect, the greatest number and variety of Russian elements can be found in those works which Rilke wrote during and just following the years of his Russian journeys and his active study of Russian literature and culture. The period between the trips, from July 1899 to May 1900, was particularly productive, bringing him the first section of the *Stunden-Buch,* the *Geschichten,* and many of the poems of the *Buch der Bilder.* The fruits of the second journey proved slower to ripen. Indeed, in the early autumn of 1900 Rilke experienced one of his characteristic periods of unease about his ability to go on writing—periods which would become longer and more severe as the years passed. In a diary entry of 1 September 1900, apparently a draft of a letter to Lou, Rilke expressed his worry and chagrin that neither during the recent Russian journey nor since his return had he been able to give form to the many impressions gathered there. He quotes a short poem and two brief fragments which had come to him during the trip, and which constitute the whole of his poetic output between May and September. The poem refers to a statue seen in a Moscow museum. One of the fragments, which he says came to him one evening in Kazan, seems to be the beginning of a meditative poem about his plans for the future. The second fragment more directly reflects the immediate surroundings; it portrays some Russian horses in red yokes, galloping through a sea-like expanse of steppe.

For the time being, these fragmentary utterances, and the few other moments of poetic suggestion which he experienced during his travels, came to nothing. But even in his bleak mood, Rilke clung to the belief that the second Russian trip would bear poetic fruit and that his paralysis would be temporary. In the diary he states, of the ideas and inspirations he had let pass by, "I didn't use them, like so much on this trip. To numberless poems I granted no hearing. . . . But *this* isn't the sum of the journey. What I paid no attention to is still in me, nonetheless. Surely I experienced it all. . . . Surely it was more than a dream. If only it would somehow come back to me."[1] And indeed, the work did begin to flow again, and with it the Russian impressions took poetic shape.

Between 1899 and 1902, Rilke made a number of translations from the Russian; wrote two dramatic fragments which contain strong Russian elements; published two perceptive essays on Russian art; and produced a number of poems which show Russian influences, including eight written in Russian. In examining the works of these years, it is important to recall that it was a crucial time for Rilke both personally and poetically. This period saw the high point and decline of his relationship with Lou and his sudden marriage to the sculptress Clara Westhoff. During the same years Rilke underwent a sometimes painful maturing process as a poet. These elements play a central role in the works of the period and are often linked with his use of Russian themes. This habit of using Russian motifs to express personal concerns permeates his works ever afterward. Under the merciless eye of Lou, he had begun as early as 1897 to sharpen his poetic style, to purge it of the sentimentality and the modish softness and obscurity which marred many of his early works. Lou had also taught him much about the art of observation, particularly of plants, animals, and other details of his environment. During 1899 and 1900 he underwent a sort of apprenticeship, learning self-discipline and trying to find his own voice, while at the same time opening himself to many new experiences. Some of these experiences brought answers to his own deepest questions, while others merely posed new questions; and all were seen through the eyes of Lou, the god-seeker.

Lou also had a practical effect on Rilke's activities. One of her motives for encouraging him in his Russian studies had been a concern for his material survival. He had no practical training, his family was not wealthy, and Lou hoped that he might be able to put a knowledge of Russian to good use. Rilke himself took this idea seriously, particularly later, in 1901 and early 1902, when an increasingly desperate domestic situation—a wife and small child and almost no income—drove him to undertake a frantic letter-writing campaign, asking all his friends in Russia to help him find work there. His idealization of that country, added to his current miserable situation, led him to exaggerate the good qualities of Russia, of whose complex realities he was barely aware. He wrote, for example, to Pavel Ettinger in January of 1902 with the following request: "I'm thinking seriously of moving to Moscow, the sooner the better. But I would have to find some sort of a post there. . . . What do you think, could a position be found?"[2] Rilke also wrote to Leonid Pasternak and N. A. Tolstoy, asking them to keep an eye out for possible openings.[3] His hopes lay in finding a job as an art critic or foreign correspondent on a Russian journal or newspaper.

He made numerous similar requests to his friend Benois. The latter, while deeply sympathetic, felt it his duty to bring Rilke to a more sober and realistic view of things; thus his replies were uniformly discouraging on this matter. He informed Rilke of the unlikelihood of finding work with a journal, for they either paid poorly (*Mir Iskusstva*), or had no openings (*Xudožestvennye sokroviščа Rossii*), or had just been shut down by the officials (*Žizn'*).[4] He tells Rilke that "life here is much more expensive than in Germany, two to three times as much. Living quarters, food, clothing, all are desperately expensive."[5] In a revealing outburst in a letter of August 1902, Benois writes, "I want to get out of here so bad it hurts [*do boli*]. I want to get away from . . . our life, from our loud, empty conversations, from our stinking banality. And you still want to settle here!"[6] As a young artist and intellectual working in Russia, Benois was in a position to know what he was talking about. But Rilke, out of the tenacious strength of his ideal vision and despair at his actual situation, was never convinced: he was only defeated by circumstances. In March of 1902, he made a last, intensely naive gesture. Via Benois—a man openly connected with the liberal aesthetic circles around *Mir Iskusstva*—Rilke sent a letter to A. S. Suvorin,[7] the most powerful publisher of the day, not realizing that Suvorin was a pillar of reactionary right-wing journalism, his ideas utterly alien to both Rilke and Benois. Rilke's paean to the "Russian soul" and his plea for a chance to work for Suvorin as an art critic must have struck the latter as the ravings of a child or madman. Suvorin never answered Rilke's letter; nor did any positions open up on any of the liberal journals. And Rilke never returned to Russia, though he went on talking of it as his "spiritual homeland."

One small portion of the dream was fulfilled, however. This was Rilke's desire to translate Russian literature. In January 1902, he wrote to his friend Gustav Pauli, director of the Bremen art gallery, about his hopes of exercising "a quiet occupation as a translator from Russian."[8] He was never to make a living at it, but he did produce a small corpus of translations from Russian which are of interest from both a literary and a biographical point of view. Rilke was eventually to make a name for himself as a translator of, among others, Michelangelo, Elizabeth Barrett Browning, Gide, and Valéry. He did not overwhelm the originals, as sometimes happens with poet-translators; rather, his gifts as a poet provided him with an astonishing sensitivity to them. But there is nonetheless a distinctly

Rilkean flavor to his versions. His translations from Russian partake of the same qualities, although some of them are of lower quality owing simply to his more limited grasp of Russian. Among his earliest attempts at translation, the Russian works already illustrate his habit of subtly changing a work so as to make it his own. They also reveal something about both his taste in Russian literature and the elements of Russian reality which most interested him, and in some we can see the embryo of his own later works.

The few extant examples of the translations from the Russian show that Rilke possessed a genuine feeling for the language, even though his spoken command of it was never fluent. The Russian works which attracted Rilke's attention as a translator were of roughly two types: those containing elements, whether in setting, subject matter, or attitude, which would have struck Rilke as peculiarly Russian, and those which interested him for other reasons, personal, poetic, or practical. The quintessentially Russian works include four poems by the peasant poet Spiridon Drozhzhin; a story by V. Yantshevetsky; passages from Dostoevsky's first novel, *Poor Folk;* and the twelfth-century Russian epic *Slovo o polku Igoreve.* Among the works which attracted Rilke for other reasons belong three poems by the leading Russian Romantic poet Mikhail Lermontov; one by Fofanov, a minor late Romantic; Chekhov's plays *The Seagull* and *Uncle Vanya;* Tolstoy's play *The Living Corpse;* and a fragment of a story by the Symbolist Fyodor Sologub.[9]

Being a translator of Russian was not a simple affair. Texts were often hard to procure and went out of print quickly. Mail service was somewhat chancy. And Rilke was not prepared for the vagaries of the Russian literary world. For example, having taken on the responsibility, in the name of the new Secession Theater in Berlin, of asking for the translation rights to Tolstoy's forthcoming play *The Living Corpse,* Rilke became embroiled in a correspondence that involved three other people besides himself and Tolstoy. This all ended with Tolstoy's decision not to publish the play after all, at the request of the family who had served as the prototypes for the characters in it.[10] Even more frustrating was the situation which arose when Rilke decided to translate a work by Benois. Around the turn of the century, Rilke was very active as an art critic for German journals. His feeling about Russian culture led him to assume the role of unofficial interpreter of Russian art to the West. Impressed by Benois's *History of Painting in the XIX Century: Russian Painting,* which appeared in December 1900, Rilke wrote to Benois asking for the right to translate it.[11] Benois was pleased at the idea, and negotiations began. But they were soon to mushroom into a nightmare of delays, misunderstandings, and inexplicable hostility, mostly on the part of Benois's publisher, Protopopov. After alienating two German publishers and spending nearly two years in long-distance negotiation, Rilke was forced to abandon the project; his energies were required elsewhere. The anecdote is typical of the problems that dogged the footsteps of the well-meaning enthusiast. Yet they never seem to have been able to dampen his ardor for Russia or to evoke a single cynical response from him.

It is obvious that the quality of the originals which Rilke selected for translation varied widely. His choice may be ascribed in part to the accident of availability, as well as to the limitations imposed by his command of Russian. Nevertheless, the selection of a number of works does strongly show Rilke's attraction to what he considered quintessentially Russian, and these choices form a pattern consistent with the views of Russia which he wove into his own works of the period.

In the works of Spiridon Dmitrich Drozhzhin, for example, he found illustrations of the virtues of rural Russia. Drozhzhin belonged to that peculiarly Russian category the peasant poet. He lived in a village on the Volga, where Rilke and Lou visited him for several days in 1900. His poetry is simple, pious, and bound to the Russian soil. In Drozhzhin, Rilke found his own ideal Russia reproduced in almost unadulterated form. Drozhzhin's peasant protagonists express a profound love for their homeland. In the poem "Accept Me," we see one such figure behind his plow and learn of his great patience in the face of the miracle of growth. Rilke renders the lines

> und werde warten, still zur Seite tretend,
> Bis sich die Aehren schwankend aus [dem Boden] heben,
> und er sich wie mit goldenen Geweben
> Vor mir verhüllt.[12]
>
> [and I shall wait, stepping quietly aside, until the ears lift swaying from the earth, and it conceals itself from me as if with a golden fabric.]

The peasant in "In the Native Village," home again after a long absence, confirms that nothing in his village has changed in all that time, and ends with a sort of humble wonder at his people, whose generations seem to merge into one another: "Die neue Sippe kommt von irgendwo / und lebt das Elend willig wie die Alten"[13] ("The new tribe comes from somewhere or other and lives misery willingly, like the old ones"). In the two poems, we can see Rilke's favorite image of the humble, patient peasant, waiting and suffering "willingly." In the third Drozhzhin poem, "The Power of Song," we find echoes of the idea, expressed by both Lou and Nina Hoffmann, that the strength of the Russian poet lies in his ties with his land and folk. Drozhzhin lists the sources of his song: the forest's roaring, the noonday sound of the Volga, the seasons. He concludes, in Rilke's version, "Wenn ich mein Lied an einem Glücke übe, / Nehm ichs vom Volk, sowie das viele Leid"[14] ("If I use my song [to express] joy, I take it from the folk, just as [I do] the endless pain"). Finally, Rilke's interest in the religious strength of the Russians can be seen in his version of Drozhzhin's "Prayer," in which Rilke's protagonist calls out to God to open his great book of wisdom, so that he may be enflamed by God's thoughts and carry them through the world, "ein wanderndes Wort" ("a wandering word"). Drozhzhin's attitude in this poem, according to Brutzer, is calm and pious, that of "a humble monk," while Rilke's tone is stronger and more ecstatic.[15] While this interpretation cannot be confirmed, it is nevertheless significant that Rilke, too, would later choose a humble Russian monk to be his voice in the *Stunden-Buch,* the work most permeated by what he had learned in Russia. The influence on the *Stunden-Buch* of these early translations can also be seen in the titles. Three of the poems which Rilke translated—one by Drozhzhin and two by Lermontov—bear the title "Molitva" ("Prayer"); so too the *Stunden-Buch,* which in its first version of 1899 was called "Die Gebete"—"The Prayers."

The story "The Petition" by V. Yantshevetsky, like Drozhzhin's poems, also shows the Russian character in a light favored by Rilke.[16] It involves a delegation of peasants who gather to give a petition to the Tsar when he rides by during a holiday procession. But there is an attempt on his life, and the peasants, overwhelmed by the event and by the sadness on his face as he passes, give up all thought of bothering him with their problems "weil der Kaiser bekümmert ist"[17] ("because the emperor is troubled"). The peasants emerge as childlike in their devotion and in the immediacy and extremism of their emotional reactions.

It is safe to say that a similar sort of characterization attracted Rilke to Dostoevsky's *Poor Folk.* He found in the loving, self-sacrificing, and ultimately isolated characters of this novel an urban variation on the theme of the humble Russian. Rilke's response to *Poor Folk* was enthusiastic. In a diary entry of 2 December 1899, Rilke remarks that he has just been reading that novel, and continues: "I know of no book which I could set beside it."[18] Later, in answer to a question about books which had been important to him, he mentions Turgenev and Dostoevsky, and adds: "The latter became very important for me later on when, prepared for him to an extreme by his land and his language, I read and reread *Poor Folk* and finally translated a portion of this unwittingly brilliant book."[19] In a letter to Benois in July of 1901, he remarks how much he admires Dostoevsky and says that "Insel in the near future will print a wonderful excerpt from the novel (*Poor Folk*) . . . which I completed with great diligence."[20] It is not known why the excerpt did not appear, and it can only be regretted that it didn't. Nevertheless, it is interesting to have proof of Rilke's early strong feelings for Dostoevsky, for the latter was to have great importance for Rilke in his later works.

By far the most ambitious and successful translation which Rilke undertook at this time was the *Slovo o polku Igoreve* (*Lay of Igor's Campaign*), which he rendered as *Das Igorlied*.[21] Rilke knew about the work from his studies of Russian history and folklore, but he probably actually read it in its entirety for the first time in 1900, when he received a copy from Sophie Schill.[22] He began work on his translation in 1902, and completed it in 1904 in Rome, after a long interruption. The work may have attracted him for a number of reasons. First, the language is vivid and rich, and must have presented a more than worthy challenge to his knowledge of Russian. Rilke made his translation from a composite source: a version of the original accompanied by a modern Russian prose version and a variety of poetic renderings by Russian writers, many of which contained inaccuracies, misunderstandings, misinterpretations, or plain lapses of taste.[23] Given this fact, it is all the more remarkable that Rilke was able to produce a version which has been cited for its faithful rendering of both content and archaic tone,[24] and which conveys the plight of its hero and the grandeur of his epoch with an intensity which "makes us virtually oblivious of the intermediator."[25]

In addition to style, subject matter and attitudes combined to attract Rilke to the work, which, he declared, "interests me uncommonly."[26] The *Slovo* is the story of a disastrous raid led by Prince Igor against the pagan Polovtsians in 1185. Igor and his allies, badly outnumbered and without the support of the other Russian princes, seek glory in an ill-timed attack on the enemy. Only Igor and his companion Ovlur escape. In rich, formulaic language, the anonymous poet evokes the wild Russian landscape, makes a plea for peace among the Russian princes in the face of threats to their homeland from beyond its border, and describes the foolhardy campaign, with its bloody battles and fatal outcome. The story of Igor's raid is portrayed against a background of complex tribal and military relationships. The Russian warriors and the wives they leave behind emerge as brave figures, full of uncontainable passions, capable of great loyalty and profound sorrow. Their actions are depicted in metaphoric language that links them closely with the earth and the elements. Igor's fate depends in part on the mood of rivers and winds; he escapes disguised as a falcon, while his companion lopes through sheltering mists in the form of a grey wolf. In her lament for her lord, presumed lost, Igor's wife, Yaroslavna, soars along the Danube like a cuckoo and begs the sun, which she addresses as *Herrin* ("mistress"), to protect her husband.[27]

It is the stark beauty of the images and the pre-Christian vision of man existing as a part of nature which most drew Rilke to the *Slovo*. Although Russia had officially been Christianized in 988 by Prince Vladimir the Great, the *Slovo*, written some two hundred years later, still reflected the role which Slavic pre-Christian elements continued to play in Russian life.

The work ostensibly treats of the conflict between Christian Russians and heathen Polovtsians, but the references to Christianity that one might expect—its role as a source of right or strength, for example, or as a comfort in adversity—are almost completely lacking. (In this anomaly the work bears some resemblance to the *Nibelungenlied.*) The work ends with Igor's return home and his ride to the icon of the Pigorozhian Virgin, but the tone and texture of the whole are permeated by earlier Slavic deities and customs and by the strong animistic sense already mentioned. Like the other works which Rilke chose to translate, the *Slovo* reinforced his image of the Russians at one with, and drawing their strength from, their land, acting in concord with it, and for its protection. In addition, Rilke had devoted more attention to medieval Russian history than to any other era. His notebooks contain extensive materials on the early period, gleaned from his reading. His interest in the period was aided by his studies of folklore, for many of the songs and narratives he read dealt with the heroes of Kievan Russ, up to the conquest of Russia by the Mongol hordes in 1224. Thus the *Slovo* appealed also to Rilke's natural inclination toward, and affection for, medieval Russia.

While I do not intend a close analysis of Rilke's *Igorlied,* certain aspects of the work should be pointed out.[28] Stylistically, it is of a piece with much of his early writing. Written, like *Die Weise von Liebe und Tod des Cornets Christoph Rilke (The Lay of Love and Death of the Cornet Christoph Rilke)* (1899–1904), in a graceful yet powerful lyrical prose, it also contains extensive alliteration, like that work. Phrases such as "hinter den Hügeln," "der Heiden Geheul," or "Selten sangen damals Pflüger sich an . . . umso öfter riefen die Raben" ("behind the hills"; "the heathens' howls"; "in those days plowmen seldom sang out to each other . . . so much the more did the ravens call"), help create a rhythm that sustains the mood. The alliteration does not always coincide with that of the original, where it tends to be random and merely ornamental. Rilke may also have been unconsciously influenced by the traditional sound of early German heroic verse, which relies heavily on alliteration combined with stressed syllables (*Stabreim*) to create its peculiarly effective rhythm.

Rilke, however true he remains in general to the original, shows a marked tendency as a translator to change or expand on an image or to realize one which is only suggested. Numerous examples of this are present in the *Igorlied.* For example, where the Russian, speaking of a monster which is flushed from the trees and flies away screaming, says, "the Div soared up—it cries in the treetops, orders unknown lands to listen" (p. 10), Rilke says, "Heulend erhob der Drache sich über die Bäume hin und zwang fremde Länder in seinen Schrei" ("Howling, the dragon arose above the trees and forced alien lands into its cry" [p. 35]. Rilke makes the

"Div" of the original, an oriental demon bird, a cross between an owl and a peacock, into a less specific dragon, and by an odd turn of phrase in the second clause, gives it a more threatening power to encompass and engulf the strange lands, which are forced "into" its cry, as if into its maw. Elsewhere the Russian describes the backdrop to the beginning of the battle: "Dark clouds come from the sea . . . and in them blue lightnings quiver to be great thunder" (p. 12). Rilke's lines read, "Schwarze Wolken steigen vom Meer . . . und in den Wolken hängen zitternd die bläulichen Blitze ungeduldig, ein grosses Gewitter zu sein" ("Black clouds climb from the sea . . . and in the clouds, blue flashes hang quivering, impatient to be a great storm" [p. 36]. Once again Rilke plays with the images, intensifying in one place (*idut*—"come"—becomes the more dynamic *steigen:* "climb"), expanding the implied possibilities elsewhere (the Russian lightnings merely quiver, while Rilke's contain greater tension, conflict: they "hang quivering," are "impatient"). In addition, through a felicitous accident of German, Rilke was able to introduce alliteration into the phrase (*bläulichen Blitze; grosses Gewitter*) while remaining fairly close to the original meaning.

A further characteristic of Rilke's work is the tendency of elements from disparate sources to merge and reinforce one another. An example is his habit of introducing impressions from the visual arts into his writing. We find a striking and complex illustration of this habit in the interrelationship between the *Igorlied* and Rilke's essay entitled "Russische Kunst" ("Russian Art"), written in 1900 and published in 1901. Although Rilke received his copy of the *Slovo* only in February 1900, he was in part already familiar with it in 1899. Brutzer notes that "in his historical notes, which must in part stem from the Bibersberg period [the months spent at Bibersberg as the guest of Frieda von Bülow in the summer and early fall of 1899], there are repeated references to the setting and historical personages of the *Slovo,* with specific quotations from it."[29] Thus we can assume a detailed, if not complete, knowledge of the work on Rilke's part before the writing of the essay.

In his discussion of contemporary Russian painters, Rilke describes a painting by Viktor Vasnetsov entitled *After the Battle of Igor Svyatoslavich with the Polovtsians,* and subtitled *On a Theme from the "Slovo o polku Igoreve."* Rilke had seen the painting at the Tretyakov Gallery in Moscow on his first visit in 1899. In the picture, corpses, Polovtsian and Russian, are strewn across a field amidst broken and discarded weapons, while two large birds of prey fight in the air above. These details are present in the epic as well. The birds may have been suggested by the epic's extensive bird imagery, for example, and the Russian corpses are identifiable by their crimson shields, mentioned in the epic. Vasnetsov, however, is more explicitly Christian in his imagery than was the composer of the *Slovo;* in the center of the picture lies a dead Russian with a cross around his neck. The pale, gentle colors which light up this portion of the painting contrast sharply with the otherwise somber scene.

Rilke describes the painting approvingly, along with others by Vasnetsov, as examples of the painter's "earnest, ruthless realism" (V, 499). He finds Vasnetsov peculiarly suited "to portray the figures of native saga and history, in conjunction with the Russian landscape" (V, 499). What is strange about his discussion of this painting, however, is that while certain details do not match the picture, they do coincide with relevant passages in the *Slovo*. The birds of prey in the painting are a mottled yellowish brown, not the "black, scuffling birds of prey" which Rilke describes in the essay. The *Slovo*, however, contains many evil and prophetic birds, including a metaphoric description of the Polovtsian enemy as a "black raven" (p. 12) which Rilke renders as *Nachtrabe* ("night raven") (p. 36). Furthermore, in the essay, Rilke portrays the helmets and weapons as bathed in "Blut und Abendrot" ("blood and sunset"). But while in the painting a murky red sun does hang on the dark horizon, there is not the dramatic, reddish effect one might expect from his description, nor is there blood in evidence anywhere. In the *Slovo*, on the other hand, the battlefield is described thus: "The black earth beneath the hooves was sown with bones and drenched in blood" (p. 14). Rilke's version is absolutely faithful to the original: "Die schwarze Erde unter den Hufen war mit Gebeinen besäet und begossen mit Blut" (p. 38). Sunsets, too, play an important role in the epic, and may have influenced the description in the essay. In short, it is not too daring to suggest that Rilke allowed his memories of striking passages in the *Slovo* to color his discussion of the related painting.

Conversely, it may be that when Rilke turned to the actual translation of the *Slovo* in 1902, the process was reversed, and his familiarity with the painting affected his interpretation of a scene in the epic. As Igor and his army approach the river Don, the Russian declares, "Already the birds in the oaks foretell his misfortune, and the wolves in the ravines howl calamity; the eagles with their screams call the beasts to the bones; and foxes bark at the crimson shields" (pp. 10–11). Rilke renders the last two images faithfully. But in the first two, he shifts the emphasis away from the ominous foreknowledge of the beasts, making them instead a direct physical threat to the doomed warriors. Rilke writes, "Igor and his army stop at the Don. And already his downfall is prepared, as fodder for the birds of the forest; out of the ravines the wolves thrust themselves threateningly; the eagles with their screams lure the beasts to the bones; and the foxes bark at the bloodred shields" (p. 35). The threat of carnage and the waiting birds are present in the original, certainly, in the eagles' alarms. But I would suggest that Vasnetsov's painting of the battleground also played a role in Rilke's choice of images. In the painting, two giant birds of prey fight in midair for possession of the warriors' bodies. In the foreground of the left-hand corner of the picture, a third bird turns its back on the field of corpses and stoops to clean its feathers as if already sated. The gruesome image of the feasting birds, only hinted at in the *Slovo,* is spelled out both in Vasnetsov's painting and in Rilke's translation. The poet's familiarity with the picture may have suggested to him this particular embellishment of the scene, thus bringing full circle this remarkable interaction of epochs, artists, and influences.

A glance at the other works which Rilke translated, or considered translating, suggests a variety of possible reasons for their selection.[30] In the small group of Romantic poems which he translated, the primary attraction may have lain, not in anything particularly Russian, but in the mood and language. Two of these translations, the two Lermontov poems called "Prayer," are not available for study;[31] but neither of the originals is particularly Russian in topic or tone. In one, the "I" of the poem prays to the Mother of God to protect a young girl, apparently one whom he has seduced. The other praises the uplifting power of prayer in hard times. Brutzer may be correct in surmising that these attempts were intended as practice in the art of translation and never rose beyond that level.[32]

The single available translation of a Romantic poem from this period in Rilke's life is his rendition of Fofanov's "Springtime and Night." The original is a gracefully ironic Romantic look at love; Rilke's version, however, bears a rather distant relation to the original.[33] The meter and distribution of rhymes are not the same as Fofanov's, and there are several passages in which—whether from an imperfect understanding of the Russian, or a need to fill out the German line, or a conscious desire to create a different impression—Rilke's images differ considerably from the original. Rilke tends to be more abstract, to use more words, and to expand on images or give them an interpretive twist, rather than simply reproducing them. The Russian *mercan'e* ("flickering") becomes *schimmert schwach* ("shimmers faintly"). "Zari negasnuščej ogni" ("the unextinguished flame of sunset") becomes "des alten Abends unverloschne Neige" ("the unextinguished remains of the old evening"). The simple *v rošče* ("in the grove") is made into "Im wirren Schatten schlanker, schwarzer Zweige" ("in the tangled shadow of slender black branches"), for once a more concrete image, reinforcing the mystery present in the original. Fofanov describes the sky as *alom jantare* ("like red amber"). Rilke turns the simple image into a simile, based on a somewhat roundabout connection. His line reads: "Der Himmel, harzklar, wie vom Stamm der Fichte" ("The heaven, clear as resin, as from the trunk of the fir tree"). Fofanov's amber (*jantar'*) has become resin (*Harz*) dripping from a fir tree's trunk. The leap from the rich, serene, semiprecious stone so common on the Russian Baltic coast to the viscous material familiar to Rilke from the forests of Germany is puzzling, and the image produced is very different.

The most important alteration occurs in the next to last stanza, where the speaker admits that, though he is disappointed in love, the mood of the spring night is urging him to give love and life another chance. Fofanov says:

> The soul, unaccustomed to dreams,
> Is ready to believe the spring night,
> And the mind hungers and the eyes,
> Often deceived, thirst for tears.

Rilke translates the adjective "unaccustomed," which is formed from a past participle, *otvykšaja* (literally "having become unused to"), by a present tense reflexive verb:

> Die Seele *löst sich* leis vom Traume los
> Bereit zu glauben an das sanfte Nachten.
> Die Sinnen hungern mir, die Augen schmachten
> Nach Tränen, wie noch nie enttäuscht und gross.
>
> [The soul softly *releases itself* from the dream, prepared to believe in the gentle growth of night. My senses hunger, my eyes yearn for tears, disappointed and large as never before.]

Although the essential statement of the stanza, and of the poem, remains the same—that the speaker is being lured back to the dangers and joys of life—the meaning of dreams is diametrically opposed in the two poems. For Fofanov, the feeling is that although he has grown out of the habit of dreaming, he is willing to try again; while Rilke implies that, as the first step on his return to life, he is consciously freeing himself from dreams. Fofanov is consistently Romantic in his equation of dreams and love with deception. Thus the return of his protagonist to dreaming is done with conscious irony; he is aware that he is pursuing an illusion. Rilke's protagonist is not ironic at all; he seems younger, and is determined to relinquish the perhaps soothing world of dream in order to pursue reality, with its inevitable tears, whatever the cost. The idea of seeing clearly and acting courageously was to acquire increasing importance in Rilke's works; in *Malte Laurids Brigge* it is one of the poet Malte's main goals.

The issue of facing reality also played a role in Rilke's attraction to Chekhov's play *The Seagull*, which he translated in early 1900, and which was to influence his own dramatic output. During the early and transitional years of his career, between 1894 and 1901, Rilke made a number of forays into the world of the theater.³⁴ In addition to a variety of rather hazy dramatic plans and ideas, he left ten plays or fragments from those years, of which three were performed.³⁵ One, *Die weisse Fürstin* (*The White Princess*), bears the stamp of the Symbolist dramas of the day, in the style of Hofmannsthal or Maeterlinck. The others strongly resemble works in the prevailing Naturalist mode: a predilection for family tragedies, poverty and exploitation, incest, suicide, young women struggling for individual freedom. The plays give great attention to minute realistic detail in stage directions and show an increasing emphasis on "inner action," the characters' interior development, in an external scene which is almost static. Two of Rilke's dramatic works written between 1899 and 1901—the fragment referred to in his diaries as the "Brautpaar-Stoff" ("Fiancé Material") and the completed drama *Das tägliche Leben* (*Daily Life*)—contain elements which plainly link them to Russian sources, specifically Chekhov and Tolstoy.

When Rilke decided to translate *The Seagull* in early 1900, Chekhov's reputation outside Russia was based almost solely on his short stories. Rilke was impressed by his reading of *The Seagull* and hoped by its publication in German to introduce Chekhov as a dramatist to the German-speaking public. In a letter of 23 February 1900, Rilke excitedly informs his friend Sophie Schill that "one of the foremost German publishers is interested in [Chekhov's] plays and urgently wants to read them. That could ease matters significantly for the plays, if I could succeed in winning this man over to them."³⁶ Work on the translation went quickly, and on 5 March, Rilke could inform Schill that it was finished.³⁷ On the same day he sent off a letter to Chekhov himself, asking the Russian writer to send him a printed copy of his dramas, "for I have the intention of translating *Uncle Vanya* as well."³⁸ There is no indication that Chekhov ever answered; and one critic avers that he was "heartily uninterested in whether or not his books were translated into German."³⁹

But despite Rilke's apparent excitement, he was already having second thoughts about using *The Seagull* to introduce Chekhov's dramas in Germany. He was beginning to feel that the play was too slow-moving, that Treplyov's suicide in the fourth act was not prepared for psychologically, and that a German audience might well take the seriously intended characters as caricatures. It was at this point that Rilke shifted his interest and hopes completely to *Uncle Vanya,* because it seemed to him important that "we introduce Chekhov to the theater with a *sure* success; perhaps *Uncle Vanya* is more suitable for that."⁴⁰ In the 5 March letter to Schill, he notes that the book edition of the two plays seems assured. He further mentions his intentions of translating *Uncle Vanya* as soon as a copy arrives, and of giving both translations to the director of the Secession Theater for consideration. In the same letter, he assures Schill that he would love to see *The Seagull* performed in Moscow, where it would be certain of being a success. (One wonders whether he was aware that *The Seagull* had been a resounding flop in its first performance in St. Petersburg in 1896.) In any case, it is clear that Rilke rejected *The Seagull* not for personal reasons but for pragmatic ones, based on his instinct for the difference between a Russian and a German theater audience.

It is not known what became of the projects to publish and to perform Rilke's *Seagull* translation, or whether Dr. Zickel of the Secession Theater ever received a copy; Rilke never translated *Uncle Vanya*. At first he was prevented by the fact that it was out of print. He may also have been discouraged by Schill's response that it was even less suitable for the stage than *The Seagull*. In any case, neither play ever appeared in Rilke's version, and his manuscript of *The Seagull* has been lost. But the play, of which Rilke declared he had "enjoyed working on it, and learned much from it,"[41] was to bear other fruit in the form of Rilke's own dramatic endeavors. At Easter 1900, just weeks after completing his translation of *The Seagull*, Rilke wrote the play *Das tägliche Leben*, which shows the definite influence of Chekhov, while at the same time forming a link in the long chain of his own works which focus on the lot of the creative person.

Tägliche Leben recounts a crisis in the artistic and romantic life of a young painter, Georg Millner. Although he has shown some talent in the past, particularly when using a certain model named Mascha, he has not worked in a long time. In the midst of his paralysis, Mascha appears, asking whether he has any more work for her. On an impulse, he tells her to come for a sitting the following day. Mascha, who is secretly and patiently in love with Georg, is overjoyed. But that night he meets Helene, a fascinating, elegant woman with whom he immediately becomes infatuated. They spend the evening together in intense conversation, in the course of which he reveals to her all his innermost secrets and demands the same of her. The next day Georg awaits Helene's visit to his studio. He is elated, believing her unusual love will give him the impetus to create once more. When she arrives, however, she astounds him by refusing to become his mistress, or indeed ever to see him again. She argues that with his insistent, possessive love he has used up all their potential future life together. In their verbal fantasies they have created a work of art, which will go on existing just as his paintings do. But now there is nothing left to do or say. As she leaves, she tells the dumbfounded painter to look around him for a more appropriate love that is close by, unnoticed. He realizes that Mascha is the person he really needs, and the play ends with their embrace.

The central question of the play is the relation of one's daily life, the rhythms of one's personal existence, to the ability to create. Georg is devoted to his art with an almost religious fervor, and he is talented, yet he is unable to produce anything because his energies are being misdirected. He is obsessed with a desire to be unconventional but, except in his art, he is totally ordinary. Consequently, he is dissatisfied with his lot and constantly seeks diversion. He is honest enough to sense that he is neglecting what is really important, and thus feels guilty and uneasy as well. When he thinks he has found a catalyst in the electrifying personality of a kindred spirit, he is gently told by Helene, as, less gently, Faust is told by the Earth Spirit, that he aims much too high. Helene turns him away from his false view of himself as a rebel, and points him toward a life consisting of simplicity, harmony, and hard work. Rilke presents here a view of creativity as craft and dedication—a view which Chekhov affirms in *The Seagull,* and which Rilke would find reinforced both in the works of Hauptmann and in Rodin's dictum, "Toujours travailler." But unlike Chekhov, Rilke also emphasizes the importance of the quiet, nurturing rhythms of family life.

Thus far there seems little to recall *The Seagull.* However, parallels exist in at least six areas. These include a prevailing mood of weary melancholy for much of the play; the relative lack of external action, with an emphasis on inner development; the use of meaningful pauses as a part of the dialogue; and the characters' habit of speaking past one another in everyday phrases and cryptic fragments. Further, and more importantly, both writers emphasize the interaction of art and love. Rilke's play echoes *The Seagull* even in details: the names and relationships of specific characters. In the latter, in particular, we can see both Chekhov's influence and Rilke's innovations.

These parallel figures or sets of figures in the two plays are numerous. Both plays focus on artists who are at odds with themselves and their art. Each is loved secretly by a woman named Mascha, whom each ignores and condescends to, or even despises. Rilke's Mascha, however, actually more closely resembles another character in *The Seagull,* the young actress Nina. Both are penniless and must support themselves. Both are strong, self-reliant, and patient; the model possesses these virtues before the action begins, while Nina acquires them in the course of the play. Finally, each play has as a secondary character a medical doctor of the older generation; like Chekhov's Dr. Dorn, Rilke's Dr. Leuthold combines affection for mankind with an ironic view of all human endeavors.

The greatest similarity between the plays lies in the characters and dilemmas of the playwright Treplyov and the painter Georg. But simultaneously, it is in their specific problems and in the solutions provided that the works most clearly diverge. It has been said that *The Seagull*, in juxtaposing two older, traditional, and successful artists—Arkadina and Trigorin—with two young, daring ones—Nina and Treplyov—"comprises as its essential element Chekhov's typology of the varieties of creative personality."[42] *The Seagull* is clearly concerned, among other things, with the nature of the creative artist. But Chekhov's artists are also human beings, engaged in complicated human relationships. Their personal problems constantly interact with, and undermine, their "artistic" lives. Treplyov desires to create "new art forms,"[43] and is disgusted by the triteness of the traditional theater. Yet his identity as an artist is threatened by his weakness as a man—his clinging love for Nina, his jealously of Trigorin, and his humiliating attachment to his mother. It is not in Treplyov but in Nina that Chekhov suggests the growth of a real artist through her single-mindedness and the sacrifice of all human ties. She has left Treplyov for a brief and ill-fated affair with Trigorin, has borne a child which soon died, and has in the process of her suffering succeeded in becoming a genuine actress. She tells Treplyov,

> I know now, Kostya, that in our work—it's all the same whether we act on the stage or write—the main thing is not fame, nor brilliance, not what I dreamed of, but the ability to endure. One bears one's cross, and has faith. I have faith . . . and when I think of my vocation, I don't fear life.[44]

But her strength has also made her solitary, and Treplyov, unable to go on without her support, commits suicide.

Rilke approaches the questions of love, art, and the "interhuman" in a different way. Rather than pitting generations and creative types against one another in a process of mutual attrition, he focuses on one crucial moment of loss and despair in the life of a single artist. Rilke makes Georg's dilemma parallel Treplyov's for a time: like Treplyov, Georg suffers a setback in his career; like him, he seeks help outside himself in the support of a strong woman; and initially, he too meets with failure—we have seen how Helene dismisses him. Yet Rilke resolves Georg's dilemma in an emphatically different way: Georg survives, and ends both more rooted in life than before and more prepared to create, while Treplyov shoots himself.

The different resolution of the two plays arises largely from the respective messages given by the departing women to the despairing artists. Nina offers Treplyov a message he is incapable of accepting because it demands of him two things he does not possess: the strength to live and work alone, and a sustaining belief in his own talent. Treplyov's art alone cannot sustain him because it is hollow, abstract, and without roots in human reality. (There are strong hints in remarks by Nina, Trigorin, and Dorn that Treplyov has never managed to find a focus in his writing; they complain that there is no real human life in his plays.) Helene leaves Georg with a much more mundane message but one that, perhaps for that very reason, he is able to put to use. She knows that in order for him to survive he must find a "happiness that keeps better pace with life" (IV, 914). A crucial fact is that at this point, Rilke provides his protagonist with a substitute for the unattainable, almost unreal Helene and the world she represents. With the patient, humble, persevering—one is tempted to say "Russian"—Mascha, Georg will be able to grow and prosper. We are intended to picture a marriage in which Georg, flattered and inspired by her humble devotion, returns with vigor to his art.

An interesting point for speculation is the fact that Rilke was careful not to make Mascha an artist herself. Treplyov's tragedy is, after all, made complete by the fact that not only is his mother an actress, totally wrapped up in herself and her career, but the woman he loves is also an artist in her own right, who chooses her vocation over a life exclusively dedicated to supporting him in his art. Rilke's alteration of the profession of the female protagonist from actress (active) to model (passive) not only enabled him to give his play a happy ending; it may also reflect misgivings about the union of two persons both deeply committed to careers. His own experiences were to bear out these fears. As we have seen, his intimate relationship with Lou, a strongly independent woman, writer, and thinker, had already shown signs of strain because of her independence, and was to come to an end only a few months after he finished his work on *The Seagull* and *Tägliche Leben*. His sudden marriage to the sculptress Clara Westhoff in 1901 was likewise to lead to disillusionment. Early in their life together, they made a pact, each promising to respect the other's solitude as artists and as people. The arrangement worked, or at least lasted, for a little more than a year. Rilke left for Paris in 1902 to do research for his monograph on Rodin, and except for common vacations and occasional brief periods together, the couple in effect ceased to be married. Though he nowhere says so, it may be assumed that the marriage failed at least in part because Clara, like Lou, was a woman with a strong sense of self, dedicated to her own artistic calling. And though Rilke needed, and sought over and over again, a woman whose intelligence and sensitivity could respond to his own, he seems also to have been unable to provide the time, energy, and attention that such a woman would have demanded of him in turn.

At this stage of his career, in the early months of 1900, Rilke was able to convince himself that an artist could live a normal life and still be productive and true to himself. Indeed, in *Tägliche Leben* he makes it a sine qua non for his protagonist. At the end of *The Seagull,* Chekhov offers an austere vision. The successful philistines, Arkadina and Trigorin, prevail; Treplyov, the hollow reed, succumbs; and only Nina promises to become a real artist, though at the expense of any personal fulfillment outside her work. In the denouement of *Tägliche Leben,* Rilke rejects this vision. But he was to discover that his own view was an idyllic one. A revealing letter written in 1926 to the Russian poet Marina Tsvetaeva, in which Rilke looks back over his life, shows how early he had begun to settle into the irrevocable isolation of an artist-recluse. He writes, "My house and the familial hearth, which had arisen in part against my will, were already . . . falling apart; and, not dissolving the marriage, which lasted less than two years, I could return to the lonely life which was real for me."[45] Rilke's life was a series of such attempts, and failures, to achieve a human relationship in which he could still work. *Tägliche Leben* represents an early confrontation with the problem. The artist with the down-to-earth companion bringing him the "happiness that keeps pace with life" seems to anticipate the compromise to which Thomas Mann was to bring his bourgeois poet Tonio Kröger two years later, when he wrote, "If anything is capable of turning a man of letters into a poet, it is this bourgeois love of mine for the human, the vital and the ordinary."[46] Rilke himself, however, despite repeated attempts to make contact with "life," was to remain an essentially lonely man for whom poetry could grow only out of the sacrifice of himself and of any permanent human ties.

Like *Tägliche Leben,* the fragment referred to in the diaries as the "Brautpaar-Stoff"[47] focuses on the relations between the sexes, and again reflects Rilke's ambiguity on the subject. An emancipated young woman, Zenaida Stollbow—the name, like Mascha's, is conspicuously Russian—is in the process of guiding her young friend and protégé, Luise, toward independence and womanhood. Luise and her fiancé, Robert, have nowhere to go to talk freely, and Zenaida has made her workroom available to them. Zenaida conceives of friendship, including that within marriage, as the highest form of human relationship. It is toward this open, intellectually vital kind of friendship, free of socially imposed falsity, that she is trying to educate Luise. But she must also protect her from Robert's heavy-handed theories. Robert and Luise have made a pact to read one another's diaries before they marry. The impetus has obviously come from Robert:

> *Luise:* As a matter of fact, we've promised to tell each other everything we've experienced so far. All the feelings. . . . Everything should be quite clear, for that's the way it should be with modern people. They should know each other completely before they get married. Fine, isn't it?
> *Zena:* Did Robert think that up?
> *Luise [hesitating]*: We . . . together. We both wanted to. Otherwise you can't really love each other.
> *Zena:* . . . says Robert?

(IV, 871–72)

The agreement is in fact fairly one-sided. We have previously learned that Zenaida has told Luise the facts of life only three weeks before, a service her mother and aunts have studiously avoided doing her. Thus it is unlikely that Luise can have much to confess, or that her diaries will reveal a great deal beyond the earnest *Schwärmerei* of a sheltered girl of Wilhelmine Germany. Robert's real motives for suggesting the exchange of diaries cannot have stemmed from a desire to get information, but to give it. They may stem at best from a desire for candor, or an intellectual satisfaction at the gesture of starting off his marriage with a clean slate. In addition, however, he may have given in to a desire not only to confess, to reveal himself, but even perhaps to test his bride's loyalties, her strength, and possibly, in a perverse way, her spiritual purity by observing her reactions to his confessions. Luise's weakness and frivolity seem to be confirmed when she begins reading aloud the "exciting" passages from Robert's diary. Zenaida is upset because she sees through Robert's ploy, and because Luise's emotional immaturity is painfully obvious to her. She feels the two are young and foolish, playing a dangerous game with their feelings and their future.

A central idea of the play is Rilke's perennial interest in finding an ideal form of human intercourse which would preserve the privacy and wholeness of all persons, while allowing them to share their lives. It is not certain what direction this theme would have taken in the completed play, but it seems clear that Zenaida, with her insistence on self-discipline, loyalty, and generosity, would have been the bearer of Rilke's current ideas on the subject. The motif of the urge to confess is not one that predominates in Rilke's works, but it is an important one in his life. The relationship with Lou had always had a strong confessional aspect; indeed, it seems likely that in leaving Rilke, Lou was in large part freeing herself from his frightening dependence on her.[48] Rilke was perhaps vaguely aware of the destructiveness of this habit, and this may have played a role in the creation of the Robert episode.

A source for the specific form of Robert's confessional urge can be found in a well-known episode in the life of Tolstoy, which Rilke, given his avid interest in the Russian writer, is sure to have known. In 1862, at the age of thirty-four, Tolstoy was engaged to marry Sophia Behrs, a girl sixteen years his junior. Sophia had been given the usual proper upbringing of a daughter of a Moscow aristocratic family. Tolstoy, on the other hand, had led a more than usually rough and debauched youth, and had set it all down vividly in his diary, interspersed with self-denunciations, coldly rational resolutions, crazy plans, and wild outbursts of self-pity. Believing in complete candor, he gave the diary to his bride to read on the eve of their marriage. Sophia was understandably appalled, but somehow managed to accept Leo nonetheless (although the effect it was to have on their marriage was anything but constructive). In Tolstoy's behavior we can already see traces of the ruthless moralist of his later years. But there may also have been more than a little of the motivation which we have attributed to Rilke's Robert: exhibitionism and a certain perversity. (In Tolstoy's case the experiment may have backfired: can he have been entirely pleased that Sophia withstood the barrage of shameful episodes he had unleashed upon her?) In any case, the anecdote about Tolstoy's diaries helped give dramatic shape to an idea with which Rilke was trying to come to terms.

In addition to the dramas, there remain a small number of scattered original works from the years surrounding the Russian journeys which display Russian influences of one kind or another. These include eight poems written in Russian, as well as German poems, poetic fragments, and a prose sketch.

In a letter to Sophie Schill dated 16 February 1900, Rilke expressed the desire to be able to write poetry in Russian: "That seems to me to be the greatest thing: to be able to make Russian verses. Who might do that!" ("Wer das dürfte!" [IV, 967–68]). Some months later, in November of the same year, the wish was fulfilled. In the space of ten days, six poems unexpectedly "came to him" in Russian. He recorded them in his diary and sent a fair copy to Lou, dedicating them to her. Then, in April 1901, two more Russian poems came. These were evidently forgotten, for the only known copy was found over thirty years later on a loose sheet of paper stuck in a book of the letters of the painter Ivanov, which Rilke was known to have been reading in the spring of 1901.[49]

The poems are in places quite vague; one has the distinct feeling that this arose from Rilke's attempts to achieve complex and oblique images in a language which he did not have fully under control. The stress patterns often do not mesh with those of the Russian language, and the poems are full of morphological and syntactical errors, particularly involving case endings, gender, and verbal aspect.[50] While these should not be overlooked, neither should they be considered the most important aspect of the works, for it is in any case amazing that Rilke was able to write Russian poems at all, after only a year of intermittent study. Their very existence bears eloquent witness to the intensity of his emotional and subconscious involvement with the Russian spirit.

The poems present an interesting mixture of allusions. Some refer directly to events during the second Russian journey; others are variations on the usual Russian motifs of patience, selfless love, a dark God, the endless expanse of the steppe, the Russian peasant, and Rilke's own joy and sense of growth in his experiences. Several poems may have been influenced by works of Russian literature, while others have nothing essentially Russian about them other than the language in which they were written. In the second through the sixth poems, Rilke combines memories from his stay with Lou at the hut of Drozhzhin[51] with motifs central to much of his work in 1899 and 1900. In the second poem, "Second Song" (IV, 948), the speaker tells of walking through the seemingly endless steppe, so vast that it makes him forget he has ever known another country. He addresses someone, apparently Lou, and calls Russia "tvoja rodina" ("thy homeland"). This address, and the fact that the first six poems were dedicated to Lou, reaffirm the identity which Russia and Lou had in Rilke's mind. All of the poems gain in significance when read in the light of Rilke and Lou's problematic relationship.

The speaker in this poem characterizes Russia as the land where "God darkens" ("temneet Bog"), and "a suffering folk came to him and took him as a brother" ("stradajuščij narod / prišel k nemu i bral ego kak brata").[52] He contrasts it with another time and another country—the gay, empty days on a southern sea, obviously Italy, an Italy which in the *Stunden-Buch* will be the epitome of all that the monk-protagonist of that book hates about Western Christianity, its art, and its ethos. The spiritual conflict between East and West forms an important undercurrent in the works of this period. Rilke had spent some time in Italy in 1898, and coming on the heels of this experience, Russia seemed to him a fulfillment of all that Italy had merely promised. In a letter written from St. Petersburg in May 1899, he declares:

> I perceive my stay in Russia as a strange completion of that Florentine spring, whose influence and success I told you about. . . . Florence seems to me now a kind of advance training and preparation for Moscow.[53]

And the juxtaposition appears more strongly stated, and more in the form of a contrast than a mere sequence, in the *Stunden-Buch*. There Rilke writes, "Der Ast vom Baume Gott, der über Italien reicht, / *hat* schon geblüht. / . . . er wird keine Früchte haben" ("The branch of the tree 'God' that stretches over Italy has already blossomed. . . . It will bear no fruit" [I, 271]). A few pages later, turning to Russia, he goes on:

> Mit einem Ast, der jenem niemals glich,
> wird Gott, der Baum, auch einmal sommerlich
> verkündend werden und aus Reife rauschen;
> in einem Lande, wo die Menschen lauschen,
> wo jeder ähnlich einsam ist wie ich.
>
> (I, 274)

[With a branch which never resembled that one, God, the tree, will also become prophetic with summer, and rustle with ripeness; in a land where people listen, where each is as lonely as I.]

In the next two Russian poems, "Conflagration" (IV, 949), and "Morning" (IV, 950), we find a similar mixture of the biographical and the metaphorical. In "Conflagration" the poet recounts a ride in a peasant cart, or *telega,* through the steppe at night; between him and the driver flows a silent communion. Suddenly the horizon is lit by the glow of a fire. The driver looks up to Heaven and thinks, "Life is hard. Why is there no salvation?" In "Morning" the poet recalls rising early and walking with Lou among the roses. He reassures her that the past is only a *bylina*—a legend—and that she needn't worry about the future. These two poems recount, on one level, events that occurred during the stay with Drozhzhin. On the fourth day of their visit with him, Rilke, Lou, and their host drove to Novinki, the nearby estate of the aristocratic artist Nikolay Alexeevich Tolstoy. A note in Rilke's diary accompanying the poem "Conflagration" indicates that it was by *telega* that they had made the trip to Novinki and back.[54] "Morning" refers to the habit he and Lou had of getting up very early and walking barefoot in the wet grass and flowers.[55]

On another level the poems are more than mere reminiscences; they also express Rilke's state of mind at the time of their writing, five months after the events described. By December 1900, he and Lou had separated, and he was caught up in one of his fits of self-doubt and artistic paralysis. The odd preoccupation of the *telega* driver with salvation, and the melancholy mood of "Conflagration" mean more in this context. Likewise, the poet's attempts in "Morning" to reassure his listener that there will be a future, and that they will share it—"Čto budet? Ty ne bezpokojsja, / . . . da budut . . . / dni sijajuščago sveta / i budem my i budet Bog" ("What is to come? Don't worry, there will be days full of radiant light, and we shall exist, and so shall God")—suddenly sound like whistling in the dark. By December 1900, Rilke knew that his future was probably not going to be shared by Lou. Yet he must have felt, at least back there on the Volga, that Russia was going to prove a new, miraculous beginning for him.

The two poems which follow, "The Face" (IV, 951) and "The Old Man" (IV, 952), are less personal; they focus on the Russian peasant—Brutzer calls "The Old Man" the "*ecce homo* of the eternal Russian"[56]— as a pious laborer with unplumbed metaphysical depths. In "The Face" the poet imagines what it would have been like had he been born a peasant. His face would have been simple, and his hands alone would have shown his love and patience. At his death, his hands would go empty to the grave, but his face would reveal the truth—not just his own identity, but "večnoe lico truda" ("the eternal face of labor"). In "The Old Man" a peasant, too feeble to go with the others to the fields, lies on the stove in his hut, dreaming of days gone by. His life has been lived in an intense silence because he never found a way of releasing and expressing the love within him.

The two poems focus on aspects of the peasant to which Rilke frequently returned. His life, a round of work and prayer, is lived out in silence. He is a riddle to those around him: "Nikto krugom ne by uznal—kto ja" ("No one around would guess who I am"). He is inarticulate, yet full of inchoate dreams: "I govoril by, byl-by kak poèt" ("And if he spoke, he would be like a poet"). Like the God whom he has "taken as a brother," the Russian peasant is dark and secretive. Together they represent the mutually dependent halves of a religion which Rilke describes elsewhere in the following terms:

> The Russian church . . . lives a life that is endlessly quiet, endlessly slow, and related to the innermost life of the people, whose soul does not get bigger like a flower, in one year, but like some trees whose growth one notices only if one has left them as a boy and come back to them an old man.[57]

The value attached to silence differs somewhat from poem to poem. In "The Old Man" it seems symptomatic of his inability to express his secret depths: "love / has been moving in his breast for over a thousand years, / and has found no lips for herself." But in "Conflagration" and "The Face" silence has a positive connotation. It is the medium of the "narrative" that passes between the poet and the *telega* driver. And the protagonist of "The Face," imagining the peasant he would have been, seems proud of the silence maintained by his hands and face, which reveal nothing until his death.

There are two nineteenth-century Russian authors whose works may have influenced Rilke on this subject of silence: the poet Fyodor Tyutchev and the novelist Nikolay Leskov. By February 1900, Rilke was already familiar with Tyutchev's works.[58] In the same letter in which he encloses a transliteration of Fofanov's "Springtime and Night," Rilke comments briefly and approvingly on Tyutchev's consciousness of form, and the beauty of his verse.[59] Brutzer suggests that Rilke found Tyutchev's language difficult, "too sublimated," and found in him too little of "the thing which attracted him as essentially Russian—the simplicity and closeness to life of the Russian."[60] But there is at least one poem by Tyutchev which may have manifested one of the qualities which Rilke himself chose to make part of his image of the Russian. This is the short poem "Silentium," written in 1836. Here the poet extols the virtue of silence, and urges the reader to conceal his dreams and feelings so as to keep them intact. In the second stanza he says:

> How will the heart express itself?
> How will another understand you?
> Will he understand what it is that you live by?
> A thought that is spoken is a falsehood;

> By stirring up the springs you will cloud them:
> Drink of them, and be silent.[61]

In the next stanza he recommends learning to live within oneself where there is a whole world of mystery and enchantment, which could be destroyed if revealed to the outside world. This is a point of view which might have underlain the portrayal of silence in "The Face" and possibly in "The Old Man" as well, if one supposes that the old man, rather than being unable to speak, in fact chose not to do so.

Nikolay Leskov was a novelist and story writer who focused on life in the provinces. His characters—peasants, poor clergymen, vagabonds—engage in a struggle for goodness against heavy odds; their surroundings and their own worldly natures are against them. Leskov often points out the positive value of silence in this struggle, most conspicuously in his novel *Cathedral Folk,* first published in 1872. This is a silence both literal and spiritual, a quietness of address and habit, and a way of striving for peace. Rilke was aware of this quality in Leskov, thanks to Lou, and may well have read *Cathedral Folk* by this time.

The first of the two Russian poems written in 1901, "I Am So Tired" ("Ja tak ustal" [IV, 959]),[62] is far removed from the Russian setting and motifs of the earlier poems. Except for the image of windless fields (*bezvetrennyx polej*), which might be a negative echo of the "windy distances" (*vetrennaja dal'*) of the steppe in "Second Song," there is nothing to suggest Russia overtly. The poem is the anguished cry of a poet who finds himself unable to write. Oppressed by emptiness, he can only listen to his own silence, which grows like fear in the night. This image foreshadows a passage in *Malte Laurids Brigge* where Malte, "abandoned" by his furniture and his possessions in the night, becomes the prey of an all-encompassing fear. The poet here is linked by this unwilled silence to the old man who dies with his secrets unrevealed, through the lack of a way to express them.

The second of these poems, "I Am So Alone" (IV, 959), likewise expresses a mood of alienation, almost of despair. Here too the poet is silent, but now silence has become a part of his character which separates him from other men. "Ja tak odin. Nikto ne ponimaet / molčanie: golos moix dlinnyx dnej" ("I am so alone. No one understands the silence: the voice of my long days"). In the mood of certain lines and in the structure (five-foot lines, alternating masculine / feminine rhymes) of this poem are echoes of Lermontov's "Vyxožu odin ja na dorogu" ("I Go Out onto the Road Alone"), which Rilke was to translate in 1919, but which he knew much earlier. In the second stanza of Lermontov's poem, the poet comments on the wondrous heavens, and asks himself rhetorical questions about his melancholy state of mind:

V nebesax toržestvenno i čudno!
. . . . .
Čto že mne tak bol'no i tak trudno?
Ždul' čego? Žaleju li o čem?⁶³

[In the heavens it is solemn and marvelous! Why is it so painful for me? Am I waiting for something? Do I regret something?]

In Rilke's last Russian poem, two images occur which are reminiscent of Lermontov. First, the marvelous skies appear, now transformed into the poet's eyes: "I vetra net, kotoryj otkryvaet / bol'šie nebesa moix očej" ("And there is no wind which opens the great heavens of my eyes"). And like Lermontov's "I," Rilke's asks himself certain searching questions. Staring out of the window at an alien scene, where something large lies in wait, he asks himself, "Dumaju: èto ja? / Čego ja ždu? I gde moja duša?" ("I think: is it I? What am I waiting for? And where is my soul?" [IV, 959]). Lermontov's persona tries to account for his gloom in the face of the wonders of nature around him; he is able to answer his own questions in the following stanzas. Rilke's persona seems to stand outside himself, divorced from his own body and its actions. His own intentions and gestures seem those of another, and he is unsure even of the 'location" of his soul. The impression is of someone very ill, perhaps feverish or drugged, whose disorientation is so great that neither body nor soul is under his control any longer. It is a state of mind that had roots in Rilke's actual experiences at the time.

His diary breaks off on 22 December 1900, and there are few letters available from the first few months of 1901. But certain facts are known about this period, which may have contributed to the mood of the last two Russian poems. In the fall of 1900, just after the break with Lou, Rilke went to Worpswede; there he met and was greatly charmed by two artists, Paula Becker and Clara Westhoff. There is evidence that Rilke was especially strongly attracted to Paula, so her letter to him on 12 November 1900 telling him of her engagement to her fellow painter Otto Modersohn must have been a profound shock.⁶⁴ It was a bleak winter for him, deprived as he was of Lou's support and abruptly disabused of any hopes of a liaison with Paula. In a letter written a little over a week after the last Russian poems, he notes that he is "convalescing at the moment after a long and not wholly minor illness, and the pen lies heavy in my unaccustomed hand."⁶⁵ Another letter written soon after this one displays a startling juxtaposition of mysterious sufferings and anticipated joys; he thanks a friend for her letter, "which came to me precisely at a time of confusion and violent change, after which I'm just now able to make out the path a few steps in front of me. I was sick and am now convalescent, and want to greet you briefly, because tomorrow I will get a dear wife."⁶⁶

In these cryptic lines we see the aftermath of a sickness which may have had its psychological roots in the disappointments of the previous autumn, taking their toll in physical ways as well as in the silence complained of in these poems.

An odd image links Rilke's last two Russian poems. In the first the poet says, "Pustaja noč' bezvetrennyx polej / ležit nad tišinoj moix očej" ("The empty night of the windless fields lies on the silence of my eyes"). In the second, as we saw, no wind comes to reveal the heavens of his eyes, to blow away the clouds which cover them. Both images produce a feeling of oppressive stillness. The poet, blinded and becalmed, awaits a wind of inspiration, or of human contact, that will set him in motion once more. Rilke seems to have hoped that his marriage to Clara Westhoff, so sudden and unprepared for, would clear his eyes and blow away his depression. But the way in which he announces his wedding in the letter to his friend is such a non sequitur that one wonders to what extent Clara was ever real for Rilke at all, and how much chance there ever was for her to replace the phantom affections of Paula, or, more difficult, the vast complex of emotions that Lou had taken away with her.

In the *Sonette an Orpheus*, written in 1922, the image of the wind of creativity will reappear. There, the poet tells a youth he must forget his first reactions to life, and let them ferment in his unconscious, so that they will reemerge as truth, a wind of creativity: "To sing truly is a different breath. / A breath about nothing. A breeze in the god. A wind" (I, 732). In the Russian poems Rilke, painfully aware of his becalmed state, lamenting the absence of a wind, seems unable at that moment to do what he will later advise the youth to do: be patient and trust to the inner process of fermentation.

One Russian poem remains to be discussed—the first of the series, written 29 November 1900 and called simply "First Song." I have left it until last because it occupies a special place in the group as a bridge between Rilke's early Russian experiences and the poems of his late phase. "First Song" is a kind of lullaby. The entire text is given in English translation here, for the purpose of extended comparison with several other texts.

> Evening. By the sea sat
> a girl, as a mother sits
> by a child. She sang,
> and now she hears
> his drowsy breathing;
> seeing the peace and hope,
> she smiles:
> it's not a smile—it is a radiance,
> the holiday of her face.

> The child, just like the sea, will
> touch the distance and the heavens—
> your pride or your sorrow,
> whispering or silence.
> You know only his shore,
> yours is to sit and wait . . .
> and so you sing a song,
> and in no way do you help
> him live and be and sleep.
>   (IV, 947–48)

The poem shares one obvious element with other works of the genre: a child is being sung to sleep by his mother. It is unusual, however, in being a narrative poem; it describes a mother watching over her child, but we do not hear her sing. Nor is the poem traditional in terms of its form, lacking both refrain and any direct address to the child, as well as the usual onomatopoetic devices found in lullabies. The mother is sometimes described in the third person and sometimes addressed as "thou," but she never speaks in the first person, as in many lullabies. The point of view is that of the poet, who maintains his distance from the events throughout. In this way he is free to pass judgment on his character directly, at the end of the poem, rather than presenting the scene as a dramatic situation and letting the character reveal herself. This device will contribute significantly to the poem's final effect.

The poem's link with Russia lies in its similarity to a well-known poem by Lermontov, "Cossack Lullaby" ("Kazač'ja kolybel'naja pesnja"),[67] written in 1838. The poem is a more or less traditional lullaby, in a Caucasian setting. A Cossack mother, in her song to her child, evokes the rough and majestic mountains in which they live; an enemy tribesman sharpens his knife, but the child's father, "an old warrior," will make everything all right. Four of the six verses concern the child's future. He will grow up and, taking arms, will ride into battle, "a hero in visage, and a Cossack at heart." She envisions how she will sew a silk saddle blanket for him, and he will wave as he rides away, wearing the holy icon she has given him. The poem is written in alternating lines of four and three feet, and each stanza ends with the phrase "Bajuški-baju," the soothing Russian equivalent of "hushaby."

Rilke's poem and Lermontov's have several details in common, besides those of the stock scene belonging to the genre: the mother who sings to her sleeping son. In both the time is evening: Lermontov has the moon looking into the cradle; Rilke begins his first line "Evening." In both cases reference is made to the child's sleep. Both women sit beside a body of water—Lermontov's beside the rushing river Terek, Rilke's beside the sea. And both poets concern themselves with the child's future, and the mother's role in it. The fact that this somewhat unusual and specific concern is central to both poems allows us to assume some connection between them. But at the same time, it is in their treatment of this theme that the two poems differ most.

The Cossack mother and her child have firm places in a traditional culture. There, women are wives and mothers; their goals—to marry and bear warriors. The mother in the poem lulls the child with visions of his future, which she can imagine fairly accurately because she knows the role he is to play. She sings to him, "You yourself recognize that the time will come, the martial life; boldly you'll place your foot in the stirrup, and seize your weapon." She can even envision what her own actions and reactions will be. She will give him a saddle cloth and an icon, go out to see him off, and that night weep bitter tears. The poem elaborates in great detail the future of the Cossack mother as it is tied to that of her son. She cannot know his precise fate, but takes for granted that it will involve bravery, battle, and separation. For the mother all this is made bearable by her pride in him and by the definite and necessary role she has to play in preparing for his future.

How different is the relation of mother to child in Rilke's poem! The child is likened to the sea: he will "touch the distance and the heavens." But this breadth of gesture or possibility is all that we know of him; and his mother knows little more—"only his shore." She doesn't even know whether her son will bring her pride or sorrow, unlike the Cossack, who will definitely cause his mother both. And most crucially of all, the mother in Rilke's poem has no role to play in her son's future: "Yours is to sit and wait . . . / . . . and in no way do you help / him live and be and sleep." She is cut off from his life in an oddly final way, unable to give him anything "for the road." The sleeping child's vague, looming future seems to have severed him from his mother—perhaps in the very act of birth—and made each of them irrevocably alone. While he is small, the mother can still watch over his sleep and sing to him, smiling and waiting. But she can do no more. The poem emphasizes the essential isolation of one human being from another, specifically in the relationship usually considered the closest and most interdependent, that of mother and child.

Erich Simenauer, in a study based on the assumptions and methods of depth psychology, devotes considerable space to the role of mothers in Rilke's works.[68] He connects the complex, at times contradictory, treatment of the figure with Rilke's peculiar, destructive relationship to his own mother. Phia Rilke had dressed and treated her son as a little girl until he was seven. Fanatical, ambitious, and bigoted, she was given to sentimental religiosity and odd fancies, and alternately spoiled and neglected little René (who later changed his name to Rainer at Lou's instigation). These and other factors combined to create in Rilke a violently ambivalent attitude toward his own mother, and toward mothers in general. Of Phia he wrote to a friend that he felt her to be an utter stranger, "who by chance brought precisely *me* into the world."[69] His most devastating commentary on her is found in a letter to Lou in 1904. He was living in Rome at the time, and felt a visit of his mother to the city as a catastrophic encroachment on him.

> Every meeting with her is a kind of regression. . . . When I have to see this lost, unreal woman, connected with nothing, who cannot grow old, then I feel how even as a child I strove to get away from her, and I fear deep within me that even after years and years of running . . . I am still not far enough from her. . . . And that I am yet her child; that some time or other a barely perceptible secret door in this faded wall that belongs to nothing was my entrance into the world![70]

We see that Rilke felt both essentially isolated from his mother and yet too close to her, threatened by her very existence.

In his works, Rilke often portrays mothers either as warm, understanding, and selfless—obviously a wistful compensation for the real Phia Rilke—or as cold and self-absorbed, a painful echo of his own experiences. At other times his ambivalence and fear show through, and the depiction of the mother is a defensive one; then we perceive his desire to distance the mother from her son and free him to live his own life. Such is the case in the Russian lullaby "First Song." And such is the situation in an important late poem as well: the third elegy of the *Duineser Elegien,* written in 1912 and 1913. The elegy distinguishes love between unique individuals, such as a young girl envisions it, from the impersonal, dark, primeval forces which flow within a man, far deeper and older than anything which the girl alone could cause in him. The poem is a powerful evocation of man's hidden drives, "jenen verborgenen schuldigen Fluss-Gott des Bluts" ("that hidden guilty river-god in the blood" [I, 693]). It is couched in terms which suggest Jung's collective unconscious, with specifically sexual coloration. And it denies the mother any role in the boy's life, beyond gestures of reassurance in his infancy.

Even in the small child, Rilke says, strong forces exist. Indeed, they were alive in him before birth, waiting for him. When the child is frightened at night, his mother works miracles of comfort. Her mere presence seems to chase the shadows into corners; she can explain every mysterious noise:

> das nächtlich verdächtige Zimmer
> machtest du harmlos, aus deinem Herzen voll Zuflucht
> mischtest du menschlichern Raum seinem Nachtraum hinzu.
>   (I, 694)

[The room, suspicious each night, you made harmless; from your heart full of succor, you mixed more human space with its night space.]

And he seems comforted. But there are places in the blood, in the inner darkness of dreams, where even a mother cannot reach.

> Aber innen: wer wehrte,
> hinderte innen in ihm die Fluten der Herkunft?
> . . . Liebend
> stieg er hinab in das ältere Blut, in die Schluchten,
> wo das Furchtbare lag, noch satt von den Vätern.
> . . . Ja, das Entsetzlich lächelte.
> (I, 695)

[But inside: who prevailed, hindered within him the floods of descent? . . . Loving, he climbed down into the older blood, into the ravines where the Fearful lay, still satiated with the fathers. . . . Yes, the Dreadful smiled.]

It is this powerful heritage that fills and guides him, and makes him different from woman (who apparently did not share his fearful and passionate heritage). He is, from birth, essentially Other, unreachable and beyond the real protection of his mother, who can do so much, superficially, to help him.

A further important aspect, found in Lermontov as well, links the lullaby and the third elegy—the use of images of water. We have seen that the Cossack mother speaks of a great Caucasian river: "Along the stones the Terek streams, / the turbid billows splash," which serves to establish the Caucasian setting. Later the river appears as the backdrop for a dreamlike dramatic vignette. In Rilke's poems, the water images are more central, being used in the first case as the major means of characterization and in the second as a principal metaphor for the unconscious. In the Russian poem the sleeping child, like the sea, will touch the distances, while his mother knows only the shore. His life will be broad and, if we pursue other possibilities of the sea metaphor, perhaps also restless, mutable, fathomless, or stormy. Woman, in the person of his mother, will be left behind, incapable of following the surge and depths of his future life.

In the elegy, too, Rilke sees the child's life in terms of water images; but here they represent his racial past and the inherited urges which he brought with him, unwittingly, into life. Dark forces, "das Entsetzliche," existed even in the amniotic fluid: "da du ihn trugst schon / war es im Wasser, das den Keimenden leicht macht" ("when you were carrying him, it was already in the water that makes the ripening one light" [I, 695]). The spirit of the undifferentiated sexual urge is a "river-god," "des Blutes Neptun" ("the Neptune of the blood"), with his "furchtbarer Dreizack" ("terrible trident" [I, 693]). The mother is at first able to defend her son against the "wallendes Chaos" ("seething chaos" [I, 694]), but eventually he is overwhelmed from within by "floods of descent." Significantly, one feature of the Ur-landscape of his unconscious is the "trockene Flussbett / einstiger Mütter" ("dry riverbed of erstwhile mothers" [I, 696]), of "foremothers," ancestresses who once bore myriads of lives but are now arid and barren. The mothers are part of the general water imagery of dark fecundity, but only so long as they are literally carrying and nourishing the children. Their power begins to wane when the river-god takes over, even before birth. And like the mother in "First Song," they fade into the background of the child's private, independent existence.

The elegy ends with a plea to the young girl, the same lover whom it began by humbling and isolating from the reality of love. The poet begs her to help the boy, now grown to manhood, by leading him "near the garden" and "restraining him." Thus woman appears to have a function in his life, but a tenuous one, a small tentative gesture of protection against those inner forces so powerfully evoked in the rest of the poem. Perhaps the gentle gesture asked of the girl corresponds in purpose and magnitude to the smile and the song of the mother in the lullaby—a loving, futile act. This much the cautious poet allows her to do, but no more.

Of the scattered works—and by this I mean isolated pieces which were not included by Rilke in any cycle or collection—written in German around this time, only a handful relate to the Russian experience. The prose sketch "Wladimir, der Wolkenmaler" ("Vladimir the Cloud-painter" [IV, 587–91]), written before July 1899, seems to function as a first tentative approach to a number of motifs which reappear in later works; several of these are associated with Russian themes. In the story, three disconcerted friends visit Wladimir in his atelier. He is a strange figure, an "artist" whose works seem to consist only of the voluminous smoke from his cigarettes and the quiet words of wisdom he speaks from behind these clouds. The three friends, a poet, a painter, and an aristocrat, who are all inspired by his words to go off and create something, resemble three painters who appear in one of the heavily Russian-flavored *Geschichten*. The role of Wladimir Lubowski in the sketch, and his relation to the Russian God of the *Stunden-Buch* and the *Geschichten* are indicated by his name. Wladimir is based on the Russian roots *vladet'* (to "possess," "control") and *mir* ("world," "peace"). Lubowski is from the word *ljubov'* ("love"). As a loving ruler of the word, or possessor of peace, Wladimir functions as a kind of god figure. This is reinforced by his identity as an artist (the Russian God of the later cycles is often both artist and artifact), as well as by several elements in his portrayal. Like God, he is attainable via his creations: "One gets at Wladimir Lubowski only through his works" (IV, 588). Like God, he sometimes sits silently behind these works, seemingly oblivious to the questioning of men. When his visitors ask him about his art and his dwelling, there is no answer except "Silence. Wladimir remains distant behind his clouds" (IV, 588). When he does speak, it is at his own pace, at a time of his own choosing, and his words are like a revelation, "nothing but secret Ascensions" ("lauter heimliche Himmelfahrten" [IV, 589]). And the words that he speaks concern a God who is dark and patient, who waits in the depths of the earth where the roots are, rather than in the cold sharp light where men seek him. These images of dark and light and the vision of God as deep rather than exalted are central to Rilke's vision of Russia's God in both the cycles mentioned.

A figure who first appears in Rilke's writings in 1899, and to whom he returns five times between then and 1907, is that of Saint George. While George is by no means a saint of the Russian church alone, Rilke's treatment of him sometimes suggests that he perceived the saint in a Russian light. The earliest work dealing with Saint George is a poem entitled "Meinem lieben Heinrich Vogeler mit einem russischen Heiligen" ("To My Dear Heinrich Vogeler with a Russian Saint" [III, 643–44]). Vogeler, an artist at the colony at Worpswede, did an etching using the Saint George motif, complete with slender maiden and gaping dragon, and this picture probably served as an inspiration for Rilke's poem. But the fact that Rilke calls George a Russian saint points to the connection with Russian sources which the motif had in his mind. In addition, many details which appear in Rilke's Saint George pieces are reminiscent of Russian icons. In icons, for example, a tall tower often stands to one side of the scene, at its foot a maiden who, according to Russian legend, prepares to lead the vanquished dragon into the city on a leash. In Rilke's treatment, these figures take on new symbolic meaning. In most of the works Rilke emphasizes the maiden's state of mind and her yearning for the hero. In one poem, the dragon is no longer a real serpent, but the symbol of her psychological and perhaps sexual torment. She is told to appeal to Saint George

> wenn die Nacht die gewaltige, plötzlich erwachende: deine
> dich wie ein unüberwindlicher Lindwurm umwälzt.
> Wenn du dich heimgesucht fühlst. . . .
>
> (II, 347–48)
>
> [When the night—the powerful one, suddenly waking: yours—overturns you like an unconquerable dragon. When you feel persecuted.]

In two poems her anxious prayer becomes a literal tower—a visible symbol of her faith, but also a sexual symbol connected with the bravery and virility of the warrior saint: "Zuseiten seines Streites / stand, wie Türme stehen, ihr Gebet" ("To the side of his struggle stood, as towers stand, her prayer" [I, 618]); and "Am steigenden Streit, der dahinstürzt, rauschend, am Ufer / steht wie ein nächtlicher Turm dein gerades Gebet" ("Near the rising struggle which plunges thither, rustling, on the shore stands like a nocturnal tower your erect prayer" [II, 348]). Thus the traditional Russian iconographic juxtaposition of George, dragon, maiden, and tower is rearranged and made to function in a new way in Rilke's poetic world, with the focus shifting from religion and folklore to include more overtly the realm of psychology and sexuality.

In "Die Znamenskaja. Der Madonnenmaler" ("The Znamenskaya. The Painter of Madonnas [III, 657–58]), Rilke likewise starts with a Russian icon; here he does not transpose his borrowed images to another realm, but concentrates on the painting itself. The word "Znamenskaya" in the title refers to one of the traditional poses in which the Virgin is portrayed, and means "Virgin of the sign."[71] In icons of this sort she stands facing us, her hands raised at her sides in an ancient gesture of prayer. As in the *Stunden-Buch,* the lyric protagonist of this poem is an icon painter. Here he embodies Rilke's conception of a pious peasant artisan. He speaks to the Virgin as he prepares to paint her in the Znamenskaya pose. In his musings he reveals certain physical aspects of the icon, such as the gold outline of the Virgin's face, the rounded folds of her robe, and her raised, praying hands.

In three main metaphors, Rilke goes beyond a mere description of the icon and reveals the speaker's attitude toward his subject. Her face is likened to "Flügeltüren, / hinter welchen hundert Ampeln sind" ("folding doors behind which are a hundred lamps" [III, 657]). This brings to mind what are called the Royal Doors, or *carskaja vrata,* which lead through the massive screen of the iconostasis, and through which the priests come and go, mediating between the people and the hidden altar. Thus the Virgin herself becomes the gate through which the painter hopes to catch a glimpse of the holy of holies. He further describes his work as a long, arduous journey; the Virgin becomes a vast land—perhaps Russia itself:

So als führte ich ein blondes Kind
will ich meine goldne Linie führen
um dein Antlitz, . . .
Und dann wandern wir noch um dein Kleid,
   . . . . .
Und der Weg um dich wird weit.
      (III, 657)

[Thus, as if I were leading a blond child, shall I lead my golden line around your countenance, . . . and then we will wander around your gown, . . . and the way around you becomes long.]

The act of painting thus becomes an act of worship and a pilgrimage. Finally, the painter reassures the Virgin that she is too great to be circumscribed or enclosed in the icon, but says that nevertheless men see in her something small and tender that allows them to approach and love her:

> Aber, o verzeih, wir glauben:
> du kannst klein sein wie die Tauben,
> . . . . .
> und wir knien (Mögst du uns strafen)
> und wir küssen dir das Kinn.
> (III, 658)

[But, oh forgive, we believe: you can be small as the doves, and we kneel (even if you punish us) and we kiss you on the chin.]

With the kissing of the Virgin's chin, the two levels of meaning—the metaphorical, in which the painter addresses the Virgin familiarly, and the literal, in which pilgrims kiss the wonder-working icon—are brought together in a single image. The attitude of the painter is at once awed and familiar, a mixture thoroughly typical of Rilke's portrayals of Russian piety.

The Russian impulse in these early scattered works, then, manifests itself in a variety of ways, appearing not only in details specific to Russia—icons, Prince Igor, memories of the journey with Lou—but also in thematic concerns such as the role of the artist vis-à-vis God, the problems of human isolation, and the artist and creativity. These themes would prove lifelong preoccupations for Rilke, as would Russia itself. Far from disappearing from Rilke's mature works of the years 1899–1922, Russia would continue to function as a major source of idea and image.

· THREE ·

THE AESTHETIC RELIGION:
Das Stunden-Buch
AND THE ESSAYS ON ART

irst published at Christmas, 1905, *Das Stunden-Buch* (*The Book of Hours*) consists of three parts: "Das Buch vom mönchischen Leben" ("The Book of Monastic Life"), originally called "Die Gebete" ("The Prayers") and written primarily in September and October 1899; "Das Buch von der Pilgerschaft" ("The Book of Pilgrimage"), September 1901; and "Das Buch von der Armut und vom Tode" ("The Book of Poverty and Death"), April 1903. Typically for Rilke, each separate part was written in a very short time: the first, consisting of sixty-eight poems, in twenty-five days; the second and third, each consisting of thirty-four poems, in eight days each. Rilke revised part one, "Die Gebete," for inclusion in the published version of 1905.

The *Stunden-Buch* has often been studied as a religious or philosophical document; here, it will be considered primarily as an aesthetic statement. It is not a program, certainly, for Rilke's work was always too spontaneous and organic, too essentially poetic, to fit any imposed framework. But the book, especially part one, may be interpreted as a metaphoric statement which unites two of his major concerns: the nature of the creative process, and the nature of God. The result is a vision of God as an endless work of art, constantly growing under the hands and in the prayers of the protagonist, who is at once poet, icon painter, devout monk, and doubting wanderer. The vision developed here owes much to Rilke's experiences of Russia, for many of the images which give the vision form arose from those same experiences.

This is the first of Rilke's major works to grow out of his confrontation with Russia.[1] It was fed by his preoccupation with the dilemma of being an artist and still somehow existing in the world, a theme present in the drama *Das tägliche Leben*. It was also fed by a habit of metaphysical questing, which in the course of his life would lead him from one manifestation of divinity to another, culminating in Orpheus and the angels. Lou's obsession with the question of faith no doubt had its effect. But the work was also grounded in tangible experiences and impressions: in the image of Russian piety gleaned from visits to churches and places of pilgrimage; in the composite Russian Everyman, patient, humble, silent, and suffering, who grew out of Rilke's reading of Tolstoy, Dostoevsky, Leskov, and others; and in the many examples of Russian art which he saw, and to which he responded with instinctive understanding—albeit a vastly different understanding from that brought to it by the people by and for whom it was created. Since the *Stunden-Buch* is above all a poetic attempt at an aesthetics of worship, a religion of art, an examination of Rilke's attitudes toward Russian art is an appropriate prologue to a discussion of the poetic cycle.

On the first Russian journey, Rilke already sensed that Russia would have a major influence on his work. In June 1899 he wrote from St. Petersburg, "I feel . . . that Russian things will give me the names for the most fearful pieties [*jene fürchtigsten Frömmigkeiten*] of my being, which have been yearning to get into my art ever since my childhood."[2] Russia seemed to him a key that had opened a locked door. On the second trip with Lou, Rilke explored the wonders of medieval cities and neo-Byzantine monasteries.

Rilke's attitude toward Russia and Russian art, as reflected in his essays and poems, may be described as basically Slavophile in that it preferred to minimize Western influences on Russian culture while emphasizing native elements. His Russia was a vast country of religious peasants bound to the land by patience and tradition. Russia was a mystical and messianic force, an exotic contrast to the familiar, highly developed, and less spiritually oriented culture of the West. The standards Rilke applied to Russian culture, and thus to its art, were not the same by which he judged the art of the West. He demanded that Russian art be rooted in Russian history and myth, and that it express national strivings and a deeply religious optimism, principles that were alien to his discussions of Western art. And for Rilke, Russia was a place relatively unspoiled by progress, ambition, and other failings which he considered to be peculiarly Western.

Rilke immersed himself in the study of folklore and icon painting[3] and in the works of the Peredvizhniki and the Slavic Revival movement. These two groups of artists, in rebellion against the Western, neoclassical formalism of the Academy, sought to develop a truly Russian artistic corpus.[4] They were aided in this by an upsurge of scholarly interest and research in the Slavic past. Rilke also took an interest in the artists of his own generation, the Symbolists and Modernists. He tried several times to arrange for exhibitions of contemporary painting and sculpture to be sent to the West, but as with his translation of Benois's history, the fates—or some mysterious hostility in the Russians he encountered—prevented his good intentions from being realized. For several months in 1900, Rilke corresponded with various people in Russia, trying to set up an exhibit of the works of artists connected with the avant garde journal *Mir Iskusstva*. The exhibit was to be shown in conjunction with a production of a Chekhov play by the new Secession Theater in Berlin, with which Rilke had some connections. He addressed his requests not only to Benois, but directly to Sergey Dyagilev, leader of the *Mir Iskusstva* group. The result was a series of delays; Dyagilev stalled, and finally refused.[5]

This episode seems to be representative of the strange relationship between Rilke and Dyagilev. It is not known what happened to cause the strain, but apparently something had transpired during one of Rilke's visits which Dyagilev had little reason to be proud of. Benois advises Rilke in a letter, early in the negotiations for the exhibit, to turn to Dyagilev directly, even though "perhaps he was not entirely correct in his behavior toward you, but really he's a dear fellow."[6] Benois suggests that Dyagilev might, in fact, be willing to cooperate on the exhibit, if for no other reason than "to smooth over his not quite honorable treatment of you."[7] But apparently the Russian entrepreneur was not prepared to smooth anything over; and in Rilke's next attempt at a cultural exchange, Dyagilev's behavior was just as puzzling. After the Berlin exhibit fell through, Rilke was able to interest members of the Vienna Secession movement in both an exhibit of *Mir Iskusstva* artists and a special issue of the Secession's journal, *Ver Sacrum*, devoted to Russian art. Negotiations for this project likewise dragged on. Filosofov, Dyagilev's colleague at *Mir Iskusstva*, wrote that the proposal would be considered, but Dyagilev himself never answered Rilke's letters and the project was eventually dropped.[8] As if in a final insulting gesture, the people at *Mir Iskusstva* consistently neglected to send Rilke a subscription to the journal, despite repeated requests from him and from Benois. Once again one comes away with some amazement at the tenacity of Rilke's interest, the extent of his energy and good will, and the strength of his love for Russian culture which allowed him to persevere in propagating it in the face of continued treatment of this kind.

Rilke's first essay on Russian art, written in January 1900 and entitled simply "Russische Kunst" ("Russian Art" [V, 493–504]),[9] is basically a study of the Slavic Revivalist Viktor Vasnetsov (1848–1927), but the discussion is preceded by considerations of a theoretical nature which illuminate Rilke's aesthetic. This introductory section develops two main ideas. First, Russia and the West are essentially different in their historical and artistic development. The West is basically secularized, while Russia is still religious. Second, the roles played in Russia by worshiper or viewer, the object of art, and the artist are quite different from those played in the West. The active role of the Russian viewer has unusual consequences for the artist and the object he produces.

In comparing the development of Russian and Western cultures, Rilke says that the history of the West is flashy, complex, "a great squandering" (V, 494). Its rapid development has come in dramatic leaps. This pattern is typified, for Rilke, in the art of the Renaissance, which is described as breathless, having lost its way and wandered into a cul-de-sac of misdirected desires and ambitions. On the other hand, Russia still finds itself living "the day of God, the day of Creation" (V, 494). Its fundamental attitude toward life and the future is an "ingathering solicitude" (V, 494), a storing of spiritual energies for the day when they will be ripe, and needed.

In Russia everything, including art, has developed slowly and patiently. Rilke compares art in the West and in Russia in the following terms:

> Whereas elsewhere a specific artistic idea, ascending in ever more mature forms, seeks to be embodied, here [in Russia] a dance of thoughts passes through a lasting form. For the folk this is the gesture of prayer, which they fill with the whole contents of their experience—for the artist, it is the old holy image, the icon.
>
> (V, 497)

Rilke sees the two forms—prayer and icon—as equally important, parallel, and related in an essential way. Prayer is the basic gesture of the Russian people, "all of whose experiences are of a religious nature" (V, 496). It is also the link between the Russian people and the country's art, for it takes place in front of, and is aimed at, the very icons which Rilke sees as the quintessential expression of that art. Thus the traditional form of Russian art is the icon, and its content is religious.

Rilke recognizes that though the old forms, the traditions, persist, they can be degraded with time, emptied of meaning or even filled with false content—by painters, for instance, who merely copy mechanically, without inspiration or understanding. But the tradition can be revitalized, the forms refilled, in two ways: by the actions of a devout man, or of a true artist. Rilke says:

> If another devout man comes again, or an artist, full of true values, he finds in readiness for his wealth the beautiful, simple vessel which is always large enough to hold everything, even the overflow.
>
> (V, 497)

Rilke's emphasis on the role of the individual in religious art is startlingly unorthodox; he does not insist on the durability of content (beliefs) that prevails through a variety of forms, but rather on the durability of the form, which can be filled with a variety of contents whose source is the individual viewer or artist.

The viewer plays an active, creative role in his relation to the work of art; he is able to imbue it with images that fulfill his own aesthetic and spiritual needs. In the old icons, blackened by centuries of varnish and candle smoke, the "content," the actual faces, have faded. Nevertheless the icons preserve their original, familiar form and purpose. The people themselves are capable of bridging this gap between form and content in order to keep alive the ritual of prayer itself, but also to project onto the icons their own, often unconscious, dreams: "The people gaze innumerable Madonnas into the hollow icons, and their creative yearning continually enlivens the empty ovals with gentle faces" (V, 496).

Rilke sees this relation of the Russian people to its traditional forms as a crucial characteristic in its makeup, which, functioning as an anchor, an absolute, allows it to embrace the wildest extremes without losing touch with its identity. He declares, "With this quiet consciousness of the ever-present form is connected the peculiar breadth of the Russian character" (V, 497). Because of its boundless faith in the visual and spiritual foundations of its experience, which include not only the familiar rituals and their artistic objects, but also the eternal land itself, the Russian people, Rilke suggests, senses instinctively that it can survive all the changes and convolutions which life brings. The notion that the Russians are a people defined by extremes of behavior which are mitigated by rootedness in the land surely owes much to the concept of *počvenničestvo,* the cult of the soil, particularly as developed by Dostoevsky.

Rilke suggests that in this instinctive awareness of his own inherited forms lies the hope of the Russian artist. He should maintain contact with his people and his cultural roots; on the other hand, he should avoid the trivialization and distortions of didacticism.[10] The Russian artist should not reject Western art per se, nor refuse to learn from it technically, but primarily he should seek models within his own tradition. The modern Russian artist who couches his visions in terms of his national past and culture has an important task and opportunity. Using old, familiar forms, he can draw the Russian viewers into contemplation of his new content, and in a natural way expand their spiritual and artistic horizons, thus bringing them into the modern age with their basic values still intact.

Rilke's emphasis on the icon as the quintessential Russian art form, and his insistence on its importance for a resurgence of the folk genius may have been influenced in part by an essay which Lou Andreas-Salomé wrote in 1898. This essay, "Das russische Heiligenbild und sein Dichter" ("The Russian Holy Picture and Its Poet"), focuses on the writer Nikolay Leskov;

in part it deals with Leskov's writings on the subject of icons and iconography. He had expressed a preference for the older examples of the art form over newer ones, because he felt the older ones were truer to the original Byzantine conception, and therefore more authentic, less corrupted by national or individual elements. Lou was very critical of Leskov's views. She, for her part, saw precisely in the more recent icons an expression of the awakening Russian *Volksgeist*.

> For in religious art, the people were beginning to come into their own and to shake off the load with which Byzantine formalism had, with a suffocating pressure, burdened art and development, because this formalism must be nourished on abstract ascetic ideas rather than on living observations. Thus it is more important that the art of the people creates out of itself a Mother of God in whom it unconsciously glorifies the ideal of a Russian peasant woman, or a Jesus who resembles, perhaps, a farmer of the Tolstoyan sort, than if it painted the finest Christs and Marys with their thin limbs and ascetic features, which so little correspond to its own gentle, soft folk types.[11]

Rilke's view of the Russians as a naive and pious people different from the rest of mankind is likewise prefigured in this essay. Lou goes on,

> in Russia (and this is something which is no longer possible in more mature, more differentiated cultures) all the yearnings and wishes, all the strength and warmheartedness of the Russian are mirrored in the naive metaphysics of the people, as in a plastic image of God.[12]

The last six pages of Rilke's essay (over half of the entire work) are devoted to the life and work of Vasnetsov. Rilke had seen his paintings at the Tretyakov Gallery in Moscow, and later his decorations in the Cathedral of Saint Vladimir in Kiev, and he considers Vasnetsov the artist who best exemplifies the ideal of Russian art. Vasnetsov, he says, is one of the new generation of Russian artists, "who are already working with Russian means, and are articulating their decided individuality in the most personal fulfillment of those inherited forms" (V, 498). Rilke praises Vasnetsov's use of familiar subjects taken from medieval history, epics, and folklore, and his refusal to be influenced by non-Russian elements. Vasnetsov's greatest achievement, in Rilke's opinion, is his work as chief decorator of the neo-Byzantine Cathedral of Saint Vladimir.[13] Among the figures which Rilke selects for special attention are those of the old Russian heroes and martyrs. Significantly, he does not mention the many non-Russian figures portrayed by Vasnetsov, except for the Virgin and Child. Nor does he note the fact that six other artists were engaged in the ten-year project of decorating the cathedral—probably because in all but one case, the styles, scenes, and subjects were more or less in the tradition of Western religious painting.

The essay "Russische Kunst," then, expresses Rilke's conception of Russia as a land and people less developed and thus richer in potential than those of western Europe. It discusses Russian art in a normative way, positing for Russian artists an ideal approach to their work, via history, legend, and the formal traditions of Russian Orthodox art. Nevertheless, the normative ideal of traditional models is balanced by Rilke's notion of both the artist and the viewer as active forces transforming these models through the imagination.[14]

In his second, rather diffuse essay on the subject, "Moderne russische Kunstbestrebungen" ("Modern Russian Artistic Endeavors" [V, 613–22]),[15] Rilke once again approaches Russian art from the standpoint of its intimate relation to the people and their history, and again emphasizes the importance of tradition for Russian artists. The essay touches on the Russians' basically pragmatic and human-oriented nature, which has tended to overshadow their purely aesthetic sense; gives a brief history of Western influences on Russian art; discusses works of several nonconformist Russian artists; and indicates a number of what he calls "paths" on which the Russian soul attempts to find an artistic outlet. One path is the icon, which Rilke, contradicting the first essay, declares to be "no work of art; but it is an important document of the Russian soul and one of the paths on which, from a distance, it is approaching art" (V, 620). Here the icon no longer functions as the primary metaphor for inherited forms, but is only one of several such forms, others being the landscape, the customs and superstitions of the peasants, and folk arts such as embroidery and woodcarving.

The second essay is less normative and more descriptive than the first, but the concern with maintaining Russian tradition emerges here too. Rilke finds it reassuring that the promising artists of the younger generation have studied abroad and obtained a great amount of knowledge and expertise, but have returned home "with their balance intact. . . . They have seen a lot, in order to be fair to their native art and their past. They don't overrate them, but they revere them" (V, 621). The essay concludes with the declaration that the Russians want an art that is "simply there, so that one can look at it" (V, 622)—that is, surprisingly enough, an art for art's sake, paradoxically grounded in old, originally utilitarian forms such as peasant crafts and the icon.

The aesthetic problems discussed in the essays reappear in *Das Stunden-Buch,* concentrated in part one. There, too, one finds the most Russian elements, as well as most of the allusions to the East-West conflict and the relation of God to art. For these reasons my focus will be on the first book, "Vom mönchischen Leben." However, parts two and three will also be examined briefly for their connections to Russia. The protagonist and setting of part one are Russian; its argument concerns the conflicting attractions of Russian and Western artistic traditions. In this respect it may be viewed as Rilke's attempt at resolving this conflict in himself. The Russian setting endows the poems with a remarkably rich texture, filled with monasteries, icons, illuminated manuscripts, flickering candles, somber bells, ancient burial mounds, Kievan catacombs, and many other artistic and human impressions which Rilke brought home with him from his Russian journeys. Against this dazzling background, the protagonist, a Russian monk and icon painter—in the earlier, unpublished version called "Apostol," but nameless in the published version of 1905—reveals his insights and his temptations. One prototype for the figure of Apostol is Dostoevsky's Father Zosima in the *Brothers Karamazov*. Other possible models include Alyosha Karamazov, who is torn between his desire for seclusion in the monastery and his calling to live and serve in the world of men, and Pushkin's holy monk Pimen in *Boris Godunov*.

The monk principally addresses his God or himself, although he occasionally turns to address another character. The poems take various forms: dramatic monologue, lament, meditation, and prayer. The main subject of the monk's reflections is the relation of God and art, or more precisely, God *as* art, for God and art are finally inseparable. Both are the creation of man, and they serve as the goal of a never-ending process of creation. The central conflict in the work is the monk's spiritual struggle between his humble role of copier, demanded by Russian tradition, and the temptations of innovation, which arise both from his own needs and from what he knows of Western religious painting. In addition, the struggle between Russian and Western art, as the monk sees it, expresses their different attitudes toward God and religion.

The struggle between inherited form and innovation can be seen in the opposition between the title of the cycle, *Das Stunden-Buch,* and its central theme. A book of hours is a very old form, traditionally a small volume carried by clergy and laymen alike to provide them with the proper prayers and meditations for each day and each hour of the day. Its form and content are rigidly set, and its theme is the exposition of fixed canonical truths. Rilke's book of prayers, on the other hand, contains the restless, inspired, and anguished meditations of a self-conscious individual who is caught between the strictures of his own religious tradition and the lures of western art.[16]

The monk's struggle is expressed in a variety of ways, but it is perhaps most clearly formulated in a long poem which occurs only in the first version of part one, unpublished during Rilke's lifetime.[17] This poem, which begins "Ehrwürdiger Vater and Metropolit" ("Venerable father and Metropolitan" [III, 360]), represents one resolution which Rilke later rejected as being too one-sided and extreme, for it implies the fearful shunning of new artistic methods and perceptions, and a fanatic embracing of tradition. Written in the form of a letter from the monk Apostol to his spiritual father, the poem states the dichotomy succinctly. Reading books about Western painting, Apostol realizes with a shock that in the West, painters enjoy God like a holiday which is fleeting and insubstantial:

> einen Sommer, der
> vorüberfliesst, wie alle Dinge fliessen—
> so dass die Hände mir vom Buche liessen
> wie von der Sünde; denn *mein* Gott ist schwer.
> (III, 362)

[a summer which flows past as all things flow—so that my hands dropped the book like a sin; for *my* God is heavy.]

For Apostol the relationship of Western painters to God is frivolous, humanizing, wasteful. As in the first essay on Russian art, where Rilke writes that the history of the West displays "a great squandering," while that of Russia is an "ingathering solicitude," so too in his letter Apostol contrasts the Western and Russian attitudes toward God, especially as they are represented in art:

> Sie haben Gott vergeudet, und wir sparen
> mit unserm Gotte und wir legen jede
> getane Tat und Alles, was uns freute,
> in kühle Kästen, glätten jedes Heute
> so wie ein Kleid. . . .
> (III, 363)

[They have squandered God, and we save our God, and we lay each deed that's done and everything that pleased us in cool caskets, smooth out each Today like a garment.]

Once again the name of the writer Nikolay Leskov suggests itself as a source for Rilke's ideas. Leskov's novella "At the End of the World" ("Na kraju sveta," 1875)[18] presents a discussion in which an aged archbishop comments to a group of friends on an album containing a collection of artistic renderings of Christ. All the works are by Western artists, and each is found to contain a major flaw in conception or interpretation. Titian shows Christ with a look of disdain on his face; a robust, curly-headed Christ, the "Jesuit version," has been separated from his biblical roots and lives on in the pampered fantasy of wealthy ladies; a medieval painter reduces Christ to an object of pity and suffering alone, and so on. All the artists fail, it is suggested, by making Christ too prone to the one-sided indulgence of one human passion or another, one quality or other. None captures his essence of perfect humanity.

Finally the old archbishop points to an icon hanging in the room, calling it the best possible representation of Christ. His reasons are of great significance for the ideas expressed in the *Stunden-Buch*. The icon is, he asserts,

> a typical Russian portrayal of the Lord: the gaze is straight . . . in the face there is expressiveness, but no passion. . . . He is somewhat peasantlike, it's true, but with all that it is fitting to bow before him. . . . Our simplehearted master understood better *whom* he had to depict.[19]

In the juxtaposition and opposition of Western religious art with its great squandering of passions, and the Russian icon as a true approximation of the divine in art, we find the same conflict which so troubles Rilke's monk. Here, too, we find the image of divinity in the guise of a humble Russian peasant, which is so central to the first part of the *Stunden-Buch*. Most important, perhaps, is the conclusion which Leskov allows his archbishop to draw from his comparison of the paintings of Christ:

> And thus, in the same measure as . . . our native art more closely and successfully comprehended the external features of Christ's portrayal, so does our native spirit, perhaps, come closer to the essence in its comprehension of the *inner* features of his character."[20]

Throughout the first part of the *Stunden-Buch,* but in his attitudes toward Russia in general as well, Rilke suggests a similar relationship between art and religious consciousness. He makes a similar point in a letter from January 1900, where he writes:

> In the Russian people, that thing might be fulfilled which I only dare to suggest in uncertain words: that its God (who is not yet completed) and its art (which is not yet completed) are developing steadily side by side, in a constant mutual influence.[21]

Apostol loves his tradition, and desires that God be allowed to remain timeless, the *Kraft* behind all finite phenomena, a refuge for all who need him—not spent by one generation. However, Apostol expresses to the Metropolitan his gnawing fear that such a thing could also happen in Russia, which had thus far maintained a very different relationship with God. The monk feels "Man fängt / auch bei uns schon an, / Ihn zu bekennen in falscher Art" ("people are already starting here, too, to proclaim him in a false way" [III, 366]). He pleads with the Metropolitan to be firm in his resolve to hold painters to their duty, and to release none from the interdictions of tradition.

In the tone of the letter and of his plea, however, one senses that the monk is not entirely sure of his own firmness of resolve, his own immunity from the desire to portray God "in einer raschen Schönheit" ("in a hasty beauty" [III, 365]). He speaks repeatedly of the fear which his ponderings have awakened in him, and remarks, "Ich musste mich euch entdecken, / weil es so drängt" ("I had to reveal myself to you, because it is so urgent" [III, 366]). When he describes God as the ineffable force which always avoids being captured in the work of art, there is a note of wistfulness: "Gott dunkelt hinter seinen Welten, / und einsam irrt des Malers Hand" ("God is dark behind his worlds, and lonely strays the painter's hand" [III, 363]). The lonely, wandering hand of the painter is Apostol's own,[22] and the artist realizes with chagrin that his own tradition is unsatisfactory, for each work of art is emptied of its sacred inspiration as soon as it is done: "In allen Bildern bleibt nur das Gewand, / mit dem die Ungeduldigen ihn umhellten" ("In all pictures, only the robe remains in which the impatient ones surrounded him with light [III, 363]).

Frightened by the puzzling and abhorrent, yet tempting, ways of Western art, Apostol clings ferociously to the teachings of the past, taking the stance of a conservative even in terms of the basically conservative Russian artistic tradition.[23] He says:

[Ich] male manchmal einen Nikolaus
oder die Heiligste im Stoglaf-Stile,—
mehr kann ich nicht.
        (III, 361)

[I sometimes paint a Nicholas or the Blessed One in the Stoglav style—I can do no more.]

The "Stoglav" referred to here is a church council of 1551 which called for strict adherence to traditional forms in icon painting.[24] It was in large part a reaction against the encroachment of an increasingly mystical and doctrinal element in painting, represented by a narrative style which, for example, employed scenes from the gospels rather than commemorating individual holy figures. This style was rather eclectic, and utilized Western iconographic themes.[25] The Stoglav declared that "in nothing will the painters follow their own fancy."[26] In 1658, another Stoglav council put it even more bluntly: "He who shall paint an icon out of his imagination shall suffer endless torment."[27] Part of the rationale behind the Stoglav's pronouncements was the consolidation of church and state in Russia at the end of the sixteenth and beginning of the seventeenth centuries, a move which was essentially a nationalist retrenchment and a strengthening of the combined sources of power. It called for strict conservatism in art as well as politics. Thus that Rilke made his monk a practitioner of the *Stoglaf-Stil* rather than allowing him to become one of the innovators is important, for behind this fact looms the image of a mighty, conservative Russian throne and church, united against incursions or threats from outside.

The religious and nationalistic messianism of the Stoglav pronouncements is echoed in Apostol's letter:

> Ein jedes Volk hat seine Pflicht und Rolle
> Und wenn wir uns um *eine* Fahne scharen
> dann ward uns wahrlich eine wundervolle:
> Wir müssen dämmernd unsern Gott bewahren.
> (III, 364)

[Every people has its duty and role. And if we gather around *a single* banner, then our lot is truly a wondrous one: darkly we must preserve our God.]

Here we find a distinct echo of the attitudes expressed by Dostoevsky through Father Zosima. In the section of the *Brothers Karamazov* entitled "From the Conversations and Teachings of the Elder Zosima," the old man defends Russian monks, who are ridiculed for their meekness, with his assertion that from them will arise the salvation of Russia and the Christian world. "In the meantime, in their solitude they preserve the image of Christ, grand and undefiled since the ancient Fathers, the apostles and martyrs. And when the time comes, they will show it to the tottering truth of the world. This is a great idea. This star will shine out of the East."[28]

Having suppressed his desire to deviate from tradition, Apostol humbly accepts the Church's pronouncements. His temptation, however, not only represents an individual problem but reflects in microcosm Russian politics of the middle of the sixteenth century. Such an extreme sentiment would have put a stamp of finality on the cycle, ending the artist's internal conflict and preventing further development of parts two and three of the *Stunden-Buch,* and this may have been the reason that Rilke chose to omit the poem from the 1905 edition. While absolute obedience to tradition may have seemed a possible solution in 1899, when the poem was written, it was no longer acceptable in 1905. By that time Rilke, who had spent several years in Paris and worked with Rodin, had undergone a change in his philosophical attitude toward tradition and innovation.

In the revised (1905) version of part one, Rilke presents a monk whose position concerning the East-West division is less rigid than that in the earlier version. But like the first version, the later one focuses on this division. Here Rilke establishes the monk very early as a representative of the Russian point of view and again contrasts him with the artists of the West. The third poem of this version beings, "Ich habe viele Brüder in Sutanen / im Süden, wo in Klöstern Lorbeer steht" ("I have many brothers in cassocks in the South, where in cloisters laurel stands" [I, 254]). The South in this context most likely refers to Italy, since Titian is mentioned later in the poem, and thus in terms of Rilke's dialectic it would actually signify the West. Russian and Western religious painters are united in this metaphor, in that they are monks ("Brüder in Sutanen"), but the laurel of fame resides only in Italy, not in Russia, and this fact distinguishes the Russian from the Western painters. Personal fame is not part of the life of the obscure Russian monk. Then the notion of Russian religious consciousness is compared to the Western one, as it is reflected in painting. Addressing his Western brothers, he says: "Ich weiss, wie menschlich sie Madonnen planen" ("I know how humanly they design Madonnas" [I, 254]). "Humanly" is ambiguous, for it can refer either to the Madonnas, who are more profane than sacred, or to the artists, who are personally and emotionally involved in their work, full of individual tastes and human dreams. In either case, the contrast with the monk's sacred, impersonal, and detached aesthetic is extreme. The Russian tradition dictates obedience to a canonized procedure and an abstract set of images. In the next poem the monk says:

> Wir dürfen dich nicht eigenmächtig malen,
> · · · · ·
> Wir holen aus den alten Farbenschalen
> die gleichen Striche und die gleichen Strahlen.
> (I, 254)
>
> [We dare not paint you willfully. . . . We take from the old paint pots the same lines and the same radiance.]29

The monk's role as painter is traditional and humble, he follows the dictates of his predecessors, and he has only hypothetical contact with his audience, for whose transcendental experiences his work serves as a catalyst. He says of a picture he has painted, "[Ich] halte es hoch, und ich weiss nicht wem / löst es die Seele los" ("I hold it up, and I don't know whose soul it releases" [I, 253]).

However, although the painter's role within the church is narrow and predetermined, he is not only a go-between for God. Rilke expands the role, giving the monk the task of actually creating God. In one poem, for example, the monk describes himself as an artisan building the cathedral that does not contain, but *is,* God. In addition, the monk does not only represent Russian tradition. While he sometimes voices the point of view of a compliant servant, at other times he imagines what his art would have been like had he grown up "irgendwo, / wo leichtere Tag sind und schlanke Stunden" ("somewhere where there are lighter days and slender hours" [I, 265]), that is, not in Russia. He allows himself to play with the images he might then have employed:

> Ich hätte dich wie eine Klinge
> blitzen lassen . . .
> Gemalt hätt ich dich . . .

... wie ein Gigant
dich bilden würde: als Berg, als Brand,
als Samum, wachsend aus Wüstensand—
(I, 265)

[I would have had you flash like a blade; I would have painted you as a giant would shape you: as a mountain, as fire, as simoom, growing from the desert sand.]

Significantly, the monk plays with images that are not traditionally Western, while at the same time moving away from his own artistic tradition. In this way Rilke conveys the monk's intermediate aesthetic position.

In Apostol's letter to the Metropolitan in "Die Gebete," the conflict between·traditionalism and innovation is resolved in an extreme manner. In "Vom mönchischen Leben," however, Rilke finds a resolution which is less drastic and which echoes the ideas of "Russische Kunst." A large number of the monk's images are old, explicitly Russian forms filled with a new, personal meaning. The monk, like the devout man and the artist in the essay, brings his own values into play amidst the old objects of his native tradition, filling them with a new content: with God. In the monk's reveries God appears, for example, as a typical Russian peasant, sleeping not only on a stove, as was common in peasant houses even in the twentieth century, but, in his mythic vastness, "auf allen Öfen" ("on all stoves" [I, 276]). In the poem which begins "Ich war bei den ältesten Mönchen" ("I was with the oldest monks"), God and the Russian land merge. In images in which the vast Eastern spaces, "rauschend am Rande des Christentums" ("rustling at the edge of Christendom" [I, 295]), are equated with God, God is the "dunkelnder Grund" ("darkening foundation") which suffers man to live and build, but which will one day demand back from all things its image, which remains incomplete in them.

Repeatedly God appears in a humble guise, almost always associated with either the peasant, the land, or a work of art. In "Ich war bei den ältesten Mönchen," he also takes the form of a simple book, a chronicle of the history of Russia, made "nicht mit Bol und Gold, nur mit Tinte aus Apfelbaumrinden" ("not with red clay and gold, only with ink from appletree bark" [I, 295]). In another poem the monk enters a cathedral as a pilgrim, and finds himself among beggars and bearded peasants who reveal God to him in their faces and gestures, "wie nie so zart, / so ohne Wort geoffenbart" ("so tender as never before, so wordlessly revealed" [I, 293]). God is present in the dark peasants, who grasp him as if with their hands, and need no words to comprehend him.

If God is traditionally portrayed as a brightness which hangs above the world, Rilke's Russian God, on the contrary, is mainly associated with images of darkness and earth.[30] For example, he is "dunkel und wie ein

Gewebe / von hundert Wurzeln, welche schweigsam trinken" ("dark and like a network of a hundred roots silently drinking" [I, 254]). Other examples include "Du Dunkelheit, aus der ich stamme" ("You darkness from which I come" [I, 258]); "Du bist so dunkel; meine kleine Helle / an deinem Saum hat keinen Sinn" ("You are so dark; my little brightness at your edge has no meaning" [I, 269]); "Ganz dunkel ist dein Mund, . . . und deine Hände sind von Ebenholz" ("All dark is your mouth, . . . and your hands are of ebony" [I, 270]); and "Du bist der dunkle Unbewusste / von Ewigkeit zu Ewigkeit" ("You are the dark Unconscious, world without end" [I, 276]). God is the darkness of chaos out of which life came, and he represents unhurried anonymity, patience, and futurity. He is also referred to in terms of earth, fertility, and organic growth: *Boden, Grund, Wurzel, Baum* ("earth," "ground," "root," "tree"). This linking of God with the earth rather than the heavens also appears as a central image in the *Geschichten,* and foreshadows the image with which Rilke concludes the *Duineser Elegien:*

> Und wir, die an *steigendes* Glück
> denken, empfänden die Rührung,
> die uns beinah bestürzt,
> wenn ein Glückliches *fällt.*
> (I, 726)

[And we who think of *rising* happiness, would feel the emotion which nearly dismays us, when something fortunate *falls.*]

There, the downward focus is positive and reiterates the consoling and fruitful attitude toward death expressed elsewhere in the tenth elegy. In "Vom mönchischen Leben" the assignment of positive value to earth and darkness, an inversion of traditional metaphors, provides another example of the monk's obligation to fill old forms with new content.

The last two poems of the first part of the *Stunden-Buch* are placed in a mythicized Russian setting. The monk prays that his soul may be like a broad, still meadow. He hopes that if he becomes quiet enough, the "old one" may come to him in the steppe. From a related prose passage in "Die Gebete" we learn that the "old one," a dark figure almost merging with the night, is "ein überalter Kobzar" ("an aged bard" [III, 373]), a traditionally blind Ukrainian singer of tales. But he is also the monk's dark God, who has dispersed himself in his songs, and fallen silent. Now he comes to receive his songs back again from the monk, who has become both singer and landscape, creator and receptacle.[31]

Between the writing of "Das Buch vom mönchischen Leben" and the second part, "Das Buch von der Pilgerschaft," lay not quite two years. By that time, the autumn of 1901, Rilke had been forced out on his own by Lou, and had married. These years were characterized by a growing conflict with reality, the encroaching necessity of making a living, and an ever greater sense of estrangement from himself and from the possibilities which had been revealed to him by his confrontation with Russia. On 13 December 1900, eight months before writing part two of the cycle, Rilke had written in his diary an entry full of despair and profound self-scorn. He found himself in an unbearable limbo of weakness, "hopelessness, spiritual shortness of breath."[32] He appears to have felt close to madness. He ends the entry: "This had to be written as a sign to myself. May God help me."[33]

The second part of the cycle reflects the author's state of mind. It shows the monk likewise estranged from his God and himself (necessarily from both, for in the first part his self-definition and self-creation had been tantamount to an ongoing creation of God as well), and likewise calling for help. One of the most frequently used words in this section is *bange*—anxious. The main imagery here is that of dispersal and fragmentation. People search for God in a variety of ways, as poet, pilgrim, hermit; but God's existence is not so assured as before: "Gerüchte gehn, die dich vermuten / und Zweifeln gehn, die dich verwischen" ("Rumors circulate that surmise you, and doubts circulate that efface you" [I, 318]).

The optimism and spiritual well-being evoked by Rilke's vision of Russia had faded. But there are still echoes of that experience in the second part. As in the first, most of the Russian elements are related to God. We find the monk trying to come to terms with the father-son relationship assumed between God and man. (The relation of children to parents is almost always a problematic one for Rilke,[34] and the relation to God is its most generalized manifestation.) But this is also a metaphor for the crucial problem of inspiration and creativity. The monk finds that to accept this relationship at all, he must reverse it, making himself the father and creator, the one who, although outgrown by his offspring and creation, will live on in the deeds of his "son." In a poem in the second part which begins "Und du erbst das Grün" ("And you inherit the green"), Rilke portrays this inversion of roles, with God as heir. The poem is basically a list of natural objects, emotions, temporal events, and physical creations that God will "inherit"; that is, since everything that is done or exists does so in his name, and ultimately returns to him, it constitutes his inheritance. Poets, painters, lovers all act for him, even though some do so unconsciously. Among the things bequeathed to God by the monk is a list of human achievements; four are Italian (Rome, Florence, Venice, the cathedral at Pisa) and four are Russian (Kazan, the Troitska-Lavra [Trinity

Monastery], another monastery at Kiev, and Moscow). All eight are repositories of art, architectural genius, and, particularly, religious culture and history.

Rilke was personally acquainted with all of the Russian examples. He had visited the ancient city of Kazan on his trip up the Volga in 1900. The Trinity Monastery referred to is probably the Trinity-Sergius Monastery near Moscow, known for its icons by the fifteenth-century master Andrey Rublyov. The face of Moscow evoked here is that of Rilke's Easter experiences, "Moskau mit Glocken wie Erinnerungen" ("Moscow with bells like memories" [I, 314]). The fourth Russian monument is "das Monastir / das unter Kiews Gärten ein Gewirr / von Gängen bildet, dunkel und verschlungen"[35] ("the monastery that under Kiev's gardens forms a maze of passageways, dark and convoluted" [I, 314]). The allusion is to the Kiev Pecherskaya Lavra, the huge underground monastery begun in caves and tunnels by an ascetic community of monks before the middle of the eleventh century.[36] Rilke had visited the monastery several times during his stay in Kiev in 1900, and walked the dark passageways with the devout pilgrims. The long-dead monks displayed in their cells had not decayed, due to a peculiarity of the atmosphere underground.

Rilke's choice of the man-made wonders for inclusion among the things God would take back from the loose grasp of time in a sense resolves the underlying conflict of the first part, that between the West, symbolized by Italy, and Russia. This image includes equally in God's inheritance the monuments of the religious and artistic traditions of both East and West.

Doubts return to the monk a few pages later, however. Referring to the Kievan monastery and the apparently immortal monks, he asks God, "Weisst du von jenen Heiligen, mein Herr?" ("Do you know about those saints, my Lord?" [I, 324]). There follows a long and detailed account of the founding of the monastery and of the flight of these ascetics further and further from the world of men and of the senses:

sie waren . . .
zurückgekehrt in ihrer Mütter Schoos.
Sie sassen rundgekrümmt wie Embryos
mit grossen Köpfen und mit kleinen Händen.
(I, 325)

[They had returned to their mothers' womb. They sat hunched, round like embryos with large heads and small hands.]

They have gone through life and returned to God by a circular path of physical transformation, from birth through renunciation to a dry perpetual sleep. Their lives have borne no fruit. The monk has serious doubts, and asks God whether these figures are still useful to him, part of his plan, or have simply been forgotten there underground.

"Das Buch von der Pilgerschaft" is full of images of people wandering, striving to reach outside themselves, searching for God. Of all these, the radical way of the fanatics who rejected life entirely can hardly have appealed to the artist-monk, with his profoundly sensual apprehension of the world. In the next poem he says to God, "Du bist der Dinge tiefer Inbegriff" ("You are the profound embodiment of things" [I, 327]). He reaffirms that *his* God is intimately connected with the world of objects. This is in great contrast to the monks in their caves; their willingness and even their physical ability to give and to create had shrunk to a deformity, represented by their useless tiny hands. It is possible that the monks also represent a warning to the protagonist, who feels a certain threatening similarity to them. He is alienated from his God and yearns to be whole again. In an earlier poem he had cried out,

> Wie hob ich meine halben Hände
> zu dir in namenlosen Flehn
> dass ich die Augen wiederfände
> mit denen ich dich angesehn.
> (I, 306)

[How I raised my half hands to you in unspeakable beseeching, that I should once more find the eyes with which I had looked at you.]

His own "half hands" and the loss of his inner vision, the eyes with which he had seen God, are mirrored in the grotesque isolation and the useless hands of the monks. Both hint at a great waste of human potential, for both worshiping and creating, and suggest that the Russian passivity Rilke so admired could in fact be carried too far.

Russian images again enter the monk's expression of his relationship with God in another poem in the second part, which begins "Du meinst die Demut" ("You intend humility" [I, 321–23]). In his diary, Rilke copied a section of a letter which he had written from St. Petersburg in July 1900, describing his trip on the Volga:

> A very broad river, very high woods on one bank, on the other side deep meadowland, in which even large cities stand like mere huts and tents.[37]

In his description of the Volga journey, the most significant aspect for Rilke is an awareness of sheer size, which he links with an experience of God himself:

> One relearns all the dimensions. One discovers: land is large, water is something big, and large above all is the sky—it seems to me as if I had

watched the Creation; a few words for all of existence, things in the measure of God the Father.[38]

These personal perceptions are echoed in the poem, where God is compared to a boat trip on a great river; he is

> wunderschön wie eine Reise,
> die er in stillen Schiffen leise
> auf einem grossen Flusse tut.
> (I, 322)

[beautiful as a journey, which he makes quietly on calm ships upon a mighty river.]

In addition to being a song of praise, the poem is a digression into memory, evoking Rilke's recognition of Russia as his spiritual homeland:

> Und manchmal lenkt das Schiff zu Stellen,
> die einsam, sonder Dorf und Stadt,
> auf etwas warten an den Wellen,—
> auf den, der keine Heimat hat. . . .
> (I, 322–23)

[And sometimes the ship steers to places which, lonely, without village or city, wait for something by the waves—for him who has no home. . . .]

In this poem, God and Russia merge in an image of welcome. For a time they must have seemed identical to Rilke, who was seeking both a faith and a home. And it is easy to understand the intensity with which he embraced this hopeful vision.[39]

The final lines of the poem also echo a passage in Rilke's diary which describes a different Russian experience: his visit to Tolstoy at Yasnaya Polyana. In the diary, he recounts the ride through the countryside toward Tolstoy's estate: "What freedom there was in me as, with quivering bells, we drove through the wavy meadows, for the first time traveling in the Russian landscape just as Gogol and Pushkin had traveled, loudly, with sounding harness and galloping horses."[40] The last four lines of the poem, which describe the troikas that wait along the river bank for travelers, convey the same mood of speed and adventure:

> Für solche stehn dort kleine Wagen
> (ein jeder mit drei Pferden vor),
> die atemlos nach Abend jagen
> auf einem Weg, der sich verlor.
> (I, 323)

[For such, little wagons stand there (each with three horses before it), which rush breathlessly toward evening on a path that has lost its way.]

There are two further poems in this part which contain, on very different levels, Russian elements. In the first, "Du Gott, ich möchte viele Pilger sein" ("God, I would like to be many pilgrims" [I, 332]), a metaphor may have been inspired by a Russian painting. In this poem, the monk vacillates between his desire to be "multiplied," so that he can attract more people's attention to his path to God, and his thankfulness that he is only himself, and therefore able to hide from their eyes. He feels surrounded by "laughers"—people who are contemptuous of his earnest search. On the one hand, he feels that as one lone man, he attracts and converts no one: "Als wäre nichts geschehn. / —lachen sie weiter" ("As if nothing had happened, they go on laughing" [I, 332]). On the other, he instinctively quails before their laughter and is glad he is alone and inconspicuous, "denn so / kann keiner von den Lachenden mich sehn" ("for thus none of the laughers can see me" [I, 332]).

Rilke likewise uses laughter to symbolize a self-satisfied and hostile mass in the essay "Moderne russische Kunstbestrebungen." There, he mentions a painting by Kramskoy called *Laughter*.[41] It shows Christ surrounded by a scornful crowd which undulates with "great and small waves of that scornful laughter with which the mob defends itself against those who are different and lonely" (V, 617–18). Just so—different and lonely—must the monk feel in this poem; he is isolated by his recognition of his need for God, which for him is also a need to create. And he is torn between these powerful needs and the desire to avoid the pain of discipleship. In a diary entry, Rilke discusses further the origin of Kramskoy's painting, and indicates what the laughter metaphor meant both to him and to Kramskoy. The Russian painter had had a growing perception that the world is permeated by a sinister and spreading laughter, and had attempted to paint this laughter in many forms and shapes, until he was overwhelmed by it. "He must seek someone for balance, he must pray for someone—recognize him, create him—who does not laugh. And in endless fear he searches and waits."[42] And in answer to Kramskoy's search, Rilke continues, a figure came and presented itself, bound, among the crowd. Thus his painting of Christ called *Laughter* came into being. Rilke describes his own reaction to that form of absurdity whose voice is laughter:

> The world is not laughter, but it is the great common accident whose loudest and most willing voice is laughter. And for the earnest, lonely man, this laughter expresses the enmity of the masses who harass him.[43]

The similarity of mood and point of view in the poem and the diary entry suggest their common inspiration in the painting by Kramskoy.

Finally, the poem immediately following "Ich möchte viele Pilger sein" which begins, "Ein Pilgermorgen. Vor den harten Lagern" ("A pilgrim's morning. Before the rough encampment" [I, 333]), contains both a reference to another of Rilke's Russian experiences, and a foreshadowing of a scene in his novel *Malte Laurids Brigge,* in which a Saint Vitus dancer undergoes a seizure. The setting is the pilgrims' camp at dawn; the wanderers wake, pray, wash themselves, and prepare for the day. Among them are types which Rilke could well have seen among the pilgrims at Easter, 1899 in Moscow, in the Kievan cave monastery in 1900, or at other places he visited in his travels: "braune . . . Frauen von Tiflis und Taschkent. / Christen mit den Gebärden des Islam" ("Brown women of Tiflis and Tashkent. Christians with the gestures of Islam" [I, 333]). Against this background Rilke presents a parable. A possessed monk has an attack in the courtyard of the hospice. In his physical and mental anguish before the unheeding eye of God, he prefigures the struggle and transcendance of the Saint Vitus dancer. Both survive a series of shocks and transformations before being freed, or accepted, by God. The monk is seen as a dancer, a fish, and a bird:

> Er flog empor, als ob er Flügel spürte
> und sein erleichtertes Gefühl verführte
> ihn zu dem Glauben seiner Vogelwerdung.
> (I, 335)

[He flew upward as if he detected wings, and his relieved feelings seduced him to a belief in his birdhood.]

After flinging himself wildly about in his isolation, he sinks exhausted before God, who finally notices him and takes him up gently, "wie eine Geige unters Kinn" ("like a violin under his chin" [I, 337]). The Saint Vitus dancer in the novel, after a desperate struggle against his body's impulses, likewise "gab . . . nach . . . er spannte die Arme aus, als ob er auffliegen wollte, und es brach aus ihm aus wie eine Naturkraft" ("gave in . . . he stretched out his arms as if he wanted to fly up, and it broke from him like a natural force" [VI, 774]). The yielding of the Saint Vitus dancer has been described as a liberation from self-control, a paradoxical enrichment through loss, where the self is seen as a hindrance to comprehension and transcendance.[44] In the case of the monk, too, the path of suffering leads, by way of the loss of self, to a release and the achievement of a new and positive state of being. We know from many comments that Rilke made that he connected Russia with the idea of suffering. In a letter to Benois discussing a famine then raging in central Russia, he remarks, "But Russia can bear everything. [She is] a great, mute sufferer."[45] It is clear that the affecting scene in the novel has its roots in this "Russian" concept, and its first expression in the pilgrimage poem of the *Stunden-Buch*.

If overt Russian allusions have dwindled in part two, they have nearly disappeared from part three of the cycle, "Das Buch von der Armut und vom Tode." But once again virtues which Rilke associated with the Russian peasant—humility, faith, patience, a lack of worldly ambition or ostentation—underlie one of this part's two main motifs, that of poverty. "Von der Armut und vom Tode" finds the monk alone, appalled and terrified at life in the modern city, to which he has evidently drifted after leaving his cell in part two. The first fourteen poems deal primaily with death, and include the important motif of a personal death and the image of death as a fruit; the remainder portrays various manifestations of poverty.

Rilke used the word poverty (*Armut*) in a very personal way which has often been misunderstood. He distinguished between *poor* in the sense of humble, simple, unspoiled, and laid open to all experience, and merely *not rich,* that is, oppressed, despised, materially deprived. When he speaks of poverty in a positive way, as "ein grosser Glanz aus Innen" ("a great glow from within" [I, 356]), it is to the former desirable state that he refers. Rilke's poor will outlive the empires of the earth, and in their unspoiled purity "werden sich wie ausgeruhte Hände / erheben, wenn die Hände aller Stände / und aller Völker müde sind" ("will rise like rested hands, when the hands of all classes and all peoples are tired" [I, 361]). His conception of poverty echoes that of Matthew 5:3, "Blessed are the poor in spirit: for theirs is the kingdom of heaven." But more important for our purposes, it echoes the attitudes of Dostoevsky's Father Zosima in his "Conversations and Teachings"; the old monk has high praise for the Russian peasant:

> All my life I've been struck by the grand and genuine dignity in our great people.... The poorer and more lowly our Russian is, the more noticeable is in him that splendid truth—for the rich among the peasants are to a great extent already corrupted kulaks and bloodsuckers.... But God will save his people, for Russia is great in its humility.[46]

Thus Dostoevsky's monk not only expresses many of the qualities also espoused by Rilke's monk, or by Rilke himself in other works; one can also say that, in part, Rilke's conception of the virtues of poverty comes directly from Dostoevsky.

The thing which most worries Apostol, however, is that these spiritually uncorrupted, humble poor will be distracted and ground down by life in the cities.[47] The monk sees the city as the enemy, actually a hindrance to creative poverty, and begs:

> Nur nimm sie [die Armen] wieder aus der Städte Schuld,
> wo ihnen alles Zorn ist und verworren

und wo sie in den Tagen aus Tumult
verdorren mit verwundeter Geduld.
(I, 362)

[Just take them again from the guilt of the cities, where everything is anger to them, and confused, and where in the days of tumult they wither with wounded patience.]

It is easy to imagine that in Rilke's mind the idealized poor belonged in an idealized setting, like that of the poor but peaceful villages of rural Russia.

The cycle closes with an evocation of Saint Francis of Assisi as a symbol of humility, poverty in the positive sense, and service. The next to the last poem begins with an erotic portrayal of the saint as a kind of nature spirit, impregnating all around him with "seines Liedes Pollen" ("the pollen of his song" [I, 365]). His death points to that of Orpheus, for he is subsumed singing into the world of flower and stream:

Und als er starb, so leicht wie ohne Namen
da war er ausgeteilt: sein Samen rann
in Bächlein, in den Bäumen sang sein Samen
und sah ihn ruhig aus den Blumen an.
Er lag und sang. . . .
(I, 366)

[And as he died, as lightly as if nameless, he was dispersed: his seed ran in rivulets, in the trees his seed sang, and looked at him calmly from the flowers. He lay and sang.]

"Von der Armut und vom Tode," and the cycle, end with a vision of the poor, looking on at St. Francis's assumption into nature. He rises like a sign in their darkness, "der Armut grosser Abendstern" ("the great evening star of poverty" [I, 366]).

Other than this major connection with Rilke's ideal of creative poverty, specific Russian allusions in this part are rare. In one poem in praise of poverty, Rilke uses the Russian word for "ruler" in the line "des Ostens weisser Gossudar" ("the white ruler of the East" [I, 354]). This ruler is merely one in a series of figures whom Rilke counts as "rich" precisely because they disregard or give away their wealth, or spend it on beautiful objects. The same poem may contain an oblique reference to the ancient Russian city of Yaroslavl, which Rilke had visited in 1900. In the poem a reference is made to

die Ersten alter Handelshäfen,
die sorgten, wie sie ihre Wirklichkeit

mit Bildern ohnegleichen überträfen
und ihre Bilder wieder mit der Zeit.
(I, 355)

[the foremost men in old trading ports, who worried about how to outdo their reality with matchless pictures, and [to outdo] their pictures in turn, in time.]

Founded in the eleventh century, Yaroslavl reached its peak as a river port in the sixteenth and seventeenth centuries, when "merchants vied with one another to erect sumptuous churches,"[48] building more than forty by the end of the seventeenth century. Aside from its architectural beauty and the exemplary activities of its wealthy men, the city may have won Rilke's affection as the place where the manuscript of the Igor tale was found.[49]

Finally, certain images in a 1903 poem in part three beginning "Ich will ihn preisen" ("I shall praise him" [I, 351]) connect it with a poem of overtly Russian subject matter, written in 1899. This is the second poem of the cycle "Die Zaren" ("The Tsars"), which begins "Noch drohen grosse Vögel allenthalben" ("The great birds are still threatening everywhere" [I, 429]). The metric pattern of the two poems is the same; each contains images of anxious April nights filled with mysterious shrieks of terror or of inspiration, and in each someone—a group of warriors fighting a monster, and the monk defending his God—must withstand the dangers pitted against him and go on to prepare a place for someone else—a peaceful society, and God, respectively. It is possible that Rilke thought of his own earlier poem when he created the later one.

Thus, in each of the parts of the cycle, written over a period of six years, a different mood prevails. The distribution and type of images dealing with Russia in the three parts reflect this difference. In the first, the monk is perceived most strongly—by himself and by the reader—as an artist, in his literal role as an icon painter, in his role as poet recording his struggles, and in his theopoetic function. There is a sense of fluidity and intimacy between the worlds of God and man, reflected in the Russian imagery. The sense of estrangement which permeates the second part can be felt in the Russian images there as well. They deal with pilgrims and ascetics, or with God seen as a river, grand and good, but beyond human scale. Another of the Russian images of part two, the metaphor of the insensitive, laughing mob, shows the artist in a different light from "Vom mönchischen Leben." Here he is an outsider, fearful and struggling for the strength to speak out. The third part reflects Rilke's altered awareness and shows the monk as concerned primarily with the world of men; the Russian allusions are sparse. Yet Russia is present on a more subtle level, informing the idealized vision of the poor and humble who shall inherit the future. Russia as Rilke chose to see it—a land of legend, vast spaces, humble people, with a complex and brilliant history, both religious and secular—forms the core of the *Stunden-Buch;* and it occupied his thoughts, fermenting and productive, so much that it overflowed into other works, most notably the *Geschichten vom lieben Gott* and *Das Buch der Bilder,* where fascinating variations on his Russian themes occur.

· FOUR ·

RUSSIA AS A SOURCE OF IMAGERY:
Das Buch der Bilder

esides the *Stunden-Buch,* the other major poetic work from the years around the turn of the century was *Das Buch der Bilder* (*The Book of Images*). It was written between 1898 and 1901, and first published in 1902. The cycle was published in its final version in 1906, greatly expanded with poems written between 1902 and 1906. This study will refer only to the later edition. The work has been somewhat slighted by critics; but it contains a number of fine individual poems, and is revealing both for its use of Russian elements and its treatment of themes which will appear repeatedly in Rilke's later works. The *Buch der Bilder* is divided into two books, each book consisting of two parts. These four sections form a rough division by clusters of topics. Almost all of the Russian themes appear in Book II, Part 1; one Russian poem appears in Book I, Part 2. The work as a whole cannot be said definitely to lead in any single direction; rather, it reflects a young man caught in a complicated set of attitudes toward his own life as a social being, toward his art, and toward God, the personal and historical past, and the world of energy and objects.

Part 1 of Book I consists of a group of poems whose central themes are death, perception, longing, loneliness, silence, and childhood. Some of the recurring figures such as angels, young girls, and children were to remain central to his poetry. The second part of Book I continues the prevailing mood of melancholy, emphasizing man's alienation from others, from the outside world, and even from himself and his past. A second major theme runs counter to that of alienation in a series of poems concerning the possibility of poetry and the nature of the poet's identity and task. Book II seems less consistent and coherent than Book I in terms of subject matter and ideas. Part 1 reasserts the theme of man's heritage and presents a variety of problematic solutions. The emphasis is on man's fateful dependence on his past. A further concern of this section is man's perception of himself and his mission in the world, indeed his responsibility for the world's functioning. The second part of Book II presents many tragic figures who, like man in the *Elegien,* "nicht sehr verlässlich zu Haus sind / in der gedeuteten Welt" ("are not very dependably at home in the interpreted world" [I, 685]). These include a widow, several blind persons, a leper, and a dwarf. Again death and perception are main themes.

In the *Buch der Bilder,* Russian themes appear which can be traced to three sources: factual and literary materials dealing with the Battle of Poltava; the *byliny*—medieval oral epics; and the history of the last two Tsars of the Rurik dynasty, Ivan the Terrible and Fyodor Ivanovich. The first of these sources, the Battle of Poltava, appears as a background in two poems which are placed in different parts of the cycle: "Sturm," Book I, Part 2, and "Karl der Zwölfte von Schweden reitet in der Ukraine," Book II, Part 1. In the Battle of Poltava, fought in 1709 in what is now the eastern Ukraine, the Russians under Peter the Great routed the combined armies of Swedes commanded by Charles XII, and rebellious Cossacks led by the hetman Mazeppa, who had joined forces with Charles in the hope of overthrowing the Russians and freeing his native Ukraine.

Several critics[1] cite the influence on Rilke's "Sturm" and "Karl der Zwölfte" of Alexander Pushkin's poem *Poltava.*[2] While Rilke knew Pushkin's works, there does not seem to be sufficient evidence for citing Pushkin exclusively as a source for either of the Poltava figures in Rilke. Rilke's knowledge of Charles could have come from a number of generally available sources, including his specialized reading in Russian history; the figure of Mazeppa was a commonplace of the European imagination, utilized by many eighteenth- and nineteenth-century writers, including Voltaire, Byron, and Victor Hugo. Rilke does not treat Charles and Mazeppa together in their historical context, as does Pushkin; rather, he devotes a separate poem to each. And Rilke's purpose in using these figures differs significantly from Pushkin's.

In Rilke's poem "Sturm" ("Storm"), several aspects of the character of Mazeppa are represented. A common anecdote told how Mazeppa, caught by the Polish husband of the woman he loved, was strapped naked to the back of a wild horse and sent galloping into the wilderness as punishment. Rilke shows Mazeppa in this guise most familiar to European readers, the one Byron so vividly exploits. Rilke focuses on the speed of the rushing horse and the reduction of all consciousness to a single perception. Mazeppa loses all contact with his surroundings, except for the alternating dark and light of the skies flying by above him. A second aspect presented by Rilke is closer to the Mazeppa of Pushkin's poem and of the history books than to the Mazeppa of legend: the patriot, military leader, and wily politician, "der du deine Kossaken gern / zu dem grössesten Herrn / führen wolltest" ("who would gladly lead his Cossacks to the greatest lord" [I, 403]). Rilke offers both views of the character, then transcends both of them by using a first person narrator who addresses Mazeppa directly, describing the endless headlong ride on the wild horse: "Dann bin auch ich an das rasende Rennen / eines rauchenden Rückens gebunden" ("then I too am bound to the raving race of a smoking back" [I, 403]). The poem, which begins as an invocation of a romantic historical figure, is transformed into a sort of epiphany, which illustrates one of the themes of the cycle, that of perception. Rilke portrays the experience of merging, both with Mazeppa and with the landscape itself. He lies on the horse's back,

> wie Ebenen liegen;
> meine Augen sind offen wie Teiche,
> und in ihnen flüchtet das gleiche
> Fliegen.
> (I, 404)

[as plains lie; my eyes are open like ponds, and in them flees the same flight.]

The poem "Sturm" is placed within a series of poems dealing with the poet's mission. This setting gives us further insight into the poem and its function. Just preceding it are the two poems "Fortschritt" ("Progress") and "Vorgefühl" ("Premonition"). In the former, the poet's tone is one of growing strength and confidence in his perceptiveness: "Immer verwandter werden mir die Dinge / und alle Bilder immer angeschauter" ("Ever more familiar do things become to me, and all the images ever more observed" [I, 402]). In "Vorgefühl" the poet compares himself to a flag that feels the coming storms long before the world down below can know of them; it is a lonely position, but one full of exaltation. These images lead directly into the Mazeppa poem. The storm of its title is surely one of those which, in the preceding poem, wring and shake the poet in his more intense consciousness. This storm, as we have seen, involves him so totally that he becomes both participant and backdrop in its drama. "Sturm" is followed by "Abend in Skåne" ("Evening in Skåne"), a sudden serenity despite its images of wind and clouds. Here the poet feels himself to be an object akin to the river, the windmills, and the endless, changing possibilities of the clouds. The poet is transformed in the space of four poems from perceiving subject to perceived object, and Mazeppa's wild ride is the agent of this transformation. Thus Rilke uses the figure of

Mazeppa as a ready-made vessel into which he pours a new concoction, an old instrument on which he plays a new tune.

In "Karl der Zwölfte von Schweden reitet in der Ukraine" ("Charles XII of Sweden Rides in the Ukraine"), Rilke turns to the Battle of Poltava. Unlike Pushkin, who glorifies the exploits of Peter the Great in a long heroic poem, Rilke focuses all his attention on Charles, and in a lyrical and impressionistic manner describes the effect of the battle on him as a person. Pushkin describes a victory, a joyous occasion from his Russian point of view, whereas Rilke's protagonist is the vanquished ruler Charles, for whom the battle is, objectively speaking, a total defeat. Yet the poems have an important element in common. This is their conception of Charles's personality. Pushkin describes him as stubborn, conceited, willful, and basically unemotional until he is faced with defeat.[3] But then Pushkin shows Charles being carried onto the battlefield on a stretcher, wounded, disoriented, and confused by the turn of events; from this place of indignity he must command his troops. Pushkin gives his face an "unusual agitation."[4] Similarly, Rilke portrays Charles as cold and cruel, a grey-eyed king on a grey horse, riding out of a grey and silent land. He is without the slightest bit of sensuality until, as Rilke puts it, "ihn das Wunder überwand" ("the miracle overcame him" [I, 422]). And the "miracle" is Charles's sudden intense awakening to the sounds, shapes, and movements of the world around him. Metal on metal rings out its being; the wind becomes a panther; flags are joyous and regal. And though Charles is aware of the dead at his feet, he does not see them—for he is enchanted, distracted by a new awareness as he rides off after the receding din of the last skirmishes, "mit seinen Wangen voller Wärme / und mit den Augen von Verliebten" ("with his cheeks full of warmth and the eyes of lovers" [I, 424]). The remarkable change we observe in Charles seems incomprehensible under the circumstances, for Rilke is careful to show that this is a military defeat, not a glorious adventure. But it is precisely in his perception of defeat that Charles is transformed.[5]

At the beginning of the poem Charles is shown as a moody dictator, indulging his cruelest whims without fear of opposition. Historically, nine years before the Battle of Poltava, the Swedes had routed the Russians at Narva on the Finnish Gulf, forcing Peter to flee and to leave all his cannon behind. Thus Charles had reason to expect another easy victory. Yet suddenly Charles has been jolted by defeat, awakened to his own limitations, his own humanity. He has learned to see, and Russia has been his teacher. The poem treats themes central to the section in which it is placed: man's perception of the world and of himself in it. There is an echo of Charles's new awareness in the poem "Der Schauende" ("The Watcher") in Part 2 of Book II. There Rilke finds the experience of a great defeat by a worthy opponent preferable to that of victory: "Was wir besiegen, ist das Kleine, / und der Erfolg selbst macht uns klein" ("What we defeat is Smallness, and the success itself makes us small" [I, 459]). Rather, what we should aim at is "der Tiefbesiegte von immer Grösserem zu sein" ("to be deeply defeated by ever greater things" [I, 460]). Charles has taken the first step on the road to real strength, internal, humble, and self-aware.

The two poems "Sturm" and "Karl der Zwölfte," which are linked thematically by the concept of awakened perception, thus portray figures closely associated with a particular event in Russian history, and touch on elements important to Rilke's overall conception of Russia. In "Sturm" we saw a profound experience of the mythic vastness of the Russian plains. In "Karl der Zwölfte," Charles XII comes to Russia as a closed and self-confident young monarch; he leaves shaken, a different man, robbed of his misconceptions. Rilke chooses to emphasize and idealize the positive aspects of this experience. Rilke, too, came to Russia as a young foreigner, not closed, certainly, but limited and to a certain extent unformed, immature. He, too, left a different man, profoundly affected and humbly grateful. It may be possible to see in his portrayal of Charles a reflection of his own experience: he, too, on one level learned to see while in Russia.

The other six poems to be discussed differ from these two in several respects. First, they form a discrete whole, grouped together in Part 1 of Book II under the title "Die Zaren" ("The Tsars"). Secondly, they draw on and portray two specifically Russian traditions which Rilke knew well: the world of the oral epics, and the history of the Rurik dynasty, which ruled from about 856 until 1598. Nevertheless, like "Sturm" and "Karl der Zwölfte," they reflect both Rilke's deep interest in Russia and his ongoing confrontation with the problems of self-perception and inheritance.

The six poems deal with the early history of Russia, from the misty, semilegendary origins to the end, in decadence, of its first royal family. On the primary level, the subject of the first two poems is Ilya Muromets, a legendary figure from the Russian medieval epics, the *byliny*.[6] The third concerns the greatest figure of the Rurik dynasty, Ivan IV, known as "the Terrible." The last three focus on Ivan's feeble-minded son, Tsar Fyodor Ivanovich. On another level, Russian history serves to illustrate the Rilkean themes of human isolation, man's relation to his past and family, and the problems of identity and perception.

Although Rilke calls the poems "Die Zaren," the first two deal not with a historical prince, but with the most popular of the epic heroes, Ilya Muromets. He is strong, patriotic, and honorable, the son of a peasant, and he becomes a knight at the court of Prince Vladimir of Kiev. The court of Prince Vladimir, the tenth-century Christianizer of Russia, is the traditional setting for *byliny,* much as in western Europe cycles of tales grew up around the courts of Charlemagne and Arthur. Rilke was deeply interested in this early literature, which he saw as an expression of *his* Russia, the Russia of the people and the distant past.

In the version of the legend on which Rilke based the first poem of "Die Zaren,"[7] Ilya, crippled and somnolent since birth, is awakened from his subterranean slumbers and magically infused with superhuman strength. He sets off on a series of adventures that leads him to Prince Valdimir's court. In the first poem, which is largely descriptive, Rilke presents a restless mythic landscape in the time before trees were tamed. Into this setting Ilya wakes, and as his strength dawns, he helps his old parents clear and plow their rebellious land before claiming his wondrous horse and riding off on the adventures that beckon to him after his long inactivity.

The poem may be taken as a metaphor for Russia's role in history as Rilke saw it. It reflects what he called in a letter "the expectant quality in the character of the Russian," who is created "to let human history go by, in order later to join in the harmony of things, with his singing heart."[8] Russia was a slumbering land, rich in potential humanity. In the final lines of the poem, Rilke expresses the same kind of scope and optimism: "Weit schreiten werden, welche lange sassen / in ihrer tiefen Dämmerung" ("They will stride far, who sat for a long time in their deep dusk" [I, 429]). In both passages there is a feeling of ripening, a sense of the existence of an appropriate hour of awakening and self-fulfillment.

In another poem from this period, the first poem in the *Stunden-Buch*, written in 1899, the same idea is applied to artistic self-fulfillment. There the poet is described at the exact moment of awakening, in transition from inactivity to inspiration. The hour has struck, and he declares, "Mir zittern die Sinne. Ich fühle: ich kann— / und ich fasse den plastischen Tag" ("My senses quiver, and I feel: I can—and I seize the malleable day" [I, 253]). Just as the poet grasps the day and pours into it all the confidence and strength of expression he has been gathering and hoarding, so too Ilya, symbol of inchoate Russia, rises and grasps first the plow, then the reins of his war horse.

In the second poem of "Die Zaren," Rilke utilizes one of the legendary adventures of Ilya in which the hero fights and captures the dread Solovey-Razboynik ("Nightingale the Robber"), who lies in wait in the treetops to swoop down on hapless travelers.[9] Solovey-Razboynik has sat on twenty-seven oaks (not nine, as Rilke has it) amid the dense, dreary forest of Bryn for thirty years, and allows no one to pass. The legend emphasizes the power of his whistling cry (it blows the roof off Prince Vladimir's palace) and his crafty, lying nature. He emerges as a folksy and human, if grotesque, figure with the mentality of a peasant bandit. Ilya captures Solovey by shooting out one of his eyes, ties him behind his saddle, and carries him off to Vladimir as booty.

The second poem is much more abstract than the first, and its allusions to the Russian source are both vaguer and more oblique. Yet without knowledge of the source, interpretation is extremely difficult. On one level, the poem simply continues the legendary adventures of Ilya begun in the first poem. We see hardy heroes withstand the horrors of Solovey and go on to aid in establishing order in the form of walls and cities, a new structure which wise rulers and even tamed monsters acknowledge. On another, more general, level closely related to this one, the poem portrays the movement of Russia out of the realm of myth into that of history, from the deeds of dragon killers to the founding of cities. On a third level, the poem confronts once again the idea of patient endurance until the moment of action, of fruition, has come.

Unlike the first poem, which narrates a series of events from the epic, the second dispenses with narration and presents selected details and episodes in fragmentary fashion. There is still the monstrous Solovey, who "oben in den Kronen von neun Eichen / sich lagert wie ein tausendfaches Tier" ("up in the crowns of nine oaks camps like a thousandfold beast"). He is still confronted by the heroes, not Ilya alone, but other unnamed "Überstarke" ("supremely strong ones"), presumably the pantheon of heroes from the Kievan cycle of *byliny*. The confrontation between the heroes and Solovey in Rilke's poem, however, differs from that of the *byliny* in that Rilke dwells less on the vivid action at Vladimir's court or on the character and defeat of Solovey, who seems to represent the last, desperate forces of chaos, than on the threat of attack from the unseen creature. This formless object of fear makes its presence known by its weird cries that go all through the incongruous spring nights as if horribly filling the darkness with pieces of itself, "hinwerfend sich und Stück für Stück sich gebend" ("throwing itself down, and giving itself, piece by piece" [I, 429]). The monster is portrayed as amorphous, yet powerful and threatening, "jenes Etwas, welches um sich griff" ("that Something that groped about itself" [I, 430]), an image very different from the Solovey of the *bylina*.

Likewise, Rilke presents the confrontation between Ilya (or the heroes) and Solovey in a very different way. In the *bylina,* Ilya, in traditional heroic fashion, simply shoots Solovey out of the tree, ties him up, and resisting Solovey's attempts at cajolery and trickery, carries him to Vladimir. He triumphs through brute force and singleness of purpose. Rilke, on the other hand, shows no battle, no action at all. The first three strophes describe the unseen but horribly tangible monster, shrieking and thrashing in the treetops. The last two strophes portray the heroes who withstand it and go on to become defenders of order. Their feat lies not in

Das Buch der Bilder

any cleverness or skill, but in their power to resist, their superhuman patience. This is emphasized by the verbs used to describe them. The heroes are the ones "die da blieben" ("who remained there"), they are not "aufgerieben" ("fretted") by the monster's cries; "sie dauerten" ("they lasted" [I, 430]). Their realization of the nature of the threat that darkens the spring nights is a long process, a sort of maturation or slow enlightenment: "Alternd nach und nach / begriffen sie die Bangnis der Aprile" ("aging bit by bit, they grasped the anxiety of Aprils" [I, 430]). As with Ilya in the first poem and with Russia in the letter to Lou, the emphasis is on patience, waiting, a slow, natural growth that allows one to understand and to prevail. It is as if Solovey no longer existed, but had simply been outwaited, endured into oblivion.[10] Thus, not only does this poem carry on a theme from the previous one, it addresses, as do so many poems in the *Buch der Bilder,* a theme which would be dealt with again from a different point of view, years later, in the fifth of the *Elegien:* that of duration and stasis.

In the third poem, leaping over hundreds of years of slow growth, war, and expansion, Rilke focuses on Ivan IV. Once more, Rilke's aim is to portray an epoch of Russian history through a seminal figure. Ivan, eccentric, cruel, crafty, and beset by terrors, pushes himself and long-suffering Russia to the brink of disaster. On another level, Rilke paints an external world that is a direct reflection and product of Ivan's sick mind, and shows Ivan trapped in a tightening net of faulty perceptions. The poet does not portray any particular moment in Ivan's career, but compresses into a few lines many fragments of reality. In the first part of the poem, we see the army of shadowy, sinister figures who surround Ivan—maliciously gossiping servants, paradoxically fleeing "favorites," women and their maids whispering in closed rooms about poisons. There is an aura of tension and falsehood, of much that is awry. In the following nineteen lines, we see Ivan himself—lonely, terrified, but terrifying in his turn, slipping silently through the palace, watching, listening.

It is through oblique but carefully chosen references that the figure of Ivan, never mentioned by name, emerges. Rilke selects a few apt details to depict the life of this dark figure. The poet notes "seine Frauen flüstern und stiften / Bünde" ("his women whisper and create plots" [I, 431]), referring obliquely to Ivan's seven wives and collection of concubines, and to the terror he aroused in those around him. Two other lines refer to one of Ivan's most characteristic and disastrous undertakings: the formation, in 1565, of a large personal guard comprised of the most hardened criminals in Russia—the *Oprichnina*. For a time, Ivan moved out of the Moscow Kremlin and lived with three hundred of the *oprichniki* in a fortress near Moscow. There he established a household run like a parody of a monastery, with the *oprichniki* dressed in monks' habits and the daily routine varying between orgies and sick religiosity. Hence Rilke's lines, "Mörder ducken unter den Dächen / und spielen Mönche mit viel Geschick" ("Murderers sneak beneath the roofs and play at monks with great skill" [I, 431]). By a mere fleeting reference to "das Eisen an seinem Stock" ("the iron on his stick"), Rilke evokes the well-known scene in which the despot killed his own son Ivan with the iron-tipped cane in a fit of anger.[11] Here once again the problem of heritage is raised; the violent old man destroys the one person he really loves, and with him, unwittingly, the hopes of his whole dynasty—for his youngest son, Dmitry, would die under very strange circumstances, and his other son, Fyodor, was a gentle simpleton with whom the line finally died out.

The historical Ivan was a brilliant and paranoiac despot, sensing spies and traitors everywhere—not without some justification: his mother and his first wife were poisoned, his boyars were constantly plotting against him, and on occasion his closest friends and advisers sided with the boyars. Always quick to believe the worst, Ivan had friends and relatives executed with impunity—even doing away, eventually, with his trusted *oprichniki*. Rilke depicts little of this directly; rather, he suggests its logical outcome. A man who can trust no one, who questions the loyalties and the very identities of those closest to him, must at some point begin to question his own identity, both absolutely and in the social context. Illustrating once more the problem of self-perception, Rilke shows Ivan angrily grabbing someone by the cloak—but then,

> im Fenster weiss er nicht mehr:
> wer ist Haltender? Wer ist gehalten?
> Wer bin ich und wer ist der?
> (I, 431)

[in the window he no longer knows: who is the holder? Who is held? Who am I and who is he?]

One detail which Rilke chooses in his portrayal of Ivan, and which in its turn illuminates Rilke's historical interpretation of the tsar, has its source in nineteenth-century Russian art. This detail occurs in the lines,

> Und er hat nichts als einen Blick
> dann und wann; als den leisen
> Schritt auf den Treppen die kreisen.
> (I, 431)

[And he has nothing but a glance now and then, but the soft step on the stairs that circle.]

In his essay "Russische Kunst," Rilke describes the painting by Viktor Vasnetsov of Ivan IV:

Das Buch der Bilder

> Supported on his dreaded staff, the tsar descends a slender spiral staircase, and soon his form, dark and steep, will cover the narrow stairway window, into whose frame, white and golden, Moscow presses.
>
> (V, 500)

Rilke's description of the painting makes clear what the spiral staircase in the poem signifies. Not only does the circling (*Kreisen*) of the stairs suggest the human circles of guilt and fear in which Ivan is caught, but it is also, for Rilke, associated with a vision of Ivan as the spirit of darkness itself. He is "dark," "steep," and his brooding form is about to blot out the brightness of the living city, seen through the narrow window. Ivan on the staircase becomes, from this point of view, a foreshadowing of the fate of his dynasty and his land.

In the last three poems of the tsar-cycle, Rilke focuses on the tsar perhaps least sung by poets and most ignored by historians: Fyodor Ivanovich, who ruled quietly from 1584 to 1598. We know of Rilke's sympathy for alienated, lonely figures, and that he, like his age, was fascinated by the weak, the sickly, and the deformed. Thus, Fyodor offers a perfect subject for Rilke's contemplation. Rilke was interested in the idea of the noble line, the joys and curses passed on in the blood, as well as the relations between parents or ancestors and children. We see examples of this in the early story "Die Letzten" ("The Last Ones"), in *Malte Laurids Brigge*, the *Cornet*, and in many poems in the *Buch der Bilder*, including "Der Sänger singt vor einem Fürstenkind" ("The Singer Sings before a Princely Child"), which is placed immediately after "Die Zaren." Tsar Fyodor was foolish, cheerful, and more or less harmless. His greatest pleasures were attending church services, ringing bells, and watching trained bears.[12] Rilke presents him as an essentially sad figure, in a series of three poems resembling three concentric circles, coming ever closer to his inner life.

The first poem is static, in the sense that we are shown neither external action, nor the feelings of the tsar, but merely the panorama of a feast and the thoughts of the noblemen. Fyodor sits, somewhat shrunken, lost in his magnificent robes just as the acrobat of the fifth poem in the *Elegien* is lost in his skin. He is surrounded by shining sycophants, restless flatterers—the boyars, who would in fact revolt after his death and plunge Russia into the "Time of Troubles." He is compared unfavorably by the boyars to his father, who had cut a vastly different figure on the throne.

In the second of the three poems, Fyodor, standing at a window in the Kremlin, hears the great bells tolling. To his vague mind, overshadowed by a gentle religious madness, "die fremde Sehnsucht" ("the alien yearning" [I, 433]), they are the voices of his ancestors, telling him that his life has nourished all of theirs. Fyodor realizes that all his forebears have drunk of his depths, have used him up in order to do their grand deeds. His reaction is one of thankfulness at having been the source of their greatness. He sees himself in everything they did, the raw material, a precious metal. Rilke here reverses the usual direction of inheritance, as he does in places in the *Stunden-Buch*.[13] He makes the son the source of the fathers' greatness; the last of the line becomes the inspiration for all that the race has accomplished. Fyodor in his gentle pride feels himself not cheated by history, but rather a vital part of it. But perhaps because of this drain on him, Fyodor's strength is minimal, and his being is essentially other-worldly.

In the final poem, Fyodor prays before an icon, one of those so encrusted with silver and jewels, so dimmed by candle smoke, that all one can see are three dark ovals in the silver, showing a pair of brown hands and a blackened face, "das uns vergangen ist; wohin vergangen?" ("which is gone from us; gone where?" [I, 436]). Rilke moves from the physical absence of the Virgin's face from the icon to a spiritual withdrawal of her help, which Fyodor senses and attempts to counteract. He strives to find the lost image in his own heart. And in the process of yearning and concentration, his own face "goes out."

> Noch sinnt und sinnt der blasse Gossudar.
> Und sein Gesicht, das unterm kranken Haar
> schon lange tief und wie im Fortgehn war,
> verging. . . .
>
> (I, 436)

[The pale ruler still ponders and ponders. And his face, which under the sickly hair had already long been deep and seeming to depart, went out. . . .]

Thus, in the structure of concentric circles, the first of the three poems devoted to Fyodor portrays him externally, with only hints of the interior reality. He is seen through the eyes of others, dreaming ineffectually on the throne, but his hand, as if even then reaching out for some other world, "mit einem unbestimmten Sehnen / ins wirre Ungewisse flieht" ("flees with a vague yearning into the indeterminate" [I, 432]). The second poem, moving into Fyodor's thoughts, reveals his surprising and profound links with his ancestors and, through them, with Russia herself. By the third poem, he has passed beyond relationships to the court and the past; he merges completely into the world of the spirit, extinguished and fulfilled. Like Mazeppa in "Sturm," Fyodor's personality, the distinctive features that separate him from the perceived world, dissolves, allowing him not merely to perceive himself as one with it, but actually to become so.

The six poems of "Die Zaren" may be interpreted on several levels. The first of these is Rilke's relation to his Russian sources. The second is his treatment of the history of Russia through the end of the Rurik dynasty;

here Rilke's extensive studies of Russian history and literature bear fruit in a sensitive evocation of a country which he had come to regard as his own spiritual home. The third level is Rilke's use of Russian materials and settings in the development of his own thematic concerns.

The thematic focus of the cycle is Fyodor; three of the six poems are devoted to him. In Fyodor, it is possible to see another representative of Rilke's Russia. At court, he is dreamy and alienated; his extreme passivity, and his joy in it, can be seen in his relation to his ancestors. His humility and religiousness are revealed in his profound need to communicate with the holy being beyond the icon, and in his detachment from the external world. Thus, although the setting in which Fyodor appears is lush, filled with panther skins, jewel-encrusted robes, sonorous bells, and magnificently decorated icons, he himself is like the face of the Virgin in the darkened oval of the icon: full of shadows, simple, elusive, yet somehow enduring amidst a richness that does not affect him.

Charles XII and Mazeppa can in their own way be linked to this image of the old Russia. Although both were outsiders in Russia, Rilke portrays them with sympathy.[14] They lived more than one hundred years after Fyodor's death, in a new, Westernized Russia ruled by a new dynasty, yet both were affected, in Rilke's poems, by the *old* Russia, which in spite of Peter's modernization was alive and powerful. The brilliance and reality of the battle at Poltava, the intensity of defeat, were for Charles a profoundly human experience that was timeless, unconnected with the modernity of the Petrine era. The vastness of the land aided Mazeppa in his transformation. Both were changed by their contacts with the huge, enduring Russia that had its roots in the times of Fyodor and his ancestors.

The *Buch der Bilder* is a loosely organized work. It does not attempt to present a unified view of its topics, but nonetheless contains a number of important poems. The eight discussed in this study are significant for three reasons: in themselves, as graceful and forceful poems; as reflections of Rilke's interpretation of Russia, emphasizing its ancient, brooding, and religious aspects; and finally, as illustrations of problems with which Rilke was grappling in other works of the time, and which constitute some of the focal ideas in his later works.

· FIVE ·

GOD AS ARTIST AND PRODIGAL SON:
Die Geschichten vom lieben Gott

At Christmas, 1900, thirteen stories appeared under the title *Vom lieben Gott und Anderes. An Grosse Für Kinder erzählt* (*About God and Other Things. Told to Grownups, for Children*). It was reprinted at Christmas, 1901, and a slightly revised edition appeared in 1904 under the new title *Die Geschichten vom lieben Gott* (*Stories about God*). This collection of stories is, next to *Malte Laurids Brigge,* Rilke's most important work of prose fiction. According to Rilke, the stories were written in seven consecutive nights, between the tenth and the twenty-first of November 1899, that is, about a month after "Die Gebete" ("The Prayers"). They were written after Rilke had seen Moscow and St. Petersburg, experienced a Russian Easter, and begun his intensive studies of Russian culture, but before he had seen Kiev and the provinces, traveled along the Volga, or visited the peasants. Thus, since most of Rilke's direct personal contact with rural and peasant Russia came after the writing of the stories, the majority of Russian elements in them, which refer in large part to peasant life and folklore, must be traced to sources in literature. These Rilke knew in abundance, even before his second trip. He had read widely in Russian literature, especially the classics, and had studied numerous secondary works on Russian history, art, and folklore. According to Brutzer, Rilke owned copies of the medieval "Nestor Chronicle," the sixteenth-century set of household rules and regulations known as the "Domostroy," and collections of medieval *byliny*.[1] E. M. Butler adds to that list the important volume of folk songs collected by the pioneer ethnographer A. N. Afanasev under the title *Russkie narodnye pesni* (*Russian Folk Songs*), and says that Rilke also knew the ballad and *byliny* collection of Pavel Rybnikov.[2]

Die Geschichten vom lieben Gott

Only one or two critics have attempted to pursue the literary or folkloric sources of the stories; and so far as I know, none has looked for possible Russian qualities in the cycle as a whole, which could serve to unite the individual stories.[3] Allusions to Russia are primarily concentrated in three tales, "Wie der Verrat nach Russland kam" ("How Treachery Came to Russia"), "Wie der alte Timofei singend starb" ("How Old Timofei Died Singing"), and "Das Lied von der Gerechtigkeit" ("The Song of Justice"). They are also present to a varying degree in other stories. In addition to the motif of Russia, three major elements, two thematic and one structural, connect the stories: the motif of God emphasized in the title, the themes of art and creativity, and the device of a narrative frame. Each of these must be considered briefly, before Russia's role in the cycle can be fully understood.

Let us begin with the structural element. The work is a collection of twelve stories (thirteen counting the "Introduction") which are placed within a *Novelle*-like frame structure. The frame is held together by the person of a frame narrator, an unnamed traveler and intellectual, who relates his stories to a variety of listeners. The frame is a complex one. In addition to the narrator and his group of listeners, all the stories are meant to be passed on to the children of the town, as the original title—*An Grosse für Kinder erzählt*—indicated. Thus there exist two sets of listeners, the adults and the children, each with its own prejudices and criteria for judging a story. And judge they do: the primary adult listeners argue with the narrator about his tales; the children send their reactions back to the narrator via the adults, and even by mail. There is, in addition, a relationship between the frame narrator and the actual reader, which, while only implied, is on a different level from any of those mentioned. The narrator and his readers are supposed to be cultural equals; we are expected to understand the asides of the narrator which go right by both of his other audiences. A final complication is the narrator's problematic relationship with the children, whom he never addresses in person. An explanation for this, or at least a literary precedent, will be suggested in the discussion of the Russian themes.

By far the most important of the primary listeners is a lame man named Ewald. He is the audience for four of the thirteen stories, including the three which contain the greatest concentration of Russian elements. And his personality reflects many of the virtues which Rilke associated with Russia. Ewald is introduced to us in the frame leading up to the fourth story, the first "Russian" story. We are given few details at this point, but these few are significant and in quick strokes create a sketch of this important character. We learn that Ewald sits all year round in a chair drawn up to his window. He can look very boyish, or turn suddenly into an old man seemingly on the verge of death, for "the minutes pass over him like years" (IV, 309). Time is a fluid for Ewald, an unconstricting element in which he is at home. Yet he is characterized by a restless desire for knowledge, has "impatient eyes," and is full of questions about the alien reality the narrator knows so well: the world beyond the window, and the world of books. In contrast to his desire for knowledge, Ewald's relation to people is hesitant. His special relation to time and to people echoes Rilke's vision of Russia as a slow land, a place of reserve, waiting, and futurity. Russia's pace is unhurried, a process of ripening; just so has Ewald's relationship with the narrator grown shyly over a period of years, until it has reached its present level of habit and trust, in which the narrator seeks out the lame man at his window to talk to him of Russia.

We gain more insight into Ewald's personality, as well as the narrator's reaction to him, in the frame for the second "Russian" story, "Wie der alte Timofei singend starb." Here the emphasis is on Ewald's closeness to the world of objects. As a cripple he is immobile. This allies him with the other immobile objects of the world, makes him "into an object far superior to the others" (IV, 316). This judgment by the narrator is meant not as a sign of condescension, but positively, for he begins the paragraph with the statement, "What a joy it is to tell stories to a lame person" (IV, 316), and continues by comparing the undependability of healthy people to the stable, thinglike quality of the lame.

In general, Ewald is further characterized by two things: his attitude of listening, and his reverence (*Ehrfurcht*). He is described as having a "listening face" (IV, 309) and he likes to shut his eyes "when a story began anywhere" (IV, 312). By closing out other sense impressions, Ewald opens himself totally to the tale, to the world of the word. Speaking of Ewald and of the lame in general, the narrator says that such a man "listens not only with his silence, but with his rare quiet words and with his reverential feelings" (IV, 316). Thus Ewald's characteristics as listener and worshiper create a character who embodies the crucial qualities which Rilke saw in the Russians, "each with a world within him . . . each deep in his humility, without fear of humbling himself, and therefore pious."[4]

Ewald thus in some ways resembles an ideal figure; one is even tempted to seek in him a direct spokesman for the author. This, however, would be unwise, for Ewald also has his weaknesses. His absolute piety at times disconcerts the more sophisticated narrator, and in one case he prefers to cling to his own ignorance rather than to hear something potentially unpleasant and disillusioning about Russia, which he has come to love through the narrator's tales. I would suggest that in providing his narrator (and his readers) with somewhat ambivalent feelings about Ewald, that bearer of so many idealized "Russian" traits, Rilke was voicing a healthy suspicion, not so much of the Russian character, as of his own role as enthusiast. In a letter to Lou, discussing his involvement with Russia, he admits that a major failing is his intense enthusiasm: "I always fall with the whole weight of my love right to the bottom of the water, and scare people."[5] A strain of irony runs through the whole *Geschichten*-cycle, balancing the generally loving tone found both in the portrayal of Ewald and in the fabric of the stories as a whole. This seems to me evidence that, contrary to the assumptions of many critics, Rilke did in fact try to maintain a certain distance and even a sense of humor about his obsessive love for Russia.

The second major element which both unites the cycle and shows the persistent effect of Russia on Rilke is the motif of God. Like that of the *Stunden-Buch*, the fabric of the *Geschichten* consists of a series of metaphors for God. As in that work, Rilke here portrays him in nature and in works of art. But here the emphasis is not on God as art, but God as artist. The tone of the stories is generally lighter than that of the poems, but a number of important motifs—art, faith, poverty, humility, the Russian peasant and his land—appear with great regularity. In the first three stories, the narrator portrays God as a mythical but fallible figure. In the first, "Das Märchen von den Händen Gottes" ("The Fairy Tale about God's Hands"), God is engrossed in creating man. His left hand, however, inadvertently lets the just-completed man fall to earth before God has had a chance to look at what he has made. Thus are introduced two themes which are repeated in subsequent stories: God's anger at his own hands, which he eventually banishes, and his desire to see what man looks like. The second tale, "Der fremde Mann" ("The Stranger"), tells a grotesque version of the life of Christ, in which God cuts off his own right hand and tells it to go to earth, take on human form, and show itself to him from a mountaintop. In the third story, "Warum der liebe Gott will, dass es arme Leute gibt" ("Why God Wants There To Be Poor People"), the theme of God's desire to see his handiwork is combined with the theme of poverty. In this case God himself wishes to inflict utter poverty on man, since this would reduce him to nakedness, and God could then see at last what man, who by this time has been hidden by clothing, really looks like. Thus in the first three tales, God emerges as an artist, temperamental, self-centered, and certainly not all-powerful. These stories are amusing, but probably among the most self-conscious and least successful in the cycle.

In each of the next three tales, God appears in the guise of a wise old man. The setting of each story is an ancient, semilegendary Russia. In the first of these, "Wie der Verrat nach Russland kam," he is a little old peasant engaged in building a church. He is a figure of wisdom, generosity, and stern justice. In the second tale, "Wie der alte Timofei singend starb,"

God does not appear overtly, and this omission leads to a discussion of the God-motif between the narrator and Ewald. Ewald feels that it is never too late for God to enter a story, and implies that perhaps he was present in the old Timofei. In the third, "Das Lied von der Gerechtigkeit," God appears as a blind bard. Like the God of the first three tales, that of the second three is an artist, or at least an artisan—once a church builder, and twice a singer of tales.

Thus far in the cycle, God has been depicted in tangible human form, as an artist. As the cycle progresses, however, he becomes increasingly abstract and distant from the world of men. In the seventh story of the cycle, God appears embodied in the sea; in the eighth, he feels trapped within Michelangelo's stone, but is freed by entering the greater space of the sculptor himself. In the ninth story, seven children, concerned about the fate of God, consciously transform an ordinary thimble into a receptacle for, and symbol of, God, thus taking direct responsibility for his existence. By the twelfth story, God can be seen only in the actions of a humble man, and in the final story, he exists only in the joyful anticipation of the characters, for whom he is a long-awaited guest.

Thus there is a large general movement in the metaphors for God, from capricious meddler to pantheistic divinity, from artistic force within a man (bard, builder, Michelangelo) to abstract mover behind or within the lives of men. The first six stories show him in some form of artistic activity. The seventh, a kind of transition to a new focus, shows him as the sea—amorphous, natural, and dependent for his divinity on human faith. In the last six, his presence becomes increasingly symbolic and abstract, until finally he no longer exists at all. A character in the last story describes her perception of God: "I feel that he existed, some time or other—now I think sometimes: he will be" (IV, 398). Significantly, this story is not, according to the narrator, passed on to the children, who are not ready for its message: that God is merely a state of mind, belief in a process.

Thus the motif of God in the *Geschichten* is closely interwoven with the other dominant motif of art and creativity. Many of the characters in the stories are artists of one sort or another: sculptors, goldsmiths, poets. Discussions of art occur in the frame, and the narrator creates the backdrop for one of his stories by a digression on Carpaccio, Giorgione, Titian, and Tiepolo. One of the strengths of the work is the variety of notes which Rilke strikes, and the smoothness with which, for the most part, he moves from one to another, mingling irony, satire, allegory, and symbolism to achieve his varying stances. This is especially evident in his pronouncements on, or portrayals of, art and artists. At times the world of artists and patrons is approached tongue in cheek. God encounters technical difficulties in creating the first man; the forehead was easy, but "it was much harder for him to make the two nostrils symmetrical" (IV, 291). Elsewhere, a mayor commissions a statue of "Truth" for the city park. When the sculptor produces a naked figure, a council of influential personages demands that Truth be clothed. And at one point, a young musician visits the narrator to ask him to join a newly formed art lovers' association. The narrator remarks to his readers that the artists' association

> arose recently out of a very urgent necessity, as you can easily imagine, and the rumor is going around that it is "flourishing." If associations don't have any idea of what to do, then they flourish. They've heard you have to do that to be a real association.
>
> (IV, 367)

The narrator goes on to tell the musician that he spends a good part of his time just resigning from precisely such organizations:

> Just imagine, . . . not a minute goes by in which I don't resign from some association or other, and yet there are still societies which, so to speak, contain me.
>
> (IV, 368)

The musician is portrayed as humorless, pompous, and fussy—in his eagerness to set everything around him in order, he twice picks up the narrator's gloves, snatches a bit of lint from his clothing, can barely keep himself from rubbing a spot of soot from his companion's nose, and leaves him at last with the avowed purpose of going back the way they had come, so that he can straighten the twisted sleeve of a scarecrow they had passed along the way. Rilke pillories in this figure the officious, orderly, self-satisfied, and overorganized side of the Germanic personality, heightening the irony by making him ostensibly represent art.

Some of these passages are intended mainly for comic effect, but most lead into, or contain within themselves, a more serious statement about the nature of art and the relation of the artist to society, himself, and God. In the story which the narrator tells the young musician, we find both obvious satire and more complex commentary. Rilke aims a few blows at various aspects of contemporary German art. The three painters are depicted as inarticulate and self-important; twice nonartists are referred to by them as "profane," thus creating of the artists by implication a sort of holy brotherhood. There is in their contemptuous reaction to reality a comic portrayal of the then-popular life versus art controversy.[6] Wandering home late one night, they are impressed by various "scenes" encountered along the way. Reality is treated wholly as a work of art, and judged accordingly. In a moonlit square,

> the illuminated surface of the pavement . . . was interrupted ruthlessly in the center by a fountain and its heavy shadow, a stroke of daring which impressed the painters uncommonly.
>
> (IV, 370)

But the intrusion of human life, in the form of a song overheard from a nearby courtyard, is dismissed by the disgusted painters as "a coarse striving for effect" (IV, 370), and the appearance of a pair of lovers turns the scene into "a pitiable illustration" (IV, 371). The painters' obsession with artifice and intention is mocked in a number of such touches.

Yet Rilke is careful to point out that these are "real artists, intended by nature, so to speak, not accidental ones" (IV, 369). That is, for all their pomposity, they are not charlatans. Thus we are urged to give some serious attention to their actions, the most significant of which is their decision to form an association of like-minded artists with similar values. They rent a farmhouse in which to work together, painting from life. (This series of events may have been suggested to Rilke by a number of similar situations with which he was familiar: the colony of artists in the moorland village of Worpswede, which he already knew in 1899, and about which he would write a monograph in 1902; the colony of Russian artists and craftsmen on the country estate Abramtsevo near Moscow, which he visited; and even perhaps the turn-of-the-century movement among Polish artists to return to the land and the people, typified by Jacek Malczewski and Stanisław Wyspiański. There may also be a suggestion here of the rural Breton preoccupations of Gauguin and Émile Bernard, as well as the open-air methods of the Impressionists.)

But once settled in their country retreat, Rilke's three painters become seriously alienated from one another, as they discover that each of them paints, and defends jealously, a totally different view of their shared reality. The differences eventually drive them to opposite ends of the earth, where, in their attempt to avoid one another, they are in danger of falling off; they are saved from destruction by the appearance of God. He distracts them by presenting himself as an artistic subject, which they all set about painting. An important point emerges out of this ironic tale. In the image of the three disparate artists all working on their pictures of God there is an echo of one of the central concerns of the monk in the *Stunden-Buch,* who worried about the correct way of portraying divinity. In the story, each artist sees very differently from the others, and we would expect their paintings of God to differ accordingly. Yet the narrator suggests that if they were ever to show one another their pictures, "who knows, maybe these pictures would barely differ from one another" (IV, 378). Thus the monk's dilemma is, in a sense, solved in this story. Though the artists' views of the world differ radically, God would bring them back together through their portrayal of him. Larger than his own creation, containing all its elements, he would reveal himself to each painter; the details of existence, the individual talents and styles, would be overcome by Rilke's God in a single all-inclusive vision. The painters would arrive, by a roundabout path, at the

Die Geschichten vom lieben Gott

position defended by the Russian icon painter, whose portraits must always reflect the same vision of the divine.

The *Geschichten* present other aspects of art, mostly as reflections of moral and ethical problems, and as symbols of the close relationship of creativity and God. In one story, a young man sacrifices his personal happiness to become a bard, literally the voice of his people. Song here represents humility and duty. In another tale, the artist's gift is clearly connected to a divine presence. God watches in fascination the movements of Michelangelo's hands, which seem to him to be engaged in prayer. The growth of Michelangelo's genius is marked by God's entry into him, and is expressed by the sculptor's sudden feeling of "unwonted humility" (IV, 349). In still another story, art, in the form of poetry and portrait painting, is seen as a record of love and harmony, and as a hedge against mortality. Finally, in the last of the stories, art is the source of love, liberation, and a renewed religious faith. It is in the man-made beauties of Florence that the protagonist rediscovers God:

> Everywhere there were traces of him. I found shreds of his smile in all the pictures, the bells were still alive with his voice, and on the statues I recognized the imprint of his hands.
>
> (IV, 398)

It can be seen, then, that the three major elements discussed thus far—the narrative frame, the varying figure of God, and the theme of art—are interwoven with each other, and are all in some way related to ideas and motifs associated with Russia in Rilke's writing. A study of the Russian elements themselves will reveal how these details function both in the individual stories and in the fabric of the cycle as a whole.

The first story which is permeated by Russian elements is "Wie der Verrat nach Russland kam" (IV, 309–16). The narrator has just returned from a trip to Russia. He becomes involved in a discussion with Ewald which touches on such subjects as the vastness of Russia, the piety and humility of its people, and the topography of that country, which borders above and below on a nation called "God." The anecdote which he is about to tell illustrates, he says, the notion that "one has the feeling that everything new is introduced by him [God], every garment, every dish, every virtue, and even every sin must first be approved by him, before it comes into use" (IV, 311). The anecdote is based on two prose versions of a common source, the sixteenth-century historical song about Ivan the Terrible, "How Treachery Was Brought into Russia" (*Otčego na Rusi zavelas' izmena*).[7] The first version is found in a collection of folk literature published by a prominent Russian ethnographer, Pavel Rybnikov.[8]

The second version, which appeared in Alfred Rambaud's study of early Russian literature, *La Russie Épique*,[9] under the title "Comment la Trahison s'est introduite en Russie," is taken somewhat abridged from Rybnikov. Rilke had read both versions. Because the Rambaud version is mainly an abridgement of the Rybnikov, with no important additions or changes, my discussion will be devoted almost entirely to the Russian source.

In the historical songs that grew up around Ivan IV in the late sixteenth century, Ivan is almost always portrayed positively.[10] But he is also seen as "violent and impulsive, though energetic and successful in his undertakings."[11] Frequently he is aided in these undertakings "by a simple soldier."[12] This pattern is retained in Rybnikov's prose version. Its central figure, Ivan IV, is seen acting impulsively (and, as it turns out, unwisely); he is superficially successful, at least in what he knowingly sets out to do; and the focus of the story is the aid given him by a simple peasant—not a soldier, in this case, but a builder—and his reaction to that aid.

In Rybnikov, Ivan decides to exact a yearly tribute from a group of foreign kings and princes. Their reply to his demands is a letter in which they ask him three riddles and set terms for a response. If he answers all three correctly, they will pay him the tribute, plus twelve barrels of gold. Otherwise he will lose not only the gold, but his throne as well. The tsar consults with his advisers, and they arrive at a set of answers. With his retinue, Ivan sets out for the assigned meeting place, a white stone in the East. On their way, the travelers come across an old peasant building a church in the wilderness; instead of carrying his supplies with him up to the tower where he is finishing the cupola, he comes down the ladder for each separate piece. Intrigued, the tsar gets into a discussion with the peasant about his way of working. The peasant then asks Ivan if he is on his way to answer the riddles; Ivan replies affirmatively, and inquires whether the peasant might help him. The peasant agrees to help, on condition that he be given one of the barrels of gold; Ivan agrees, is given the correct answers, and departs for the east, where he amazes the foreign rulers with his wisdom. But on the way home, Ivan and his boyars decide that it would be foolish to give the peasant a whole barrel of gold, since he has no need of it, while they have an army to feed. Instead they give him a barrel two-thirds full of sand, with a layer of gold on top. The peasant sees through the ruse and declares that Ivan has brought treachery to Russia, warning that neither he nor anyone else will ever be able to root it out again. Ivan tries to make amends, but the peasant declares he can live without gold; what he needs is "not your gold, but truth" ("ne . . . tvoja zlatnica, a . . . pravda").[13] The peasant and his church thereupon disappear. Ivan concludes

Die Geschichten vom lieben Gott

that the peasant had been God himself ("zaključil, čto èto byl sam Bog");[14] chastened, he bows and turns homeward toward his throne.

The plot of Rilke's anecdote is similar; there are, however, a number of major changes. In Rilke's version, when Ivan calls upon his advisers to solve the three riddles (Rilke includes neither the text of the letter, nor the riddles), their answers displease him, so he has them taken out onto Red Square and beheaded one by one. He becomes so engrossed in this activity that he suddenly finds himself, fairy-tale fashion, riding to meet the rulers without having received any answers to their riddles. On the road, he still does not lose hope, however, for as the narrator points out, "there was still the possibility of meeting a wise man; for at that time many wise men were in flight, since all the kings had the habit of having their heads cut off if they didn't seem wise enough" (IV, 312–13). When Ivan, in Rilke's version, comes upon the old peasant, he is irritated by the peasant's inefficient method of building, and addresses him with a shout of "Dummkopf." The peasant nonetheless volunteers to give Ivan the correct answers to the riddles, and wants no reward for them, until Ivan orders him to wish for something; at that point, the peasant asks for one of the barrels of gold.

Rilke omits the scene at the white stone, where Ivan triumphs over the princes. We next see Ivan back at the Kremlin, where he has locked himself into his chambers and poured out all twelve barrels of gold onto the floor, "so that a regular mountain of gold arose, which threw a big black shadow across the floor" (IV, 314).[15] He sneaks out into the courtyard at night, scoops sand into a barrel until it is three-quarters full, lays gold over the sand, and the next morning sends the barrel to the peasant. The peasant sees the messenger coming and calls out to him to return to Moscow with his fake barrel of gold; he doesn't need Ivan's gold, but rather "truth and integrity" ("Wahrheit und Rechtlichkeit" [IV, 315].[16] Ivan has disappointed him, and has introduced treachery into Russia; and if Ivan now discovers that he cannot trust anyone, it is his own fault. The messenger rides off, but when he turns around, he discovers that the peasant and his church have disappeared. Panic-stricken, he gallops back to Moscow and stammers to Ivan "rather incomprehensibly" what had happened. The messenger concludes "that the presumed peasant had been none other than God himself" (IV, 315).

Rilke's anecdote differs in plot, characterization, and tone from Rybnikov's story, and it is in the changes Rilke makes that his originality is displayed. Let us look, for example, at the figure of Ivan. In the traditional historical songs, Ivan is portrayed positively. This does not mean that his fearsome character is overlooked, but his faults are seen against a background of grandeur. Rambaud, in his introduction to the Rybnikov tale, speaks of Ivan's well-known obsession with spies and traitors, and suggests that the purpose of the original Russian storyteller was "to depict that uneasy and feverish preoccupation of the Terrible, to scoff at what people believed to be a sinister habit of the tsar."[17] In scene after scene, using the tools of irony and exaggeration, Rilke changes this image of Ivan, making him a more modern, less grand figure, burdened with guilt, yet ludicrous and petty. For example, in Rybnikov, Ivan demands a yearly tribute to Russia, but he makes no threats. The foreign princes, almost as if in arrogant mockery, not only reply with a challenge of their own, but also, with a touch of insulting condescension, offer to pay him an extra twelve barrels of gold if he can guess their riddles. Self-confidently, they add a direct threat: "If you can't figure out these three riddles . . . you will be forced to abdicate."[18] The aggressive princes thus represent a menace to the tsar, and indirectly to Russia, and this fact would have aroused sympathies for the tsar in the Russian audience. In Rilke, however, Ivan alone is the aggressor. "The terrible tsar wanted to impose a tribute on the neighboring princes, and threatened them with a great war if they wouldn't send gold to the white city of Moscow" (IV, 312). In the princes' response we find the riddles, but no extra promises, and no threats. By omitting the princes' threat to the future of Russia, Rilke removes a source of sympathy for the tsar; by adding the element of Ivan's saber rattling, he turns the princes' response into an act of self-defense, and places Ivan in the wrong from the beginning.

Rilke also greatly alters the scene of consultation between Ivan and his advisers, once again shifting responsibility to Ivan's shoulders. In Rybnikov, Ivan, upon receiving the princes' letter, summons "his boyars and princes and wise men." There is some disagreement—"someone says something, but it pleases the tsar little"[19]—but eventually "by general consultation" they arrive at a set of answers to which the tsar can agree. In Rilke, the princes and boyars have disappeared, and the "scholars and advisers" appear only long enough to be beheaded.[20] Ivan is placed plainly in the center of the action, and the eventual guilt is his alone. Rilke's vengeful and impatient tsar might be said to have emerged from Rybnikov's mildly displeased one, but Rilke carries a character trait to absurd extremes and makes Ivan the caricature of a despot.[21]

In the scene between Ivan and the peasant, Rilke makes a number of important changes. Several of these involve a change in tone from the Rybnikov tale, which, although a prose retelling of the historical song, still retains some elements of its oral folk origins. Other major changes in Rilke's version of the scene are in characterization and in the development of the plot. The first difference occurs in the sentences introducing the scene. The original Russian says literally that "Tsar Ivan traveled, whether long or short, near or far" ("dolgo li, korotko li, blizko li, daleko")[22] before coming to the peasant's church "in an empty place." The phrase is a folk formula indicating a journey into the indeterminate; it carries with it an aura of expectancy. The indeterminacy of the journey and the conveniently deserted place where Ivan meets the peasant create the feeling of a trip into a timeless land where anything can happen. These elements are omitted by Rilke, resulting in both a sense of greater distance from the events and a more matter-of-fact tone. In addition, Rilke's narrator introduces the scene ironically, and his tone further distances us from it. In his preparation for the scene, he mentions that Ivan hopes to meet a fleeing wise man, and the first sight of the peasant is presented casually, as if in passing, at the end of the sentence: "It's true he didn't catch sight of such a wise man, but one morning he saw an old bearded peasant who was working on a church" (IV, 313). The ironic introduction of the figure of the peasant, and the few concrete details which Rilke uses to describe him ("old," "bearded," wearing a "long caftan") lead in an opposite direction from the folk genre's supernatural, fairy-tale mood. The sense of indeterminacy and the supernatural which permeate the folktale are not totally omitted, however, but merely deferred to a later point in Rilke's more sophisticated anecdote, and concentrated in the final scene, where they produce a very different effect.

A second important alteration occurs in the exchange between Ivan and the peasant. In Rybnikov, the tsar is courtly, calling the peasant "little old man, my brother" ("brat staričok") and greeting him with "may God help you" ("Bog v pomoč'").[23] Rilke's tsar, as we have seen, becomes impatient and greets him with ridicule. Gone is the formulaic politeness of the folk genre, where the tsar would not have been portrayed as crude and lacking in finesse.

The most important change is in the character of the peasant. In Rybnikov, Ivan asks the peasant, who seems to know where the tsar is going, to help him. The peasant agrees, but only on condition that Ivan give him the barrel of gold. He torments Ivan by reminding him how much hangs on his knowledge of the correct answers: "If you give me one of the twelve barrels, then, if you please, I'll explain to you the riddles and you will go on ruling; if not, then your reign will come to an end." Ivan responds, "As you wish, old man . . . take any of the twelve barrels, but just tell me the riddles,"[24] and upon receiving the answers, thanks him. Here, the peasant is portrayed as crafty and acquisitive, the tsar as a desperate man caught in a bind and willing to promise anything.[25] In Rilke's anecdote, the relationship has changed. Here the peasant, without bargaining, volunteers the answers to the riddles. The tsar is amazed, and asks what the old man wants as his reward. When the latter replies "nothing," and unconcernedly starts back up the ladder, the tsar orders him to accept a reward:

> "Stop," ordered the tsar, "that won't do. You have to wish for something."
> "Well, little Father, if you command it, give me one of the twelve barrels of gold which you will get from the princes in the east."
>
> (IV, 314)

Thus, where Rybnikov's peasant was greedy, and resorted to something approaching blackmail, Rilke's is generous, and would have given his help for nothing if he had been allowed to. But Ivan, unable to comprehend or trust a gift freely given, asserts his authority and forces the old man to choose a reward. Rilke is parodying here the folktale trope of the magic wish. In both versions, Ivan comes to regret his promise, but in Rilke's, his regret is doubly ironic because Ivan is not only the source of the promise, but its enforcer as well.

Rilke also changes the episode of falsification of the barrel of gold. In Rybnikov, Ivan consults with his retinue, on the road back from the east, as to the amount of gold the peasant should be given—Ivan's army needs the money more than the peasant does—and the necessity of deceiving him. Thus, Rybnikov shows Ivan as a miserly and imperious ruler who errs through too great a concern for the costs of governing; his act is public and is perpetrated with the help of his advisers. In Rilke, however, both the motivation for the deception and the setting in which it is carried out are different: Ivan rides all the way back to the Kremlin and from "forgetfulness" pours out the twelfth barrel along with the others. His first reaction is to refill it, but "he hated to have to take away so much gold from the magnificent pile" (IV, 314). Rilke's version emphasizes both Ivan's deviousness and his solitude. His reason for the ruse is personal greed, and he carries it out himself in the dark of night—a petty man, doing a shameful deed in secret.[26] Rybnikov's tsar boldly presents the barrel to the peasant himself, with flowery and hypocritical salutations: "May the Lord help you, old man. I humbly thank you for your explanations. I received everything that was promised me. Now you, too, come, old man, and accept the barrel of gold which I promised you."[27] Rilke's tsar, too cowardly to face the peasant, sends the barrel with a messenger instead. In the two versions, the tsar is equally dishonest; but while Rybnikov's is a brazen figure, Rilke's is timid and fearful. In general, Rilke's Ivan remains more isolated from those around him; he dramatically rejects his advisers' aid in solving the riddles, later conceives and carries out his ruse by himself, and carefully avoids confronting the peasant a second time. This isolation, as well as a pervasive fearfulness, was also emphasized in Rilke's poem about Ivan in "Die Zaren." There Ivan is surrounded by shadowy, threatening figures, but he remains alone:

Und er hat . . .
nichts, was er zu rufen wagt,
nichts als die Angst vor allen diesen,
nichts als die tägliche Angst vor Allen,
die ihn jagt durch diese gejagten
Gesichter . . .
                              (I, 431)

[And he has . . . nothing that he dares call out, nothing but the fear of all these, nothing but the daily fear of them all, which hunts him through these hunted faces.]

The final major change concerns the discovery of the ruse and the peasant's judgment of Ivan. In Rybnikov, the peasant confronts Ivan directly and accuses him to his face of having introduced treachery into Russia by his faithlessness. Likewise, Ivan himself recognizes the peasant's true identity; like the patriarchs in the Bible, he has intimate dealings with God. Rilke's Ivan, as we know, sends the barrel with a messenger; it is possible to attribute to the latter's journey mythic proportions and significance, for he is sent "into the region of vast Russia, where the old peasant was building his church" (IV, 314). The rider's goal is the boundless, undifferentiated spaces of all Russia; it is as if, wherever he rides, he will find the old man building his church. The sense of indeterminacy surrounding Ivan's journey which Rilke omitted from the scene first introducing the peasant is recaptured here and shifted to the messenger's journey, setting the tone for the final supernatural revelation.

But this revelation, and the effect of the peasant's judgment, differ in important ways from their counterparts in Rilke's source. The judgment pronounced by Rilke's peasant comes to Ivan only through an intermediary, the messenger; and it is only the latter who comes to the conclusion that the old man must have been God. Rilke combines several elements to produce the particular effect of this scene. He juxtaposes the tsar's material richness with his spiritual poverty by depicting Ivan, who is waiting in Moscow for the return of the messenger, as wearing golden robes but sitting alone and suffering from a bad conscience. Rilke isolates the tsar, and distances him from the experiences. Having throughout the story made Ivan solely responsible for his troubles, Rilke now deprives him of the possibility of an ethical insight or of purgation. Ivan remains without the personal experience of God, and is left alone with his guilt.

But the most important aspect of Rilke's handling of his source is the fact that he places the story within a frame and creates a narrator who controls the point of view, a device which, by preventing any single reading of the tale, opens it up to multiple meanings. The narrator's basic tone, in this story and in the cycle in general, is one of light irony. He is gregarious, and his anecdotes are frequently meant as helpful parables, illustrations of arguments that he hopes will aid or enlighten his audience. On the other hand, we know from other sections of the cycle that he is subject to fits of shyness about himself and his stories. He cannot, for example, bring himself to talk to children directly, but continually asks other adults to tell his tales, as at the end of this story, where he asks Ewald to pass on the Russian anecdote. It is difficult, given what we know of the narrator, to explain his aversion to telling his tales directly to their avowed audience. In the frame following the first story, we have an inkling of this aversion. The narrator has just received a letter from the village children, apparently asking him to come and tell them his stories. He declines, and his reasons are very strange:

> I don't have a nice nose, and if, as occasionally happens, it also has a little red pimple at the end of it, then you would stare and gape at this pimple the whole time, and not hear at all what I was saying a little further down. And you would probably dream about that little pimple.
>
> (IV, 296)

He obviously feels that his slight physical peculiarities will endanger his success as a storyteller. A few pages earlier he has refused an invitation to talk to the children directly, saying he embarrasses easily. Yet the personality of the narrator as it emerges in other parts of the cycle is often ironic, occasionally satirical, only rarely ingenuous or seemingly naive. He does not, by and large, appear to be as shy as he implies in these two situations.

A look at Nikolay Gogol's story "The Nose" may afford some insight into this image of the nose and pimple. In Gogol's story,[28] written in 1836, an official, Kavalyov, awakens one morning, reaches for a mirror "to look at a pimple which had appeared on his nose the previous evening," and discovers that his nose is missing. The plot continues in a fantastic, absurdist mode in which the nose takes on a life of its own. There have been many interpretations of this story, but the one that is the most applicable to the case of Rilke's narrator is that "The Nose" is a delightful piece of conscious nonsense[29] and that "nose-humor" has a rich tradition of long standing in Russia.[30] Thus Rilke, in giving his narrator such odd and unconvincing excuses, may well have had Gogol and "The Nose" in mind, aiming both at a similar kind of absurd playfulness, and, more importantly, at establishing a distance between the narrator and his earnest little audience, via mystification. We shall see that that is very much in character for the narrator, and that he was in fact concerned with maintaining such a distance even from his friend Ewald.

In the frame preceding the tale of Ivan and the old peasant, Rilke also lays the groundwork for the effect of multiple meaning by establishing contradictions between the frame and the tale. The narrator prepares for the anecdote by establishing a series of metaphoric identities. He speaks of "God" as the land above the mountains and below the abysses of Russia. He also remarks that for a simple people it is hard to distinguish between their land and their ruler. Finally he compares the imports from "God"—bread and ceremonials, and broad Russian gestures of respect, which make no distinction between God and the tsar—with the imports brought in from the West, which become "stones, as soon as they cross the border. Now and then precious stones, but still only for the rich, the so-called 'educated' " (IV, 310). The narrator's scorn and antipathy for the West echo the thoughts expressed by the monk in the *Stunden-Buch*. What emerges from these loosely connected images is that God, land, and tsar are identical. This equation is subsequently contradicted, however, in the Russian anecdote, where God appears as a peasant, whose activities are coterminous with the land, but where the tsar, a separate character, resembles nothing so much as a Moscow merchant trying to cheat a customer.

The divergence of the frame and the anecdote is tied closely to another divergence, that of the narrator and Ewald, and the anecdote's tone owes much to this difference between speaker and listener. Ewald is a plain man, earnest and naive. Several times he misunderstands the narrator's irony, or takes one of his turns of phrase literally, The God-land image, for example, makes him uneasy, and at the narrator's remark that God must approve every new sin in Russia, Ewald stares at him "almost shocked" (IV, 311). And while the narrator claims that his aim in telling the anecdote is to illustrate the meaning of this unorthodox idea, the tale in fact does not illustrate this. Rather it shows God present and involved in the inception of the new sin—treachery—and sadly acknowledging—not the same thing as approving—its addition to the list.

This shift between frame and anecdote is necessary because, while Ewald is the narrator's immediate audience, there also exist two other audiences: the children of the town, and the sophisticated reader, both of whom understand the tale in different ways. The children, for whom the "stories about God" were conceived, are fascinated with details about the divinity. They have no trouble finding God in all sorts of guises, in every story, and are thus easily satisfied. Unlike Ewald, they are utterly at home in the world of unconventional metaphors and fantasy.

The sophisticated reader, on the other hand, is the audience closest to the narrator himself in experience and temperament. It is for him that the latter couches his simple tale in ironic terms, and comments on the action in humorous asides—for certainly neither Ewald nor the children are capable of apprehending this level of the narrative. Thus, for example, he provides an irrelevant prediction that the peasant will probably never finish building his church, comical expertise in the assurance that it was common practice for dissatisfied kings to behead their advisers in droves, and a humorous explanation of why the tsar greets the peasant as "Dummkopf": "That's how they usually address the peasants in Russia" (IV, 313). It should be noted that in this passage, the humor is not at the expense of the peasant, but of Ewald, who is expected to believe it. These are fine examples of Rilke's straight-faced humor, which has unfortunately been largely ignored. Eudo Mason, in the only article on the subject to date,[31] mentions as typical of Rilke's humor elements similar to those which I have pointed out as characteristic of the narrator in the *Geschichten:* irony, subtlety, and a tendency toward self-parody.

The last incident in the frame that reveals Rilke's device of a multiple audience which allows multiple readings of the tale is that of the flight of the narrator from his own story, which occurs at the very end. He concludes the anecdote with the messenger's assertion that the peasant was God, and Ewald asks, "Do you think he was right about that?" (IV, 315). Ewald's question seems to embarrass the narrator, whose own hurried reply serves to undermine his relation to the story: "Perhaps—but, you know, the people are—superstitious—however, I have to go now, Ewald" (IV, 315). His deprecating manner may be a defense against his being identified too closely with the folk material of his tale and thus limited to one level of narrative truth. His stories, and even his metaphoric flights of fancy within the frame are, after all, conscious fictional constructs. He is a storyteller, and as Rilke's alter ego, he is a sophisticated, rather self-consciously modern artist. His anecdote was told partially tongue in cheek, with a conscious desire to entertain. Thus when Ewald presses too hard with his unsophisticated interpretation, and tries to involve the narrator in it as a reality, the narrator panics and, extracting a promise that the tale will be passed on to the children, quickly disappears: " 'Goodbye!' And with that I left" (IV, 316).

The narrator is, in his own way, "treacherous," for he fully intends for his anecdote to be understood on different levels by different people. But none of these interpretations is invalid, nor do they cancel one another out. The story of the introduction of a specific sin into a specific country by the wickedness of one individual can be understood on a naive level by the children; Ewald is only a little less easily convinced. For the reader, however, who takes for granted the existence of treachery in all peoples and nations, the anecdote functions as an amusing distillation of this more general truth, and can also be seen, perhaps, as a paraphrase of the story of the Fall—that is, of the introduction of sin per se into the world by the first man.

In addition, the reader who is familiar with Rilke's works can see in the purposeful utilization of the Russian tale a reflection of Rilke's attitudes toward Russia. In the frame, the narrator suggests the identity of God, the Russian land, and the tsar; in the anecdote, he identifies God with a Russian peasant, a figure rooted in the land. This God figure, besides being wise, cheerful, generous, and forthright, embodies other traits which Rilke saw in the Russian peasant per se: simplicity and a patient acceptance of reality bordering on passivity. The peasant-God is saddened by the tsar's deception, but he also accepts it in all its ramifications for the future: "From century to century his example will find many imitators all over Russia" (IV, 315).

What, then, has Rilke done in the course of his adaptation? First, he has created a new psychological portrait of Ivan IV, modifying the figure traditional in folk literature—impatient, imperious, miserly, a little vain, and brazenly dishonest, but also courtly and capable of learning from experience—into a figure who is cruel, personally greedy, cowardly, slow-witted, and rude. Second, Rilke has presented an affectionate variation on his frequent theme of the peasant. The existing framework of the supernatural tale, with its peculiar telescoping of the peasant and his God into one figure, lent itself well to Rilke's purposes. The sixteenth-century image is very close to Rilke's own imagery in the first part of the *Stunden-Buch,* where the lyric protagonist addresses his God, "Du bist der Bauer mit dem Barte / von Ewigkeit zu Ewigkeit" (*"*You are the peasant with the beard, to all Eternity" [I, 277]). Finally, he transforms a simple folktale into a distinctively Rilkean work of art by creating a "treacherous" narrator who addresses himself to three different audiences, satisfying their different expectations, and who then, like the peasant in the anecdote, vanishes at the end.

In the second overtly "Russian" tale, "Wie der alte Timofei singend starb," as in the previous story, a conversation with Ewald leads into the narrative. Ewald demands to know where the narrator got the story about Ivan and the peasant. The narrator explains that stories used to be "alive" and pass from mouth to mouth until, crushed and quenched by the "heavy, unsingable words" (IV, 317) of modern man, they died out at last,[32] and were given a solemn burial by scholars, in a book.[33] Ewald then asks the age of the tale about Ivan, and the narrator replies, "Four hundred to five hundred years old."[34] Ewald is skeptical when he hears that it could have found a place to rest for all those centuries in the unquiet hearts of men. But the narrator assures him it was so, for men in those days talked less, danced slow, stately dances, and in general showed themselves worthy of such tales. (Here the qualities which Rilke admired in Russia are represented specifically by an idealized vision of the Russian middle ages.) The narrator tells Ewald that such songs and tales were hereditary in Russia in certain families. The ability to sing and the knowledge of a large number of stories by heart constituted one's inheritance, and showed one's ties to family, community, and folk. Conversely, the "disinherited" lacked these skills and this knowledge. The narrator proceeds to illustrate this information with a tale about two members of such a family: the old village singer Timofei, and his rebellious son Yegor.

Against his father's wishes, Yegor marries and goes off with his wife to Kiev. Timofei's reaction is to curse his son and to stop singing. Thus he spends his days and nights sitting silently on the stove, growing old and sick; and the youths of the village, despite their pleading, learn no more songs from his lips. Four years later, Yegor suddenly returns, having left wife and child to fend for themselves in Kiev. He has heard from a pilgrim, Ossip, how things are in the village since Timofei stopped singing: it was "as if it hadn't a soul any more, our village. Nothing throbs, nothing moves, no one weeps any more, and there isn't a real reason to laugh, either" (IV, 322). Yegor, evidently feeling within himself the powerful flow of tradition, duty, and community, tells his wife "my turn has come" (IV, 322) and returns home to learn all his father's songs. The two men remain locked in their hut all winter long, until, shortly after singing his best song, Timofei dies. In the spring, Yegor emerges into the village and sings the old songs, but with a new tone. Yegor sings

> all those tunes which no one, be he Cossack or peasant, could listen to without weeping. And in addition he supposedly had a gentle and sorrowful tone such as no one had yet heard from any other singer. And this tone always occurred, quite unexpectedly, in the refrain, which made its effect particularly touching.
>
> (IV, 324)

The tale then glides over into the frame once more, as Ewald and the narrator debate the source of the new tone, which had not come from Yegor's father.

The presence in Yegor's singing of this personal, melancholy sound raises for Ewald the question of its source, and for the reader that of its relation to the Russian tradition. Ewald suggests that it arose whenever Yegor thought of his lost wife and child, whom he had abandoned in order to do his duty. One critic regards the new tone as un-Russian, seeing in it an expression of Rilke's own view of the artist, his inability to imagine anyone taking over materials from someone else without changing them.[35] While this does in fact reflect Rilke's modus operandi, there is no essential conflict with the Russian tradition. Indeed, inventiveness and creativity on the part of the individual *skazitel'* ("narrator") played an important role in the development of each particular song cycle.[36] In addition, the specific

Die Geschichten vom lieben Gott

element of melancholy belongs equally to the tradition of Russian song. In a story entitled "Singers," from Ivan Turgenev's *Sportsman's Sketches,* for example, a young man sings a "plaintive song" and in his voice there is

> authentic profound passion, and youth, and strength, and sweetness, and a kind of fascinatingly detached, melancholy sorrow. The true, hot Russian soul sounded and breathed in it, and seized you by the heart, seized right at its Russian heartstrings.[37]

His listeners are all struck by the tone, and the tears roll down their cheeks as he sings. Thus we see in Rilke's story that, though Ewald's surmise is probably accurate and fits the events, Rilke also had several details of the actual tradition to fall back on.

The story about Yegor performs several functions. In the context of the narrative frame, it is part of the narrator's continued response to Ewald's growing curiosity about everything Russian. In addition it gives, in combination with the information provided in the frame, an interesting and reasonably accurate, if poeticized, view of the Russian oral tradition. And it focuses on one of Rilke's recurring themes, the problematic relation of father to son. The plot concerns a son's disobedience and a father's curse; the threatened loss, not only of a son's inheritance, but of that of his whole village through him; the ultimate reconciliation; and the continuance of the inherited tradition. There are three distinct levels on which the story functions. First, the episodes of the plot closely resemble those of a fairy tale of the quest variety. In a typical quest tale, the hero is often the only son of a poor peasant; he leaves home and goes off in search of adventure. Having passed a test of some sort, he returns home and reaps the benefits of his return.[38] Here Yegor, an only son, leaves home to seek his fortune in Kiev, passes a test—by making a moral decision that will change his life— returns home, learns his father's songs, and dons the melancholy mantle of his inheritance.

Secondly, both the traditional fairy tale and Yegor's variation seem clearly to be based on the biblical story of the Prodigal Son, a motif of which Rilke was very fond. Like the young man in the Bible, Yegor leaves home against his father's wishes. And like the Prodigal Son, when he returns home, he is welcomed without reproach. Yegor's repentance brings him back into the fold, but at a cost at which, like Ewald, we can only guess. We never learn why Timofei had opposed his son's marriage in the first place, or why it should necessarily have stood in the way of Yegor learning his father's songs and carrying on the family tradition—although it may reflect Rilke's as yet unconscious doubts, discussed earlier, about the possibility of combining the life of a poet with that of a family man. All we know, in this case, is that ultimately Yegor opts for duty over love.

On the third level, the story is connected, both by allusion and by plot, to a source in Russian folk literature, the *bylina* about Dyuk Stepanovich.[39] This *bylina* is mentioned twice in Rilke's tale, first by the pilgrim Ossip, who reminisces about the good old days, when Timofei used to sing "the song about Dyuk Stepanovich, for example" (IV, 321). The second time it is alluded to is in the final days of Timofei's life. As the old man's strength fails, he keeps returning unconsciously to the same song: "Now he mostly sang the same strophes about Dyuk Stepanovich, which he especially loved" (IV, 323). No other *bylina* is mentioned by name. Since Rilke rarely uses specific details gratuitously, the repetition calls for investigation.

Dyuk was one of the heroes of the Kievan cycles of *byliny,* and like most of the Kievan heroes, his exploits exist in a variety of versions. The basic outline of the tale as it is usually told is as follows: young Dyuk, the only son of a wealthy queen in Galich (sometimes Chernigov, or India) leaves home (sometimes with, often without, the blessings of his mother) to seek adventures at the court of Prince Vladimir in Kiev. Once there, he disdains the wine and bread he is offered, and brags instead about the high quality of everything back home. In some variants, Vladimir sends emissaries to investigate Dyuk's claims, which are found to be true. In most versions, Dyuk also undergoes a series of armed contests, in which he is victorious. Assured of lasting fame at Kiev, Dyuk returns home to his mother.

Rilke had access to a large number of variants of the Dyuk tale, in Rybnikov's collection and from other sources. In a comparison of his story about Timofei and Yegor with these songs, a number of oblique similarities occur. Both Dyuk and Yegor leave home against their parents' wishes. The goal of both is Kiev. Dyuk's mother's patronymic in at least two variants is Timofeevna (daughter of Timofei); Yegor, as the son of Timofei, would have a full name of Yegor Timofeevich. And when Dyuk leaves Kiev and goes home, people sing songs about him for more than a century; Yegor, on his return home from Kiev, personally carries on the singing tradition. It seems clear that Rilke's story was based at least in part on the Dyuk tales; that he made this tale the favorite of a character within that story merely reinforces the connection. Timofei had sung it in the "good old days," before Yegor had gone away. But only after Yegor's return do we learn that it is his favorite, the one to which he continually returns as life ebbs away. Perhaps at this point he has unconsciously recognized in it the parallels with his own and his son's lives, and feels in it the joy of reconciliation. It is not difficult to see why Rilke would have chosen thus to embed the Dyuk tale in the very foundation of his story. This Russian folkloric retelling of the Prodigal Son story must have seemed to him an ideal vehicle for a

Die Geschichten vom lieben Gott

similar venture of his own. Thus he builds his tale of a Russian prodigal on the already existing example of the folk tradition. Yet he changes both the biblical story and the Russian legend, adding a layer of associative richness and turning the traditional materials, as he had done with the historical song about Ivan, into a new and wholly Rilkean product.

The third major "Russian" story is "Das Lied von der Gerechtigkeit." The frame surrounding this story, and its relationship to the story proper, are much more complex than is the case with the other stories in the cycle, and must be examined in detail. The frame contains a discussion about death and an illustrative anecdote about a drowned girl. The story proper follows, interrupted almost at once by objections from Ewald and a digression on Russian history by the narrator. As before, the frame focuses on the figure of Ewald, revealing in him once more the idealized Russian characteristic of patience. Here it is the fact that Ewald is a cripple that links him to the Russians.[40] He has developed a great affection for Russia. He now requests another story about "those Russian singers" (IV, 325), and reveals his dream that one of them might suddenly visit him in his humble room. The narrator assures him that such a thing is possible, since Ewald has a special fate unlike that of other men. His it is "to be a still point amidst all haste" (IV, 326). The narrator reassures Ewald that "something always happens to those who wait" (IV, 326). The Russian parallel is further underscored by the narrator's reference to the Iberian madonna, a wonder-working icon housed in a shrine at the entrance to the Moscow Kremlin. The icon was periodically taken out and displayed at weddings, funerals, and on other ritual occasions. The narrator tells Ewald, "Even the Iberián madonna has to leave her little chapel" (IV, 326), whereas Ewald can stay in his room and summon the world to himself.

Even death is obliged to come to Ewald, since he cannot go to seek it. The idea that death will visit him amidst familiar surroundings is reassuring to him. It reaffirms his belief that death is no different from other human experiences. Ewald's dream of a calm and reasonable death that harmonizes with his life echoes the way in which Timofei in the previous story had died, lying on the stove in his old familiar hut, singing the songs that had been the focus and strength of his entire life. In addition, we recognize in this image of death—an integral part of the individual's life and personality—a theme which was gradually becoming central to all of Rilke's thought.

The discussion of death is then continued in the anecdote told by the narrator about a seventeen-year-old girl who had committed suicide. Overwhelmed by her impressions of life, she drowned herself in a secluded pond, in order to find peace in which to contemplate life undisturbed. The romantic image of the drowned girl is a common enough one, but among its sources may be several Slavic versions. In Karamzin's sentimental tale "Poor Liza," a girl abandoned by her lover drowns in a pond; this story caused among the youth of eighteenth-century Russia as much of a cult of tragedy of love as did Werther's death in eighteenth-century Germany. Taras Shevchenko's poem "Katerina" also portrays a girl who is abandoned and who drowns herself. And a character in Gogol's story "A May Night, or the Drowned Maiden" shares this fate.

Rilke's use of the anecdote here poses a problem of interpretation, for unlike most of the topics discussed in the frame, it seems to have little to do with the story which follows. It grows out of the previous discussion of death, of course; its immediate inspiration is a comment by Ewald that a dead person seems to him essentially no different from one who has merely withdrawn to meditate on something in solitude. Thus the anecdote is a variation on the idea of death as a continuation of life. But its connections with the story are harder to determine. There are two possible ways in which the anecdote may be said to lead into the story, both based on rather circuitous associations. The story contains neither drownings nor other deaths, nor girls disappointed in love; rather, it deals with a nationalist uprising in the seventeenth-century Ukraine against Polish oppressors, and the role played in this rebellion by a *kobzar,* old Ostap. It is in one of the suggested sources of the anecdote, Shevchenko's "Katerina," that a first connection may be sought.[41] In Shevchenko's poem, a girl, Katryusa, abandoned by her Russian lover, drowns herself in despair. Her orphaned son then becomes the servant of a *kobzar,* wandering and singing from village to village. The patriotic poet throughout the poem compares Katryusa to the Ukraine itself, abandoned by those who loved it, threatened from outside with extinction. The faithless Russian lover parallels Russia itself, age-old enemy of Ukrainian independence; the child left behind becomes part of his country's traditions at their very roots, in touch with the people and their songs. To move from this plot to Rilke's story would take an extensive shifting of roles and reassigning of symbolic values, but Rilke may have made that mental leap. Russophile Rilke would not have approved of Shevchenko's anti-Russian sentiments, but he might have seen in the poem something which he could appropriate and transform. Rilke separates out the elements of plot and imagery found in Shevchenko's work—the rejected and drowned girl, personification of oppressed Ukraine, her son who carries on her blood and traditions, the *kobzar*—and distributes them to the frame (the drowned girl) and the story (the *kobzar,* the Ukraine suffering under foreign—albeit no longer Russian—oppressors).

Ewald, hearing the anecdote, does not at first know how to react, and asks whether it is "also a story" (IV, 329); his emphasis is obviously on *story,* i.e., not an actual event. The narrator responds, "No . . . that is a feeling" (IV, 329). In response to Ewald's question as to whether this feeling couldn't be transmitted to the children, he replies that it could, "by means of another story," whereupon he launches into his narrative. "It was at the time when in southern Russia they were fighting for freedom" (IV, 329). But here he is interrupted immediately by Ewald, who is dismayed at the thought that the peasants might rebel against the tsar. This would have contradicted both his conception of the Russian people, and the narrator's own earlier tales, and he declares that in that case, he would rather not hear the story at all: "For I love the picture that I have created for myself of things there, and want to keep it undamaged" (IV, 329).[42] This is an obvious misunderstanding of the narrator's intentions, and he is forced to drop back and fill in some history for Ewald. It is in this lyrical digression about the land and people of the Ukraine in a time of tension and imminent rebellion that the "feeling" of the anecdote is echoed and transformed.

The narrator explains to Ewald that his story is set at the time of a Cossack rebellion against Polish rule. He paints a bleak picture of the foreign overlords:

> The Polish Pans . . . were hard masters. The oppression and the greed of the Jews, who even had control of the church keys, which they turned over to the Orthodox only upon payment, had made the young people around Kiev . . . tired and thoughtful.
>
> (IV, 329)

Rilke's tone here, and the anti-Polish and anti-Semitic slant, while unattractive, are perhaps understandable given his sources. Rambaud speaks of the great enemies of the Cossacks as "the lord, the Jesuit, the Jewish leaseholder,"[43] and writes at length about the hated Jews, including their role as keepers of the church keys. Gogol, in his novel *Taras Bulba,* set in the same era and location, says, "Even the holy churches are not ours. . . . Nowadays they are leased to the Jews. If you don't pay the Jew beforehand, you cannot serve mass."[44] Gogol then goes on to portray a bloody and spontaneous pogrom carried out by the Cossacks, with the tacit approval of his narrator. (As a matter of fact, the Poles used the Jews to exploit the Cossacks, requiring them to collect taxes for the use of the church keys, and to turn the tax money over to their Polish masters.)[45]

Rilke's narrator describes the mood and character of the Ukrainians who inhabit the steppes around Kiev. Like most non-Slavs of his day, Rilke made no distinction between Russia and the Ukraine, and thus we quickly recognize in these "deep, dark, silent" people of the southern steppe his familiar Russian peasants. They are portrayed as small dim figures against the backdrop of their vast land.[46] Rilke emphasizes the immensity against which their only protection is the icons, which stand like "God's milestones" (IV, 330). Their normally silent, passive state of mind is disturbed at the time of the story by waves of repressed resentment against the Poles, and by amorphous feelings of expectation. The city of Kiev "sank ever further into itself and devoured itself in conflagrations, as in sudden, mad thoughts behind which the night only grows ever more boundless" (IV, 330). The narrator goes on, concerning their strange restlessness, "Sometimes wild songs plunge into the dim people and disappear deep inside them" (IV, 330). It is perhaps these aspects of the historical digression that form a link between the "feeling" of the anecdote and the world of the story. The girl in the anecdote was characterized by stillness and watchfulness toward the world around her. Suddenly her inner peace and darkness were destroyed by a harsh and violent intrusion from that world, and "the whole weight of the outside world fell through her into her dark heart and shattered like glass" (IV, 328). Similarly the peasants and the city both find their inner calm churned into turmoil by disturbing, alien thoughts and feelings. As the girl finally acted, seizing death as the most straightforward way out of her unease, so the peasants and the Cossacks act, choosing rebellion and the possibility of violent death.

After this historical digression, the narrator finally, without interruption, takes up the story proper. It concerns the inhabitants of a small village in the steppe. Peter Akimowitsch, a shoemaker, icon painter, and patriarch, has a son, Aljoscha, born to him late in life. The boy has been unable to find a niche for himself in the village society. He can't learn to paint like his father, his proposal to a village girl is rejected amid peals of laughter, and neither the Cossacks at the Sicz[47] nor the monks at the nearby monastery will take him. He leads a solitary life, wandering about the steppe with his gun. One evening an old *kobzar* named Ostap visits Peter and his family. He sings a stirring song about justice which attracts the whole village to Peter's hut. Ostap sings the song three times, and each time it has a different quality; first it is a lament, then an accusation, finally a series of curt commands. The village men, roused by the story the song tells of Polish greed, cruelty, and exploitation, arm themselves and go off to join the rebellious Cossacks. In the dark of night, Aljoscha too steals away to join them. Ostap goes his way, singing his song from village to village.

The story abounds in Russian and Ukrainian references, both literary and historical. The most convoluted concerns the figure of Ostap. His song has been traced to one sung by a historical bard, the *kobzar* Ostap Mykytovyč Veresáj (1803–1890).[48] Rambaud had heard his performance of the song "Pravda" ("Truth," or "Justice") at an ethnographic congress in Kiev in 1874, and was deeply impressed by it and its singer. In *La Russie Épique* he gives a translation of one version of the song.[49] Veresáj sang in Ukrainian, a language which Rilke did not know. This fact, plus the closeness of Rilke's poem to Rambaud's French transcription, make it fairly certain that Rilke used Rambaud as a source. But Rilke's version diverges somewhat from Rambaud's in terms of imagery, and some of Rilke's turns of phrase seem closer to the original than to Rambaud.

For example, one Ukrainian version several times mentions Justice's enemy, "schtchyra neprawda" ("hearty" or "outspoken" "untruth," or "injustice").[50] Nothing of the sort appears in Rambaud. But Rilke depicts Injustice as laughing at Justice, and the Pans as laughingly inviting Injustice into their palace. The image of a laughing, mocking enemy is not too far removed from the original's "hearty" one. One is reminded, too, of the significance for Rilke of laughter as a symbol of mockery and rejection, such as we found in a passage in the *Stunden-Buch* and in Rilke's comments about Kramskoy's painting of Christ. In another version, Justice is seen shedding tears;[51] again, no such image appears in the version presented by Rambaud. But Rilke says, "Justice . . . beseeches" (IV, 335)—a posture related in its humility to weeping. Either Rilke was able, with his knowledge of Russian, to make out enough of the Ukrainian to get the basic imagery, or he had access to an unknown Russian or other translation of the text. A third possibility is that he simply hit upon remarkably similar images of his own. In any case, Rilke's version does show traces of the originals.

In other particulars, Rilke's portrayal of his *kobzar* can be seen to rest heavily on Rambaud's discussion. For example, Rambaud describes Ostap Veresáj's appearance before the assembled scholars: "a poor vagabond," with his Ukrainian peasant costume and his worn blind face, acting out a role which was, according to Rambaud, not that of creator or poet, but of one who "must preserve the treasure of folk poetry which his predecessors have passed on to him."[52] Rambaud describes Veresáj's rendition of another song, the singer's own favorite, "The Storm on the Black Sea." Here he points out certain habits of performance, such as the nervous rustling of the musician's fingers on the strings and the repetition of lines which seem to have a particular importance. His style was apparently very affecting; he was able to suggest a broad range of emotionally charged situations, from the crash of the waves to a repentant prayer sent up through the raging storm. Rilke's Ostap, too, is an old man, a blind wandering singer, whose usual repertoire consists of traditional heroic songs. His playing is characterized by purposeful repetition, and he too possesses a style which can arouse deep emotions. In his discussion of Veresáj's song "Pravda," Rambaud emphasizes its emotional content, its power to hypnotize, touch, and arouse the Ukrainian listeners with its monotonous melancholy and its nationalistic pathos. He mentions that in the period two hundred years before, when Veresáj's song was born, peasants were so stirred by its sentiments that they slipped away by night to join the Cossacks. He calls the traditional *kobzars* "the tocsin of Ukrainian liberty."[53] Rilke portrays an identical situation.

The parallels cited show beyond a doubt that Rilke's Ostap was based on Ostap Veresáj, as he is depicted by Rambaud. As such, the figure is an evocation of the idealized bard as political hero. But the Ostap episode in Rilke's story is not an exact reproduction of the Veresáj section in Rambaud, and there is, especially, a major difference in historical circumstance between the two episodes. Thus there exist other possible sources for Rilke's Ostap. In Gogol's *Taras Bulba* a character who is agitating for war declares to the assembled Cossacks, "It seems there is no justice in the world,"[54] thus voicing precisely the opinion that underlies both Veresáj's song and Ostap's. The story of Ostap is set, not in the nineteenth century when his prototype Veresáj lived, but in the seventeenth, in the days of the song's origins, and of the action of *Taras Bulba*. Rilke may have hoped to achieve the fullest dramatic effect from the song by placing it in its original political and emotional context. But he may also have wished to avoid the embarrassment of a fictional protagonist who, like Veresáj, was calling people to arms against the Russians. For despite the fact that he was able to poke fun at himself through the figure of Ewald, Rilke still did not want to be too critical of his idealized Russia of pious peasants and a loving, fatherly tsar. The real enemy in Veresáj's day, however, was precisely the Russian state and the tsar, who were trying for political reasons to stamp out "minority" cultures within the borders of the Russian Empire. Rilke avoids having to deal with this unpleasant fact by placing the story in a time when he could hate the enemy with a clear conscience. This is the same motivation that was at work in his transformation of Shevchenko's "Katerina."

There are numerous literary and biographical echoes in the character of Aljoscha as well. Like his namesake, Alyosha Karamazov, he is the last offspring of an elderly patriarch. Alyosha Karamazov, a novice at a monastery, is ordered to go out into the world to do good works. Rilke's Aljoscha, while not even accepted into the monastery which he tries to enter, finally finds his possibility of being useful in leaving home to join a rebellion in the world outside his village. A biographical echo appears in the fact that the boy was supposed to become an icon painter like his father Peter, but he has so little talent for it that after his one attempt, the results of which Peter hurriedly paints over, he is allowed only to fill in an occasional halo. In this there is a curious, oblique echo of the early life of Taras Shevchenko (who did, however, become a skillful painter later on). As a child, Taras, son of a Ukrainian serf, was sent around to various clerks in the surrounding villages to learn icon painting, with very little success. Eventually, he beat up one of his teachers and ran away; and he became, like Rilke's Aljoscha, a radical Ukrainian patriot.[55] Finally, there is a slight parallel to a scene in *Taras Bulba*. There only the mother is saddened when her sons, named Andrey and, it is worth noting, Ostap, go off to join the Cossacks. As Rilke's Aljoscha is slipping away in the dark to follow Ostap's call, he is surprised by a sudden embrace. He turns to see his mother running back into the silent hut; the rest of the family doesn't even acknowledge the fact that he's gone until the following evening. (Such an emphasis on a loving and sorrowing mother is also consistent with Rilke's wishful thinking in his treatment of mothers and sons.)

A number of details have been mentioned in relation to Gogol's novel *Taras Bulba*, which Rilke had read, and of which he saw a staged version in St. Petersburg in 1899.[56] But a kinship between the works rests in larger gestures as well: in the setting in the Ukraine during the time of the Cossack rebellions against the Poles; in the authors' sympathy with the values of the people, roused against the foreign enemy; and in the lyrical evocation of the steppe. Final proof that Rilke did in fact draw on the novel in his writing of this story lies in another set of details, the Ukrainian names mentioned by Rilke's narrator. The girl whom Aljoscha courts is the "daughter of the Cossack Golokopytenko" (IV, 332), and the tales Ostap usually recites are about the hetmans and heroes "Kirdjaga, Kukubenko, Bulba . . . Ostranitza, and Naliwaiko" (IV, 334). Of the six, only Ostranitza (Jakiv Ostrjanycja) and Naliwaiko (Severyn Nalyvájko) are historical figures.[57] They also appear, in somewhat distorted form, in *Taras Bulba*. The other four names are fictitious—and all are found in Gogol's novel. Thus Rilke paid a small tribute to his fellow writer by prolonging the fictitious life of his characters.

Finally, the story contains echoes of Rilke's own works of the period. The emphasis on icons is familiar from the *Stunden-Buch* and the essays. Aljoscha's father, Peter, is portrayed as a well-balanced man who divides his time between painting icons and making shoes—and who incidentally has maintained his good posture in the process, because he isn't always working in the same position. He may echo Lev Tolstoy, who after his conversion spent much time at homely tasks such as cobbling. The icon to which blind Ostap bows when he enters the hut is Rilke's favorite, the Znamenskaya.

The remaining stories of the cycle contain Russian elements in varying degrees and forms. In general, they can be divided into two categories: overt allusions to Russia and to Russian objects or customs; and thematic or structural devices which tie the respective stories to Russian motifs in other works. The former are of a simpler nature than the latter. For example, a figure who appears at various times in Rilke's works is that of Saint Nicholas, the patron saint of Russia. In the *Stunden-Buch*, the icon-painting monk mentions him specifically. A character in "Das Lied von der Gerechtigkeit" wishes to be buried with an icon of the saint, so as to recognize "the especially honored one" (IV, 331) when he gets to Heaven. In the story, God, in the process of making man, gets distracted and allows things on earth to get out of hand. At this point, "Saint Nicholas, who is particularly esteemed by God, stepped up to him" (IV, 291) to give him a report on the sad state of affairs on earth. God's irritable reply causes Nicholas to stalk out, slamming the door to Heaven and shaking loose a star, which falls on the head of an unsuspecting fox terrior. Thus, in the very first story of the cycle, Rilke not only establishes Saint Nicholas, a Russian saint, as God's favorite, but also portrays both of these characters as possessing very human failings. This is a comic reflection of the monk's view, in the *Stunden-Buch*, of God as an everyday sort of person—a peasant or a neighbor. The particular human frailties attributed to Saint Nicholas—impatience and a short temper—produce a catastrophe in the dog's demise. The episode, aside from its humor, has a serious message. The virtue par excellence of the Russian is patience; when it is too sorely tried, and the Russian loses control and betrays his nature, the result is disastrous.

In another story, "Der fremde Mann," Russia emerges through a number of smaller details as a symbol for human warmth and brotherliness. A distressed stranger comes to visit the narrator just at nightfall. In an attempt to make him welcome, the narrator offers him tea with lemon, a custom which he says he learned in Russia. He then lights a lamp and puts it "in a distant corner, somewhat elevated" (IV, 298), where it gently illuminates the darkness with a warm, reddish glow. The red lamp set high up in a corner recalls the Russian custom of placing the family icon in a "Holy Corner" with a candle or lamp before it. Upon his return from Russia, Rilke had set up a so-called Russian corner in his own room, which included icons and an icon lamp. The image also occurs in "Das Lied von der Gerechtigkeit," where old icons stand in the corner of every house, and "no house can exist without them" (IV, 330). In "Der fremde Mann" the offering of tea, the mention of Russia, and the lighting of the ceremonial light in the cornr combine to create a feeling of warmth and protection around the uneasy guest: "And the face of my guest, too, seems to be surer, warmer, and a great deal more familiar" (IV, 298–99). The evocation of Russia has put the stranger at ease, and has brought the two men closer together.

Allusions of the second type, those which depend on structural or thematic links, tend to be more complex and far-reaching than the type just discussed. But they can also interact with allusions or motifs of the simpler kind. For example, the story "Der Bettler und das stolze Fräulein" ("The Beggar and the Proud Young Lady") contains overtly the motifs of poverty and humility; the attitude toward them here is the same positive one which Rilke developed in the *Stunden-Buch*. But the story is related to Russian themes in another, far more complicated fashion. First, like the story of old Timofei, it treats song as a symbol of tradition, community, and continuity. In the Russian tale, the narrator describes to Ewald the way in which the ancient songs were kept alive for centuries, "the whole time underway from mouth to mouth" (IV, 317). Occasionally they would come to rest "in a heart where it was warm and dark" (IV, 317). There the narrator emphasizes the sharing and passing on of a work of art, and the protective and nurturing darkness of the human heart—the same dark heart which God prefers to the bright, cold human mind. In "Der Bettler," the narrator speaks once again of songs that had been alive: this time not traditional songs of heroism, but poems by individual poets in praise of the fleeting moment. These poems too had a connection with the dark subconscious; their topic is life, with its "dark background with the roaring of the blood" (IV, 381), and they arise "out of the poet's darkness" (IV, 380). Like the old Russian songs, they were perpetuated by anonymous singers and took on new life: "The poet began a song, and all those who sang it completed it" (IV, 380). One is struck by the conception of singing as a communal act which underlies the two stories.

The second connection with Russian motifs also rests on a startling juxtaposition of the ritualized folk songs of peasant Russia and the sophisticated and frivolous lyrics of fifteenth-century Florence. A contrast between two specific songs reveals their common relation to a major motif of the *Stunden-Buch*. The songs in question are Ostap's "Lied von der Gerechtigkeit" and a poem by Lorenzo dei Medici, "Quant' è bella giovinezza" ("How Beautiful Is Youth"). My rationale for bringing the two together lies in the way in which each is described by the narrator. He carefully prepares the mood for the impact of Ostap's song:

In the six long strings of the bandura a tone began, grew, and returned briefly and as if exhausted from the six short strings. And this effect was repeated in ever quicker beats, so that one finally had to close one's eyes, for fear of seeing the sound plunge down somewhere from the melody which it had scaled at a delirious pace.

(IV, 334)

In describing Lorenzo's poem, the narrator uses terms very similar to those in which he describes Ostap's. Here life itself, the topic of the poem, is seen as an instrument, "this violin with the bright singing strings" (IV, 381). Lorenzo's poem is then presented as follows:

> The uneven strophes climb upward in giddy gaiety, but there, where this gaiety becomes breathless, each time a short, simple refrain takes form, which inclines down from the dizzying heights and, fearful of the abyss, seems to close its eyes.
>
> (IV, 381)

In the two passages we find significant repetition, beginning with the strings—of the bandura, and of the violin of life—and progressing via a breathless upsurge to a point of excitement which threatens to become vertiginous, and forces the eyes to close—in one case, the eyes of the listener, in the other the "eyes" of the poetic refrain. In Ostap's case, this description refers to the instrumental prelude of mounting intensity, which fixes all attention on the *kobzar* before he begins to sing. The narrator's description of the prelude is impressionistic and emotionally charged, and serves to bring the reader into the circle of breathless peasants who flock to listen. The intensity of the prelude prepares the listeners for the message of the song which follows, a song that is a weapon of conscience and a call to moral action. In the other story, it is the *structure* of Lorenzo's song to which the description is applied; and the narrator's understanding of the message of the lines is prefigured in his perception of their form. For, mirroring the form described by him, the message of the song is a cry of joy in youth, followed by a sudden evocation of decay, sinking down to the sobering knowledge of the passage of time and the uncertainty of tomorrow.[58]

In both stories, the narrator focuses on the effect of the songs on their respective audiences, and it is here that the great difference in intention and effect of the two stories lies, and here that they serve as foils for one another. The villagers undergo a transformation from melancholy to fury as the *kobzar* skillfully plays on their sense of honor and patriotism: "A wild fury broke out of the quivering words and seized them all and transported them into a broad and at the same time fearful rapture" (IV, 336). Their response is to arm and go to war; through the traditional activity of the bard, they are united as a community, aware of their brotherhood and of an identity worth defending. In contrast, the Italian youths, although they live several hundred years before the Ukrainian revolt, seem part of a world in some ways far more modern, more anxious and fragmented. Their world is in flux, a world of shifting political alliances, and their sense of a waiting abyss pushes them into a panic:

> Is it any wonder that a haste overtook the people who sang this poem, an attempt to pile up all festiveness on this Today, on the single rock on which it pays to build?
>
> (IV, 381)

They realize that their human attachments are fluid and uncertain; and even their painters make an attempt

> to unite all their princes and wives and friends in one painting, for people painted slowly, and who could know if at the time of the next picture they would all still be so young and colorful and united.[59]
>
> (IV, 381)

The sense of urgency of each era is conveyed through the depiction of a song and its effect. The two episodes share a number of images which call attention to their internal relation. But what emerges from the comparison is, once again, the dichotomy which occupied Rilke during these years, and which lay at the bottom of the *Stunden-Buch* and the essays on Russian art: the conflict between West and East, Italy and Russia, the loneliness and fragmentation implicit in individualism, and life as brotherhood, continuity, and common purpose. And once again the latter triumphs; the peasants respond to the call to unite, and even the Western protagonist of the other story gives away his wealth to the poor and abandons his frivolous ways to become a pilgrim, and eventually a saint.

Another device which links a number of stories is a set of metaphors which first emerges in the *Stunden-Buch*. Over and over the monk seeks to capture God, if only for an instant, in his true form. But he finds God everywhere, and his verses portray him in ever new guises. In one poem, the monk tries to express his sense of the complexity of his subject: "Thou art the deepest one which soared, / the envy of divers and of towers" (I, 283). In the paradox of soaring depths, the monk finds a satisfying image for this being who is both higher and deeper than anything else, present and prevailing everywhere. Images of God as both high and low reappear in the *Geschichten*, reaffirming and illustrating his omnipresence. In the frame preceding the story "Wie der Verrat nach Russland kam," Ewald and the narrator discuss what Russia borders on. Ewald lists the directions of the compass one by one, but the narrator replies that looking at maps has spoiled people: "But a country is no atlas. It has mountains and abysses. It has to bump into something above and below, as well" (IV, 310). After some hesitation, Ewald guesses that it is on God that Russia borders above and below. God becomes a spatial concept, on which Russia abuts with its vertical extremities. In "Das Lied von der Gerechtigkeit," the narrator in his digression uses a similar image to describe the steppe and its inhabitants: "In this land where graves are mountains, the people are abysses" (IV, 330). The mountains are paradoxically graves, and the people themselves are spiritual abysses, "deep, dark, and taciturn" (IV, 330), who climb up onto the grave mounds to see into the steppe. Filled with uneasiness, they mount their own past, the resting places of their ancestors, to get a look at the future, which is shrouded in uncertainty.

What we see developing here is a sort of topographical mythology which appears in other stories in the cycle. In "Eine Szene aus dem Ghetto von Venedig" ("A Scene from the Ghetto of Venice"), the characters climb up to God. Because of Venetian laws which limited its horizontal expansion, the ghetto of Venice had to expand upward; its houses were built "one on the roof of the other . . . in innumerable tiers" (IV, 342). In the process, the ghetto dwellers discover a new dimension, a new set of borders: "Their city, which did not lie on the sea, grew slowly into the sky as if into another sea" (IV, 342). Melchisedech is the wisest and most honored man in the ghetto; thus the inhabitants accede to his wish always to live in the highest of its dwellings. And so it is that Melchisedech and his granddaughter, Esther, are constantly underway like pilgrims, moving upward from one house to another. But their climb has another significance, for it acts as a kind of purification and transfiguration. They eventually climb so high that it seems that "at the level of their foreheads a different country began, about whose customs the old man spoke in dark words, half psalming" (IV, 340). "Up" in this story implies a journey into another realm, to a place of solemn mystery, and yet to brightness and beauty as well, for when they arrive at the topmost roof, they see "a still, silver light: the sea" (IV, 344). Melchisedech goes to the edge of the roof and prays, while a crowd gathers in the street below to wonder at him. And the narrator ends his story with the question, "Did he see the sea, or God, the Eternal, in his glory?" (IV, 345). The question is left open. Herr Baum, the adult to whom the story is told, seizes on the rational explanation—the sea; but the children, when asked the question, reply without hesitation, "Oh, the sea *also*" (IV, 345). For them it is quite natural that God can be found simply by climbing up out of the shadows into Heaven. The rooftops of Venice, like the mountains of Russia, border on God.

But in Russia the abysses, too, had the same glorious neighbor. This other possibility—that God is to be reached by going downward—is expressed in the frame to the tenth tale, "Ein Märchen vom Tod und eine fremde Nachschrift dazu" ("A Tale about Death and a Strange Postscript"). The narrator and his companion, a grave digger, discuss varieties of worship and different gestures of prayer. The narrator paints a vivid picture of a dismayed God who looks down to see men coming at him with their pointed hands folded in prayer and the gothic spires and roofs of their churches, "all equally steep and sharp like hostile weapons." God, who possessed "a *different* bravery" (IV, 359), flees out the back door of Heaven. Since that moment he has been underway through the darkness, which reminds him wistfully of men's hearts.

> Ever thicker becomes the darkness around him, and the night through which he pushes his way contains something of the fragrant warmth of fruitful soil. And not much longer, and the roots will stretch toward him with the beautiful old gesture of broad prayer. There is nothing wiser than the circle. The God who fled from us into the heavens will come back to us out of the earth.[60]

(IV, 360)

In Rilke's symbolic topography, the world is a circle. Man is a part of this landscape, with his warm, dark depths. But he occasionally loses sight of his own nature, with unfortunate results. God is at home in a traditional heaven, but is not limited to it; he is also of the earth, dark and fruitful.

Another motif frequently associated with Russia is that of waiting. We have seen how, in the *Stunden-Buch,* and elsewhere, Rilke perceived the Russians as a people with a great future, for which they wait in passivity and faith. In the last of the *Geschichten,* "Eine Geschichte dem Dunkel erzählt" ("A Story Told to the Dark"), a situation is depicted in which the waiting is better than the goal. The protagonist, Klara, holds the conviction, not that God exists, but rather that he "will be." Klara and Georg, her disillusioned visitor, had been childhood friends. She now draws a parallel between her present state of happily awaiting God, and an event from their childhood. Her parents had been awaiting the visit of a distant, rich relative. Everything was prepared, lit up, shining; the air was tense with anticipation, but the guest still didn't arrive. Klara recalls:

> The later it got, the more wonderful a guest did we expect. We even quaked, lest he come before he had reached that last degree of magnificence which he approached with every minute of his absence. We weren't afraid that he might not appear at all. We knew for certain that he was coming, but we wanted to leave him time to become great and powerful.

(IV, 396)

Georg points out that the guest never did, in fact, arrive. But for Klara that is part of the charm of the episode, and the basis for her peculiar religious faith: "But it was still beautiful! . . . the waiting, the many lamps, the silence, the festiveness" (IV, 396). For her the important thing, that which feeds her imgination and raises her life to the heights of pleasurable expectation, is the potential arrival of the guest, the potential existence of God. In Klara are combined two key elements in Rilke's conception of faith: a kind of pantheism that enables her to see divinity in everyday things such as the objects she had seen in Florence, and a great patience that grows out of the belief, not in God, but in the idea of God.[61]

Rilke's champions in the stories and their frame are children and the childlike; artists and craftsmen; the humble and simple of heart—those who wait, as well as those who act when the time is ripe, in a spirit of creativity, communality, and justice. All of these characteristics can be seen to relate to his ideal of Russia. They are not limited to the Russian experience; but Rilke, particularly at this period in his life, was greatly attuned to that experience and derived from it a set of characters and images in which to clothe his ideas about God and art.

The motif of the prodigal son should be mentioned once more in this context. Rilke makes use of the motif in a number of places, the most well-known being *Malte Laurids Brigge* and a poem in the *Neue Gedichte* written in 1906, "Der Auszug des verlorenen Sohnes" ("The Departure of the Prodigal Son" [I, 491]). The theme is rarely recognized as being central to the *Geschichten,* but it is present there in several forms. God relates to his hands as if they were his sons, gives them orders, becomes angry and banishes them when they disobey him. The parallel is made quite plain when his right hand is sent to earth, is crucified, and returns to the father just in time to keep him from bleeding to death. The thimble which represents God is lost and then retrieved. And Georg in the final story has been sent away as a child, and is now trying futilely to recover his childhood and his past by returning to his home town. The most significant and well-developed version of the motif in the *Geschichten* is found in the story of Timofei and his erring son Yegor, where Rilke both introduces into the basic story peculiarly Russian elements, and experiments with psychological aspects not present in the original legend. We shall find that he continues to experiment with the motif, and that it becomes, in fact, one of his major concerns. The motif can be viewed, in addition, as a variation on Rilke's concern with childhood, particularly with the necessity of reliving his own, in which childhood and home both come to represent the larger sense of loss which is basic to Rilke's view of the world. It is possible to see the treatment of God in the *Geschichten* as another variation on the prodigal theme. God appears in a variety of forms, moving from a strongly individualized, anthropomorphic figure to progressively more abstract conceptions, until he is only an idea; from a humorous, in some ways neoclassical divinity to a process and an artistic product, to the mere promise of his own future existence. Though present in some form in each story, he becomes gradually more and more distant from man.

But on one occasion, Rilke makes it clear that the prodigal God will come home again. This is in the frame to the tenth story, where we found God fleeing from men and their Heaven, and setting out on his long and paradoxical journey through the dark, back to the world of men again. This God of the warm darkness is the Russian God of the *Stunden-Buch*. Among his characteristics there were the silence, patience, and passivity that he shared with his worshipers, as well as the quality of fruitfulness. It is striking that these characteristics, attributed by Rilke both to the Russian and to his God, are traditionally feminine, motherly ones. And the God who flees in alarm from the spearlike, masculine steeples and praying hands will return to the world via a circle, out of the darkness, making his way among the fruitful clumps of earth and the roots with their gestures of welcome. Rilke's Russian God is to be reborn by way of the female earth, Mother Russia.

How conscious Rilke was of the import of his images on this level is impossible to say. But in a letter to Paula Becker written late in 1900, he speaks longingly of Russia, where his thoughts reside though his body is in a different reality. There he says, "Every homeland has a good and warm effect, like every mother. But I must seek my mother, mustn't I?"[62] Homeland equals mother; and every person, one would suppose, possesses both. But Rilke felt he had never really had a mother in the way he imagined this figure ought to be, nor had his homeland come to him automatically: he had to discover it for himself. The homeland of all his instincts, he remarks elsewhere, was Russia. It does not really surprise us to find Rilke—so preoccupied with both the relation of fathers and sons, and his own yearning for a mother—casting God as a Prodigal Son who is to be redeemed by the welcoming embrace of Mother Earth.

· SIX ·

THE SEARCH FOR SELF:
Die Aufzeichnungen des Malte Laurids Brigge

n 1902 an event occurred which constituted a turning point in Rilke's life and art: he moved to Paris, the city where he would live off and on for the rest of his life. It commanded in him a grudging loyalty and affection, and drastically changed the shape of his visions. In general terms, one could divide Rilke's works into those written before his imagination was seized by Paris, and those which came afterward. (The revisions of the *Stunden-Buch* and the *Geschichten,* as well as the translations of the *Slovo,* were done mostly in Paris. But these works were begun in the strong afterglow of the Russian experience, and really belong to the earlier period.) All his works after about 1903 fall chronologically under the shadow of Paris, and some of them reflect directly Rilke's fascination with the beauty and brutality of the city. These include, most notably, the novel *Die Aufzeichnungen des Malte Laurids Brigge* (*The Notebooks of Malte Laurids Brigge*), two volumes of *Neue Gedichte,* and certain of the *Duineser Elegien.* It was natural that the enthusiasm of Rilke's youth, including his love affair with an exotic and idealized Slavdom, should fade before the harder and more demanding aspects of both Paris and his own increasing maturity. But Russia was not forgotten. In the works conceived after 1902 we still find its strains, at times muted, at others reemerging overtly and strongly.

Malte Laurids Brigge is Rilke's major prose work; it was begun in 1904 and completed in 1910. The book is divided into two parts. In the first part, Malte, a young Danish poet recently arrived in Paris, struggles to come to terms with the ugliness and absurdity he finds there, the omnipresent disease and poverty, and the impersonality of everything, including even death. Against this background, Malte also undergoes a crisis of identity, as he tries to discover his own role in the city as a poet, a stranger, and an exile from family, roots, and self. He suffers a fearful attraction/repulsion for the silent poor, the outcasts in the streets of Paris who seem to surround him, beckoning to him as to one of their own. He decides that his major task, as a man and as an artist, is to relive, and finally deal with, his own childhood, as a way of reaching out to reality. One aspect of his problem stems from the warring sides of his heritage: the rational Brigges, who fear and loathe death, the supernatural, and any mixing of past, present, and future; and the somewhat fey Brahes, his mother's family, for whom time is a continuum, and death merely one of many passing events in the course of a fluid existence. (This attitude reappears, refined and reinforced, in the *Elegien,* where the angels are described as not perceiving boundaries between living and dead, and in the *Sonette,* dedicated to a god whose essence is the mortal cycle.) Part one of *Malte Laurids Brigge* combines diary entries recording Malte's day-to-day encounters, fears, and insights with flashbacks to various events in his childhood and youth. These center on his family, on their attitudes toward death and, one might almost say, their performances of it, and on his own growing sense of alienation.

Part two likewise utilizes a mixture of Parisian present and personal memory, with the added device of historical sketches. Anecdotes from medieval and Renaissance history serve as meditations on, and illustrations of, his own fears and problems.[1] The themes of the first part are intensified, and to them is added a developing philosophy of nonpossessive love, illustrated by images both of failure (the family of the prodigal son, who never learn to understand him) and success (the great women lovers of history, who were able to transcend both a need for requital, and the very object of their love itself).

A great deal has been written about *Malte Laurids Brigge,* from a variety of viewpoints.[2] The book has been seen variously as the successful or unsuccessful apprenticeship of a writer striving to know himself and his métier. It has been approached as a study in existential prose, with Malte as alienated modern man per se. Some critics concentrate on the religious or metaphysical overtones, singling out the parable of the prodigal son, which ends the second part, as a parable of Malte's own progress. Others focus on the novel as a symbolist work, lyrical and hermetic. Rilke himself regarded the book as a watershed. Into it he poured the pain, terror, and insights of his own experience, artistically distanced, filtered through the ordering lenses of European art, literature, and history. He felt its completion, after having "lived" with Malte for so many years, as a personal relief: "Only now can everything really begin," he wrote in 1910.[3] Yet in a letter to Lou in 1911, he seems unsure whether the book has been a purgation (in the manner of *Werther* for Goethe) or merely a gateway to further trials. He asks whether Malte, "who is after all made partly of my dangers, perishes there, as it were, to spare me the downfall, or whether with these notebooks I have only just gotten into the stream that will tear me away and force me beyond."[4] It was, as we now know, both purgation and symbol of the future. Rilke was to pursue throughout his career the same basic question addressed in *Malte Laurids Brigge:* "If we are continually insufficient in loving, uncertain in deciding, and incompetent in the face of death, how is it possible to exist?"[5]

But what interests us primarily here is the extent to which Russia played a role in this pursuit, and the forms this role took. We have seen that early in his career Rilke found in certain characteristics of the Russian psyche comforting or inspiring ideas about man's ability to grow in humble dignity, simplicity, and patience. The question remains, however, as to how the values he found in Russia relate to the basic questions of his middle and late works—the coming to terms with love, childhood, and death, and the striving to understand his own necessary relation to the external world and to his inner, final truth. Russia clearly was still a productive source for Rilke when he wrote *Malte Laurids Brigge*. There are two episodes in the novel containing overtly Russian elements: a historical sketch about the death of Grisha Otrepev, the False Dmitry, and the story of Malte's neighbors in St. Petersburg. Both occur in the second part of the book, and both serve as variations on the basic problem of Malte's life, that of identity. The two episodes focus on various aspects of this problem: fame and the crowd, which threaten and define; the dizzying and paralyzing awareness of details of reality that impinge on the personality and send it out of control; the problem of recognizing and accepting oneself. The episodes are permeated by Malte's personality. They arise from his memories of his childhood reading and of a personal experience in Russia. In the retelling, Malte exercises editorial powers, carefully selecting only certain facts and details from the many possible ones and interspersing these with subjective interpretations.[6]

Much of what is Russian in these anecdotes comes from Rilke's reading in Russian history and literature. The anecdote of Grisha Otrepev is, of the two episodes mentioned, the more obviously related to specific events and texts. Tsar Ivan IV had a son, Dmitry, who was supposedly murdered while still a child by the minions of Boris Godunov. A series of legends and superstitions grew up around the figure of Dmitry, and over the years a number of pretenders, or "False Dmitrys," cropped up, laying claim to the throne. The first of these was Grisha Otrepev, a Russian monk who fled his monastery and escaped into Poland. He returned as "Dmitry," miraculously saved from violent death, and seized the throne upon the death of the usurper Godunov. With him came his bride, the Polish noblewoman Marina Mniszek. At first welcomed by the superstitious people, Dmitry and his bride were eventually deposed in a coup led by Prince Shuysky; Dmitry was killed, and his remains shot out of a cannon symbolically aimed westward, back toward Poland, the land of enmity and false faith.

Rilke's version focuses on the period after Grisha's return to Russia and his seizure of power. In order to assure his acceptance as tsar, he orders the real Dmitry's mother, Tsarina Maria Nagoy, to leave her cloister and acknowledge him in public; this she does. The next scene already shows Grisha's demise. He leaps from a palace window, and is helped up and surrounded by his guards, the Streltsy, who still believe in him and refuse to relinquish him to Shuysky. Then the tsarina renounces him before the assembled crowds. He is shot, and his masked and mutilated body lies on the square for three days. It is in the joining and interpretation of these events that Rilke creates something new.

There are several possible sources for this anecdote. The story of the Russian monk who dared to steal the throne of the tsars was already known in western Europe in 1605, the year Dmitry seized power.[7] Like the figure of Mazeppa, whom Rilke utilizes in the *Buch der Bilder,* Dmitry had become the common property of the European imagination, and he served as the theme for many writers, including Lope de Vega, Schiller, and Hebbel. In addition, Rilke had read a number of works on Russian history.[8] His most likely sources are an article on Dmitry by Rauschnik in the *Allgemeine Encyclopädie der Wissenschaften und Künste,*[9] and the *History of the Russian State,* by the major historian Nikolay Karamzin, published in 1843. Between the two, they contain all the factual information which Rilke uses. Many details are found in both, although certain information on Marina Mniszek (misspelled "Mniczek" by Rilke) is in Rauschnik alone, while only Karamzin contains a reference to masks.

Rauschnik's encyclopedia article is fairly neutral in tone, and is limited in scope by its genre. Karamzin's treatment, considerably longer and more detailed, is definitely partisan. Writing from the point of view of a patriotic Russian of the early nineteenth century, Karamzin emphasizes three things: the fact that Dmitry was only a pretender, with no royal blood and no right to the throne; the crucial political struggle for hegemony between the Orthodox church and Roman Catholicism, introduced and fostered by Dmitry; and the fiercely nationalistic element which underlay the hatred of the Russians for Dmitry and his coterie of Poles, and which made it possible for Shuysky to stir up enough resentment to overthrow Dmitry.

One can imagine that Rilke, with his strong sympathies for everything Russian and his horror of any sort of imposition from the West, would have found Karamzin's spirited narrative and its "lucky" outcome in the defeat of the Polonicized usurper highly attractive. Nevertheless, there existed for Rilke a strong attraction to Dmitry himself, the lonely figure with his self-inflicted dilemma. However one views the historical and political situation, it had taken amazing courage for Dmitry to rise from obscurity to the throne of Russia simply on the strength of his own assertions. This daring, along with the motif of identity and disguise, seem to have appealed greatly to Rilke, engrossed as he was at this time in trying to move his fictional character, Malte, through the thickets of his search for himself.

In his transformation of history into fiction, Rilke does not change facts, but he shapes and balances them to fit his needs. He is selective, and develops a constellation of ideas, traits, and details which would be useful to Malte who, as the narrator of the Grisha story, turns all meditations on the outside world ultimately inward toward himself again. A minor detail in Karamzin, for example, grows into a symbol for Grisha's ordeal, as presented by Rilke; this is the matter of the mask, and of masks in general. Karamzin relates that, after the execution, the body of Dmitry lay "on a table, with a mask, a whistle, and a bagpipe, as a sign of his love for the traveling players and for music."[10] Rilke uses the mask literally, beginning and ending his account with a reference to it; Grisha's corpse lies "mangled and stabbed, and a mask before its face" (VI, 882). But the mask is more than a mere historical detail. A critic has pointed out that the mask is, for Rilke's Dmitry, "factually a deceit, but internally—the truth . . . the pure realization of life."[11] For Dmitry struggles with the same problems that plague Malte: authenticity, self-knowledge, the inner freedom to discover or determine by oneself who and what one is, and the ability to remain true to that discovery. It is primarily in his emphasis on this theme that Rilke, in his retelling of the story, deviates from historical and literary sources.

Identity is one of the principal themes of the novel as a whole, and as symbols for this, masks and mask-like faces appear at various places in the book. The relevance of the Grisha story for Malte lies in its relation to this theme, and to an experience which Malte recalls from his own childhood. Malte had often hidden in a storeroom at his grandfather's house, and dressed up in the old clothes he found there. His imagination was stimulated and delighted by this game, and he soon noticed that each disguise, confirmed and defined in the mirror, immediately took him into its power. Yet he felt that a kind of liberation dwelt in the indefiniteness and multiplicity of the costumes: "The more variedly I modified myself, the more convinced I became of myself. . . . I didn't notice the temptation in this rapidly growing security" (VI, 804). One day he accidentally becomes entangled, trapped in his costume; he is terrified to realize that the unknown creature in the mirror has become reality. "For a second I had an

Die Aufzeichnungen

indescribable, painful, and futile yearning for myself; then there was only he: there was nothing but he" (VI, 808).

Grisha's tale, as related by Rilke, bears a number of similarities to this one, even while the historical facts remain intact. First of all, Grisha is in disguise: he claims to be Dmitry, and stakes his life and fortune on being believed. And, like Malte, his joy and power, his remarkable success, lie in his free choice of roles. I conclude this from Malte's statements which suggest that it is precisely by being limited to one role, caught in his mask, so to speak, that Grisha is undone. This happens, Malte suggests, through the affirmation of his identity by Marina, the tsarina, and the Streltsy, all of whom by their public acceptance declare him to *be* what he appears to be: Dmitry. Malte wonders

> whether his insecurity didn't begin precisely with [the tsarina's] acknowledgment of him? She lifted him out of the fullness of his invention; she limited him to a weary imitation; she reduced him to the individual who he *was* not; she made him into a betrayer.
>
> (VI, 882)

As long as Grisha chooses to be Dmitry, he is free. Like the child Malte, he is playing at history and at reality. Inside the strange robes, there is a self which he knows, and which does not have to coincide with the momentary face he wears. But like Malte, who is made single, limited, and real by the creature staring back out of the mirror, Grisha, by the public declaration of the tsarina, is suddenly reduced to a single persona, and that one a lie.

Rilke says little about Marina, Grisha's Polish bride, but what is there places her in a role similar to that of the tsarina vis-à-vis Grisha. Rilke says that she too "denied him in her fashion, because as it turned out later, she didn't believe in him, but in everyone" (VI, 883). The Marina of the sources is an empty opportunist, believing in no one. In Pushkin's play *Boris Godunov,* for example, she claims she can marry only Dmitry, "the heir of Moscow's throne."[12] Nonetheless, she promises herself to Dmitry, "a truant monk,"[13] knowing that not his actual identity but his name and public persona will be her ticket to a throne. He himself could be anyone, or no one. From Rauschnik's article we learn that some time after Dmitry's death, Marina publicly acknowledged another man, also pretending to be Dmitry Ivanovich, as her husband.[14] Thus in a sense the historical Marina, too, "believed in everyone," as long as they seemed to further her ambitions.[15] For Rilke's Grisha, this cynical acceptance by Marina constitutes a different kind of betrayal from that of the tsarina. By accepting the mask, she negates the real person within.

The third source of belief and betrayal is Dmitry's personal guard, the Streltsy. The historical Shuysky, who knew that Dmitry was an impostor, spread rumors about him and eventually led the rebellion which unseated him. When Dmitry leaped out of the window, the guards surrounded him in the courtyard and refused to give him up, provided he really *was* the son of the tsarina. When the tsarina recanted and denounced Dmitry, the guards were satisfied that he was an impostor, and handed him over to the boyars. Dmitry expressed the wish to confess to the people on Red Square, but was not allowed to, and was immediately shot instead. Rilke shifts these historical details around, giving them a relationship and meaning they did not have before. In his version, the guards believe implicitly in Dmitry—a fact which, as one critic has noted, is deeply ironic, since Dmitry by that time had reached a low point of self-esteem. He is "he who has lost his innermost reality and is, at this instant, purely overwhelmed" ("nichts als ein Überwältigter").[16] Yet the old soldiers, who had known Ivan the Terrible in all his glory, persist in seeing Dmitry, too, as "real." Dmitry is so overcome by this irony that "he would like to enlighten them" (VI, 883). Thus whereas in Karamzin's account, the impulse to confess came *after* Grisha's exposure and capture, where it could have served at best as a sort of last confession, a clearing of the slate, in Rilke's version it becomes an act of pity and the voice of authenticity. Grisha wants to free himself once and for all of the encumbering lie of his royalty, and at the same time to free his followers of the lie they are living by believing in him. The Streltsy's faith is so strong, indeed, that it spreads to the advancing, angry crowd and tames the people's rage: "Suddenly no one else wanted to step forward" (VI, 884). Shuysky is shown "despairing," momentarily alone against Dmitry and the people. Only the voice of the tsarina as she denounces Dmitry breaks the tension and throws all present into action once more. Rilke's guards and his attacking crowd are at once more naive and more good-hearted than the real ones described by Karamzin. The historical Streltsy were a pragmatic lot and were determined to save Dmitry only if he deserved it; i.e., if he really was the tsarevich. Rilke's Streltsy appear almost like heroes from the days of Ilya Muromets—loyal, epic figures, "these gigantic Streltsy . . . these old men" (VI, 883–84). Nor was the historical crowd stopped for a second by any displays of affection for Dmitry; his closest adviser, Basmanov, was murdered on the steps of the palace as he tried to talk to the crowd. And after Dmitry's execution, Karamzin shows the people going wild, robbing and killing anyone who looks vaguely Polish.[17] Rilke's crowd, in contrast, seems more humane, more prone to gentle emotions.

    The different character and reactions of Rilke's guards and crowd from the ones described by Karamzin may arise from two causes. First, Rilke may have chosen to ignore the reports of the maddened crowd in order not to do violence to his own image of the patient Russian peasant.

The second reason may have been an artistic one. If, before any testimony from the tsarina, the guards and the crowd had voluntarily renounced their belief in Dmitry and simply redefined him as "impostor," they would in effect merely have removed one public mask and replaced it with another. They would have reduced him to "Grisha the monk," just as the tsarina at first had elevated him to one role, "Dmitry, son and heir." Either role robs him of his alternatives, and of the freedom to choose or change. Had the people rejected him, the tsarina's subsequent denunciation would only have sealed the fact for good—prime evidence of his deceit, but given after the fact, when no one needed to be convinced. Such a situation would, in Malte's eyes, have had no dramatic tension. The tsarina's denunciation would have been an anticlimax. Thus, he allows the guards and the people to remain convinced of Dmitry's genuineness; in doing so, they ironically intensify with their love his state of imprisonment within the alien persona. Coming in this situation, then, the tsarina's voice raised in denial is both a contradiction and a release. It strips Dmitry of the identity the others claim for him, cutting through the opinion of the masses and releasing him again to be simply Grisha: the man with imagination and courage, or, as Malte puts it, "the will and power once more to be everything" (VI, 884).

It has been claimed that Grisha's essence is his loneliness.[18] But in addition to this essential loneliness are two other qualities which make him of great interest to Malte: his artistic sense of the world and the fact that he is an orphan. Grisha possesses, like a child or an artist, or like Malte himself, a love of the multiplicity of the world. He feels the need to remain free and fluid behind all masks, so as not to endanger the flow of riches. The other quality, that of orphanhood, is linked with this one. In defining what gave Grisha his initial strength, Malte remarks, "I am not unwilling to believe that the power of his transformation consisted in the fact that he was no longer anyone's son" (VI, 882). He is no one's son because, having denied his parents by denying himself and taking on another man's name, he has orphaned himself. That Malte finds this a source of strength, and the tsarina's claim to be his mother a threat, fits in with several things we have already seen in Rilke. He is concerned with parent-child relationships: one thinks of Yegor and Timofei; the mothers and their children in both the first Russian poem, "First Song," and the third poem of the *Elegien;* the odd reversals of father-son roles in the *Stunden-Buch.* Malte's problematic family heritage, and his relations with his father and mother, so different from one another, form another important motif. The highly eccentric version of the biblical Prodigal Son parable which ends the novel can be said to echo Malte's pronouncement about Grisha, for the prodigal son becomes free and strong only when he no longer allows himself to be defined by his family. Thus the Russian anecdote is interwoven with several of the main themes of the novel, and gives Malte material on which to work out his own problems, artistically and at some distance.

Throughout the novel, the fact that Malte is a poet determines the nature of his quest. He is preoccupied with problems of perception—the courage to see honestly—and of communication—the courage to relate with sensitivity to people as they are. He realizes that he will never achieve his true poetic calling, nor become a whole person, until he has mastered these things, which are of course intimately related to one another. Malte already possesses an almost morbid sensitivity to the needs and fears of other people. In one vivid episode, for example, he follows a sufferer from Saint Vitus's dance down a crowded Paris street, aware that the man is about to have an attack. Agonizingly attuned to the man's terror and embarrassment, he mimics his odd telltale movements, hoping to fool passersby into thinking them natural—a sudden stumble over a crack, an exuberant hop—and thus deflect attention from the man ahead. He wishes that he could, purely by the strength of his will, prevent the man from having an attack: "I laid my little bit of strength together like money and, looking at his hands, I begged him to take it, if he needed it" (VI, 773). But Malte's strength is too little, and the man's inner forces too great, and he throws himself into his fit with a kind of abandon.

We know that Malte's father possessed the same kind of sensitivity, the same odd, impulsive generosity. On the frequent occasions when Malte's Grandmother Brigge would begin to choke at dinner, his father would mentally put "his own orderly windpipe" at her disposal (VI, 821). We find a similar kind of vicarious participation on the part of the monk in the *Stunden-Buch,* who addresses his "neighbor God" and says if he sometimes disturbs God by knocking on the wall in the night, "it is because I rarely hear you breathing, and I know you are alone in the hall, and if you need something, no one is there" (I, 255). Malte is capable of a profound sympathy with other people; but this sympathy is rooted in horror. He can imagine himself in their position; indeed, in the case of the poor of Paris, he feels they recognize this affinity and are trying to make him affirm it. Malte's reaction to this sensitivity is expressed in an inability to face the reality of other people. He flees instead into the safety of his imagination, and constructs there a fictional version of them which he can control.

There are many examples of Malte's resistance to seeing and conveying the truth about people. One is the episode of the cauliflower vendor. Malte begins to write about a blind vendor he had seen pushing a cart along the street; but in the midst of his description, he realizes that he is not being honest: "I'm falsifying, if I say that; I'm suppressing the wagon that he pushed, I'm acting as if I hadn't noticed that he called out cauliflower" (VI, 748). But even in his outburst of frustration at his own weakness, he fights the impulse and defends himself: "But is that essential? And even if it were essential, isn't it a matter of what the whole thing was for *me?*" (VI, 748). He is, at this point, still a victim of his ego, and falsifies reality even as he sees it. It will be a long time before he learns to forget all he sees and let it ferment within him before becoming art of its own accord, as Rilke recommends in the *Sonette*.

Malte genuinely desires to open himself to reality, however terrifying or unpleasant it may be; but at the same time, he clings to his past, his habits, the symbols which give him the illusion of wholeness and safety. The conflict between these urges brings on a mysterious illness, for which he must be treated at a crowded, dreary clinic. The doctors do not understand what is wrong with him; the clinic waiting room is full of grotesque, vaguely threatening figures; and while he waits, Malte is overcome by two insights. The first is the realization that his being ordered to come to this clinic is "the first open confirmation that I belonged to the 'throwaways' " ("zu den Fortgeworfenen" [VI, 758–59]). The second is the sudden return of all the terrors of a haunted childhood, rolled into a shapeless horror which he calls "das Grosse" (a difficult phrase to translate—perhaps "the Big Thing" or "the Monstrous"). Its essence is the irruption of the absurd into Malte's life. He had thought it left behind in childhood; but since he has decided that he must face that childhood squarely for the first time, all its evils have returned along with it. Thus terror and the grotesque become part of Malte's daily reaity, along with the problems of honest perception and an authentic relation to people. A further aspect of Malte's unhappy situation is his feeling of uprootedness. There are numerous references to other days, when he was part of a family, or to the sort of peaceful, traditional, and unambitious life he thinks he would like to lead. Thus, in addition to searching for himself, Malte is seeking a place of his own within human society.

I have suggested that the historical and fictional figures whose lives appeal to Malte do so because of his instinctive realization of their potential similarity to himself, in some stage or isolated aspect of his development; he uses them as tools of self-discovery. This term is used in its basic etymological sense: Malte's self is dis-covered, uncovered; the layers of propriety, falsity, cowardice, and misunderstanding are removed, gradually and painfully, through his personal encounters and through his confrontations with history and literature. Walter Sokel very convincingly shows that Malte, in the course of the novel, goes through a process of *Ent-Ichung*—"devolution of self"—a "process of persecution and breaking of the I, for the release of a power which far surpasses the I."[19] He shows how certain events and characters which horrify both Malte and the reader—the hovering beggars, for example, who seem to represent a total loss of self, or the seeming humiliation of the Saint Vitus dancer—are in fact positive, indeed invitations to transcendence, if read, as Rilke once suggested, "against the current."[20] The constant self should be regarded as a mere facade, a social convenience which each of us struggles to maintain. Thus, though the defeat of the Saint Vitus dancer by the forces within him seems to be a tragedy, Sokel shows how it can be regarded, on the contrary, as a release, a breakthrough of what is within man, which is far greater and more creative than the brittle shell of the conventional "self." Malte is caught in the middle of this process, and cannot yet see the transcendent aspect of the events of his life. The whole process of the novel, in fact, is the process of his learning to see. Thus the entries in his diary, the "Aufzeichnungen," are all experiments in a new mode. Very often they seem partial or total failures, from his limited point of view. But they are successes from ours, who look at them from outside, as facets of Malte's personality and signs of his artistic development.

The second overtly Russian episode in the novel, concerning Malte's neighbor in St. Petersburg, is one such variation on the themes which constitute Malte's quest. Like all of Malte's fictional, historical, or "biographical" digressions, it tackles important problems; it reveals the stage which Malte has reached in his transformation. And it is equally revealing, on another level, in what it tells us about Rilke's knowledge of, and empathy for, certain aspects of nineteenth-century Russian culture. This episode concerns a period Malte had once spent in St. Petersburg; his neighbor on one side was a petty official named Nikolai Kusmitsch, who spent all his days lying on his bed. Malte had speculated about him, but one day learned what he believed to be the true story from a student who was the man's friend.

Any discussion of the Nikolai Kusmitsch story will neccessarily be complex, for Malte's own reactions to it are ambiguous. It combines a number of important Russian elements; and it does not stand alone, but forms part of a digression on the habits and worth of neighbors. Malte begins this digression by likening neighbors to a kind of contagion, a "canine pneumococcus," that attacks one through the ears. He then begins reminiscing about some that he has had in the past, and finally mentions the two he had in St. Petersburg: the one who simply stood in his room and played the violin, and Nikolai Kusmitsch. Malte's remarks about his neighbors are not so cynical as his initial comparison of them to the canine pneumococcus might suggest. In fact, they show an anxiety on his part for these unseen people which brings to mind his behavior vis-à-vis the Saint Vitus dancer. It does not surprise us that Malte is extremely aware of his

Die Aufzeichnungen

neighbors. Paris and St. Petersburg have overwhelmed him with their multitudes; he is morbidly sensitive to the people he meets, and a chance encounter can be shattering to him. How, then, should he not be sensitive to the people who surround him on all sides, separated only by a wall, floor, or ceiling, and whose habits he involuntarily learns by listening?

Like everything else in his life, Malte's relations with his various neighbors are unusual and difficult. He never seems actually to meet them; rather, he creates his own fantasies about them. Only occasionally, as in the case of Nikolai Kusmitsch, is the conjecture obliterated by the truth. Yet he becomes personally, if secretly, involved in their lives. When, for example, prompt and regular neighbors suddenly stay out late at night, Malte relates, "I pictured to myself what might have happened to them, and left my light burning, and was anxious as a young bride" (VI, 864). Once again Malte, afraid and lonely and increasingly aware of his fears, participates vicariously in the lives of others. What Malte does in relation to these people is, of course, just what we have seen him doing in relation to the people on the street, such as the cauliflower vendor: he creates a reality to suit his own needs, rather than attempting to find out what really exists. One of the neighbors whom he recalls, for example, was a medical student studying for his exams. Purely on the basis of certain odd sounds emanating from the next room, Malte had, without any corroboration, invented a tale of desperation and collapse, concerning a student with a nervous tic, a metal box thrown down again and again in anger, and a mother who comes to comfort her son and take him home. During the days of his obsession with this neighbor, Malte had stood on his own side of the wall, sending his will through it to help the student control his nervous tic and concentrate on his studies. Significantly, Malte admits that he has now almost forgotten this neighbor, that "it was no genuine sympathy that I felt for him" (VI, 875). The man, whoever he was, had served merely as an excuse for Malte to create a life, a myth. Now that he is gone, all Malte feels is a strong urge to see the empty room and encounter there the little tin box—an object which he himself may actually have brought into existence.

One begins to wonder about Malte's great sensitivity, his habit of offering his strength to strangers. His generosity seems so often to take the form of anonymity and wishful thinking. Rarely does he directly approach anyone with a concrete gesture of compassion, love, or aid. It seems that what appeared to be a strength in his character may turn out to be another weakness which he must overcome or discard. He must still develop a more human form of love, and this will come only when he sees and acknowledges the real human being in front of him. Rilke was very fond of Dostoevsky, and in reading him encountered many of the same questions which plague Malte.[21] In Dostoevsky, love and real neighborliness often conflict with mere abstract humanitarianism. We also find in him the concern that each man have a place of his own, a "place" in a metaphysical sense. According to one critic, Dostoevsky, in conceptualizing man's individual sphere of freedom, "starts from the Christian concept of the 'neighbor,' i.e., by accepting as the basic ethical datum the concretely individual existence of a multitude of ethical subjects. Ethical rationalism understands only love for man in general, while the 'neighbor' is strange and distant. It is, however, precisely the concrete individuality of the 'neighbor' that should be the object of our ethical action."[22] The critic cites various passages from Dostoevsky on the difficulty of loving one's neighbors, the real men standing next to one. For example, Versilov in *A Raw Youth* states, "Love for humanity must be understood as love for that humanity which you have created in your soul. . . . To love people as they are is impossible."[23] A character in the *Brothers Karamazov* declares, "The more I love humanity in general, the less I love man in particular."[24] Malte gradually becomes aware that such an attitude is a common one; it shocks him, but he is forced to recognize its prevalence in the world and in himself. It is easier to love the faceless mass than to do the more difficult thing of loving the people whom one encounters every day, with their imperfect and irritating individuality. Malte's difficult goal is to love "man in particular"; but Versilov's statement that we can love only our inner perception of a person is strongly reflected in Malte's dilemma, his inability to acknowledge the people who try to assert their reality—the cauliflower vendor, the blind newspaper seller, the old woman with her pencils. In the *Brothers Karamazov*, Alyosha declares that love must be free of all judgmental qualities; and Malte echoes this, at the point of one of his important breakthroughs. Having finally had the courage to look, really look, at a newspaper vendor for whom he had, as usual, imagined a reality, he is overcome by the man's otherness, and his right to be as he is. Malte cries out, "if only we would learn, above all, to endure and not to judge" (VI, 903).

The case of Nikolai Kusmitsch is somewhat different from that of the medical student. Malte had as usual set out to create reality for the unseen neighbor,

> and God knows what might have crawled forth, if the student who sometimes visited him hadn't come to the wrong door one day. He told me the story of his acquaintance, and it turned out to be rather comforting.
> (VI, 865)

Malte is immensely relieved to learn what he believes to be the truth from the student. This is the tale he tells Malte. Nikolai Kusmitsch, a petty official, had one day taken it into his head to change the years remaining to

Die Aufzeichnungen

him into minutes and seconds, like small change. In the process he has a conversation with his double, a broader and more stately version of himself, on matters of wealth. Nikolai Kusmitsch then finds that he is wasting time, tries to economize, and finally decides that he has been cheated by his double. As he ponders ways of getting his small-time changed back again into years, and considers the meaning and importance of numbers, he suddenly becomes aware of the moving world around him: first of time as it whisks past his face with a windlike motion, then of the ceaseless motion of the earth under his feet; and finally he recalls the tilt of the earth's axis. Overcome by dizziness and nausea, he lies down and closes his eyes, determining never to get up again. And there he lies, sometimes on good days reciting aloud verses from Pushkin and Nekrasov.

Though Malte doesn't actually see or meet Nikolai Kusmitsch, he chooses to regard *this* story as true because he knows that for once it is not the product of his own uneasy imagination. Yet precisely this tale is so fantastic and so permeated by echoes of Russian literature that one has the feeling that the student has had a wonderful time pulling Malte's leg. Critics have tended to seize on the striking images of changing years into seconds, and Nikolai's obsession with numbers. One writer links the anecdote to "the growing time-consciousness and the passion for reflection characteristic of western civilization. . . . In Russia, [Rilke] thought, these features were far less pronounced and when they did acquire prominence in individuals their effect was pernicious."[25] Rilke did see an essential difference in the Russian and Western concepts of time. One thinks of his many remarks concerning the relative timelessness of Russia, and its place outside the boundaries of "normal" historical development. One can also well believe that Rilke felt the influence on Russia of a Western (or merely modern?) sense of hurry, of schedules, divisions, and deadlines, to be pernicious, for it would have seemed to him a profanation and distortion of Russia as he chose to see it.

However, a fact of which Rilke was well aware from his extensive reading in Russian literature, and one which the critic does not mention, is that not only speed, schedules, and bureaucratic categorization, but also the whole gamut of modern and urban abuses were already present in Russia, and already the target of critical or satirical writing long before Rilke chose to caricature them in Nikolai Kusmitsch. The episode is in fact permeated by the atmosphere and punctuated by details from a number of works by nineteenth-century Russian writers. That the tale is placed in St. Petersburg is already significant. There is only one other indication in the novel that Malte has ever been to Russia, and that was deleted in the published version. But for the story of the obsessed little clerk we are suddenly transported to that northern city so rich in gloomy associations, so much the city of Pushkin, Gogol, and Dostoevsky. St. Petersburg, built on a swamp with slave labor, was from its beginnings the pet project of the arch-Westernizer Peter I. It was not only a city full of government bureaucracies, but the symbol of something unnatural and antihuman. In this, and in its crowded squalor, St. Petersburg stands as an entity parallel and comparable to Malte's Paris.

Into this quintessentially literary setting, Rilke places Nikolai Kusmitsch. The character, "this little civil servant," with his apparently uneventful life and a fatal penchant for reflection which leads him into the realms of the absurd, comes from a long line of illustrious ancestors—petty officials and silently suffering "little people" of nineteenth-century Russian literature. His closest relatives come from the pages of Dostoevsky: Golyadkin, the poverty-stricken office worker whose double tricks him out of name, reputation, and freedom ("The Double"); and the complex figure of the Underground Man, a poor clerk whose self-conscious perversity makes him irrevocably miserable ("Notes from Underground"). Other close relations come from Gogol: Akaky Akakevich, the clerk whose only purpose in life becomes the acquisition and then, after it is stolen, the reclamation of a winter coat ("The Overcoat"); and Kavalyov, the petty civil servant whose nose runs away from him ("The Nose").

Rilke appears to have taken a number of ideas from Dostoevsky's "The Double," both in its serious underlying motifs, and in details of plot and characterization used to illustrate these motifs. In "The Double," we find a more protracted investigation of the problems which beset Nikolai Kusmitsch. Golyadkin, a petty official in a St. Petersburg bureaucracy, is obsessed by paranoid fantasies about a plot to ruin his reputation. He is brought to a bad end by the appearance of a double, Golyadkin, Jr., who insinuates himself everywhere in Golyadkin, Sr.'s life, with much more success than the latter himself has ever had. The Double ousts Golyadkin, Sr. from his job, makes a favorable impression on his superiors, and even wins the favor of the young society lady whom Golyadkin, Sr. has been clumsily and unsuccessfully courting. Dostoevsky was, in this story, exploring for the first time a theme which was to permeate his later work, and which he himself regarded as the most important he ever dealt with. In 1877, in *The Diary of a Writer,* he wrote, "The idea [of "The Double"] was very clever and I have never propounded anything more serious in literature."[26] Golyadkin is driven mad by a combination of his weak character, his terror and anxiety before the outside world, and his insecure and humiliating position in the bureaucratic structure. As a cog in this structure, utterly dependent on it and incapable of dealing with it effectively, he is, in the words of one of the critics, "the passive bearer of the rational principle—and its victim."[27] The form his madness takes is the appearance of the Double who possesses all the traits he himself lacks—eloquence, aggressiveness, and an ability to focus and utilize his ambitions, and to work busily and productively within the self-perpetuating world of the bureaucracy. Dostoevsky focuses on the development and logical outcome of Golyadkin's breakdown. Golyadkin's "place" in life is usurped by the Double, his identity sucked away, and he ends by being removed entirely from the normal world.

He has gone through a painful process of *Ent-Ichung*, which arises both from within (his basic indecisiveness and instability) and from without (the crass, destructive real world, and the junior Golyadkin, who seems to exist objectively, outside Golyadkin, Sr.'s sick fantasy). By robbing Golyadkin of his role at the office, at home (his servant refuses to serve anyone of such a doubtful moral caliber that he would tolerate a double), and in society—in other words, by stealing his identity in the eyes of others, however unflattering that identity may have been—the Double turns Golyadkin into a phantom. This is a totally negative experience; there is none of the liberating expansiveness which Sokel suggests awaits Malte in the process of *Ent-Ichung*. This is partly because Golyadkin clings to the old, public (though distorted) image of himself. He persists in regarding that identity as a continuous one despite his abandonment by the world at large. Secondly, Golyadkin is still not free, despite this abandonment. The outside world continues to define him; it has simply decided he is mad and must be removed. He is thus turned over to the ministrations of the sinister and merciless Dr. Krestyan Ivanovich Rutenspitz. Golyadkin's story ends with his being taken away to an insane asylum.

Nikolai Kusmitsch experiences a number of similar emotions and events. Like Golyadkin, he is a petty official, and like him, he is disturbed by threats from all sides. For example, Golyadkin, hurrying miserably through a typically nasty St. Petersburg night, meditates gloomily on the fog, which is "fraught with colds, swollen faces, fevers, quinsies, inflammations of every possible sort."[28] When Nikolai Kusmitsch feels time blowing past his ears, his reaction is a similar one of despair and personal insult:

> That this should happen precisely to *him,* who perceived every sort of wind as an insult. Now he would sit there and it would go on blowing like this his whole life long. He envisioned all the neuralgias which he would get from it; he was beside himself with anger.
>
> (VI, 869)

Elsewhere, when Golyadkin's one chance at reasserting himself in his own name is ruined by the noisy interruption of a polka band, he is crushed, and "everything in the room became agitated like the sea."[29] When Nikolai

Kusmitsch becomes aware of the earth's movements, it likewise spells disaster for him, for he was "somewhat delicate on just that matter, he even avoided streetcars. He reeled about the room as if on deck, and had to hang on left and right" (VI, 869).

Rilke's choice of details renders the character an amusing one, while not robbing him of his symbolic value. We find ourselves smiling at a person who regards the wind as a personal affront, gets seasick on trolleys, and assumes that because of the importance of the subject, there must be a directory entry for matters of time under "K" for "Kaiserlich" ("Imperial"). In the latter detail, we detect the direct influence of Gogolian absurdity. In Gogol's story "The Nose," Kavalyov goes to a newspaper office "to publish a thoroughly detailed description [of the nose] so that anyone meeting it could at once present it to him—or at least let him know where it was."[30] For characters such as these, brothers to all the hapless bureaucrats of nineteenth-century Russian literature, there is always an office which can deal with the problem. After all, their lives revolve around "the service," they are urban creatures whose every activity reflects in some way their work, their rank, their acquaintances within the government bureaucracy. And they have implicit faith in the ability of that rational structure to solve all temporary aberrations from normal life; there *is* no other approach to reality. Indeed, Nikolai Kusmitsch's remark that it was "out of the question that, for example, one should meet a seven or a twenty-five in society" (VI, 868) is ironic, if one recalls that for the nineteenth-century Russian, one's place in the Table of Ranks, one's "number" from one to fourteen, was all-important, determining whom one saluted, socialized with, visited, or married.[31] Nikolai Kusmitsch's initial mistake is to change his years into "small change," and to indulge in a feeling of wealth because of his action. One of Golyadkin's inexplicable acts is very similar; one morning he "changed all his big notes into small ones, and though he lost on the exchange, his pocketbook was considerably fatter, which evidently afforded him extreme satisfaction."[32] It is typical of the painfully self-conscious Golyadkin to want to appear impressive. Nikolai Kusmitsch's transaction takes place in the privacy of his room, but there is an element of pomp, or of self-satisfaction, about it nonetheless. He is pleased at having decided that he will live another fifty years—a discovery which he regards as an "act of generosity which he rendered himself" (VI, 865). And this self-satisfaction drives him to the fateful act of changing his years into seconds, for "now he wanted to outdo himself" (VI, 865), and he sets to figuring out what his "capital" amounts to. He, too, falls prey to the "rational principle," in the sense that he becomes obsessed with dealing with life in terms of numbers. He keeps careful records of his time, till finally he is no longer capable of perceiving the world as a whole at all, but only as a collection of separate parts and movements. He can no longer see the face of the clock and read its simple message, for the whirring of its parts. Organization, consequential thought and planning, rationality have tipped over into irrationality and a fragmentation of reality; his life becomes a parody of analysis, with synthesis no longer possible.

As with Golyadkin, a double is one of the manifestations of his growing peril. The Double appears almost gaily, as a product of Nikolai Kusmitsch's exuberance at having discovered the secret of time. Nikolai plays a game of talking to himself as if there were two of him—a shabby little Nikolai Kusmitsch sitting on the horsehair sofa, and a stately, condescending one in a fur coat. The Double thus begins as a part of Nikolai Kusmitsch, a rich, generous, imposing version of himself. After he decides that the Double has cheated him, however, the latter takes on an independent existence as a big-time swindler; no doubt already "arrested somewhere," he slips out of Nikolai Kusmitsch's grasp, never to return. Here, too, no synthesis is possible; the parts separate and go their own ways. Morally Nikolai Kusmitsch has in fact lost part of himself, for in his growing concern for his "wealth" he has become miserly. He goes to great lengths to save time: "He arose earlier, he washed himself less thoroughly, he drank his tea standing up, he ran to the office and arrived much too early" (VI, 866). These absurd time-saving attempts remind one of the lengths to which Gogol's Akaky Akakevich goes to save money for his precious overcoat:

> [He] gave up drinking tea and burning candles in the evening, and if he had to do any work, he must go into the landlady's room and work by her candle. . . . He must walk as lightly and carefully as possible, almost on tiptoe, on the cobbles and flagstones, so that his soles might last a little longer than usual [and] he must send his linen to the laundry less often.[33]

Nikolai Kusmitsch has become suspicious and vindictive, and can no longer even imagine that other self, "the one in the fur coat, the generous one" (VI, 866). Thus a positive part of him has been sacrificed in an act of limitation. As with Golyadkin, so with Nikolai Kusmitsch are habits and ways of seeing stripped away; but they are replaced with something narrower in terms of character (though infinitely wide and uncontrollable in terms of their relations with the world). Nikolai Kusmitsch is laid bare to "das Grosse," the same huge, fearful universe which Malte has known since childhood. But while Golyadkin is destroyed by his too-close dependence on other men, and Malte continues to seek, as the artist he is, for new ways of distancing and examining his role in the world, Nikolai Kusmitsch is merely left stranded. He ends in a gentler madness than Golyadkin, but madness just the same. He is consigned, not to an asylum, but to his own sofa, the only place where he is able to bear the movement of the earth—a sad but also ludicrous "place of his own."[34]

On another level, Malte himself appears to resemble both Nikolai Kusmitsch and several Dostoevskian figures. His ambiguous position in relation to this episode has already been suggested. He is, for example, aware of the humor inherent in the story of his odd neighbor, and some of his comments are wry and understated. Yet he takes the story seriously, and feels "uncommonly reassured" by knowing the truth. We know from context that this is meant seriously, for we are aware of his fear of his unruly imagination and his struggle to face reality as it is. Yet Malte has not yet mastered the art of seeing, and he is often not able to draw the right conclusions from what he encounters. Several times Rilke makes gentle fun of his protagonist, by making him fall into a trap of his own making and never realize it. Malte tells us that Nikolai Kusmitsch, having become physically aware of the instability of existence, is unable to cope with it, and flees to a horizontal position, where he literally closes his eyes to the world. There he seeks, in the monotonous and mechanical recitation of poetry, a false order and stability in a chaotic world; he recites "in the tone of voice in which children recite poems when people demand it of them" (VI, 865), and "with equal emphasis on the end rhymes" (VI, 870). Malte's reaction is: "What luck that he knew all those poems. But then he had always been particularly interested in literature" (VI, 870). We can understand Nikolai Kusmitsch's relief and gratitude at this one refuge, but we can hardly call it an "interest in literature." Malte's reaction contains, perhaps, an ironic commentary by Rilke: how much of Malte's wisdom and growth is acquired, if not directly from books, then in his own reworking of what he finds in books? And when he feels threatened by the strangely sinister people who encroach on him in the streets of Paris, Malte flees—to the library: "And then I am amongst these books; I have been taken away from you, as if I had died, and sit and read a poet" (VI, 745).

There are other signs that Malte continues to misinterpret at least part of what he learns. He says he has never had such a pleasant neighbor as Nikolai Kusmitsch, "who certainly would have admired me, too" (VI, 870). The remark suggests mutual respect, "neighborliness" in the Dostoevskian sense. But only a few sentences earlier, Malte has told us that since his neighbor had been confined to his horizontal position by vertigo, "an exaggerated admiration [has] developed in him for those who went about and bore the movement of the earth" (VI, 870). Of course he would have admired Malte! He was one of those remarkably vertical—and in Nikolai Kusmitsch's eyes, necessarily less sensitive—folk who are not bothered by the motion of the earth underfoot. They, and Malte, either don't notice it, don't show it, or aren't upset by it. In any case, they are

Die Aufzeichnungen

either dull or stoical. Dostoevsky's Underground Man sums up his own dilemma: "To be conscious of too much is an illness."[35] Similarly, but comically, Nikolai Kusmitsch is laid low by his sudden hyperawareness of the world, of its threatening abstract possibilities. As we have seen, however, Malte is less "vertical" than Nikolai might imagine, for in Paris Malte likewise falls prey to an illness that arises from his awareness, as his childhood fears return to him. These fears concern his perceptions and expectations of reality; ordinary objects are perceived by him to be full of threatening potential for destruction, horror, betrayal. One of these, in fact, is "that some number begins to grow in my brain, until it has no more room in me" (VI, 767). In his confrontation with "das Grosse" lies, perhaps, a key to his attraction to the tale of Nikolai Kusmitsch.

It is also in his illness that Malte is related directly to Dostoevsky's Golyadkin, without the intermediation of Nikolai Kusmitsch. There are two scenes in the "The Double" in which Golyadkin is examined by a doctor. In the first, he visits Dr. Rutenspitz, the man who will eventually take charge of him as a mental patient. Golyadkin has sought out the doctor for unknown reasons—he does not seem to suffer from any physical ailment, though the doctor has already prescribed a medicine and told him to relax and find some recreation. The content of Golyadkin's interview with the doctor, who regards him with perplexity and suspicion, is a nearly incoherent litany of his ambitions, jealousies, frustrations, and his conviction that there is a plot afoot to ruin him. It is evident that his disease is one of the spirit, based on fear of other people and on a profoundly distorted sense of himself. In the second scene, Golyadkin is terrified and humiliated by a group of officials who stand to one side of the room discussing him with the doctor, "nodding significantly and glancing from time to time at Mr. Golyadkin."[36] There is of course a vast difference between Golyadkin and Malte, whose untreatable and vague disease is also spiritual, but who is neither grotesque nor mad. But Rilke may nonetheless have utilized these strange, vivid scenes when he made Malte undergo his ordeal at the clinic. Malte must face a group of curiously obtuse and noncommittal doctors; his description of the whole encounter begins, "The doctor didn't understand me. Nothing. And it *was* hard to relate" (VI, 758). Like Golyadkin, he has no luck in conveying to the doctors the true nature and urgency of his affliction. For Golyadkin, the doctor is a figure firmly entrenched in the upper middle class, an intimate of those high officials whose attention and approval Golyadkin so covets. For Malte, too, the doctors are connected with the establishment. They *belong,* and have the power to command that he come to the clinic, that he mingle with the suffering dregs there, that he join them, admit his brotherhood with them. The doctors are allowed to ask questions, to make judgments, to label

Malte and define him. But whereas Golyadkin's doctors serve to exclude him finally and utterly from normal human intercourse, Malte's unwittingly move him further along the path to a face-to-face encounter with his own inner identity. Malte is embarked on a self-confessed journey to find the reality of himself and others; but at times he must be given a push. Some confrontations he seeks voluntarily, in his assays into history and literature; others, like Nikolai Kusmitsch or the clinic, force themselves on him. But each adds some important element, if not to his growing maturity, then at least to the quest itself.

· SEVEN ·

DEATH AND AUTHENTICITY:
Malte Laurids Brigge

he first entry in Malte's notebooks begins, "So this is where people come to live—I'd say, rather, it was a place for dying" (VI, 709). In this fashion Rilke presents in the very first sentence a motif that permeates the whole novel. Death has long been recognized as a major theme of the book, and a great deal has been written on the subject. My purpose here is not to go over the same ground, but to examine specific aspects of the motif, in search of possible Russian inspiration or parallels. These in turn may illumine the complex web of ideas and attitudes toward death in Rilke's work.

Malte, made aware of the aggressive presence of death all around him in Paris, also evokes it repeatedly in his childhood reminiscences and his historical digressions, trying to place it within the context of human life, his life. There are seventeen deaths in this short novel, ranging from the impersonal and anonymous (the *Massentod*—"mass dying"—in the cities; the flies in autumn) to the individual and particular (Malte's Grandfather Brigge); from deaths personally touching or involving Malte (mother, father, several other relatives, his dog) to those felt only at a distance like a scene in a tapestry (Grisha Otrepev, Christian IV, the suffocated armies at Ghent). But in their incredible variety and frequency, each serves Malte as an excuse to meditate on death, to approach its cold, black core from a different angle.

In the first specific death he describes, that of the old Chamberlain Brigge, Malte presents the idea of death as something intrinsic in each person, "that one had his death within him, as the fruit its core" (VI, 715). He also suggests in this passage that each person possesses and must die his *own* death, one as unique and appropriate to himself as his life and person-

153

ality are (or ought to be). But Chamberlain Brigge's death also reveals the uneasy and uncharitable relationship between the dying and the survivors; in this sense it is an "unsuccessful" death. The deaths in the novel represent a variety of possibilities on the scale of authenticity; and all are important for Malte, as they force him to come to terms with another, deeper facet of the individual reality of himself and others.

These ideas are of course central to much of Rilke's work. Death, a topic to which he returned often, was for him linked to two other great questions: the nature of art, and of the divine. In a letter written to Lotte Hepner in 1915, Rilke expresses in parable-like form some crucial ideas on death and God. He seeks to explain how the gods—man's creations—and death came to be what they are for us today: "something not of this world, but something later, from elsewhere and alien."[1] He suggests that men have always created divinities into which they posited "whatever is dead and threatening and destructive and terrible, violence, anger, the suprapersonal stupefaction . . . the Unknown."[2] But originally these things had been an integral part of man. And though man recognized the relationship secretly, he did not know how to deal with it. Thus he preferred to extract these elements from his daily life and put them somewhere outside it, as being "too large, too dangerous."[3] The next step, says Rilke, was that these aspects of man, isolated and condensed outside him, acquired a menacing influence over him, and now came from outside, as if something no longer his. He had objectified them and given them power, and then tried uneasily to ignore their existence. Rilke says here of death,

> It lives and yet, in its reality, beyond our experience, . . . never really acknowledged by us, spoiling and outstripping the meaning of life, from the very beginning it, too, was banished, expelled, so that it wouldn't constantly interrupt us in finding that meaning.[4]

Contained in this vision are several things of importance: the concept of death and God or gods as coeval and similar; the implication that death is really a natural part of life, not something originally separate from and opposed to it; the idea that the terror-inspiring aspect of death is a creation of man; and the emphasis on man's attempts to shut it out, as something unfitting and distasteful. We recognize here, in slightly altered form, the basic Rilkean vision of death, familiar from his works and eminently present in *Malte Laurids Brigge*. The most important of these ideas for Malte is the last one. In many of the deaths in the novel, we see either Malte or the people he describes instinctively rejecting death. The servants and villagers on Ulsgaard, while yearning for the finality of death to silence the chamberlain's screams and bring them peace again, are horrified and drained of energy and will by his lengthy and imperious dying.

The mother of a girl who dies in a trolley in Naples reacts with anger and disbelief, shaking and rearranging the girl's body until "finally she drew back her arm and struck the fat face with all her might, so that it wouldn't die" (VI, 859).

Malte's grandmother, Margarete Brigge, thinks often about her own death, but she believes the time of its arrival to be a matter of choice, and her prerogative as mistress of the house. When Malte's mother falls fatally ill, Margarete is insulted that "the young woman was usurping precedence from her, who intended to die at a point which was in no way as yet determined" (VI, 823). Margarete had thought, perhaps, to cheat death or at least hold it indefinitely at bay, by her manner of propriety and unhurried aloofness. Death, like the other figures in her life, was expected to follow orders. Now Malte's mother was dying out of turn and with unseemly haste, shaking Margarete's vision of the controlled nature of existence.

There exists within Malte a dichotomy which stems from his two disparate sets of relatives, and which typifies the two attitudes toward death in the novel. Walter Sokel sees this dichotomy as best represented on the one hand by what he calls "the Brahe principle" of a fluid sense of time, without boundaries, the "falling away of the barriers between the dimensions of regulated time, in favor of the experience of the unity and simultaneity of all existence,"[5] and on the other hand, the "quasi-existential temporal dimension of Briggean dying, which is aimed at the future."[6] This dichotomy is reflected in the few deaths which occur within the circle of Malte's mother's side of the family (the Brahes), and those which take place among the Brigges. It is also reflected in the attitude of the two families toward the dead themselves. Malte's mother relates how Ingeborg, her cheerful younger sister who had had the knack of making everyone around her happy, had faced death: calmly, indeed willingly—"I don't want to any more." Ingeborg knew herself better than those around her, who had tried to hide from her the fact that she was dying. She knew, and told them so, and seemed to feel no incongruity in her dying. Malte tells of the repeated appearance at Urnekloster of the long-dead Christine Brahe, and of the odd atmosphere there, expectant and accepting, in which the centuries mingled as a matter of course. And the Brahes, with their calm acceptance of ghosts and their blurring of the lines between forms of existence, perceive that other people do not regard death with due respect. Malte's mother expresses her fear: "Oh, Malte, we just depart, and it seems to me that everyone is distracted and busy and doesn't really pay attention when we go. As if a star fell, and no one saw it and nobody made a wish on it" (VI, 788). A typical Brahe, she senses the sadness, the waste of a death that goes unnoticed, that is not integrated into life, even if only by the wishes or the fantasies of others.

Very different is the attitude of Malte's father, a Brigge. He reacts to the appearances on Urnekloster with horror, and when his wife is dying, his pride is wounded at having to admit that she is "very much disfigured" (VI, 812). Contemplating his own end, he so greatly fears a confusion of death and life, their possible inadvertent mingling, that his last wish is to have his heart pierced to insure that he is really dead. He fears, not death itself, but the mixing of life and death; he has a horror of incompleteness and of the adulteration of the self, which he regards as finite and real. Indeed for most of the characters in the novel, death must not be allowed to mix with or spoil life. It is an inconvenience, an indiscretion, an act of violence to the sensibilities of the survivors. It is above all an antisocial act. Death occurs among, and in relation to, other people, in a social setting of one sort or another; and it is on the social context, the dying individual's relation to himself and society, that Rilke focuses.

This emphasis on self-perception either in the dying person or in his fellow men links the deaths in *Malte Laurids Brigge* to several Russian literary prototypes. Two in particular are of interest to us here: Dostoevsky's *The Insulted and the Injured,* and Tolstoy's *Death of Ivan Ilich*—the first for its literal and formal contributions to an episode in the novel, the second for the importance which its basic premises had for Rilke. The link to Dostoevsky appears in one of the most vivid scenes in Rilke's novel, in which Malte witnesses the death of an old man in a café. It occurs at a moment when Malte is feeling particularly vulnerable. He has just come from the profoundly upsetting discovery of the stained walls and gutted, naked rooms of a block of demolished flats, which had forced their hidden lives on his senses. His mysterious illness is about to attack him, and everything—the vulgar carnival crowds, his smoky stove and cold apartment, his greasy hand-me-down furniture—seems a threat to his person, his privacy, and his sanity.

Entering a crémerie, a cheap café frequented by the decent poor, Malte finds that his usual seat has been taken by someone else. Seating himself nearby, he experiences one of his moments of intense awareness: the old man who has taken his seat is dying, right there in the café. Without looking at him, Malte is able, against his will, to follow every step of the process of terror and withdrawal which is taking place in the other man. For once he is able to face reality, forcing himself to look at the man—but to his horror, he discovers that his imagination had been right. Reality corroborates his fears, and he sees death progressing. Malte flees precipitately, pierced above all by the kinship he feels with the dying man. The worst thing is that the man takes leave of the familiar world passively: "He sat there like that and waited for it to happen. And didn't resist any longer. And I'm still resisting" (VI, 755). Malte's outcry reveals how deeply related he feels to the man embarked on his inexorable departure. Malte, too, feels threatened with a process of withdrawal: "After all, I could only understand that man because in me, too, something is taking place that is beginning to distance and separate me from everything" (VI, 755). He instinctively draws a parallel between the process of death, and that of *Ent-Ichung,* which he cannot yet bring himself to accept, even though he knows he must endure it: "If my fear weren't so great, I'd console myself with the idea that it's not impossible to see everything differently and still live. But I'm unspeakably afraid of this transformation" (VI, 755). Suddenly death and the fear of death acquire a new dimension. *Ent-Ichung,* radical change, like death, is a frightening and narrow passageway into a new consciousness; Malte knows his way lies there, but he is not yet capable of acquiescing. Indeed the novel is itself the chronicle of his journey toward that new form of consciousness.

It is at first startling to realize that much of the external form and a number of details in this crucial crémerie episode come from *The Insulted and the Injured.* The first chapter of that novel presents an anecdote which, with some obvious differences of purpose, is in essence the same. The first person narrator, Ivan, recounts an episode which occurred one evening in a small neighborhood café. An old man, whom Ivan had often noticed previously, goes into the café and, as is his habit, takes a seat and remains there motionless, staring into space, with his emaciated dog at his feet. Ivan follows him and watches as one of the German guests in the café becomes offended because he thinks the old man was staring at him. He complains, causing the old man to rise in confusion. As he starts to leave, he discovers that his faithful dog has just died of old age and hunger. The man flees, and the narrator runs after him into the night, catching up with him in a dark alley, where the old fellow dies in his arms.

Certain similarities are readily evident: the first person narrator; the old man sitting, lost in his own inner world, in a bright café; the sudden incursion of death into a mundane setting. On closer examination, we find that a large number of details in Rilke also have their parallels and perhaps origin in Dostoevsky. Malte is a poet, Ivan a novelist. Both are lonely wanderers in a large city, and recount something which happened to them on an evening in early spring: "It was Carnival and evening" (VI, 751), says Malte; and Ivan notes, "Last year, on the evening of March 22, something very strange happened to me."[7] Both are conscious of their own poverty and are depressed by the living quarters they are forced to take because of it. Malte complains about the smoking stove which has driven him from his room, and declares that "if I weren't poor I would rent a different room" (VI, 753). Ivan has just spent the day "walking around town trying to find a lodging . . . and, of course, it had to be as cheap as possible."⁸ The old man in the Russian café sits without ordering and stares unseeing; Malte notices his neighbor's "motionlessness," and knows instinctively that "horror had numbed him" (VI, 755).

In both episodes, the authors make a point of a person being displaced from his usual seat. Malte's place has been usurped by the dying man; this both establishes the bond between them and symbolizes Malte's gradual disorientation and displacement. Ivan notes that the old man's favorite place was by the stove, and that whenever he found someone else sitting there, he would move slowly to another by the window. On the night of his death, Ivan sees that "the old man was already sitting by the window."⁹ That is, he had been displaced from his usual seat, pushed to the periphery of the warm human circle in the café, as if in preparation for the coming final displacement. The central part of Dostoevsky's anecdote, in which he parodies the prosperous and sentimental German patrons of Müller's Café, is lacking in Rilke's story. Typical of Dostoevsky's dislike of foreigners, it could serve no purpose in the context of Rilke's work. Even so, one may detect a slight echo of it in Malte's abhorrence for the jolly, insensitive crowd which surrounds and hinders him in the street outside the crémerie.

The most important parallels in the two anecdotes are certain peculiar qualities shared by the narrators, and the portrayals of death. In both stories, we sense the incongruity of death in a public place, as well as the isolation of the dying men. Malte's neighbor, experiencing his own death, feels everything becoming "incomprehensible . . . strange and difficult" (VI, 755). The old man at Müller's, devastated by the death of his dog, is unreachable either by the Germans who shout at him, or by their clumsy generosity (they offer him cognac and propose that he have the dog stuffed). "The old man listened to all this obviously without understanding it, trembling all over as before."¹⁰ In each case, it is the narrator who feels a bond with the old man—Malte, the bond of kinship and a shared fate; Ivan, a vague but nonetheless powerful connection. Earlier that evening Ivan had had a premonition about the old man: "Why was it that at that meeting with him I had felt at once that that same evening something not quite ordinary would happen to me?"¹¹ And latter when the man tumbles out of the café, it is Ivan who runs after him, and in whose arms he breathes his last.

Both narrators possess an unusual degree of sensitivity to their surroundings, which can lead them into awkward and painful but also enlightening situations. And both consciously connect their sensitivity to illness. Ivan has an "ominous cough," and at first puts down his presentiments to his sickness: "I was ill, however, and sensations in illness are almost always deceptive."¹² He then attributes his staying at the café so long to the fact that he was "more and more overcome by illness," which he somehow connects with "a cheap concern over trifles which I had noticed in myself lately, which hindered me from living and looking clearly at life."[13] On fleeing the café, Malte, caught up in the carnival crowd, finds himself "heavy with sweat, and a dulling pain circulated within me, as if something too large were pushing along in my blood" (VI, 752). He believes he cannot live much longer, and the next episode finds him in the clinic, to which his mysterious illness has driven him.

However, the two authors make different use of their narrators' sensitivity, even while using very similar devices to convey that quality. For example, when they enter their respective cafés, both Ivan and Malte have just come from a walk around the city, in which they have made certain observations about the houses they have passed. Malte is shaken and demoralized by the sight of the naked life revealed in the half-demolished walls. Ivan, on the other hand, has found in the streets of St. Petersburg one of the few bright spots in his day: "All the houses seem suddenly to sparkle, their grey, yellow, and dirty green hues for a moment lose all their gloominess; it is as though it suddenly became clear in one's soul, as though one were startled."[14] Each character is being prepared for the coming intense confrontation in the café; but the tenor and ramifications of the confrontations will turn out to be different for each of them, and thus the psychological preparation of each is different as well. Dostoevsky confronts his hypersensitive narrator with the two unexpected deaths (of the dog and his master) so as to further the development, not of his main character, but of his plot. Having ascertained the old man's name and address, Ivan proceeds to move into his vacated flat, and thence to become entangled with his family, enemies, and fate. These entanglements constitute the bulk of the novel's action, and grow out of the chance encounter in the café. As we have seen, Rilke makes the encounter into a metaphysical crisis for Malte, one which leads him further along his destined path of *Ent-Ichung*.

The other Russian source for the visions of death in *Malte Laurids Brigge*—and I use the term "source" in its broadest sense—was Leo Tolstoy: his personality and his life, and among his works, *The Death of Ivan Ilich* in particular. We have seen the emotional importance of Tolstoy for Rilke. A central event of each of his journeys to Russia was a visit to the aging, eccentric writer, whom he regarded as the "eternal Russian."[15]

It is not known exactly how much of Tolstoy's other work Rilke had read, but there are references which indicate a long-term acquaintance. According to Ingeborg Schnack, Rilke was already reading Tolstoy while at the commercial school in Linz in 1891. She also quotes a letter from him to Leonid Pasternak in February 1900, in which he remarks, "What a joy it is to read Tolstoy's prose in the original."[16] Brutzer asserts that "already as a young man Rilke got acquainted with Tolstoy from his books. Tolstoy was fashionable at the time."[17] She declares that the first thing by Tolstoy Rilke had read in Russian was *The Cossacks,* and cites as works on Rilke's personal book list Tolstoy's essays "Thoughts about God" and "Slavery of Our Time," and the novel *Resurrection.*[18] In his diary for 7 April 1900, Rilke notes: "I'm currently reading *War and Peace.* I'm in the first volume, and my greatest sympathy belongs to Prince Andrey. I have marked all the passages that are valuable to me."[19] And in a letter to Helene Voronina written in July 1899, he remarks, "I have also read a lot of Tolstoy, whose little sketch "Lucerne" particularly impressed me."[20]

Yet in answering a questionnaire sent him by Hermann Pongs in 1924, Rilke declared quite plainly that, as regarded Tolstoy, "it would be false to ascribe an influence on my works of that time to my visits to him; ultimately he only corroborated for me the discovery of Russia, which was decisive for me."[21] In the same questionnaire, he notes that he had, just before his second journey, acquired a copy of Tolstoy's "What Is Art?" which he calls "a disgraceful and foolish brochure."[22] In his essay "Über Kunst" ("On Art"), Rilke reacted strongly to this document, which as a dedicated poet and an aesthete he was bound to regard as an aberration and a betrayal.

Despite the sparseness of information about his reading, and his assertion to Pongs that Tolstoy had left no mark on his works, there is abundant evidence to the contrary. In one of the poems of the *Stunden-Buch,* for example, there is an obvious echo of Tolstoy's story "Yardstick," which Rilke recommended to Lotte Hepner in 1915. The first person narrator of much of the story is a horse that develops a theory about why human beings are the way they are. He is particularly puzzled and dismayed by their habit of referring to things as "mine."

> At that time I could not at all understand what it meant that *I* could be called the property of a man. The words "my horse" applied to me, a living horse, seemed to me as strange as the words: my earth, my air, my water.[23]

He decides that humans attach very great importance both to words and to possessions. Among the words they value most are "my, mine, which they use for various objects and creatures, even for land, people, and horses." Later he concludes that the source of this peculiar habit is "the lowly and bestial human instinct which they call the . . . right of private property."[24]

Rilke often expressed dismay at the arrogance of human beings toward each other and toward the objects of the physical world. These feelings were eventually to find expression in two of his principal motifs: the emphasis on the inner nature of the "things," and the philosophy of "possessionless love," which involved the total release of the beloved from any sort of possessive relationship. In a poem in part two of the *Stunden-Buch,* the monk reassures God that the latter cannot be captured, held, or possessed, despite men's habit of calling everything "mine."

> Du musst nicht bangen, Gott. Sie sagen: *mein*
> zu allen Dingen, die geduldig sind.
> Sie sind wie Wind, der an die Zweige streift
> und sagt: *mein* Baum.
> So sagen sie: mein Leben, meine Frau,
> mein Hund, mein Kind, und wissen doch genau,
> dass alles: Leben, Frau und Hund und Kind
> fremde Gebilde sind, daran sie blind
> mit ihren ausgestreckten Händen stossen.
> (I, 337–38)

[You need not fear, God. They say "mine" to all things that are patient. They are like wind that brushes the branches and says: my tree. Thus they say: my life, my wife, my dog, my child; and yet they know quite well that all this—life, wife and dog and child—are alien creatures with which they blindly collide with their outstretched hands.]

One senses a close kinship between the attitudes of the two protagonists, with the distinction that, though the monk recognizes man's propensity for claiming possession, he finds it ultimately irrelevant to the things thus claimed: "You need not fear, God." The horse, like God in the poem, is appalled and a little frightened. Rilke's treatment of Tolstoy's motif occurs on a different level from the original, but the moral attitude is the same. Rilke presents neither allegory nor social commentary, but a declaration of independence on the metaphysical plane.[25]

One of the most important sources for our knowledge of Rilke's thoughts on Tolstoy is the letter to Lotte Hepner mentioned earlier. There Rilke characterized Tolstoy as a man whose life was permeated "by a finely distributed death, [like] a strange spice within the strong flavor of life,"[26] a man who was horrified at the realization of "pure death," so that his whole relationship to it was suddenly transformed into "a grandly pervading fear."[27] These statements are very revealing of Rilke's perception of Tolstoy, and of the latter's importance for his thought. There are many possible sources for his vision of Tolstoy as a man obsessed by death. Lou had depicted him as such in her essay on Tolstoy; and certainly Tolstoy's works are full of significant encounters with it. Rilke also knew Birukov's edition of Tolstoy's memoirs and correspondence, *Vie et Oeuvre,*[28] and thus he knew of the network of deaths which crisscrossed Tolstoy's long life. In addition to the deaths of many relatives, Tolstoy had experienced in 1869 a personal crisis. It began as a sort of nightmare of death which befell him while he was staying at a rural inn.[29] The experience he underwent—a first realization of death as a personally inescapable reality—was not, certainly, unique to him. But this realization combined with many other experiences to color his thought and writing to a great degree, and to play a role in his ultimate about-face: his abandonment of both art and orthodox Christianity, and in their place, the development of his own version of salvation via poverty, service, love, and the renunciation of a traditional life "in society."

Lotte Hepner in 1915 was apparently embarking on a study of the nature of death. It is in this context that Rilke recommends to her that she read "much by Tolstoy—the two volumes 'Steps of Life,' *The Cossacks*, 'Polikushka,' 'Yardstick,' 'Three Deaths.' "[30] He also mentions "Work for the Night Is Coming" and "Master and Man." There are, says Rilke, "a few significant people who have pondered about death purely, quietly, and nobly. First of all, one: Tolstoy. There is a tale by him which is called *The Death of Ivan Ilich*."[31] It is understandable that Rilke should have been impressed by the story. It is a powerful, precise recounting of a man's struggle toward the final acceptance of his own mortality. Here we find some of the elements which are central to Rilke's portrayal of death in *Malte Laurids Brigge:* death as a process both of alienation and of insight; and a social background which serves as a foil and a commentary to a spiritual struggle. The tale shows the growing pain, isolation, terror, and eventual spiritual clarification of a succesful man who must face the apparent absurdity and unfairness of dying, after a life spent observing all the social conventions and acquiring petty social prizes. Tolstoy places this process of enlightenment against a social background that is sharply observed and cruelly portrayed. Ivan Ilich's family and friends are seen as indifferent, tasteless, selfish, and impatient. He is aided through the crisis only by the kind and healthy peasant Gerasim, whose attitude toward death is matter-of-fact and compassionate, and who has no part in the uncomfortable lies perpetuated by everyone else.

Ivan Ilich, before he dies, makes several important discoveries and decisions. After a great struggle, he recognizes that the life he had lived was neither so exemplary nor so desirable as he had always believed. He has experienced honesty at the hands of Gerasim, and discovers within himself pity for his wife and son, where before he had only longed for pity for himself. Now he finds the strength to act, that is, "to release them and deliver himself from these sufferings."[32] Tolstoy's growing scorn for smug materialism is expressed in Ivan's progress, and his ideal of selfless service appears in Gerasim's cheerful, simple kindness and in Ivan's more drastic resolve to relinquish his hold on life itself in order to spare his family any further sorrow or unpleasantness. Having made this decision, Ivan discovers that neither his fear of dying nor death itself exists any longer. What is important is not dying one's own death, but rather comprehending and taking responsibility for one's own life.

Both attitudes and details from the story found their way into *Malte Laurids Brigge,* often with significant modifications. Ivan's dying is seen by those around him as a tedious, unseemly business. Similarly, the death of Malte's mother is a long-drawn-out process which is regarded with distaste by her family. The death in the crémerie, with its heavy debt to Dostoevsky, also contains an element taken from Ivan's ordeal. Ivan, gradually succumbing to terror when confronted with the truth that he is dying, feels that there is a "terrible, fearful, and unheard-of thing . . . taking place within him, incessantly sucking at him and irresistibly drawing him away."[33] Malte sees in the face of his neighbor in the café "horror at something that was happening inside him. . . . Yes, he knew that he was withdrawing from everything" (VI, 755). In both instances there is an awful knowledge of an internal process whose end result will be separation from other men and from one's familiar reality. Death is perceived here as a "going away," a departure that is made horrible by its having to be undertaken alone.

Except for the peasant Gerasim, Ivan is alone in his admission that he is not just suffering from a temporary indisposition, but is really dying. The family, servants, doctors, and visitors all continue to play their roles, which require constant dissimulation. Ivan is so outraged at their pitiless falsity that he longs to cry out, "Stop lying! You know and I know that I am dying."[34] Similarly, Malte's mother had told him of the girl Ingeborg, who was known to be dying, but "we all went around and concealed it; then she sat up in bed one day and murmured, 'You needn't make such an effort, we all know it, and I can reassure you, it is good the way it's happening' " (VI, 787). The tones of the anecdotes obviously differ greatly. Ivan is suffering not only great physical agony, but an even worse mental anguish at being isolated from everyone around him through their lies and false sense of propriety. An essential part of Ivan's story is his gradual coming to terms with his past and with the shallowness and hypocrisy of his whole society. Ingeborg, like Ivan Ilich, is more honest than those around her, who hide the truth of death from her and each other. But her tone in speaking the truth is gentle and reassuring, and seems to arise, not from anger or isolation, but from a desire for communion and peace.

The different treatment of the two episodes arises, I believe, from the very different characters involved, and the way in which the previous life of each is envisioned. Ingeborg had always been a source of joy for her family; Ivan and his wife had quarreled almost constantly, and his relations with his colleagues and acquaintances had been based almost solely on propriety and good form. These differences are consistently maintained in the depiction of their dying attitudes. But for all the difference in characterization, there are important parallels: the dishonesty of the survivors, the desire of the dying person to face and speak out the truth, and even their ultimate attitudes toward their families. For Ivan too arrives at a final peace, as he realizes that his duty is to die and release his loved ones from their anguish.

There is another episode in *Malte Laurids Brigge* which forms a more significant parallel to the story of Ivan Ilich, and in which it is also possible to discern some major differences in Rilke's treatment of death. This is the episode of the death of Malte's paternal grandfather, the Chamberlain Christoph Detlev Brigge, at Ulsgaard. The chamberlain is dying of dropsy. In his last weeks, he orders his servants each day to carry him from one room to another, and can find rest only in the delicate chamber where his mother had died. Each night, his screams penetrate beyond the walls of the ancestral home, reaching all the way to the village, where they waken the peasants, frighten pregnant women, and cause cattle to miscarry. The exhausted, despairing villagers long for Christoph Detlev's death; but this death, personified as an imperious summer visitor to Ulsgaard, won't be hurried; it "had come for ten weeks, and it stayed the full time" (VI, 700).

The first and most obvious similarity to Ivan Ilich's death is the protracted screaming, which penetrates and upsets the lives of those around the dying men. Ivan's widow relates how "he screamed unceasingly, not in his last minutes, but for hours. For three days he screamed incessantly. It was unendurable. . . . You could hear him three rooms off."[35] A second parallel is the unspoken reaction of other people to death. Ivan becomes aware that everyone is waiting for him "at last to release the living from the restraints caused by his presence and to release himself from his sufferings."[36] The servants at Ulsgaard, peeking in at the chamberlain lying in the dusk, and knowing that the screams will soon begin again, "wished that that weren't anything but a large suit, over a spoiled thing" (VI, 718). And the villagers who loved and pitied him begin to pray for his death.

The treatment of the similar stories is different in several important ways, including tone and style. Whereas Tolstoy's is a masterpiece of psychological observation and realistic detail, Rilke's has about it a mythic quality. Christoph Detlev's dying takes on the timelessness and horror of a surrealist nightmare. Ivan's screams can be heard "three rooms off," but Chamberlain Brigge's voice travels seemingly superhuman distances, distressing the whole region with its force. (There may be in this voice an echo of the dragon in the *Slovo*, who forces whole regions into its cry, or of Solovey-Razboynik, who subjugated the Forest of Bryn with his shrieking.) Tolstoy is primarily concerned with his protagonist's painful journey from unselfconscious philistinism to absolute honesty and self-sacrifice.

Rilke's protagonist is never seen from his own point of view, and seems unaware of anything but his pain. Rather, it is his *death* which becomes the focus—death as a person in its own right. This death takes over the old man's body and the whole of Ulsgaard. It is his voice that tyrannizes the village for ten weeks: "Christoph Detlev's death had lived on Ulsgaard for many, many days now . . . and during that time he was more of a lord than Christoph Detlev had ever been; he was like a king whom they call the Terrible, later and forever" (VI, 720).[37] Ivan Ilich must learn not to cling to his life, which was in any case false and wrongly lived almost from the very beginning. For Christoph Detlev, and for Malte, who tells his story, death itself is the important thing. The villagers react to the death as to an elemental event: awakened by the screams, they huddle around a lamp "as during a storm" (VI, 718). Like the fulfillment of a curse, or the denouement of a legend, Christoph Detlev's death battles with the very forces of life throughout the entire village. Pregnant women are locked away in the farthest rooms for protection from the uncanny contagion, but can still hear the screams and prefer to join the others in their fearful vigil. The cows whose time had come were "helpless and closed," and the villagers "tore the dead fruit from one along with all her entrails, when it simply wouldn't come" (VI, 719).

Even the nature of the respective diseases reflects the different intention of the two portrayals. Ivan Ilich, who apparently died of cancer of the abdomen,[38] shrivels and wastes away. In a parallel process, he is divested of his roles as magistrate, husband, father, bridge partner, host—losing all his former authority as he is more and more reduced to his own inescapable company, and to the inner struggle which cannot be shared. But it is precisely through this reduction, this jettisoning of conventional externals, that Ivan Ilich is forced to face himself and fight his way through to an individual insight and final peace. Tolstoy's purpose is a moral one, and he uses Ivan's disease as a symbol for a social and metaphysical process. Christoph Detlev suffers from dropsy. *His* body becomes swollen, massive, and ungainly, and in his death he becomes far more imperious and demanding than he had ever been in life. He threatens even to burst the physical bounds of his surroundings: "The long, old manor was too small for this death; it seemed as if they would have to build on wings, for the body of the chamberlain became ever larger" (VI, 715). Finally, Rilke makes it clear that he is not concerned with Christoph Detlev, but with death on a much vaster scale, death as the essence of life. "That wasn't the death of just any dropsical man, that was the angry princely death, which the Chamberlain had borne and nourished within him all his life" (VI, 720). But—and this is crucial—this angry death is not seen as an alien thing, an unjust incursion. Even the old man himself, Malte suggests, would have regarded it as proper and necessary: "How would Chamberlain Brigge have looked at anyone who had required of him to die a different death from this one. He died his difficult death" (VI, 720). Unlike Tolstoy, Rilke does not seek to negate death; rather, as he does in many of the deaths in *Malte Laurids Brigge,* he seeks to acknowledge it, to make his characters, especially Malte, accept it as their own, an essentially human and essentially personal event in the process of living.

The episode of Christoph Detlev's death does not culminate in a moral, any more than do the other deaths in the novel. It is important that there are many deaths; in a sense this diffuses the impact, since our sympathy and horror are not focused on any central character who dies, but on a variety of secondary figures, some not even named. The deaths in the novel are like variations on a theme, functioning for Malte almost as exercises in perceiving and accepting death. Malte is the central character here, and it is not his death but his reaction to the idea of death that Rilke emphasizes.[39] Malte's trial as man and poet involves learning several important lessons: to look at and accept the world as it is; to relive and reify his childhood; to learn how to use his fear. All are related to the problem of death; for death, we are told, is an integral part both of life and of ourselves as individuals, and must be accepted as such. It exists in us already as children, and manifests itself in shadowy prefigurations even then, as "das Grosse." Rilke uses fear here in an unusual way, making it into a potentially positive force, an artistic raw material. By this he means not petty, daily fears nor semiconscious anxieties, but the great personal fear that grows from consciousness. Malte recalls that as a child he was teased and insulted: "That was because I was still bad at fearing. But since then I have learned to fear with the real fear, which only grows when the force which begets it grows also" (VI, 861). It is the awareness of death, his own death, that gives birth to this giant fear. As we have seen in the death of the old man in the crémerie, Malte is appalled both at the man's dawning comprehension of the growing distance between him and the objects of the everyday world, and at his acquiescence to this distance. Malte knows that he himself is still too tied to life, still loves it too much to be able to accept death, as the old man does. Yet he senses that comprehension and acceptance are desirable for his growth as a man and an artist, an idea which he expresses in the unusual image: "Oh, this time I shall be written . . . only a little is lacking, and I could comprehend all this, and approve of it. Just one step, and my profound misery would be joy. But I can't take that step" (VI, 756). Malte's crisis as a poet and his existential confrontation with death merge here in one image. He seeks continually to find himself as a writer, one who perceives and portrays others. Yet part of his ordeal is precisely to learn to accept himself as a man, in a sense perceived and portrayed by forces beyond his will. He must learn to give himself up and be subsumed, "be written" instead of writing.

And as there is a relationship between his art and his death, so too is there a relationship between these and God. The language which Rilke places in Malte's mouth to explain his conception of the great, productive fear is very much like that which he uses in the letter to Hepner to describe the common origins of God and death. We saw in the letter how Rilke delineates the process by which man, put off by the more ferocious aspects of his own nature, had isolated them, and then rejected them in the person of Death. God and Death, who both began as aspects of man himself, were turned into alien, unreachable beings. In the relevant passage in the novel, Malte decides that the great fear that has overtaken him and with which he lives is actually the source of his greatest human strength, of "all our strength, which is still too strong for us" (VI, 862). He goes on to describe in terms very similar to those used in the letter, his conception of the origin of Heaven and Death:

> We have thrust our most valuable thing ["unser Kostbarstes"] from us. . . . Now ages have passed over it, and we have gotten accustomed to less. We don't recognize our property any more, and are horrified by its extreme largeness. Can't that be?
> (VI, 862)

In both cases the main point is that man has created for himself an untenable situation, has made a needless rift in his existence and introduced into it terrors that are groundless. This is not to say that these forces which were isolated and have solidified into awesome entities in themselves are to be taken lightly. They were precisely "unser Kostbarstes," which "one . . . perceived, bore, indeed recognized for the sake of a certain secret relationship and inclusion: one was this, too, only that one didn't know what to do, right off the bat, with this side of one's experience: they were too big, too dangerous, too multifaceted."[40] Here Malte achieves a certain amount of insight into the human condition, and his own; he has taken a step toward liberating himself from his small, formless fears and his artistic paralysis, in his idea of drawing strength from the great fear, and thus winning back himself the awesome powers to which he, as a human being, has a claim. Rilke's advice to Hepner was to pursue the meaning of death as she had already begun to do, on a variety of paths. The implication there, too, is that by doing so, she can regain an invaluable part of herself as a human being. And the bulk of Rilke's suggestions to her in this task focus, as we have seen, on Tolstoy.

Two of the most interesting examples of Tolstoy's presence in Rilke's work are found in the two versions of the final scene of *Malte Laurids*

Brigge, the so-called "Tolstoi-Schluss" ("Tolstoy Conclusion"), which Rilke ultimately omitted from the published version of the book (the two fragments were not published until 1962). These versions, while overlapping in certain details, differ considerably in others.

The first version of the "Tolstoi-Schluss" (VI, 967–71) deals primarily with Tolstoy's religious crisis and his attempt to stamp out his own artistic genius. His name is never mentioned, but from biographical details and from the substance of the fragment, it is clearly Tolstoy who is being depicted. Rilke describes the struggle of Tolstoy, the artist and god-maker, with the "Tempter" ("Versucher"), a somewhat Dostoevskian visitor who comes to Tolstoy and persuades him that it is immoral to bother with the fates of fictional characters, when real people are unable to deal with their own. The writer succumbs, and tried to pour his creative energies into work that is utterly unsuitable for him—"these paltry manual skills" (VI, 967)—such as cobbling. But his genius keeps trying to resurface, and he is oppressed by a vision of death in which the inhabitants of the next life would be embarrassed by his incompleteness, his "rudimentary soul." Before the temptation, Rilke suggests, Tolstoy might have met this fearful warning through his work, his life's project of creating "his secret God" (VI, 968); but now he seems short-circuited into an endless repetition of his own terrors, a vision of his own death, rather than following his correct instincts to fulfill himself by creating God through art. It is significant that in discussing Tolstoy's problem, Rilke returns to the central metaphor of the *Stunden-Buch.*

As a background to this mightly struggle of a great man to suppress himself, we see the inhabitants of the house at Yasnaya Polyana, and in particular one figure, Tatyana Alexandrovna, a mild, just woman who had lived in the house and filled it with her love, and who had, perhaps, foreseen this death-crisis and tried to warn against it. But now she is dead, and Tolstoy is alone with his battle; and he acquiesces, accepting hurriedly and in anxiety "the ready-made God who could be had right away" (VI, 970), rather than summoning the courage to live his own life and create his own difficult God. The fragment ends in the first person voice of Malte, who worriedly hopes that Tolstoy may yet come to his senses and free his art and his true nature again. (Tolstoy was still alive when this was written in 1909; he died in 1910, at the age of 82).

Rilke's attitude toward Tolstoy's uneasy choice of an ascetic moralism over creativity is obviously both sad and disapproving. It is evident that he regarded this dilemma in Tolstoy's life, rather than any single work by the man, as the most important factor for himself and his fictional hero, Malte. It is illuminating to look more closely at the details which he chose to include in this highly symbolic and crucial episode. At one stage in his internal crisis, Tolstoy, brooding on his narrow, diminished existence, is shown reminiscing about his past. He recalls "the boy who had died at thirteen: what for, with what right?" (VI, 968), and "the grim days in Hyères" occur to him, "when his brother Nikolay suddenly changed, gave in and let himself be cared for" (VI, 968). These refer to two related incidents which occurred in France in 1860. Tolstoy's beloved brother Nikolay died of consumption in the French resort town of Hyères—the first personal encounter with death that really touched Leo (he didn't count the deaths he had seen as a soldier, or even the death of another brother, Dmitry, from whom he was totally estranged by temperament). At the time, a thirteen-year-old boy he had met at Hyères also died. Rilke had read of the two events in Tolstoy's memoirs. Together they represented a shock and the beginning of a crisis. Tolstoy had loved but neglected his brother, and felt his death deeply. Nikolay's courage and dignity in his suffering had impressed him; he recounts how the sick man had insisted on dressing himself and in various ways sparing others the sight of his weakness. Finally the illness became too strong, and Nikolay had to call Leo to help him dress—an event which touched Leo and brought him suddenly closer to his brother through the act of serving him in his helplessness. It is this event to which Rilke refers in the fragment. The same episode is found the *The Death of Ivan Ilich,* where it is the peasant Gerasim who gladly helps dress his sick master. The death of the thirteen-year-old boy is like a repetition in a minor key of the shocking, seemingly unfair and unnecessary death of Nikolay. They caused Leo to question the nature of life, the reason for death, the point in trying to live a good life at all. Nikolay had been a good man, and at the moment of death, "he had perceived that swallowing-up of his being in nothingness. And . . . if he could find nothing to hang on to, what will I find? Even less."[41] Tolstoy goes on to declare bitterly, "And the truth which I have acquired during the thirty-two years of my existence is that the situation in which we are placed is horrible."[42] Rilke chose these events out of many possible ones with which he was familiar. They represent a turning-point in Tolstoy's development, his first conscious struggle with the problem of death. He is shown here at the moment of inception of the idea of renunciation and withdrawal which, in *The Death of Ivan Ilich,* Rilke finds good and useful (because turned into art), but which in Tolstoy's own life Rilke rejects as morbid, loveless, and unproductive.

Further, Rilke spends much time on the figure of the loving woman, "whose still existence in her room had been like a protective spirit in the house" (VI, 969). The person referred to was a distant relative of Tolstoy's, Tatyana Alexandrovna Yergolskaya, who was raised as an orphan by Tolstoy's paternal grandparents. She fell in love with Tolstoy's father,

Nikolay; but he was forced by bankruptcy to marry a wealthy, middle-aged woman instead. This woman, who was Tolstoy's mother, died fairly soon after bearing Nikolay five children; after a few years, Nikolay proposed to Tatyana (known to the Tolstoy children as Aunt Toinette). Though she still loved him, she refused his offer. But she placed a note, telling of the offer and her refusal, in a little beaded bag and kept it secret till her death. Nevertheless, she spent the rest of her long life with the family, bringing up the Tolstoy children and providing stability in their lives. Tolstoy had much to say about her in his memoirs, and declares that it was during the long evenings spent in her room that he received "the best of his thoughts, the best movements of his soul."[43] Elsewhere he states that "her principal trait was love."[44] He relates an anecdote in which the gentle, aging woman asked that she be given a different, more humble room so that when she died, she wouldn't "spoil" for future generations the nice room where she had lived. In *Malte Laurids Brigge,* Rilke uses all these events and details in the fragment, putting them together in a way which reproduces the feeling of Tolstoy's memoirs, but also adding an overlay of metaphoric and philosophical meaning which makes the scene echo certain aspects of his novel as a whole. Tatyana emerges not only as an uncommonly devoted and selfless woman in the life of a famous man, but as one of Rilke's "great lovers," "these strong renouncers" (VI, 969), elevated to the novel's pantheon of selfless lovers along with Sappho, Bettina, and Marianna Alcoforado. She is made into something more than human, a "guardian spirit." This good genius watches over the fate of the Tolstoys and of reckless, brilliant, and unstable Leo in particular, and warns him not to suppress what is best in himself.

Thus we find in the first fragment, couched in actual events from Tolstoy's life, the Rilkean themes of death, fear, selfless love, and artistic self-fulfillment, all of which are central to *Malte Laurids Brigge*. Tolstoy's life seems almost to have offered a ready-made vehicle for a Rilkean parable. But the first fragment was superseded by a second (VI, 971–78) which approaches Tolstoy's struggle with a vastly different focus and framework. It begins as a first person narrative, as Malte recalls his own visit to Tolstoy at Yasnaya Polyana. Aside from the fact that we know he had "St. Petersburg neighbors," this is the only indication that Malte had ever been to Russia—and this inconsistency of plot may indeed have been part of the reason that the fragment was later rejected.

The second fragment can be divided roughly into four segments. The first, which shows Malte traveling through the Russian countryside and onto the estate, to be met at the door by the old man himself, closely resembles Rilke's account of his own visit to Yasnaya Polyana in May 1900. The second part shows Malte's grudging fascination with a crudely powerful portrait of a nun in Tolstoy's dining room; this detail likewise appears in Rilke's reminiscences. The third segment finally arrives at Tolstoy's inner struggle, which was the main point of the first fragment. The fourth comprises a slightly reduced and altered version of the Tatyana episode.

That the "factual" account of Rilke's visit to Yasnaya Polyana in 1900 constitutes something of a problem has been noted by previous critics. There are at least six versions of what happened that May morning, some differing only slightly, others substantially, from one another.[45] Rilke and Lou had arrived, uninvited and unannounced, in the midst of one of Tolstoy's famous rows with his wife, and found themselves, as E. M. Butler puts it, "barely granted admittance, herded up the stairs, shooed out of doors, scolded like two children, and banished into a waiting-room."[46] After a long, nervous wait, they were invited to accompany Tolstoy on a walk in the woods. He did not even remember them from their visit in Moscow the previous year. This rather disappointing, not to say abortive, pilgrimage was portrayed by Rilke a number of times over the years. The versions include a letter from Rilke to Sophie Schill, dated 20 May 1900;[47] a diary entry, apparently a draft of a letter to Lou, dated 15 September 1900;[48] an unpublished letter to Suvorin, dated 5 March 1902;[49] Maurice Betz's account of an oral description by Rilke in 1925;[50] and Charles Du Bos's description of a conversation with Rilke, also in 1925.[51] For comparison, there is Lou's account of the incident in her book *Lebensrückblick,* published in 1951.[52] In a sense, the version in the second *Malte Laurids Brigge* fragment constitutes still another.

Rilke portrays the visit most positively in the two 1900 versions. The second *Malte Laurids Brigge* fragment bears great resemblance to these. But even the earliest versions show an awareness of audience and display certain key differences. In the letter to Schill from Tula, written only a few days after the visit, Rilke was full of both enthusiasm and respect, and doubtless also of a desire to give a positive account to the person who had functioned almost as a Russian chamber of commerce, sending him books and pamphlets, taking him to meetings, arranging his contact with Drozhzhin. The occasion of a second description of the event was a letter to Lou, in response to her report that Tolstoy had fallen gravely ill. Rilke, musing that perhaps they really had said farewell to him, launches immediately into a reminiscence of their visit. This description is more dramatic than the first, the rhythm more rash. In the letter to Schill, the huts of Yasnaya Polyana had huddled "like a herd"[53] in a field of ubiquitous grey. For Lou, Rilke evokes Gogol and Pushkin, and the Russian landscape, and remembers ringing bells, galloping horses, and the "startled village."[54] For Schill, Rilke and Lou had dismounted from the carriage at the gates and approached the estate "quietly like pilgrims."⁵⁵ For Lou, Rilke recalls their trepidation at the thought of the meeting before them, their desire (like children who know they must do something, but wish they could get out of it) not to have to go on to "the old man to whom all this is leading."⁵⁶

The second "Tolstoi-Schluss" begins on a significantly introspective note, as Malte asks, "Why all at once does that strange May morning occur to me? Should I understand it now, after so many years?" (VI, 971). The question could as easily be that of Rilke to himself, asked nine years after the episode which was so upsetting to him, and which he continued to retell for so long. That Malte suddenly asks it is certainly startling; but once we accept the fact that he has apparently visited Tolstoy in Russia, it is not surprising that his attitude is inner-oriented and analytic. We know already that Malte uses all his experiences as a means of introspection. There was, apparently, something in the visit which evaded understanding, something he has been pondering more or less consciously ever since. Thus a certain tension is set up by these opening lines; we await an explanation.

The fragment then passes on to Malte's memories of the journey in an "adventurous *telega*" (VI, 971) through the village, now barely mentioned, to the familiar gates. But this description of the journey has something exceedingly strange, something Gogolian and dreamlike about it that distinguishes it from the two more or less factual accounts, and that places it in the ambiguous realm of fantasy (not just of fiction, but of unreal adventure only imagined by a fictional character). One senses that perhaps Malte never was in Russia at all. The trip is characterized by an odd rhythm of stops and starts, rushing and dawdling, all without any obvious reason. Malte recalls that he didn't understand "why it [the *telega*] sometimes drove so frantically fast and suddenly, without transition, quite slowly" (VI, 971). The mood is reminiscent of the romantic type of magical or bewitched journey, such as that which the "Taugenichts" experiences on his way to the mysterious castle.⁵⁷ At times Malte has the leisure to notice the individual forget-me-nots on the hillsides, "then again it was as if, with the wind of our haste, we tossed aside the feeble huts which came up close to the path, and finally, just as unexpectedly, the ride became gentle" (VI, 971). He arrives at the gates almost before he knows it, as if in a fairy tale, and demands to be left there. Like the visitors in the letter to Lou, Malte feels the need of quiet, and a sense of hesitation, awe; he stalls as long as he can, even leaving the path to find out what kind of plants are growing in the woods. But Malte, too, inevitably arrives at the very door to his adventure.

The initial confrontation with Tolstoy is different in all three versions. For Schill, Rilke presents Tolstoy as a fatherly old man whose eyes bestow a blessing on the strangers. For Lou, who knew better, Rilke emphasizes homely or ironic details—a friendly dog, and the glass door inadvertently slammed in Rilke's face by the old count, who evidently thought Lou was by herself. Malte's description of the meeting is wholly subjective; that is, we are presented in detail, not with what happened to him, but with his perceptions of the old man. He sees Tolstoy as having grown visibly older (implying that he has seen him before, and thereby strengthening the biographical parallel with Rilke). He sees in his face the traces of "sicknesses . . . thoughts of death . . . sleepless nights" (VI, 973), thus preparing the way for a discussion, as in the first fragment, of Tolstoy's moral crisis. The old man emerges in Malte's description as a slightly grotesque and elemental figure, almost like one of the Slavic wood spirits, the *lešy,* or like Vrubel's painting of the god Pan. His eyes "have become too wide," his brows froth up "like anger." His nose gives the impression of "unusual mass," his gaze is like "white spotlights," and his long beard contains "a great power" (VI, 973). This image is far removed from the dissimulated grandfatherly Tolstoy of the Schill letter—small, bent, old, with a "shadowless eye."[58] Malte's Tolstoy is in fact closer to the figure described to Du Bos in 1925, with his "violent eye" of "an indomitable sensuality."[59] Yet Malte's memory also calls forth a bizarrely contrasting image of the back of Tolstoy's aged head, as he led Malte up the stairs; he recalls the delicate curls of touchingly shy "indoor hair" (*Stubenhaar*) behind his ears. Tolstoy the wood demon, the indomitable; and Tolstoy, a tame little old man—this jarring shift of perception calls up in Malte himself a strong reaction: "Never again did I experience in such simultaneity pity and terror" ("Mitleid und Furcht" [VI, 973]). Pity and terror: it is certainly not by accident that Rilke chose terms which evoke the essence of classical tragedy. For in the figure of Tolstoy, Malte experiences both; and the character of Tolstoy is seen, in both of the fragments, as a tragic one, rent by a tragic flaw, a noble figure in the process of destroying himself. Later in the second fragment, Malte declares that Tolstoy's mad actions arise from pride, and he continues, "He didn't notice how much impatience and vanity were there, that he tore the love out of his work so as to show it purely, and do violence to everyone with it" (VI, 976).

In each of the three acounts, the next section after the meeting with Tolstoy is a scene in an upstairs room where Lou and Rilke, or Malte, are taken to await the count's return. In the Schill letter, this section is very brief, relating only that they spent the time with Tolstoy's oldest son. In the letter to Lou, Rilke recalls the two hours spent drinking coffee and strolling with Leo Lvovich, amidst long embarrassed silences. Rilke had examined several of the family portraits hanging in the upstairs room, one of them of a nun. Rilke's attitude in the letter is objective, knowledgeable; he mentions the era of the portrait ("from the time of Alexey Mikhailovich"),[60] the iconographic style, the resemblance to the strictly traditional icon figures of Saint Sophia. Only when he gets to the figure's hands does he abandon the objective tone. He sees in the hands, too large for the figure and too realistic for the traditional style, a sign of the artistic individuality of the painter breaking through. The hands are out of proportion, earthy, as if the saint now carried them as a burden, and could bear with them a very large prayer.

Malte, too, becomes engrossed in the picture of a nun, at first with an ulterior motive. He senses that, in his relation to Tolstoy, it is somehow "too late," that there is something he must try to forget or suppress. So while he waits, he wanders along the row of portraits, trying to distract himself. The picture of the nun takes him by surprise, for it really interests him. The description of the figure here is more visual, more narrative, and less specific in its historical references than in the letter. The painting is not "obviously painted by an icon painter,"[61] but merely "obviously by a Russian hand" (VI, 974). It is no longer from the era of Alexey Mikhailovich, but "toward the end of the seventeenth century" (VI, 974). But when he comes to the hands, Malte's description becomes much more detailed and involved than does Rilke's in the letter. Their anomalous size and individuality is "a miracle" (VI, 974). The anonymous painter has suddenly become "the simple serf painter," who dared to take the reality of those hands seriously and portray them as they were. Whereas the account of the painting in the letter remains rather cool and aloof, it is used in the fragment as a metaphor and a transition to the crucial subject, Tolstoy's betrayal of his artistic genius. Malte now realizes that at the time, he had thought he was merely covering his embarrassment by staring at this picture of an unknown abbess. Now for the first time he admits (and here we return to the opening idea of the fragment, which promised a revelation) that the painting had real significance for him in its contrast to the spirit of the house in which it hung. The painter, humble though he may have been, had followed the dictates of his meager genius, had dared to create, and in those hands was "the decisive, the thrilling experience of the painter . . . who became aware of the world, who tried his hand at it for the first time with all the happiness and all the affliction of his being" (VI, 975). And Malte compares him with Tolstoy: "Here someone, whose heart had opened to the glory of a pair of hands, had spent his many years in trying to deny himself" (VI, 975). Malte goes on to a discussion of Tolstoy's struggle, similar to that in the first fragment, but more personal and more accusing. The incorporeal Tempter of the first fragment is gone, and in his place we see Tolstoy pacing in deathly terror the mundane floors of the very rooms where Malte walks in memory. Rilke then uses again the scenes from Hyères and Tolstoy's vision of a wasted life.

The final portion of the fragment focuses on Tatyana, whose love is this time flatly declared to have been in vain. The scenes from her life are evoked in a series of questions, many of which are phrased negatively (with *nicht*), as if to call into doubt her very existence, or perhaps to remind Tolstoy that she had existed and chastise him for ignoring, misunderstanding, and thus negating her. This sense of misunderstanding is strongly underlined at the end of the fragment. Here Tolstoy finds and reads the secret note in the little beaded bag, and instead of grasping the greatness of her love, which had allowed her to reject her own deepest wishes and yet remain near her lost lover and sacrifice her life for his children, he "almost condemned her. He accused her of having been able to love only for his father's sake" (VI, 978). Rilke based even this harsh detail on fact; Tolstoy in his memoirs says of Tatyana's love, "I must say to my regret that it was love for a single man, for my father. . . . One sensed that in us she loved only him."[62] In the fragment, he does not understand what she is telling him by allowing the note to fall into his hands: that she herself has fulfilled *her* essential task, "her inner work," by caring for the children as she promised Nikolay and herself she would do.

Rilke suggested earlier that Tolstoy's struggle to mutilate and destroy the love and art in his life was merely a distorted form of vanity, which in itself just calls more attention to him. A truer humility might have led Tolstoy to succumb quietly to the gift within himself, like Michelangelo in the *Geschichten*, to follow its dictates and suppress instead the stubborn rebellious will to re-form his life: "Despotically, he had disposed of his life, and was aware of himself, and had desired otherwise" (VI, 975). The values implied in these accusations echo Rilke's general ideal view of Russia and the Russians: Tolstoy is not humble (and even a giant can be humble in accepting his greatness—God himself appears in the *Stunden-Buch* as a peasant); he does not accept the unique gift of his talent, but tries, rather, to deny the powerful inner force and make himself into something inappropriate and inferior. In so doing he is, in fact, ironically committing the sin of blind pride.

We have before us the two Tolstoy fragments—undeniably stemming from Rilke's personal experiences and his metaphysical quarrel with Tolstoy. But the fact remains that Rilke, having once written them, did not include either in the novel.[63] Why, then, did he write them in the first place—that is, why were they planned as a culmination of Malte's odyssey, how were they intended to continue, if not complete, Malte's tale—and secondly, why were they left out? These questions must ultimately remain unanswered; I can but suggest some partial answers. We have seen that the two fragments contain several themes and figures clearly connected with the novel: a great and generous lover following in the footsteps of the historical women Malte so admires; a central concern with death and the fear of it; the necessity, thwarted here, of turning fear and the other experiences of life into art. Thematically and formally, the fragments might easily have fitted into this work, which is in any case made up of fragments.

The first "Tolstoi-Schluss" ends on a note of anxiety. Malte has imagined that somewhere in the neglected park there is a monument to the day when Tolstoy gave himself back to nature, in all the love and power of his art: "So there might still be the certainty that he now existed" (VI, 971). But Malte's hopeful imagining is a mirage, for his next thought envisions Tolstoy as truly lost, having squandered and cheapened his talents on an easy God, and disappearing "in undated destiny" (VI, 971).

The second fragment likewise ends on a note of despair, with the scene of Tolstoy reading and rejecting his aunt's secret. The final line is: "He no longer understood it" (VI, 978). A thing which in its purity and truth he might once have grasped is now beyond him. Tatyana is portrayed as someone who loves strongly, purely—so much so, that all else, including her own possessions, becomes unreal, unnecessary: "Her worthless things were collected modestly; it looked as though she were leaving them behind only because she didn't want to think that anything belonged to her" (VI, 969). Tolstoy is far from comprehending such a love; for him, it must have had an ulterior motive, a concrete and narrow object, to give it such strength. By the end of the novel, Malte is much farther along in his comprehension of the nature of love than this Tolstoy can possibly be.

Both fragments focus, in varying degrees, on the struggle of Tolstoy between, on the one hand, his true self, which is all-encompassing, observant, and creative, and which includes in its great passions a great productive fear; and on the other, a closing-in of walls, limits, petty and confused doubts, a misguided pride, and an obsession with conscience that throttles art. Malte's struggle has been to see and accept reality, including the reality in his past and in himself, and to arrive at a state in which his writing can be pure, accurate, generous to the world it portrays. To Malte, whom we meet already in the process of consciously trying to change and to see, Tolstoy must have seemed a familiar figure from his own past; but he also represents failure and betrayal—all the more so because he had so much to betray.

176

· E I G H T ·

SUBTLE ECHOES:
THE MIDDLE AND LATE POEMS

In the preceding chapters we have seen that Rilke frequently chose works of Russian literature or events in Russian history as the raw material for his own work, reflecting and transforming them. In addition he gravitated toward certain qualities which he perceived to be typically Russian. He selected these qualities from the numerous disparate and often contradictory ones observable in Russian life and literature, and utilized them in his art. They were also present in his mind as he developed a personal modus vivendi, working out his problematic relationships to people, the physical world, and God. These two types of Russian influence, the specific and the thematic, are most overt in the works begun before about 1904.

In the poems begun after this time, the Russian reflexes become fewer. Russian references in the letters tend to have a nostalgic tone, as when he recalls an event or scene from his travels or his reading, or shares with Lou or the Pasternaks his continued love and concern for Russia. But the Russian influence is not dead, nor is it random or insignificant when it does appear. Indeed, those elements that initially attracted him—humility, patience, the many-faced Russian God—continue to be strongly in evidence in these later works.

One of Rilke's great problems throughout his life was the conflict between his human ties, whether to parents, wife and child, or friends, and his powerful need for the solitude in which to write. He suffered under the tensions thus caused, but almost inevitably opted for solitude, for his calling. It was primarily for this reason that his life as husband and father was doomed almost from the start. In 1906 the marriage was still sufficiently intact so that Rilke, Clara, and their daughter, Ruth, spent their vacation together, traveling and visiting friends. But Rilke's letters show how worried he was about the loss of time implicit in such travels; and even before the trip began, we find him firmly setting forth his insistence on privacy. In a letter to Clara from 29 June 1906, he expresses his determination to continue working during the vacation.[1] This determination is couched in terms that evoke his perception of Russia, and reveal how seriously and deeply he had absorbed the "Russian" virtue of patience as a necessity for his work.

> However, we'll see what comes of my unconditional decision to lock myself in for such and such a time each day, wherever and under whatever conditions . . . for the sake of my work: whether it really comes or whether I just make the appropriate gestures, unfulfilled. Haven't I known ever since Russia, with such great conviction, that the prayer and its time and its reverent gesture, passed on unabridged, was the necessary condition for God and for his return to this one or that, who hardly expected it any longer, and just knelt down and stood up, and was suddenly full to the brim? Thus will I kneel down and stand up again, daily, alone in my room, and will keep sacred whatever happens to me there: even his not having come, even the disappointment, even the abandonment. There is no poverty which would not be fullness, if one took it seriously and worthily and didn't make it into an irritation, and sacrifice it.[2]

We find here a merging of the qualities of patience and humility, unexpectedly yet smoothly united with Rodin's dictum, "toujours travailler," which so impressed Rilke. Rilke hoped desperately to create for himself a discipline that would sustain him, whether in solitude in Paris, or surrounded by family, friends, and patrons. Patience and humility must be supplemented by an unremitting dedication to the gestures of work, the workman's unvarying routine, which, like the gestures of prayer, might by their very form create an atmosphere auspicious for the coming of God, or the miracle of poetic inspiration. Such a combination of faith and hard work formed the backbone of remarkable strength thanks to which Rilke was to survive the long fruitless years between 1912 and 1922.

A few weeks after this letter to Clara, in the middle of July, Rilke wrote a poem which expresses the same ideas. This was "Der Stifter" ("The Founder"), published in *Neue Gedichte* (*New Poems*) in 1907.

> Das war der Auftrag an die Malergilde.
> Vielleicht dass ihm der Heiland nie erschien;
> Vielleicht trat auch kein heiliger Bischof milde
> an seine Seite wie in diesem Bilde
> und legte leise seine Hand auf ihn.
>
> Vielleicht war dieses alles: *so* zu knien
> (so wie es alles ist was wir erfuhren):

zu knien: dass man die eigenen Konturen,
die auswärtswollenden, ganz angespannt
im Herzen hält, wie Pferde in der Hand.

Dass wenn ein Ungeheures geschähe,
das nicht versprochen ist und nieverbrieft,
wir hoffen könnten, dass es uns nicht sähe
und näher käme, ganz in unsre Nähe,
mit sich beschäftigt und in sich vertieft.
                                                          (I, 508)

[That was the commission to the painters' guild. Perhaps the Savior never appeared to him; and perhaps no sainted bishop ever stepped gently to his side as in this picture and laid his hand quietly upon him. Perhaps this was all: *thus* to kneel (just as it is all that we learned): to kneel: so that one held one's own contours, which wish to surge outward, in one's heart, all tensed like horses held in check. That if something colossal happened, which was not promised and never pledged, we could hope that it wouldn't see us and come nearer, right up close to us, preoccupied and engrossed in itself.]

In "Der Stifter," Rilke sets before us one of those medieval paintings in which the artist has placed his patron, perhaps a wealthy and pious nobleman or merchant, within a religious scene. The donor is portrayed kneeling before the Savior, while a bishop lays his hand upon his shoulder. Rilke acknowledges the purely fictive, symbolic nature of the patron's religious experience. But he finds in the man's intensely concentrated kneeling, his listening self-control, the potential for these events. The man doesn't simply kneel; he does so with a conscious effort at subduing his inner "contours," which are likened to strong and unruly horses. The hope contained in this gesture of submission is that a miracle *might* happen. If an "Ungeheures" did occur—that is, if Christ or a saint were to appear—the man could be quiet, humble, unnoticeable enough that the miracle, like some delicate woodland creature, would not be frightened away. His silence, concentration, and readiness for the miracle would allow it to come close to him. Rilke includes himself in this hope, by shifting from the external portrayal of the patron in the first two stanzas to "we" and "us" in the third. It is the same hope, the same determination to be humble and prepared, that he expressed in the letter to Clara. The coming of a miracle to the patron, or of inspiration to the poet, are both unpredictable; neither can be called forth on command. But both are possible, and attainable only through the "Russian" gesture of silent supplication and the conscious suppression of one's internal chaos.

Russia and the motifs associated with it were still on Rilke's mind several months later, in Capri, where he was spending the winter as a guest of one of his patrons. From there he wrote to Leonid Pasternak of his continued warm feeling for Russia, despite time and distance. He can barely speak Russian any more, he writes, "But thinking! Believe me, I often think in Russian." Further on, he says: "Sometimes I feel the lack of a Russian for really profound expression, for great mutual understanding."[3] In the same month, December 1906, Rilke wrote three poems, published later as "Improvisationen aus dem Capreser Winter" ("Improvisations from the Capri Winter" [II, 11–16]), which he designated "something like a new Book of Hours."[4] Like the *Stunden-Buch,* they are prayers addressed to a towering earth-god who lives in many forms: "Gebirge, Gestein, Wildnis, Un-weg: Gott" ("Mountain, stone, wilderness, impasse: God" [II, 11]). As we have seen, the monk in the first part of the *Stunden-Buch* was wrapped up in the discovery of his own creativity, which was aimed at God. In the second and third parts, he turned both more inward, toward a struggle with his instability, and outward, toward the life and death of ordinary suffering mortals. In the three Capri poems, Rilke combines these attitudes; he speaks both as man seeking God, and poet longing for a voice and a direction, a sign. He begs God to make use of him in his own way. Insofar as they are a humble cry to a dark god, the Capri poems are of the same substance as the Russian monk's prayers, and as the hopes expressed in the letter to Clara.

There are a number of poems from this period which focus in various ways on faith, patience, and the individual's relationship to himself, his calling, and his god. Several of these are connected in new and complex ways to Russian motifs and Russian sources. One such poem, "Der Ölbaum-Garten" ("The Olive Grove"), has several complex sets of Russian roots. Written in May or June of 1906, about the same time as the letter to Clara, and just before "Der Stifter," the poem could be seen as an inverted companion piece to the latter. Both were included in the same collection, the first *Neue Gedichte.* Whereas "Der Stifter" concerns itself with the possibility of miracles, that is, the power of the individual, through patient faith, to prepare himself for inspiration, whether divine or poetic, "Der Ölbaum-Garten" is a poem about the loss of faith. And it is couched in the most drastic terms possible, for the person who loses his faith is Jesus Christ.

The poem is based on the story of Christ's vigil in Gethsemane, from Luke 22:39–46; but it is a changed, desanctified version, "a poem . . . which apparently has broken with all biblical tradition."[5] As in the gospel, Christ is seen going up into the olive grove, to wrestle alone with his fate. The evangelist describes how he ultimately submitted to this fate, as hard as it seemed: "Father, if thou be willing, remove this cup from me; nevertheless not my will, but thine, be done" (Luke 22:42). But Rilke's Christ does not submit. He has lost touch with God and is reduced to a lonely, despairing man, overwhelmed by a sense of futility in the face of a task too large for him:

> Ich finde Dich nicht mehr. Ich bin allein.
> Ich bin allein mit aller Menschen Gram,
> den ich durch Dich zu lindern unternahm.
> (I, 493)
>
> [I can find you no more. I am alone. I am alone with the affliction of all men, which I, through you, came to ease.]

The evangelist relates that an angel came to comfort and strengthen Christ in his hour of struggle, a sign of the concern and presence of God even then. Rilke, however, writes,

> Später erzählte man: ein Engel kam—.
> Warum ein Engel? Ach es kam die Nacht
> und blätterte gleichgültig in den Bäumen.
> (I, 493)
>
> [Later they claimed: an angel came. Why an angel? Oh, the night came and leafed indifferently in the trees.]

Christ is abandoned, not only by God, but by the angels and the world of things:

> Denn Engel kommen nicht zu solchen Betern,
> und Nächte werden nicht um solche gross.
> Die Sich-Verlierenden lässt alles los.
> (I, 494)
>
> [For angels do not come to such worshipers and nights to not grow great around them. Those who lose themselves are dropped by everything.]

This demythologizing of Christ is typical of Rilke's attitude toward him, which was always skeptical and often openly hostile. (An exception is in Rilke's discussion or use of icons, where Christ, Mary, the saints, and God all seem to merge in a large undifferentiated divine essence.) One critic calls Rilke's usual attitude an "almost malicious hostility to Christ and Christianity."[6] Another has stated that in Rilke's view, Christ got in the way of a direct relationship between man and God.[7] Christ brings to man a "finished" God, like the "ready-made" one of Tolstoy's compromise—one laden with centuries of completeness and definition. In this way he hinders the delicate creative relationship between man and God which Rilke postulates in the *Stunden-Buch* and after. Thus it is not totally surprising that Rilke should choose to make him the vehicle for a parable about the loss of faith; the poet here exercises his prerogative to alter traditional material, and gives his old enemy an ironic comeuppance.

Rilke also brings to bear once more the motif of the prodigal son. The poem ends:

> Die Sich-Verlierenden lässt alles los,
> und sie sind preisgegeben von den Vätern,
> und ausgeschlossen aus der Mütter Schooss.
> (I, 494)

> [Those who lose themselves are dropped by everything, and they are abandoned by the fathers, and excluded from the mothers' wombs.]

Christ is by implication compared to the Prodigal Son who has also lost himself in losing his goal and the sense of his actions. But whereas the prodigal can go home again, Christ has forfeited his right to parents, past, and identity.

Although fully Rilkean in stance and motifs, the poem does not stand in a literary vacuum. Bernhard Blume demonstrates its kinship to an iconoclastic tradition beginning with the 1796 publication of Jean Paul's "Rede des toten Christus" ("The Speech of the Dead Christ"), and including Nerval's "Le Christ aux Oliviers" and de Vigny's "Le Mont des Oliviers" (both 1844).[8] He also notes the probable influence on the poem, and on Rilke's Christ-image in general, of the writings of Lou, particularly her essay "Jesus der Jude" ("Jesus the Jew") from 1896. In this essay, Lou notes the emphasis of the Jewish religion on earthly fulfillment of prophecy, on the reification, in *this* life, of the word of God. Beginning from this conception of the non-transcendent nature of traditional Judaism, she proceeds to paint a portrait of Jesus as the simple Jewish believer par excellence, the Jew who felt himself one with God. He was confident that God's promise would be fulfilled then and there. Lou writes,

> No doubt about it, that Jesus took quite for granted [the visible fulfillment of God's word], and that he could consider his mission as completed only with political victory. . . . How should he ever believe it possible that God would leave him in the lurch, with his childlike, sacred activity?[9]

He was confident of his success, not as the only son of God, a special divine personage, but as simply a son of God, that is, a Jew. Thus when Jesus on the cross cries out, "My God, why hast thou forsaken me?" it is because he realizes that he has been tricked, that his death is worse than pointless, and that God's dominion on earth is not to come through him, if at all.[10] There is certainly an echo of this profound and utterly human disappointment in Rilke's Christ.

But there are other works, Russian ones, which suggest themselves as sources for details, mood, or attitudes in the poem. These are Ivan Kramskoy's painting *Christ in the Desert,* and the chapter in the *Brothers Karamazov* entitled "The Devil, Ivan's Nightmare." Rilke's liking for

Kramskoy has been noted; and one of the works which he singles out for mention is Kramskoy's *Christ*. In the essay "Moderne russische Kunstbestrebungen," he says, "there is by this painter a Christ, an abandoned meditator, whom his thoughts have pursued into the wilderness" (V, 617). The painting shows Christ seated alone on a boulder, hands tightly clenched, face sad and drawn. The predominant color is grey—the cold, dusty grey of the rocks which fill the entire foreground, the purple-grey of the empty horizon, the pinkish grey of the broad desert sky. Christ's robe itself is a dark bluish grey, gathered around his drooping shoulders as if against the cold of dawn. Turning to the first lines of Rilke's poem, we find that grey also predominates there:

> Er ging hinauf unter dem grauen Laub
> ganz grau und aufgelöst im Ölgelände
> und legte seine Stirne voller Staub
> tief in das Staubigsein der heissen Hände.
> (I, 492–93)

[He went up under the grey foliage all grey and dissolved in the olive grove, and laid his dusty brow deep in the dustiness of his hot hands.]

There are, of course, superficial differences between the painting and the poem: they portray two different episodes in Christ's life—the vigil in the desert and that in the garden—and the painting contains no foliage. We know, however, that Rilke felt free to change and combine the materials he used for his own effects. Paul Böckmann, for example, points out in his discussion of the poem that Rilke's version of the Gethsemane episode is strongly colored by his awareness of still a third scene; the Crucifixion. Rilke writes his Gethsemane poem, according to Böckmann, "in reminiscence of the words on the cross, 'My God, why hast thou forsaken me,' " presenting "a monologue by Jesus . . . that only gives witness to his forsakenness."[11] It is thus not unlikely that the visual details such as the pervading greyness and the profoundly gloomy aspect of Kramskoy's Christ may have found their way into Rilke's version of Christ in the garden.

The other important Russian source for Rilke's poem is the *Brothers Karamazov*. Dostoevsky's god was a Christian one, and his vision of the salvation of Russia and world through love, a Christian ideal; in this, Rilke would not have agreed with him. But there are both major motifs and striking literary devices in the *Brothers Karamazov* which Rilke utilizes in his Gethsemane poem. Dostoevsky, speaking in a letter about the novel, once asserted, "The main question which will pervade all the sections is the same with which I have struggled, consciously and unconsciously, all my life long—the existence of God."[12] Many of the major characters in the novel fall into one of two categories—spokesmen for faith, and its enemies. The two who will concern us here are the philosophical Ivan and his half-brother, the epileptic Smerdyakov—each in his own way a representative of the "enemy" camp.

Each of these figures is portrayed as a deeply Russian character, suffering from the complexity and contradictions inherent in the Russian soul; each harbors a paradoxical attitude toward the existence of God. Smerdyakov is a sneering skeptic, but he is also a kind of mystic. He is once compared by the narrator to a figure in a painting by Kramskoy called *Contemplation*. There, a Russian peasant appears deep in a meditative trance, at a wintry crossroads. The narrator sees Smerdyakov as just such a contemplative, a character who "may suddenly . . . throw away everything and go off to Jerusalem to be saved, or maybe he'll set fire to his native village, and maybe he'll do both."[13] Ivan is portrayed sometimes as an agnostic, and sometimes as an out-and-out atheist. To his father's question, "Is there a God or not? But be serious now!" he answers, "No, there is no God."[14] But in a conversation with the holy Father Zosima, the old monk perceives Ivan's indecision and torment over the question of faith.[15] Again, in a discussion with his brother Alyosha, Ivan emphasizes that it is not God he rejects, but his world, in which evil and brutality reign.[16]

Both Smerdyakov and Ivan tell anecdotes which in their focus on the loss of faith can be connected with Rilke's agnostic and despairing Christ. In a comic masterpiece of sophistry, Smerdyakov argues that a man should be forgiven for renouncing his faith under pain of death. For, he reasons, even by thinking of rejecting Christ, he causes himself to be anathematized; and thus by the time he actually speaks the words renouncing Christ, he is already no longer a Christian, and has nothing to renounce, and therefore nothing to be ashamed of. Ivan expresses himself with equally intricate but more sinister reasoning in his "Legend of the Grand Inquisitor." Here he portrays a church establishment and a cynical philosophy which in the name of Christ have perverted the Christian message, enslaving men in order to make them happy. Faced with Christ himself, who has suddenly returned to earth, the Grand Inquisitor explains that he must burn Christ at the stake, for he is the greatest danger of all to Christianity. At one point in their dialogue, the Inquisitor attempts to persuade Christ that he was wrong in rejecting Satan's temptation to rule via miracle, mystery, and authority. In his exposition, the priest reminds Christ of the time

> the wise and terrible spirit set you on the pinnacle of the temple and said to you, 'If you want to know whether you are the Son of God, throw yourself down, for it is said that angels will support and carry him, and he shall not fall nor hurt himself. And then you'll prove how great is your faith in your

father.' But you, having heard it, rejected the proposal, and resisted, and did not throw yourself down. Oh, of course, you acted as proud and magnificent as a god. . . . Oh, you understood then that, having taken but one step, just a single move toward throwing yourself down, you would immediately be testing God, and would have destroyed all your faith in him, and you would have been smashed on the earth which you came to save.[17]

In Smerdyakov's anecdote the ex-Christian escapes via a technicality, and will receive only the lightest of punishments. In that of the Grand Inquisitor, had the devil's temptation succeeded, his trick—which is a "trick" built into the very structure of faith, in Ivan's view—would have resulted in Christ's ignominious death, and the failure of God's plan.

Despite the difference in tone, the two anecdotes express essentially the same thing. For the cynical Smerdyakov, the question of faith is a game of words. A state of grace is only a state of mind, and it ultimately doesn't matter whether one has it or not. If one believes, one is automatically a Christian, with all that that implies; and if one *doesn't,* one *isn't,* and the whole question is irrelevant. For the honestly struggling Ivan, there is a catch built into the contract of faith in God's word. It is true, so long as you believe it is; but trying to put in into practice will automatically prove you no longer believe, and will remove you from grace. Christ in Ivan's anecdote may have had faith, or, then again, he may simply have been smart enough to recognize the catch and avoid the trap. Rilke's Christ, too, had faith once; but he has somehow lost it, and has been left holding the bag: "I am alone with the afflictions of all men / which I, through you, came to ease, / Thou who art not. O nameless shame!" (I, 493). A critic, discussing the *Brothers Karamazov,* says of Ivan, "Reality escapes the man who has lost the highest reality—God."[18] The same thing has happened to Rilke's Christ. He has been abandoned in his self-abandonment, not only by God but by everything (*alles*). For Rilke the two were synonymous; God was an ever-growing protean divinity, present throughout the physical world. It is consistent with this view that all of the world, all of reality, should have left the faithless one to his fate.

There is a further similarity between the poem and the novel; this is the device of the paradoxical dialogue between a character and an interlocutor in whom he does not believe. In the poem, Christ addresses God as "Der Du nicht bist"—"Thou who art not"—and asks him "warum Du willst, dass ich sagen muss / Du seist, wenn ich Dich selber nicht mehr finde" ("why do you want me to say you exist, when I can't find you any longer myself" [I, 493]). Paul Böckmann, writing of the poem, notes:

> The biblical scene is totally limited to the anguishing situation of the man who is thrown back on himself, but in such a way that the forsaken "I" speaks to a Thou which actually does not exist, indeed, which it denies. . . .

> The man who is losing himself can only make known his anguish by speaking to the Thou which he calls into question.[19]

Christ cannot find God anywhere, even in himself, and he feels trapped in an undertaking accepted under the direction of this very God. His fate is sealed, but the instigator, and the significance, have disappeared.

There are several instances in the *Brothers Karamazov* where a character carries on a similar dialogue. Ivan admits to Alyosha that the Inquisitor does not believe in God, though he speaks at length to Christ and acknowledges his identity, indeed even proposes to kill him precisely because of his divinity. And later Ivan finds himself in such a conversation. Tormented by the dawning realization of his own guilt in his father's death, he imagines that he is visited by the Devil. The Devil wants Ivan to admit his existence, but Ivan believes he is talking to a mere hateful figment of his own imagination, that is, to someone who doesn't properly exist at all. Yet Ivan addresses the Devil directly and at length, only partly aware of the paradox of trying to convince himself *and* his interlocutor that the latter doesn't exist. "Not for one moment do I take you for a reality. . . . You are a lie, you are my illness, you are a phantom. I simply don't know how to destroy you, and I see I must go on suffering for a while."[20]

In talking to Christ, the Grand Inquisitor strives to uphold the empty shell of a faith he no longer holds, but which forms the reason and vehicle for all his actions. Ivan, striving to maintain his sanity and struggling with his guilt, imagines the Devil in order to give himself a foil and a sounding board for his chaotic thoughts. Rilke's Christ, out of long habit, or despair, or lack of anyone else to appeal to, continues to complain to the God he cannot find. All are, in a sense, attempting to perpetuate or recreate a reality which will allow them to continue to play a certain role. The Grand Inquisitor is disconcerted by Christ's response to his long argument—a single forgiving kiss on the lips; and the Inquisitor releases the prisoner, while nevertheless continuing to cling to his vision of his mission on earth. Ivan ends his dialogue, which was at times passionate and violent, by falling seriously ill, and then by confessing his guilt in the murder of his father. Rilke's Christ alone fails utterly; the tone of the rest of the poem is both sad and condemning. But the similarity of his situation and his one-sided, futile conversation, with those of Dostoevsky's characters points to fruitful reading of the Russian work.

Work on the eighty-three poems of the *Neue Gedichte* (*New Poems*) was begun in 1903 and completed in 1907; they appeared in print in December 1907. The one hundred six poems of *Der neuen Gedichte an-*

derer Teil (*The Second Part of the New Poems*) were written between July 1907 and August 1908, and were published in December 1908. These works came at a time in Rilke's career when he was attempting to extirpate the subjective element from his poetry, and to focus on the essence of the poetic object. They are what is generally called *Dinggedichte*—thing poems. Rilke opens each of the two volumes with a poem about Apollo—the first book with "Früher Apollo" ("Early Apollo") and the second with "Archaïscher Torso Apollos" ("Archaic Torso of Apollo"). In them, and in the materials surrounding their creation, we find Rilke addressing once again the relation of art to divinity, a combination of motifs that, as before, draws heavily on his conception of the Russian God of the *Stunden-Buch*.

The following discussion of Rilke's Apollos is admittedly conjectural. But I feel that an excursion into the complicated relationships between Rilke's love for antique art and his views on Russia can shed new light both on the Apollo poems and on the Russian theme.

In a letter to Lou in 1903, Rilke declares that the aspect of antique objects which most attracted him was their anonymity and absoluteness: "that one can contemplate them quite as unknowns; one doesn't know their purpose . . . no unimportant voice interrupts the silence of their collected existence, and their duration is without a backward glance, without fear . . . they *are*. And that is all."[21] This taste for an art which he comprehended as pure, ahistorical, existing for itself alone, would be intensified by Rilke's discovery of the works of Cézanne in 1907. For a number of years this attitude conditioned Rilke's approach to his own work, producing the somewhat cold perfection of the *Dinggedichte*. Yet in the same letter, there are strong indications that antique art was not totally impersonal and ahistorical, even for Rilke, and that it had, in fact, connections in his mind with Russia. Writing from Rome, he remarks, "Yet I think somehow that even now in Rome, face to face with antique objects, I am preparing myself for Russia, and for returning there."[22] But it was, in turn, Russia's peculiar quality of timelessness, of standing outside history, that made this equation possible. In the same letter, Rilke discusses the development of art and of man's perceptions over the centuries:

> Relationships revealed themselves . . . connections were made, and the history of endless races of objects were discernible below human history, like a stratum of slower and quieter developments, which take place deeper, more internally and surely. Of this history, Lou, perhaps the Russian will some day become a part, who . . . as one who becomes and suffers, is descended from the Things and related to them . . . by blood. The waiting nature in the character of the Russian . . . would thus receive a new and certain enlightenment; perhaps the Russian is created to let human history pass by, in order later to join in the harmony of things with his singing heart.[23]

It is with these remarks by Rilke as a background that I suggest reading the second Apollo poem, with its overt emphasis on an object of antiquity.

Archaïscher Torso Apollos

Wir kannten nicht sein unerhörtes Haupt,
darin die Augenäpfel reiften. Aber
sein Torso glüht noch wie ein Kandelaber,
in dem sein Schauen, nur zurückgeschraubt,

sich hält und glänzt. Sonst könnte nicht der Bug
der Brust dich blenden, und im leisen Drehen
der Lenden könnte nicht ein Lächeln gehen
zu jener Mitte, die die Zeugung trug.

Sonst stünde dieser Stein entstellt und kurz
unter der Schultern durchsichtigem Sturz
und flimmerte nicht so wie Raubtierfelle;

und bräche nicht aus allen seinen Rändern
aus wie ein Stern: denn da ist keine Stelle,
die dich nicht sieht. Du musst dein Leben ändern.
(I, 557)

[We did not know his unheard-of head in which his eyes swelled [literally, his eyes' apples ripened], but his torso still glows like a gas lamp in which his gaze, just turned down, persists and gleams. Otherwise the bow of the breast could not blind you, and in the slight turning of the loins a smile could not go toward that center, which bore generation. Otherwise this stone would stand disfigured and short beneath the transparent fall of the shoulders and would not shimmer thus like the hides of beasts of prey; and wouldn't burst all its boundaries like a star; for there is no place that does not see you. You must change your life.]

The poem deals with a work of art and as such, falls into the subject group of poems about *Kunstdinge,* art objects (as opposed to objects of daily life or of nature). Like the things mentioned in the letter to Lou, the statue is so old as to have been purified by time; its purpose is lost, it simply *is.* Men's influence on it, as makers or destroyers, has ceased. The movement is now in the opposite direction, from autonomous object to receptive human being.

The Apollo figure has a direct, urgent effect on the reader/viewer. The figure is only a fragment, yet in its compactness and intensity, it contains great force, as if, as in Rilke's central metaphor, the god's gaze had merely been retracted into his torso, turned down like a flame that still illumines from within. This figure is not simply the god of light; he holds a subdued fire that makes his light both a bursting star and a beast of prey. He is a mixture of beauty and peril, and focuses his bright and ambiguous attention on *us*—"for there is no place that does not see you." The last line comes as a shock, and several interpretations offer themselves. One critic emphasizes the image of Apollo as source of poetic inspiration, and considers that "the god of light, god of poetry, god of ecstasy of the heart, has merged with the ecstatic heart of the poet and is acting directly in the world."[24] Others emphasize the idea of self-creation and entelechy, and consider the message of the last line an admonition to spiritual rebirth. One traces it to a Greek saying, "Man, become essential! Become what you are!"[25] These interpretations rightly focus on the artistic and personal possibilities of the poem, representing in microcosm a theme and a struggle perceptible throughout Rilke's career.

Discussing the two Apollo poems, Hermann Pongs makes the following assertion: "The most astonishing shift which Rilke makes, after having sung the 'dark god' in the *Book of Hours*, is the glorification of light. . . . As an introduction to both books [of the *Neue Gedichte*] Rilke places the figure of Apollo, the god of light, at the same time the god of poetry."[26] I have in the course of this study identified this dark God as an essentially Russian phenomenon. If what Pongs says is true, then by implication the dark, protean God and what he represents—warmth, silence, rootedness, patience, futurity—had been overcome in the *Neue Gedichte,* replaced entirely by the brilliant god of the sun. But Rilke's Apollo is not that simple; let us trace his roots.

Two external impulses can be discerned in Rilke's Apollo: Friedrich Nietzsche and Dostoevsky. Several critics have examined the relation of Rilke to Nietzsche, but the connection which I intend to examine is slightly different from that which concerned them.[27] Erich Heller, referring to an unpublished letter from Rilke to Ellen Key, probably written in the winter of 1903–1904, claims that Rilke "indulges . . . in an eschatological vision of Apollo's ultimate triumph over the chaotic dominion of Dionysus." Heller asserts that in the letter, Rilke uses "almost exactly the same words as Nietzsche's conjuration of the Dionysian Apollo." There, Rilke predicts a time when chaos will "stand with millions of ripe, fine, golden forms . . . a totally fermented and enflamed apollonian structure."[28] The "Dionysian Apollo" to which Heller refers is the result of Nietzsche's long-standing concern with the basic dichotomy of human existence. Nietzsche expressed this dichotomy in terms of the impulses represented and governed by the dark, passionate, chaotic Dionysus, and Apollo, the bright god of intellect, order, and art. For him the two eventually merged into a synthesis of all these qualities—the Dionysian Apollo; Rilke in 1903 was obviously excited by the Nietzschean vision of chaos molded into beautiful forms.

We know that Rilke had read Nietzsche; and he must certainly have been exposed to Lou's opinions on the man and his writings, for she had been Nietzsche's friend in a brief but intense relationship in 1882, had written an important work on him,[29] and had herself absorbed much in their short time together. In Rilke's notes from his reading of Nietzsche's "The Birth of Tragedy" in 1900, we find him making a significant connection between Dionysus and the Russian spirit. In one passage on the nature of the theater, Nietzsche says that a sense of unity is important within a theater audience. The onlookers should share a set of values and a perspective, if they are properly to grasp the message of a play, particularly of a tragedy. Rilke's response to this was that since this is unlikely today, there must be a go-between to interpret the play for the onlookers. He cites the Russian people as ideally suited to this role. Their nearness to their own past and myths represents a cultural unity which would allow them to act as interpreters between play and audience. He envisioned a group of Russian peasants as a sort of Greek chorus, dancing in front of the stage, conveying to the audience the sense of wonder and unity of great drama. In their primal simplicity, they could serve as intermediaries between an audience lacking the essential oneness of vision, and a work of art whose basic requirement is precisely unanimity of world view and impact. By way of evidence, he asks, "Might not the Dionysian element be the moving factor in the *xorovod* of the Russians?" (VI, 1175).[30] And it is but a step from the Russian spirit to Rilke's Russian God. It is true that, being Christian in origin and ritual if not in overall conception, he lacks both the cruelty and the violent sensuality of Dionysus. And though he inspires in the poet—the monk of the *Stunden-Buch*—strong and contradictory emotions, he is not associated with anything like the maenads and their bacchanals. But though Rilke's Russian God is not the same as Dionysus, neither are they unrelated. Both are represented in a number of manifestations: Dionysus is traditionally both mortal and god, joyous and cruel, lion and vine. Both are profoundly linked to the earth, to the darkness of roots, and the growing cycle of life. And both serve as poetic inspiration: Dionysus for the poets at his springtime revels celebrated in the Greek theater, Rilke's Russian God as cause, object, and product of his aesthetic religion.

The question remains, however, as to how the Russian God is related to Apollo. In his notes from Nietzsche, as in the letter to Ellen Key of 1903, Rilke emphasizes that aspect of Apollo which represents the ordering principle: beauty, form, a subduing and transformation of chaos. In the notes he says, "Along with the strength of Dionysian force, that is, of the rhythmically flowing element which is hostile to form, beauty and a strictness of form must also grow, in resistance" (VI, 1174). The "Archaïscher Torso Apollos" is a remarkable expression of this balance of power, the combined power of the two gods. The broken torso of Apollo appears in a fragmented form that, though initially incidental, lends itself to a new statement of intention by the poet. Apollo was seen by Rilke primarily as a shaper, one who submits the amorphous and dangerous world to the discipline of form—a god of intellect. But in the poem he appears without a head, his powers of mind not lost but transmuted, "zurückgeschraubt," into his body. Rilke emphasizes the power emanating from this body, even making the pivotal eighth line of the sonnet, the poem's center, focus on the "middle" of the statue, "that center, which bore generation." The purely cerebral god has changed. This is a Nietzschean Apollo, a god of formal beauty with a strong admixture of the physical. The final line, "You must change your life," thus takes on added meaning in this light. Some readers have regarded the coolness of the *Neue Gedichte* as a flaw,[31] and Rilke himself eventually found the works of this period lacking in humanity. In a letter to Princess Marie von Thurn und Taxis dated 30 August 1910, he writes, "Perhaps now I'm learning to become a little human; my art previously came into being only at the price of insisting on nothing but things; that was willfulness and, I fear also, arrogance, dear God, and it must also have been an incredible greed."[32] Was Rilke in 1906 already toying with a move away from formal perfection and play, from the world of the *Dinge,* toward a more whole, human art—one which, like Nietzsche's synthetic god, combined two natures in a precarious but ecstatic balance? And knowing Rilke's association of Dionysian ecstasy with the Russian spirit, I believe that one can say that, far from being superseded and displaced by the sun god, the Russian God has, along with Dionysus, permeated him with the darkness of earth.

There is one further link between Rilke's Apollo and Russia, consisting of a strange similarity of point of view and subject matter found in a passage in Dostoevsky. Rilke had read the first German biography of Dostoevsky, Nina Hoffmann's *Th. F. Dostojewsky. Eine biographische Studie.* The biographer notes that while Dostoevsky had a distinct antipathy toward consciously utilitarian art, he maintained that true moral and artistic worth were inherent in great works of art, without requiring any tendentiousness on the part of either the artist or the interpreter. Hoffmann quotes an anecdote by which Dostoevsky had hoped to illustrate this idea.

> Some one might, for example, when he was still a youth, in those days when "existence's images were still fresh and new," have seen the Apollo Belvedere; and the noble and endlessly beautiful image of the god might have irresistibly impressed itself on his soul. . . . The impression which the youth received was hot, it shook the nerves, made his skin run cold. . . . Perhaps, in such an experience of high beauty, at such a convulsion of the nerves, there is in men an inner transformation, some sort of exchange of

molecules, some galvanic current which in one second makes what *is* into something else, makes a piece of iron into a magnet. . . . This special impression of a god surely doesn't disappear without a trace. And who knows: when this youth, perhaps twenty, thirty years later, and one of the main movers in some great event in public life, chooses to move in one direction and not another, it may be that among the mass of causes which made him act in this way . . . he quite unconsciously retained *that* impression too, which he had received twenty years before from the image of the Apollo Belvedere.[33]

The exact prototypes for Rilke's Apollos are not known for certain, although several versions of the Apollo Belvedere have been suggested.[34] What matters is the similarity in symbol and in emphasis between Dostoevsky's anecdote and Rilke's second Apollo poem. Both choose the antique figure of the god as the vehicle of a moral lesson. Dostoevsky's youth experiences a "galvanic current" which changes his innermost moral structure, so that twenty years later the effects of it are still perceptible. Rilke's Apollo is given the power to command, "You must change your life," and the viewer, or the reader, is immediately aware of the fateful moment and the action incumbent upon him. Dostoevsky is concerned about a man's social actions, and the overwhelming beauty of Apollo has an effect on his protagonist's public morality. Rilke is characteristically concerned about the individual in relation to himself. But both authors found in the image of Apollo currents which they believed capable of radically changing the lives of those who encountered them. The parallel is so striking that I would venture to suggest that Dostoevsky's treatment played a role in Rilke's choice of object.

Three original poems remain to be considered in this examination of the Russian elements in Rilke's works. These are "Nächtliche Fahrt. Sankt Petersburg" ("Nocturnal Drive. St. Petersburg") in the *Neue Gedichte, II* (1907); Sonnet XX of the first part of *Die Sonette an Orpheus* (1922); and the fifth elegy of the *Duineser Elegien* (1922). Together they reiterate some of the major themes which I have pointed out in the course of my study. They also demonstrate that in the middle and late poems, Rilke still most definitely depended on his peculiar kinship with Russia to provide him with settings, motifs, and ways of seeing.

"Nächtliche Fahrt" describes—evokes, perhaps, is a better word for the oblique complexities of this poem—a carriage ride through the streets of St. Petersburg during the midsummer period of White Nights, when the sun goes down late and rises again not long afterward.

Damals als wir mit den glatten Trabern
(schwarzen, aus dem Orloff'schen Gestüt)—

während hinter hohen Kandelabern
Stadtnachtfronten lagen, angefrüht,
stumm und keiner Stunde mehr gemäss—,
fuhren, nein: vergingen oder flogen
und um lastende Paläste bogen
in das Wehn der Newa-Quais,

hingerissen durch das wache Nachten,
das nicht Himmel und nicht Erde hat,—
als das Drängende von unbewachten
Gärten gärend aus dem Ljetnij-Ssad
aufstieg, während seine Steinfiguren
schwindelnd mit ohnmächtigen Konturen
hinter uns vergingen, wie wir fuhren—:

damals hörte diese Stadt
auf zu sein. Auf einmal gab sie zu,
dass sie niemals war, um nichts als Ruh
flehend; wie ein Irrer, dem das Wirrn
plötzlich sich entwirrt, das ihn verriet,
und der einen jahrelangen kranken
gar nicht zu verwandelnden Gedanken,
den er nie mehr denken muss: Granit—
aus dem leeren schwankenden Gehirn
fallen fühlt, bis man ihn nicht mehr sieht.
(I, 601–02)

[Then as we, with the smooth trotters (black ones from the Orlov stud-farm)—while behind high gas lanterns, city-night facades lay, tinged with earliness, mute and no longer suitable for any hour—drove, no: slipped by, or flew, and round cumbrous palaces we bent into the blowing of the Neva Embankment, torn along through the waking night, which has neither heaven nor earth—as the urgency of unguarded gardens seething from the Summer Garden rose up, while its stone figures, vanishing with unconscious contours, disappeared behind us as we drove—: then this city ceased to be. All at once is admitted it never had been, begging for nothing but peace; like a madman, whose bewilderment is suddenly untangled, which betrayed him, and who feels a years-long, sick, quite unalterable thought which he need never think again: granite—fall away, until it's seen no more.]

Upon untangling the many parenthetical and adverbial phrases and subclauses, we find a picture of the anomalous city, built on a swamp at the end of the seventeenth century, by force and the fiat of Peter the Great. Rilke evokes the massive linearity of the granite city with its governmental-Baroque offices and palaces. We see them paradoxically racing by, lit by gas lamps, as the carriage in which the poet is riding passes them on its way to the Neva Embankment. We smell the heavy, moist fragrance of flowers in the Summer Garden (the Letny Sad, a famous park in the city). All this transpires against the hazy, disconcerting unreality of light and objects typical of the White Nights.

One critic has pointed out how the overlapping and intertwining clauses of this first section of the poem produce an impression of breathless flight.[35] He also notes correctly that the *Umschlag,* or fulcrum, of the poem occurs at the end punctuation of dash and colon, the—: of line fifteen. All the roundabout evocation, the laying on of detail that is rich yet hesitant, leads up to the statement, "—: then this city ceased to be." What follows is merely exposition of this statement, an extended simile which likens St. Petersburg, giving up all ideas of ever possessing any reality, to a madman who suddenly loses his lifelong obsession. The feeling is one of sudden buoyant relief. Another critic relates the uneasy and oppressive feeling of the first half of the poem to Rilke's own experiences there.[36] Citing letters in which Rilke mentions his impressions of St. Petersburg (Rilke preferred Moscow, in part, no doubt, because he found it more truly Russian), the critic notes that Rilke found the city heavy and tiring:

> The nights become uneasy and sleepless, and maintain a secret gleam, which is the bridge from day to day. And there is an activity in everything that won't allow itself to rest.

> It was inexpressibly frightful to live these days . . . after this unexpected and hurried departure and with the almost hostile impressions of this heavy city. . . . You can't believe how long the days can be in St. Petersburg. And yet not much can be fit into them. Life here is a continual being-underway, under which all goals suffer. One goes, goes, drives, drives, and wherever one arrives, the first impression is that of one's own tiredness.[37]

A fact which the critic does not mention in his citing of Rilke's reactions is that at this time Rilke was alone in the city, feeling out of sorts and very much abandoned by Lou, who had gone off abruptly to visit relatives, leaving him to fend for himself in the strange place. This was the "unexpected and hurried departure" mentioned in the letter.

The poem gives concrete form to a combination of perceptions: of the manic mood and uneasy sociability of the people of St. Petersburg during the brief period of warm weather and short nights, and of St. Petersburg itself as an essentially uneasy city, living a false life. The former image could very easily have arisen from Rilke's personal experiences; his frame of mind was peculiarly unsuited to enjoying the life of the city. The second idea, of St. Petersburg as an unreal, unstable place, has much deeper roots, which Rilke was aware of, in the old and thriving Russian literary image of the city.[38] Pushkin, Gogol, and Dostoevsky used aspects of the city as background or as central fact in many works.[39] Each learned from his predecessor, though they wrote from differing points of view. In each we find details and characteristics which are echoed in "Nächtliche Fahrt."

Pushkin loved St. Petersburg, and praised the grand vision of Peter in his narrative poem "The Bronze Horseman," subtitled "A Petersburg Tale" (1833). There we find the lush gardens, the vast mansions, and the "Neva . . . clad in granite" which Rilke portrays. Pushkin also alludes to the odd world of the White Nights, "the transparent twilight of meditative nights, the moonless lustre."[40] Gogol focused on the ambiguous and illusory nature of the city, the social masks worn by its inhabitants, the grandiose facade which conceals misery, greed, and grotesquerie. His story, "Nevsky Prospect" (1835), about two young men who fall prey to the allure of the Nevsky, St. Petersburg's fashionable main thoroughfare, ends:

> It deceives at all times, this Nevsky Prospect, but most of all when night falls on it in a condensed mass, and detaches the white and straw-colored walls of the houses, when the whole city turns into noise and glitter, myriads of carriages pour from the bridges . . . and when the devil himself lights the lamps, to show everything in a false light.[41]

Dostoevsky's novels are set in a St. Petersburg that is usually gloomy, unhealthful, and oppressive. When, on the contrary, it is warm and bright, as in the novella entitled *White Nights* (1848), the protagonist feels abandoned when "everybody" in town leaves for the countryside. He is led by the strange euphoria in the atmosphere to fall in love, against his better judgment, and is subsequently misused by the girl he loves. (Rilke may have felt a particular attraction to this story, considering the disintegration of his relations with Lou which coincided with his stay in the city.) In a feuilleton written in 1860, Dostoevsky recounts a "vision" of St. Petersburg which he experienced while walking along the Neva:

> The taut air quivered at the slightest sound, and columns of smoke like giants rose from all the roofs on both embankments and rushed upward through the cold sky, twining and untwining on the way, so that it seemed new buildings were rising above the old ones, a new city was forming in the air. . . . It seemed, finally, that this whole world with all its inhabitants, strong and weak, with all its domiciles, the shelters of the poor or gilded mansions, resembled at this twilight hour a fantastic, magic vision, a dream which would in its turn vanish immediately and rise up as steam toward the dark blue sky.[42]

In his novel *A Raw Youth,* he suggests:

> What if this [Petersburg] fog should part and float away? Would not all this rotten and slimy town go with it, rise up with the fog, and vanish like smoke, and the old Finnish marsh be left as before, and in the midst of it, perhaps, to heighten the picture, a bronze horseman on a panting overdriven steed?[43]

Even Lou, who cannot strictly be considered a Russian writer, made her contribution to the tradition of depicting St. Petersburg as an aberration. In her work "Im Zwischenland" ("In the Land Between"), published in 1902, she gives the following picture of her home city:

> Everything seemed contrived and inauthentic to her, the city itself a hollow deception. "Have you seen Petersburg on a 'White Night?' Around June, when it stays as light as day? Oh, that is something strange. . . ." Everything becomes light and colorless, everything hovers. "Are you made of granite?" one says to St. Isaac's Cathedral. . . . "Aren't you made of grey paper?" . . . And that's how everything is . . . so upsetting, not at all orderly any longer, one gets a fever. A dream. Yes, in order not to go mad in St. Petersburg, one has to be a bureaucrat![44]

An element which all of the writers mentioned have in common in their portrayal of the city is the theme of madness. Lou, writing in 1902, was of course well aware of the tradition, and her references to madness and to bureaucrats is conscious literary play. But for the others, madness was a central fact associated with the very spirit of the city. Even Pushkin, admirer of the city, focuses his "Bronze Horseman" on a young man who goes mad directly as a result of its influence. Evgeny, a young clerk, loses his beloved in a flood which sweeps through the low-lying city. Driven mad by grief, he blames Peter personally for founding his city on such a vulnerable site; and raving, he rushes through the streets pursued by the sound of the bronze hooves of a giant statue of Peter the Great.[45] In Gogol one finds many examples of obsession, falsity, and madness. Part of the satirical thrust of "The Nose" is against Petersburg society and its bureaucrats, of which the wayward nose becomes a part. In "Nevsky Prospect," a young artist is driven mad by the falseness and decadence of the city. *Diary of a Madman* portrays the decline and eventual mental extinction of a clerk in the bureaucracy. One of the first signs of his growing derangement is the heading in his diary, "Martober 86 between day and night,"[46] a hybrid, hovering state of being with no definite contours, which reflects the amorphous aura of the city during the White Nights. Dostoevsky, too, peoples his St. Petersburg with madmen and eccentrics, such as the heroes of "The Double" and "Notes from Underground," who are in their way typical of the bewildered and paranoid denizens of the city.

Rilke knew all these writers; and he cannot but have been impressed by the recurring theme of the illusory city, apparently full of unhappy, obsessed people. It is not, I believe, unreasonable to suggest that these literary impressions entered into his own poetic evocation of the city. The vocabulary of the poem clearly reflects the Russian tradition of irreality. Rilke uses "dissolved" (*vergingen*) twice, "neither heaven nor earth," "vanishing," "unconscious," "ceased to exist," "never existed." The ambiguous nature of the city is expressed in the juxtaposition of such heavy and seemingly real objects as "cumbrous palaces" and the stone statues in the Summer Garden, with a mood of general instability, a world out of control. The facades of the buildings are "mute and not suitable for any hour," strange fragrances "seethe" up from the gardens, dissolving in the grey air; and even the statues have "unconscious" or "helpless" (*ohnmächtig*) contours and vanish in the twilight. It is, seemingly, the same pernicious city that preoccupied Gogol and Dostoevsky. But, as usual, Rilke goes two steps beyond his sources. Seizing on the familiar image of the man driven mad by the unhealthful and deceptive nature of the place, he transforms the city itself into a madman whose lifelong obsession is "granite"—that is, the mistaken conviction of its own reality. And in a second bold departure from tradition, Rilke cures the madman of his obsession. The city suddenly admits that it has always been a chimera, and is thereby freed of the tangle of pretense, the granite-like weight of lies which have characterized it ever since it was built.

Between "Nächtliche Fahrt" and the last manifestations of Russian influence in his work, Rilke returned unexpectedly to an early love. In a letter of 21 January 1919, he informs Lou that he has just translated "the Lermontov poem that for a long time had been inscribed in my notebook: 'Vyxožu odin ja na dorogu' ["I Go Out onto the Road Alone"]."[47] The translation, which is appended to the letter, constitutes one of his best renderings of Russian poetry, while at the same time typifying his approach as a translator by its subtle shifts in emphasis and purpose. It is striking that, eighteen years after his last active study of Russian, his command of the language was good enough to produce such a skillful translation. At this time, the beginning of 1919, Rilke had been living in virtual exile for five years. Prevented by the hostilities and by his Austrian citizenship from returning to Paris, he had spent the entire period of the war in Austria and in Munich, which he hated. He regarded these years as a violent breach in the normal course of his life, and had arrived at a psychological and emotional nadir. It is noteworthy that at this point he should once again turn to a Russian poet. He had carried Lermontov's poem around with him for years, but only now, when nothing in his life seemed to offer solace, did he decide to translate it. He was probably motivated as much by its reassuring contact with the Russian tradition as by its contents, which in part reflected his uneasy state of mind.

Mikhail Lermontov was a Tsarist officer who, because of the incautious expression of his radical beliefs, was exiled to the Caucasus, where he was killed in a duel in 1841—the same year in which the poem was written. It is both a typical Romantic revery, and the personal expression of the exiled poet. The lyrical "I" travels along a road alone, feeling around him the vastness and solemnity of the night. Within it, he perceives his own dissatisfaction, which he tries to analyze. He expects nothing from life, nor does he regret anything he has done. Finally he declares that he is seeking peace and freedom; but the peace of the tomb is not what he desires. Rather, he would like to slumber endlessly without dying; his breath would continue to flow, a voice should whisper to him of love, and an oak tree should bend over him, forever green.

Rilke's version contains significant deviations from the original, but this is not immediately apparent. Indeed the German is in some ways remarkably faithful to the original, capturing the mood closely. Rilke even succeeds in retaining both the meter (trochaic pentameter) and the rhyme scheme (*a b a b,* with feminine and masculine rhymes alternating), in a tour de force of formal skill. Despite this achievement, however, both the rhythmic feeling of the poem and the final stance of the "I" depart considerably from the original. The difference in rhythm derives in large part from differences in the two languages. Russian has a strongly sounded stress, and a system of vowel reduction in all unstressed syllables. In addition, Lermontov follows the Russian custom of at times leaving out stresses in a poetic line, and replacing them with unstressed syllables or secondary stresses. These elements combine to produce a very different sound from that of the more regular pattern of the German. Lermontov's lines average five words each, whereas fifteen of Rilke's twenty lines are six to eight words long; the added pauses between words in German, plus the Russian habit of elision, also contribute to the different sound. Compare, for example, the first lines. Lermontov's line of ten syllables has only five words, and of these, he stresses only three: "Vỳxožu odìn ja na doròdu" ("I go out onto the road alone/lonely"). To say more or less the same thing in ten syllables, Rilke uses more words, several of which have the feeling of filler. And even given only a secondary stress on the preposition *auf,* the German rhythm is much more regular: "Eìnsam trèt ich aǜf den Wèg den leèren."

Brutzer maintains that except for the final stanza, Rilke is "very true" to Lermontov's original content. This is so to a great extent; but there are important differences which make of Rilke's version a poem in itself. Among these are Rilke's tendency to abstraction, compared with Lermontov's greater simplicity and concreteness. (It is interesting to consider whether this difference would have been so striking had Rilke translated the poem during the period of the *Neue Gedichte,* when he was himself writing poems of great concreteness.) Lermontov's "the earth sleeps in a blue radiance" becomes "hingeruhte Erde in der Himmel Herrlichkeit" ("earth, stretched out to rest in the splendor of the heavens"). The visual image of the moonlight shining palely through the mist is replaced by an intangible and slightly inflated "splendor." When Lermontov says "the night is still. The wilderness listens to God," Rilke has "[ich] seh die Leere still mit Gott verkehren" ("I see the void quietly associate / commune with God"). The simple realism of night and the forest, with its creatures implied in the act of listening, which in the original establishes the isolated setting for the soliloquy, is replaced by a much more abstract "void" which "communes" with God. Rilke also shifts the emphasis in certain passages. Consider the first stanza:

> Einsam tret ich auf den Weg den leeren,
> der durch Nebel leise schimmernd bricht;
> seh die Leere still mit Gott verkehren
> und wie jeder Stern mit Sternen spricht.
>
> [Alone I step out onto the empty road which, shining softly, breaks through the fog; I see the void quietly commune with God, and how every star speaks with stars.]

As Brutzer points out, the word *Gott* is the only stressed syllable with a dark vowel in this stanza.[48] This focuses the reader's attention on God, as if on a quiet center around which the stars circle. This emphasis, however, stems from Rilke alone. In the original, the word "God" (*bogu*) comes at the end of the third line and the movement of the poem carries the reader on to the next line almost immediately. We do not dwell on the word. It appears, moreover, in an oblique case (*bogu* is the dative of *bog*) which makes it a feminine rhyme; and finally it is one of five stressed *o* sounds in the stanza. Thus Lermontov does not emphasize God structurally, as does Rilke; the emphasis is consistent with Rilke's continuing preoccupation with divinity.

Another important difference is the relatively active or passive nature of the "I" in each poem. In the third stanza, Lermontov writes, "I seek freedom and peace! / I would like to seek oblivion and go to rest!" Rilke turns this active statement, with its repetition of "I" at the beginning of each line and its emphatic punctuation, into a passive situation. He writes, "Freiheit soll und Friede mich umfangen / im Vergessen, das der Schlaf verspricht" ("Freedom and peace should surround me in the oblivion that sleep promises"). The Romantic persona seeks flight to another form of existence, but he does so, despite his melancholy, with a Romantic's gesture of rebellion and pride. Rilke's persona, exhausted by life, wishes to succumb to the "promised" embrace of sleep, to be "surrounded" passively by freedom and peace. Rilke's pervasive mood of weariness shows through in his poem, in contrast to Lermontov's stance.[49] In the fourth and fifth stanzas, the Russian poet describes the oblivion he seeks. The passage begins with a Romantic cliché, the cold sleep of the tomb; but in the very way in which it is presented, the cliché is negated. The fourth stanza begins, "But *not* the cold sleep of the tomb" (italics mine). Rather, Lermontov goes on, he desires a sleep where "in my breast the forces of life would slumber." Lermontov uses verbs of sleeping throughout the poem, drawing subtle parallels between the speaker and other parts of nature. The earth "sleeps" in stanza two; life's forces "slumber" in stanza four; and for the space of two whole stanzas, the speaker describes his own ideal, sought-for sleep. It would include a sweet voice that, "delighting his ear," would sing to him of love, and a "dark oak" which would bend over him, whispering. The overall impression gained from the poem is one of on-going life, as if the speaker were to become part of a winter world, hibernating with the beasts of the forest and the juices in the roots of plants—asleep, but full of life.

Rilke omits all the sleep images except those referring to the speaker, thus reducing the importance of his relation to the rest of nature. More important, Rilke changes two images slightly but definitively, and in so doing introduces both a different mood and a new theme into the poem. In Lermontov's endless sleep he would have "life's forces" slumbering in his breast. Rilke renders this as "dass ich alle Kräfte in mir habe" ("that I have all forces within me"). The change from "life's" forces to "all" forces seems at first a weakened, generalized image. But it may have a more purposeful significance. By deliberately substituting "all" for "life," Rilke seems to imply a conscious distinction. "All" is larger than "life"; and what else is there besides life, but death? Rilke's sleeper wants to be full of the whole gamut of experience that human beings are subject to, and posits this all-inclusiveness as a criterion for his ideal sleep. Even though Rilke's sleeper too rejects the clichéd "cold sleep of the tomb," he senses that death is an integral part of human experience, and therefore desirable. Thus we find embodied in a poem about eternal life the Rilkean theme of the eternal presence of death, and the necessity to will it and welcome it.

The other image which Rilke subtly changes is that of the oak tree. Lermontov's last two lines read, "And it is necessary that, eternally green, a dark oak should bend and whisper." Rilke's rendition is: "Und ich wüsste, wie die immergrüne / Eiche flüstert, düster hergeneigt" ("And I would know how the evergreen oak whispers, mournfully bent toward me"). The last line is beautifully constructed, rising in an arc or a crescendo and falling back softly again to where it began. The vowels in the two halves of the line echo one another, and the internal rhyme of *düster* and *flüstert* has the effect of a ritardando, allowing the line to linger in our memories. But precisely because it lingers there, we come away from Rilke's poem with a different feeling. Lermontov's oak is *temnyj*—dark or swarthy; only in a tertiary meaning does it have the feeling of somber or sad, which would normally be rendered by *mračnyj* or *pečal'nyj*. Rilke's *düster,* on the other hand, implies primarily gloomy, mournful, melancholy, or dismal, as opposed to the more neutral *dunkel* ("dark") which he might have used. Thus the slight change in mood in the last line underscores the deeper awareness of life and death implied in Rilke's version.

"Nächtliche Fahrt" is Rilke's last poem which is directly indebted to Russian literature, and "Vyxožu" is his last translation from Russian. But after the long silence lasting from 1912 to 1922, when Rilke's poetic forces returned to him like a hurricane, Russia was still there, and figured in both the major products of that time, the *Sonette* and the *Elegien*. The two books of *Die Sonette an Orpheus* (*Sonnets to Orpheus*), written in about three weeks in February 1922, focus on the figure of Orpheus, and on the power of song and of praise. God in his specifically Russian form has been left behind, but several essentially Russian characteristics have survived in new forms in the *Sonette*. The protean Russian God of the *Stunden-Buch* and the *Geschichten* was sometimes portrayed as a bard. In one poem at the end of "Das Buch vom mönchischen Leben," his songs had been absorbed by the earth, and the monk promises to recapture them and return them to him. Similarly, Orpheus, the "god with the lyre," represents the eternal death and rebirth of song; his songs continually return to earth with him, only to be reborn in the spring. The Russian God also represented perpetual change; in this, he was so dynamic that the monk half shrinks from recognizing it: "Auch wenn wir nicht wollen: / *Gott reift*" ("Even when we don't wish it, *God ripens*" [I, 262]). The voice which sings the praises of Orpheus has grown stronger, less timid and confused than the monk's. It boldly proclaims the rightness of change as the essence of the god; and it goes further in suggesting that change is crucial for artists and all human beings. The twelfth sonnet of the second part urges, "Wolle die Wandlung" ("Will the transformation" [I, 758]). But the "Russian" virtue of patience is emphasized as well. At the same time that the poet urges us to be changed willingly, indeed, to change the world ourselves by internalizing it, he cautions,

Alles das Eilende
wird schon vorüber sein;
denn das Verweilende
erst weiht uns ein.
Knaben, o werft den Mut
nicht in die Schnelligkeit,
nicht in den Flugversuch.
(I, 745)

[All that is hasty soon will be past; for only that which lasts initiates us. Boys, oh don't throw your courage into speed, or into an attempt at flight.]

And speaking of a cosmic garden that seems to go on bearing fruit for us in spite of our clumsiness, he asks, astonished,

> Haben wir niemals vermocht, wir Schatten und Schemen,
> durch unser voreilig reifes und wieder welkes Benehmen
> jener gelassenen Sommer Gleichmut zu stören?
> (I, 762)

[Have we never been able, we shadows and phantoms, by our too quickly ripe and then wilted behavior, to upset the equanimity of those patient summers?]

Patience, and an openness without haste: these are among the main values expressed in the *Sonette*. Though the cosmology has taken on a different shape, the values basic to the "Russian" Rilke still prevail.

Within this general atmosphere there is one poem with a specifically Russian theme. This is Sonnet XX of the first part.

> Dir aber, Herr, o was weih ich dir, sag,
> der das Ohr den Geschöpfen gelehrt?—
> Mein Erinnern an einen Frühlingstag,
> seinen Abend, in Russland—, ein Pferd . . .
>
> Herüber vom Dorf kam der Schimmel allein;
> an der vorderen Fessel den Pflock,
> um die Nacht auf den Wiesen allein zu sein;
> wie schlug seiner Mähne Gelock
>
> an den Hals im Takte des Übermuts,
> bei dem grob gehemmten Galopp.
> Wie sprangen die Quellen des Rossebluts!
>
> Der fühlte die Weiten, und ob!
> Der sang und der hörte—, dein Sagenkreis
> war *in* ihm geschlossen.
>   Sein Bild: ich weih's.
>   (I, 743–44)

[But to you, Lord, what shall I dedicate, say, who taught the creatures to hear? My memory of a day in spring, at evening, in Russia—a horse. The white horse came over from the village alone, a hobble on his fore fetlock, to spend the night on the meadows alone; how his curly mane struck his neck in time with his high spirits, with his gallop clumsily hindered. How the springs of stallions' blood sprang! He felt the distances, and how! He sang and he listened—your saga's cycle was enclosed within him. His image—I dedicate.]

In the poems which precede this one in the cycle, the poet has presented, in a variety of ways, his vision of Orpheus at work in the world and in us. The poems are full of life and nature: trees, earth, roses, running water, constellations, fruit. Orpheus is the god who can unite the fragments of the world, changing the character of man and of other creatures. The symbolic act manifesting his power is the taming of the savage beasts through song. The first sonnet of the cycle portrays this act; the animals, fascinated, creep out of their hiding places:

> Tiere aus Stille drangen aus dem klaren
> gelösten Wald von Lager und Genist;
> und da ergab sich, dass sie nicht aus List
> und nicht aus Angst in sich so leise waren,
>
> sondern aus Hören. . . .
> . . . und wo eben
> kaum eine Hütte war, . . .
> da schufst du ihnen Tempel im Gehör.
> (I, 731)

[Beasts of silence crept out of the clear, opened woods, from nest and lair; and it turned out that not from guile and not from fear were they so still, but from listening. . . . And where there had just been hardly a hut . . . you created for them temples in their hearing.]

This is the same god who teaches man how to live and perceive more fully through constant metamorphosis, through turning all experiences into life itself and thence into song: "Tanzt die Orange . . . / Ihr habt sie besessen. / Sie hat sich köstlich zu euch bekehrt" ("Dance the orange . . . you have possessed it. It has converted itself to you exquisitely" [I, 740]). The *Sonette* describe and praise the exploits of Orpheus. In the twentieth, Rilke seeks an object worthy of being offered up to the god of poetry. In the exuberant Russian horse he finds an object that is suitable on two counts. First, it is cousin to those beasts which responded to Orpheus in the first sonnet. Despite the fetters, it is strong and vital, full of "springs of stallions' blood." It almost dances its way from village to meadow: "How his curly mane struck his neck in time with his high spirits." This creature, receptive, awake to the world ("he felt the distances"), and full of song, is himself a natural vessel of the god.

The second reason for the particular suitability of the Russian horse as an offering to the god lies in one of the underlying themes of the cycle. An idea which emerges in the *Sonette* is the importance, for the poet, of letting impressions ripen. Not experience alone begets poetry, but the memory of the experience, filtered through time. One of the sonnets urges,

> Dies *ists* nicht, Jüngling, dass du liebst, wenn auch
> die Stimme dann den Mund dir aufstösst,—lerne
> vergessen, dass du aufsangst. Das verrinnt.
> In Wahrheit singen, ist ein andrer Hauch.
> Ein Hauch um nichts. Ein Wehn im Gott. Ein Wind.
> (I, 732)

[*This* isn't it, Youth, the fact that you love, even though your voice then wrenches your mouth open—learn to forget that you began to sing. That will pass. To sing truly is a different breath. A breath about nothing. A breeze in the god. A wind.]

As far back as the writing of *Malte Laurids Brigge,* Rilke had expressed similar ideas. Early in his stay in Paris, Malte realizes that

> it's not enough that one has memories. One must be able to forget them . . . and one must have the great patience to wait for them to come again. For memories in themselves aren't yet the thing. Only when they have become blood in us, glance and gesture, nameless and no longer distinguishable from ourselves, only then can it happen that in a very rare moment the first word of a line of poetry arises amongst them and emerges from them.
> (VI, 724–25)

Once again, all depends on patience and ripening: the virtues of the Russian people and their God. And the horse-sonnet is itself the product of just these virtues. On the evening of 11 February 1922, Rilke wrote to Lou to announce that the miracle had happened: he had just completed the long-awaited *Elegien,* begun ten years earlier, and, unexpectedly, twenty-five sonnets as well. (The other thirty sonnets were written between the fifteenth and the twenty-third of February.) In the letter, he tells Lou he has made

> the horse, you know, the free happy white horse with the hobble on its foot, who once sprang at us, toward evening on a Volga meadow, at a gallop—: I've made him as an "ex-voto" for Orpheus!—What is time?—When is the present? Across so many years he leaped toward me, with his whole joy, into my wide-open feelings.[50]

It seems very fitting that the image of the Russian horse, coming to the poet unbidden from the depths of memory, should be made into a gift for Orpheus, for his appearance embodies the basic tenets of the cycle. In the poem, Rilke praises the earth, and turns the fruits of his experiences, now ripened, into song.

The *Duineser Elegien* (*Duino Elegies*) represent the high point of Rilke's poetic art, and the culmination of ten years of spiritual struggle.[51] Begun at Castle Duino on the Adriatic in 1912, they haunted their creator for ten years, coming to him in short, frustrating spurts of inspiration in

1913 and 1915, then falling stubbornly silent until February 1922. The intervening years were hard for Rilke; he wrote very little, was constantly ill with nervous ailments, considered and then rejected psychoanalysis. During this time he considered publishing the *Elegien* as fragments, since he despaired of ever finishing them. Then came the miracle. Testimony to the force with which the coming of the *Elegien* overwhelmed Rilke is the well-known letter, written on 11 February to his longtime friend and patroness, Princess Marie von Thurn und Taxis.

> Finally, Princess, finally the blessed, how blessed day, when I can send you the completion—as far as I can see—of the elegies: ten! . . . Everything in a few days, it was an inexpressible storm, a hurricane in the spirit . . . all the fibers and tissues in me groaned—there was no thinking about food, God knows who fed me.[52]

And here, at his greatest moment, it seems that among the powerful winds of inspiration that overtook Rilke and carried his major work to its completion may have been one blowing across time and space, from Russia. The product was the fifth elegy, with its family of acrobats and agile lovers. This poem is known to have been based on a painting by Picasso, *La Famille des Saltimbanques*. Numerous critics have pointed out the elements which the poem and the painting have in common; and the dedication of the poem to Frau Hertha Koenig, owner of the painting, is a tribute on Rilke's part to the profound effect the work had on him. In addition, several critics have shown that certain details of the poem stem from Rilke's own encounters with an actual family of acrobats in Paris, that of Père Rollin.[53]

Picasso's painting shows a group of five acrobats in costume, grouped at the left-hand side of the picture into a rough D-shape, the "Dastehns grosser Anfangsbuchstab" ("great initial letter of Thereness [*Dastehn*]" of the elegy. A sixth figure, a woman in a tall straw hat, sits apart at the lower right-hand corner of the picture. The relation of the elegy to Picasso's painting is clear. However, there are elements in the poem which are sought in vain in Picasso. These are the acrobats' carpet, which forms a central theme in the poem; the erotic theme, which is likewise important to the elegy; and the presence of an audience. An unnoticed source for the elements not found in Picasso may be a Russian painting entitled *Tanec* (*The Dance*), painted in 1889 by the Russian modernist Mikhail Vrubel (1856–1911).[54]

Vrubel was deeply interested in old Russian art and was connected with the Slavic Revival movement, but at the same time his interpretation and use of tradition were highly original and personal. He was a brilliant eccentric who, eventually becoming obsessed with the figure of the Demon (from Lermontov's poem of that name), ended his days in a madhouse.

Vrubel does not appear in Rilke's essays on Russian art, but he is among the painters mentioned in Rilke's private correspondence.[55] Rilke was familiar with Vrubel as one of the artists who had worked on the neo-Byzantine cathedral of Saint Vladimir in Kiev along with Vasnetsov. In addition to Vrubel's paintings there, Rilke had seen his decorations in several other churches, as well as some of his secular paintings.[56] There is no evidence that Rilke knew this particular painting, but the coincidence of details in Vrubel's and Picasso's paintings, and in *Tanec* and the fifth elegy, indicate that Rilke's acquaintance with *Tanec* is more than likely.[57]

The painting *Tanec* at first glance bears a remarkable similarity to Picasso's *Saltimbànques*. The eight figures are grouped in a rough capital D, the lines and contours of which divide the picture in the same proportions and directions as do those of Picasso's acrobats. In the lower right-hand corner is a figure (a musician playing on a pipe) wearing a tall conical hat. The main figures are two acrobats, standing at left and center in the middle ground. One is a man in tights, facing the viewer, his arms crossed on his chest in a nonchalant pose. The other is a naked woman standing on an oriental carpet. Her body is turned away from the viewer at a forty-five degree angle, but her face is turned toward us over her lifted shoulder. She stands poised in an attitude of tension and preparedness, as if about to leap into the air or do a back-flip on the bright carpet. The other figures, aside from the pipe player already mentioned, are spectators, facing the performers obliquely from the right side of the painting. Among them, as among Picasso's figures, is a small boy with a look of intense concentration on his face.

The cluster of images mentioned above that is lacking in Picasso's painting but present in Vrubel's—the carpet, the audience, and the erotic possibilities—occurs in the final portion of Rilke's elegy, in the thirteen lines beginning "Engel! Es wäre ein Platz . . ." ("Angel! There might be a place . . ." [I, 705]). Rilke shifts his focus from the fate of the acrobats to that of some nameless lovers, themselves in the guise of performers. Carpets appear in both parts of the poem, and are not limited to the last thirteen lines. The first carpet is the threadbare one on which the acrobats perform—their miserable bit of turf, the site of their ever-repeated tricks, "diese[r] verlorene . . . Teppich im Weltall" ("this lost carpet in space" [I, 701]). The second carpet is a mythical one, an "unsäglich[er] Teppich" ("unutterable carpet" [I, 705]), on which the lovers, like acrobats of the heart, might finally perfect all the marvelous movements which they can't accomplish here, in real life. Satisfied and fulfilled on that carpet, they might receive the thanks and good wishes of their audience, composed of the dead.

Picasso's figures stand together, isolated from any other human beings, not performing, but seeming rather to be resting on the road from one town, one performance, to another. Their audience is merely potential—though perhaps not far away, for three of the figures stare off the canvas toward the right, as if seeking their next customers there. Vrubel's figures, like Rilke's, are caught in the midst of performing, at an instant of calm between motions. The woman with her taut body and lifted arms is, like the figure in the poem, "aufrecht, da und gezeigt" ("upright, there and displayed" [I, 701]). Her audience is present, visible to us in its fascination with what is going on. Rilke calls attention several times to the idea of an audience—first in the image of the "Rose des Zuschauns" ("the rose of watching" [I, 701]) surrounding the performers at its core, then in the concluding thirteen lines. Here the audience of the "unzähligen lautlosen Toten" ("innumerable silent dead") show their appreciation of the lovers' act by throwing them their carefully hoarded "Münzen des Glücks" ("coins of happiness" [I, 705]).

The metaphorical movement from acrobats to lovers is important, for it is likewise a movement from a state of being that is barren, lonely, and mechanical, to one that is artistic, authentic, and fulfilling. In Picasso's painting there is little to suggest such a movement. His figures stand in a stiff, distracted group. There is nothing in the least erotic between them. They seem to represent only the first half of Rilke's metaphor, the lonely wanderers. In Vrubel's painting, the limitation of the number of performers to two, and the fact that they are a young man and a naked woman, seem to bring it closer in spirit to Rilke's metaphorical statement in the last thirteen lines. They are performers—but they might also be lovers. There is a potential in them for embodying both the images used by the poet.

The fifth elegy stands at the center of the cycle; one critic calls this poem the "balance point" of the *Elegien,* and locates the fulcrum of the cycle at the center of the poem.[58] The elegy falls into two unequal parts, the first focusing on the repetitive and unfulfilling lives of the acrobats, and the second on the hopeful image of a place where the mythical lovers might succeed. The two parts reflect the two paintings—a Western and a Russian one—which function as sources for the poem's basic imagery. The figures of the first part of the poem, the wanderers, subject to the ceaseless will of an unknowable fate, reflect the dejected figures in Picasso's painting. The acrobat-lovers of the last thirteen lines, though their success is only potential,[59] represent the persistent hope that communion and release are possible. These figures, who exist, if only for a moment, in a higher realm of fantasy, reflect the world of Vrubel's painting.

The location and juxtaposition of these two sets of figures may be suggestive of the structure of the *Elegien* as a whole. In the poems preceding the fifth elegy, and culminating in the images taken from Picasso, we find an increasingly bleak picture of human existence; man is alienated from himself and nature, and his view of both life and death is dishonest and self-defeating. Beginning with the images taken from Vrubel, the second half of the cycle (with the exception of the temporary regression into despair of the eighth elegy) expresses greater and greater assurance, culminating in an affirmation of existence at the end.

Thus as late as 1922, when the fifth elegy was written (it was the last to be composed), we find Rilke, at the heart of his most important work, returning to the dichotomy which had fascinated him in 1899. Here, as in those early works, he contrasts the art of Russia and the art of the West, each of which embodies a particular ethos. And it is in the Russian, not the Western, painting that he finds a basis for a positive resolution of the problem of the *Elegien*. Vrubel's *Tanec* has little in common with Rilke's early ideas on Russian art, yet Rilke apparently saw in it the spiritual qualities he was looking for in 1922, just as he had found, in a very different Russian art, the spiritual qualities he was seeking twenty years before.

In the works which Rilke wrote after the *Elegien* and the *Sonette*, during the last four years of his life, we find virtually nothing Russian. This is not to say that he had no more contact with Russians, or that their land and culture ceased to be of interest to him. With his French friend Maurice Betz, for example, he spoke at length about what Russia meant to him, and discussed his current Russian friends, such as the emigré puppet mistress Julia Sazonova or the dancers Clotilde and Alexander Sacharov.[60] The spring and summer of 1926 brought him his last great Russian friendship, in the correspondence with the emigré poet Marina Tsvetaeva.[61] Out of this friendship two poems arose: the small French dedication which begins, "Marina, voici galets et coquillages" ("Marina, here are pebbles and shells" [II, 678–79]) and the long poem "Elegie an Marina Tswetajewa-Efron" ("Elegy to Marina Tsvetaeva-Efron" [II, 271–73]).

But Russia itself seems to have faded finally from his poetic works. One major reason may have been that many of his works after 1922 were written in French. The language associated with his beloved Paris was also the language of the western Rhône Valley of Switzerland, the region where he lived out his last years in the Castle of Muzot. One of his last poetic cycles, for example, *Les Quatrains Valaisans* (*Quatrains from Valais*), written in 1924, focuses on this region, on the cyclical life of the land and its people. Another, *Les Fenêtres* (*The Windows*), was written for and dedicated to a French-Polish friend, Baladine Klossowska, while another was entitled significantly *Tendres Impôts à la France* (*Tender Duties to France*). France and French associations largely occupied him during these years between the great release of the *Elegien* in 1922 and his early death in December 1926.

But even up to the end, Rilke maintained a profound and conscious love of Russia. On 14 March 1926, in a letter to his old friend Leonid Pasternak, then living in exile in Berlin, Rilke wrote:

> And now I want to assure you right away how much . . . everything that has to do with old Russia (the unforgettable mysterious *skazka* [fairy tale]) and everything about which you remind me in your letter has remained close, dear, and sacred to me, fixed forever in the foundations of my life![62]

And in August 1926, four months before his death, he hired a young Russian girl to act as his secretary. In the evenings in Sierre, she would read to him "from the memoirs of Prince Volkonsky, and passages of Turgenev, interspersed with Russian poetry whose rhythm and music he felt so deeply."[63] He had hoped to return to Russia, and had mentioned to various friends his plans to write a book about his experiences there. Death, his old familiar companion, interrupted these plans. But Russia had become so much a part of him that his last letter to Lou, written on his deathbed, is signed "Proščaj, Dorogaja moja"—"Farewell, my dear one."[64] Far from being a passing fancy, his love for Russia, once awakened, never left him. And between the first intoxication of his early studies and the last "proščaj," it had played a profound and varied role in the creation of his most basic beliefs and in their literary expression.

Abbreviations

BjD	*Briefe an einen jungen Dichter.* Frankfurt, n.d.
B der B	Rainer Maria Rilke. *Das Buch der Bilder.* In *Sämtliche Werke.* Ed. Ruth Sieber-Rilke and Ernst Zinn. 6 vols. Frankfurt, 1955–66.
Briefe 1902–06	Ruth Sieber-Rilke and Carl Sieber, ed. *Briefe aus den Jahren 1902 bis 1906.* Leipzig, 1929, 1930.
Briefe 1906–07	Ruth Sieber-Rilke and Carl Sieber, ed. *Briefe aus den Jahren 1906 bis 1907.* Leipzig, 1930.
Briefe 1907–14	Ruth Sieber-Rilke and Carl Sieber, ed. *Briefe aus den Jahren 1907 bis 1914.* Leipzig, 1933.
Briefe 1914–21	Ruth Sieber-Rilke and Carl Sieber, ed. *Briefe aus den Jahren 1914 bis 1921.* Leipzig, 1937.
Briefe aus Muzot	Ruth Sieber-Rilke and Carl Sieber, ed. *Briefe aus Muzot. 1921 bis 1926.* Leipzig, 1936.
B und T. 1899–1902	Ruth Sieber-Rilke and Carl Sieber, ed. *Briefe und Tagebücher aus der Frühzeit. 1899 bis 1902.* Leipzig, 1931, 1933.
DE	Rainer Maria Rilke. *Die Duineser Elegien.* In *Sämtliche Werke.* Ed. Ruth Sieber-Rilke and Ernst Zinn. 6 vols. Frankfurt, 1955–66.
GB	Ruth Sieber-Rilke and Carl Sieber, ed. *Gesammelte Briefe.* 6 vols. Leipzig, 1936–40. Indi-

ABBREVIATIONS

	vidual volumes are cited as *GB* followed by volume number.
Hofmannsthal-RMR	Rudolf Hirsch and Ingeborg Schnack, ed. *Hugo von Hofmannsthal—Rainer Maria Rilke. Briefwechsel. 1899–1925*. Frankfurt, 1978.
MLB	Rainer Maria Rilke. *Die Aufzeichnungen des Malte Laurids Brigge*. In *Sämtliche Werke*. Ed. Ruth Sieber-Rilke and Ernst Zinn. 6 vols. Frankfurt, 1955–66.
NG	Rainer Maria Rilke. *Neue Gedichte*. In *Sämtliche Werke*. Ed. Ruth Sieber-Rilke and Ernst Zinn. 6 vols. Frankfurt, 1955–66.
RMR-Lou	Ernst Pfeiffer, ed. *Rainer Maria Rilke—Lou Andreas-Salomé. Briefwechsel*. Zurich and Wiesbaden, 1952.
RMR-Taxis	Ernst Zinn, ed. *Rainer Maria Rilke und Marie von Thurn und Taxis. Briefwechsel*. 2 vols. Zurich, 1951. Individual volumes are cited as *RMR-Taxis* followed by volume number.
RMR-Volkart	Rätus Luck, ed. *Rainer Maria Rilke. Briefe an Nanny Wunderly-Volkart*. 2 vols. N.p. [probably Frankfurt], 1978. Individual volumes are cited as *RMR-Volkart* followed by volume number.
RrR	Sophie Brutzer. *Rilkes russische Reisen*. 1934; rpt. Darmstadt, 1969.
S an O	Rainer Maria Rilke. *Die Sonette an Orpheus*. In *Sämtliche Werke*. Ed. Ruth Sieber-Rilke and Ernst Zinn. 6 vols. Frankfurt, 1955–66.
SB	Rainer Maria Rilke. *Das Stunden-Buch*. In *Sämtliche Werke*. Ed. Ruth Sieber-Rilke and Ernst Zinn. 6 vols. Frankfurt, 1955–66.
SW	Ruth Sieber-Rilke and Ernst Zinn, ed. *Sämtliche Werke*. 6 vols. Frankfurt, 1955–66. Individual volumes are cited in parentheses by volume and page number only.
Tagebücher	Ruth Sieber-Rilke and Carl Sieber, ed. *Tagebücher aus der Frühzeit*. Frankfurt, 1942.

Notes

NOTES TO CHAPTER 1

1. Sigfrid Hoefert, *Russische Literatur in Deutschland*, pp. viii ff.
2. Maximilian Harden, quoted in V. Dudkin and K. Azadovskij, "Neoromantizm. Legenda o 'russkoj duše,' " p. 689.
3. H. F. Peters, *Lou. Das Leben der Lou Andreas-Salomé*, p. 256.
4. Rudolph Binion, *Frau Lou: Nietzsche's Wayward Disciple*, pp. 215 and 217. "Volynsky" was a pseudonym which Akim Flexer often used.
5. Ibid., p. 215.
6. The essays which grew out of the collaboration at Wolfratshausen include the following: "Russische Dichtung und Kultur, I"; "Russische Dichtung und Kultur, II"; "Das russische Heiligenbild und sein Dichter"; "Russische Philosophie und semitischer Geist"; and "Leo Tolstoi, unser Zeitgenosse."
7. See Peters, *Lou*, for an extensive discussion of her relationships with these and other prominent men of the period.
8. Peters (*Lou*, p. 294), suggests that Rilke's deep attachment to, and idealization of, Russia—the vast feminine country with its Eastern mysteries and its simple, earthy charms—was but a metaphoric projection of his feelings for Lou, and that his direct contact and obsession with both of them faded simultaneously. I do not believe this to be the case. Rather, Lou helped awaken in Rilke an interest in Russia that became a permanent part of him.
9. Ibid., p. 31.
10. In an interesting sidelight on her relations to the Naturalists and the sort of effect she had on her contemporaries, Peters suggests (pp. 221–28) that Lou may have been the prototype not only for the free-thinking Russian student Anna Mahr in Gerhart Hauptmann's play *Einsame Menschen,* but also for Wedekind's Lulu.
11. Peters, *Lou*, p. 105.
12. Lou Andreas-Salomé, "Russische Dichtung und Kultur, II," p. 885. Ironically, her vision of the West as a tired culture looking to Russia for renewed vitality was echoed in the characteristic stance of the Russian Modernists, who, acutely conscious of their own exhaustion and decay, looked even further east, to the steppes of Asia, for cultural renewal—albeit at the price of their own destruction. Bryusov's "The Coming Huns" (1904), Bely's *Petersburg* (1913), and Blok's "The Scythians" (1918), to name but a few, represent this vision.
13. A. L. Volynskij, *Russkie kritiki.*
14. Lou Andreas-Salomé, "Russische Geschichten," p. 153.
15. Andreas-Salomé, "Leo Tolstoi."
16. Ibid., pp. 1147–48.
17. Ibid., pp. 1150.
18. "Russische Dichtung, I," p. 577.
19. Quoted by Robert Heinz Heygrodt, "Rilke und Russland," p. 7.
20. Andreas-Salomé, "Russische Dichtung, I," p. 579.
21. Among the works which Rilke read were some of the most important histories and anthologies of the day. They included Zabelin, *Domašnyj byt russkix carej v XVI–XVII*

stoletijax; N. M. Karamzin, *Istorija gosudarstva rossijskago;* W. R. S. Ralston, *The Songs of the Russian People;* a standard collection of ballads and verse tales, compiled by P. N. Rybnikov, *Pesni sobrannye P. N. Rybnikovym;* and the folk tales collected by A. N. Afanasev, *Narodnye russkie skazki.* Histories or interpretations of Russian literature which Rilke read included Alfred Rambaud, *La Russie Épique. Étude sur les chançons héroïques de la Russie;* Nina Hoffmann, *Th. M. Dostojewsky. Eine biographische Studie;* and Melchior de Vogüé, *Le roman russe.* For his knowledge of Russian art Rilke used, among others, the standard histories by O. P. Novytskyi, *Istorija russkago iskusstva s drevnejšix vremen',* and Petr Petrovič Gnedič, *Istorija Iskusstv: zodčestvo, živopis', vajanie.*

22. Vogüé, *Roman russe,* p. 72.
23. *Tagebücher,* p. 173.
24. Kurgans: ancient Slavic burial mounds.
25. Hoffmann, *Th. M. Dostojewsky,* p. 5.
26. Ibid., p. 6.
27. Ibid., p. 205.
28. Ibid., p. 9.
29. Ibid., p. 109.
30. *GB* I, p. 393.
31. Over the years his correspondents included Tolstoy, Goncharov, Gorky, Volynsky, Trubetskoy, Benois, and Malyutin. He also continued to make new Russian friends, including many in the Paris emigration. These included dancers, actors, writers, and even a puppet-mistress. Parenthetically, it is interesting to know that he also met Vogüé, whose book on Russia he so admired (*RMR-Lou,* pp. 105–06).

NOTES TO CHAPTER 2

1. *Tagebücher,* pp. 197–98. Rilke's method of writing was both idiosyncratic and consistent. The traditional metaphor for inspiration, the summoning of one's muse, was inappropriate for him. Instead, he waited patiently for poems to come to him, and despite his great attention to craft and hard work, he saw himself essentially as a receptacle. Images and whole poems came when they were ripe, and not before. The passivity, openness, and trust implicit in such an approach are crucial aspects of Rilke's creative personality; they may also be seen as a key to his intense response to Russia.
2. Konstantin M. Asadowskij, "Briefe nach Russland. S. W. Maljutin im Briefwechsel zwischen Rilke und Ettinger," p. 207.
3. K. M. Azadovskij, "R. -M. Ril'ke i A. N. Benois. Perepiska 1900–1902 gg.," p. 97.
4. Ibid., p. 91.
5. Ibid., p. 97.
6. Ibid., p. 101.
7. Ibid., pp. 98–99.
8. Letter of 11 January 1902, *GB* I, 194.
9. None of Rilke's published translations have been collected; they are available only in scattered form. The manuscripts of *Poor Folk* and *The Seagull* are lost; *Uncle Vanya* and *The Living Corpse* remained only ideas, never actually carried out.
10. Konstantin Azadovskij, "Rajner Marija Ril'ke. Pis'ma v Rossiju," pp. 241–42.
11. Azadovskij, "Ril'ke i Benois," p. 85 ff.
12. Brutzer, *RrR,* p. 79. Rilke's versions of all four poems by Drozhzhin are found in Brutzer, pp. 79–80.
13. Brutzer, *RrR,* p. 79.
14. Ibid., p. 80.
15. Ibid., p. 81. I cannot evaluate Brutzer's interpretation, as I have been unable to obtain the Russian originals of Drozhzhin's poetry.

16. "Die Bittschrift" ("The Petition") appeared in the supplement to *Bohemia*, 5 January 1902. I have been unable to obtain a copy of this newspaper, but Brutzer quotes from, and summarizes, the story.
17. Brutzer, *RrR*, p. 83.
18. *Tagebücher*, p. 173.
19. Hugo Heller, "Die Bücher vom wirklichen Leben" (Vienna, 1908), quoted in Brutzer, *RrR*, p. 46.
20. Dudkin and Azadovskij, "Neoromantizm," p. 695.
21. Since its discovery in the form of a sixteenth-century manuscript in 1795, the work has been surrounded with controversy and drama. This manuscript was destroyed in the burning of Moscow in 1812; the two surviving copies differed considerably from one another. The actual form of the medieval original—prose or verse—has not been determined. Theories about its origin abound, and there are a number of passages in the work which remain obscure. Rilke's translation of the *Slovo* was not available until 1949, when André von Gronicka published it with annotations in "Rainer Maria Rilke's Translation of the 'Igor' Song (Slovo)." In 1953, it appeared in R. M. Rilke, *Werke. Auswahl in zwei Bänden*, II, and in 1960 as a separate edition along with the Old Russian and a modern Russian translation in Insel Bücherei No. 689, under the title *Das Igorlied. Eine Heldendichtung*. All references to the *Slovo* and to Rilke's translation are to the Insel edition, and page numbers will be given in the text in parentheses. (References to the *SW* continue to be cited in the text by volume number and page given in parentheses, as explained in the Preface.)

    For a brief overview of the history of the *Slovo*, see the "Nachwort" to the Insel edition of Rilke's *Igorlied*. For an overview of the main controversies, a summary of German attitudes toward the *Slovo*, and a discussion of Rilke's translation, see von Gronicka, "Rilke's Translation of the Slovo." For an English translation, see *The Song of Igor's Campaign: An Epic of the Twelfth Century*, trans. Vladimir Nabokov.
22. Mentioned in a letter to Sophie Schill, 23 February 1900, *GB* I, 80.
23. For a discussion of Rilke's relation to his sources see Caryl Emerson, "Rilke, Russia and the Igor Tale." The version Rilke used was the "Russkaja klassnaja biblioteka" (St. Petersburg, 1901).
24. A. S. Magr, in his comments on a fragment of the translation published in the Supplement to the *Prager Presse*, 16 February 1930 (cited in Brutzer, *RrR*, p. 85).
25. Von Gronicka, "Rilke's Translation of the Slovo," p. 185.
26. Letter to Sophie Schill, 23 February 1900, *GB* I, 80.
27. Yaroslavna's lament was Rilke's favorite passage; to Schill (ibid.), he calls it "the most beautiful thing" in the *Igorlied*.
28. A certain amount of analysis of the *Igorlied* has already been done by Brutzer, von Gronicka, and Emerson. Both Brutzer and von Gronicka focus on Rilke's deviations from the original; von Gronicka provides corrections for a number of lines. One of Rilke's errors, corrected but not discussed by von Gronicka, presents a curious possibility. In the original Old Russian text, two pagans are seen racing toward the river: "Gzak runs as a grey wolf, Končak shows him the way [*emu sled pravit*] to the Great Don" (*Igorlied*, p. 12). The modern Russian translators whom Rilke used, including Gerbel and Mej, render this correctly. But Rilke reverses the relationship, translating it as "Gsa macht sich wie ein grauer Wolf davon und Kontschak ihm nach auf den grossen Don zu" ("Gsa runs away as a grey wolf, and Končak *after him* toward the great Don" [ibid., p. 36]). It is possible that Rilke was led astray by the excerpts given in French by Rambaud in his discussion of the poem in *Russie Épique*. There the passage reads, "Le khan Gzak accourt, 'comme un loup gris,' et Kontchak *le suit de près* sur les bords du Don" (p. 200; italics mine). This may indicate that Rilke consulted not only Russian translations of the poem for his own work, but French ones as well.
29. Brutzer, *RrR*, p. 73.
30. Likewise we can learn something from a list of the writers he chose *not* to translate. Rilke

at one time asked Benois for suggestions about what to translate; Benois listed essays by Merezhkovsky and Rozanov, the interpolated narratives in Dostoevsky's *Diary of a Writer,* and works by Bely and Leonid Andreev (Azadovskij, "Ril'ke i Benois," p. 101). Rilke responded somewhat coolly to Benois's suggestion that he translate the religious thinkers Rozanov and Merezhkovsky, and spent three pages expressing his basic suspicion of all philosophical systems. (See: R. M. Rilke, *Worpswede. Auguste Rodin. Pis'ma. Stixi,* pp. 177–79.) Given Rilke's aversion at this time to the Russian Modernists, it is not surprising that only one of their number, the Symbolist Fyodor Sologub, is found among his translations from those early years. Rilke attempted a version of part of a short story entitled "Červjak" ("The Worm"—incorrectly given by Brutzer, and perhaps by Rilke as "Červ' "). It is significant that the story does not belong to the author's more overtly decadent works, but is a rather naturalistic tale about the mental anguish and obsession of a school girl. (The translation appears only in Rilke's "Anfängerheften," the notebooks he used when first studying Russian, and is thus unavailable for examination.) Later Rilke's taste would broaden. In 1919 he translated two short poems by Zinaida Gippius; they remain unpublished. In 1922, Sologub's novel *Slašče jada* (*Sweeter Than Poison*) appeared in Munich in a German translation by Fega Frisch. In it a small poem by Sologub, "Esli b, serdce, ty ležalo" ("If, My Heart, Thou Layest"), appears without acknowledgment on page 67 and again on page 369. The poem was translated by Rilke for his friend Frau Frisch, with the request that she publish it without using his name. The manuscript is located in the Van Mises Collection of the Houghton Library at Harvard. In 1925, Rilke had only praise for the poetry of young Boris Pasternak. The work of Marina Tsvetaeva, with whom he corresponded during 1926, he found attractive, but ultimately too difficult to read in the original. He did not attempt to translate either poet, as far as is known.

31. The Lermontov poems appear in Rilke's "Anfängerheften." Brutzer considers them mere linguistic exercises of no artistic merit. Since the notebooks are currently unavailable for examination, this judgment cannot be tested.
32. The third Lermontov poem, "Vyxožu odin ja na dorogu," was not translated until 1919, and so will be discussed in chapter 8.
33. Rilke's translation of "Vesna i noč'" ("Springtime and Night") is available only in Brutzer, *RrR,* p. 81. He sent a transliteration of the Russian to Schill on 23 February 1900, with the remark, "Yesterday, I translated a pretty poem by Fofanov" (B und T. 1899–1902, p. 27).
34. Not a great deal is available on Rilke's dramas. See: Howard Roman, "Rilke's Dramas—an Annotated List"; Howard Roman, "Rilke's Psychodramas"; Frank H. Wood, "Rilke and the Theater"; Ursula Münchow, "Das 'tägliche Leben.' Die dramatischen Experimente des jungen Rilke"; Rainer Maria Rilke, *Nine Plays,* trans. Klaus Phillips and John Locke, p. ix; Rilke's own comments on the theater and on specific plays in *SW* V; the *B und T. 1899–1902;* and the extant plays and fragments in *SW* IV.
35. Münchow, "Das 'tägliche Leben,'" p. 9. These were *Im Frühfrost,* written in 1895, performed in 1897; *Jetzt und in der Stunde unseres Absterbens,* 1896; and *Das tägliche Leben*—a disastrous performance—in 1901. Erich Simenauer in *Rainer Maria Rilke. Legende und Mythos* (p. 330), claims that a drama *Gleich und Frei* was also performed, and panned, in Prague in 1896.
36. *GB* I, p. 79.
37. Ibid., p. 83.
38. N. A. Alekseev, "Pis'ma k Čexovu ot ego perevodčikov," p. 105.
39. Eberhard Wolfgramm, "Tschechow und die Deutschen," p. 117.
40. *GB* I, pp. 83–84.
41. Ibid., p. 83.
42. Simon Karlinsky, commentary to *Anton Chekhov's Life and Thought,* trans. Michael Heim, p. 281.
43. A. P. Čexov, *Izbrannye proizvedenija v trëx tomax,* III, p. 408.

44. Ibid., p. 454.
45. Letter of 17 May 1926. In K. N. Azadovskij and E. B. Pasternak, "Iz perepiski Ril'ke, Cvetaevoj i Pasternaka v 1926 godu," p. 251.
46. Thomas Mann, "Tonio Kröger," p. 79.
47. This work is entitled "Fragment" in the *SW* (IV, 867–76).
48. See Rudolph Binion, *Frau Lou*, especially part 2, "Womanhood."
49. Brutzer, *RrR*, p. 100. Brutzer published Rilke's Russian poems for the first time, gave German translations, and attempted to place them within the context of Rilke's views on Russia. She concerns herself mainly with origin and content. Two later scholars, Samson Soloveitchik and Everett Bushnell Gladding, approach the poems strictly from the point of view of the quality of the Russian, in "Rilke's Original Russian Poems." The poems have since been published, with German translations and notes, in *SW* IV, 947–71.
50. The most glaring, and also most amusing, of his errors is his use of the word *tjažba*, meaning lawsuit, in the line "Ja tak ustal ot tjažby bol'nyx dnej" (IV, 959). What Rilke probably wanted was *tjagoty* or *tjažesti*, meaning weight or burdens; but he ends up by saying: "I am so tired of the lawsuits of sick days" (pointed out by Soloveitchik and Gladding, "Original Russian Poems," p. 521).
51. For four days in July 1900, Rilke and Lou stayed with the peasant poet Spiridon Drozhzhin in his village of Nisovka on the Volga. Rilke had by that time published his translation of two of Drozhzhin's poems in the *Prager Bote*. For an account of the machinations which finally led to this visit, see E. M. Butler, *Rainer Maria Rilke*, as well as Drozhzhin's memoir, "Der deutsche Dichter Rainer Maria Rilke. Erinnerungen," in *Das Inselschiff*. However it actually came about, the experience was a vivid and important one for Rilke.
52. The Russian is incorrect. As Soloveitchik and Gladding point out ("Original Russian Poems," p. 516), the verb should be *vzjal*, not *bral*, to maintain the correct verbal aspect. It should be noted, however, that these writers were using the version given by Brutzer, which deviates in a number of instances from that one published in the *SW*, which is based on a corrected copy sent to Lou.
53. Letter to Frieda von Bülow, 27 May 1899, *GB* I, 68–69.
54. *Tagebücher*, 5 December 1900, p. 343.
55. In his very interesting reminiscence of the visit, Drozhzhin describes this habit of theirs; the practical Russian remarks that he wasn't convinced of the efficacy of going barefoot, and preferred to wear his high boots, as usual (Drožžin, "Erinnerungen," p. 228).
56. Brutzer, *RrR*, p. 99.
57. "Moderne russische Kunstbestrebungen," *SW* V, 619–20.
58. A number of years later, in 1919, Rilke would return to Tyutchev. In a letter to Fega Frisch, the translator of Sologub, he enclosed two translations from the Russian: the Sologub poem, "Esli b, serdce, ty ležalo," and the first four lines of a poem by Tyutchev which begins "O veščaja duša moja" ("O my visionary soul"). The manuscript is at the Houghton Library, Harvard.
59. Letter to Sophie Schill, 23 February 1900, *GB* I, 80.
60. Brutzer, *RrR*, p. 54.
61. Tjučev, "Silentium," in *The Penguin Book of Russian Verse*, pp. 132–33. Translation by Dimitri Obolensky.
62. In the *SW*, the editor has added German titles to the Russian poems. He translates "Ja tak ustal" as "Ich wurde so müd" (IV, 959). Brutzer likewise renders the line this way. But while *ustal* can be read as the masculine form of the past tense of the verb *ustat'* ("to grow tired"), it is also the short form of the adjective *ustalyj* ("tired"). Common usage and the context of Rilke's poem make the latter more appropriate; hence "I am so tired" rather than "I grew . . . ."
63. M. Ju. Lermontov, *Izbrannye proizvedenija*, I, 196.
64. *Paula Modersohn-Becker in Briefen und Tagebüchern*, Eds. Günther Busch and Liselotte von Reinken, pp. 243–45.
65. Letter to Rudolf Alexander Schröder, 22 April 1901, *GB* I, 157.

NOTES TO PAGES 49–61

66. Letter to Gräfin Franziska Reventlow, 28 April 1901, *GB* I, 158.
67. Lermontov, *Izbrannye proizvedenija*, I, 143–44.
68. Erich Simenauer, *Legende und Mythos*, pp. 231–310.
69. Magda von Hattingberg, *Rilke und Benvenuta*, p. 211.
70. *RMR-Lou*, 15 April 1904, p. 143.
71. The particular Znamenskaya icon to which Rilke is referring is probably one in the Znamenskaya Monastery in Moscow, of which he wrote to a Russian acquaintance in 1899, "I love that one above all others" (quoted in Vladimir Boutchik, E. L. Stahl, and Stanley Mitchell, "Letters of Rainer Maria Rilke to Helene XXX," p. 158).

NOTES TO CHAPTER 3

1. The most significant investigation of the Russian influences on the *SB* is found in Ruth Mövius's study, *Rainer Maria Rilkes Stunden-Buch. Entstehung und Gehalt*, published in 1934. She points out that overt Russian topics are concentrated in part one, and discusses poems which relate directly to the experience, noting the importance of the East-West dichotomy. She finds virtually no Russian elements in the second and third parts, and feels that Rilke's Russian experiences, expressed overtly as "astonishment, which became joyously aware of itself, at a new earth recognized as home—that is, Russia" (p. 43), are present there only as a backdrop or an already assimilated emotional fact and expressed only unconsciously. What Mövius says of the Russian aspects of the cycle is, as far as it goes, accurate and enlightening. But she neglects to examine a number of poems which reflect Russian impulses. See also: M. Rudnickij, "Russkie Motivy v 'Knige Časov' Ril'ke."
2. Letter to Frieda von Bülow, *B und T. 1899–1902*, p. 17.
3. In addition to the icons with which he became familiar through histories and art books, Rilke saw many religious paintings in the churches, monasteries, and museums he visited. He became fairly knowledgeable about them, and as early as May 1899 remarked in a letter that he had learned to tell the Virgin of Vladimir from that of Smolensk, and was immersing himself in the study of Russian art, including "the representation of Christ in the Russian church" (Boutchik, Stahl, and Mitchell, "Letters to Helene," p. 155).
4. The Peredvizhniki ("Wanderers") served as important predecessors for the Slavic Revival movement, which flourished at the end of the century. The principal members of the latter group included at one time or another Serov, Repin, Nesterov, Vrubel, Antokolsky, the brothers Apollinary, and Viktor Vasnetsov, all major names in Russian art of the period. The common interests of the group included the history of Muscovy and Kievan Rus; among the genres they practiced were painting, sculpture, and stage design based on historical and folkloric themes, and architecture in a pseudo-archaic style. For excellent treatment of the period from the 1800s to the first decade of this century, see the special issue of *Apollo* for December 1973, on Russian art; and G. H. Hamilton, *The Art and Architecture of Russia*.

   Rilke showed particular interest in two artists, Ivan Kramskoy (1837–87) and Alexander Ivanov (1806–58). Brutzer (*RrR*, pp. 30–31), quotes an unpublished letter to Leonid Pasternak, dated 3 March 1900, in which Rilke states his intention of writing a series of essays about Russian artists, beginning with these two. In a letter to Sophie Schill dated two days later, Rilke thanks his friend for sending him a copy of a brochure she had written on Ivanov. In the same letter, he says he wants to write an essay on Kramskoy "which may perhaps even turn into a book" (*GB* I, 24–36).
5. Azadovskij, "Ril'ke i Benois," pp. 79–82.
6. Ibid., p. 81.
7. Ibid., p. 82.

8. Ibid., pp. 82–85.
9. "Russische Kunst" was expanded in July 1901, and published in October 1901.
10. In an essay entitled "Über Kunst" ("On Art"), written in 1898 as a reaction to Tolstoy's "What Is Art?" Rilke had firmly rejected the didactic approach to art; "We must articulate that the essence of beauty does not lie in the effect, but in existing" (V, 428).
11. Andreas-Salomé, "Das russische Heiligenbild und sein Dichter."
12. Ibid.
13. The cathedral was built between 1862 and 1883 as a monument to the Christianizing of Russia by Saint Vladimir in 988. See the illustrated study by S. V. Kul'zenko, *Sobor sv. kn. Vladimira v Kieve*.
14. In a letter to Benois written 15 November 1901, Rilke states that he has revised his ideas about Vasnetsov; but he maintains that the first, that is, the normative and theoretical, part of the essay is still correct (Azadovskij, "Ril'ke i Benois," p. 93).
15. The essay was probably written at the end of 1901, and was revised and republished in 1902.
16. There is also an echo in the title of an image used by Rilke in a letter to Helen Voronin on 18 May 1899. At that time, Rilke understood very little Russian; in the letter he turns this lack to his advantage, by finding in the sounds of the Russian language, which for him were still amorphous, a communication more profound than mere words: "Your language is for me only sound—but I don't have to invent a sense for it; there are hours where the sound itself becomes meaning and image and expression. And now I know that these hours are *Russian hours*, and that I love Russian hours greatly" (quoted in Boutchik, Stahl, and Mitchell, "Letters to Helene," p. 154). The "hours" of the *Book of Hours* were, in a sense, a continuation of these Russian hours: inspired by Russian things, and full of Russian meanings.
17. This is the only poem which gives us either the monk's name or that of his monastery. He dates his letter, "In the cloister of the Holy Anargyra, on the death-day of Saint Charitinas, October 5" (III, 368). Mövius (*Rilkes Stunden-Buch*, pp. 252–53), provides the information that the "holy Anargyra" are Saints Cosma and Damian, third-century martyrs who were brothers and doctors, and who dispensed their services free. They are in addition the patron saints of Bohemia, and thus perhaps known to Rilke from his Prague days. Finally, they are among the most popular saints in Russia, after whom numerous monasteries and villages were named. From her sources, Mövius concludes that the particular monastery of Saints Cosma and Damian in which Rilke places his protagonist was probably one near Yaroslavl on the Volga. The choice of a monastery dedicated to martyrs whose most notable act was the dispensation of charity is significant in the light of the subsequent development of the second and third parts of the *SB*, whose central themes are death, poverty, and charity.
18. Nikolaj Leskov, "Na kraju sveta." In *Sobranie sočinenij v odinnadcat' tomax*, V, 451–517. Rilke undoubtedly read Lou's discussion of the story in her article on Leskov, "Russische Heiligenbild." It is possible that Rilke had read only this article. But it seems more likely that he had read the story itself, perhaps spurred on by the article, which portrays Leskov's fiction in a light that must have been highly attractive to Rilke. Leskov, a writer who vividly and sympathetically portrayed the world of the provincial Russian clergy and the nature of Russian Christianity in such works as *Cathedral Folk, The Enchanted Wanderer,* or *The Sealed Angel*, expressed ideas closely corresponding with those which Rilke entertained on the subject. For the most thorough study of Leskov to date, see Hugh McLean, *Nikolai Leskov. The Man and His Art*.
19. Leskov, "Na kraju sveta," in *Sobranie sočinenij,* V, 454–55.
20. Ibid., p. 455.
21. Ingeborg Schnack, *Rainer Maria Rilke. Chronik seines Lebens und seines Werkes,* I, 96.
22. This interpretation is supported by a similar phrase spoken by the monk in a poem which appeared in the 1905 version of part one: "Was irren meine Hände in den Pinseln? / Wenn ich dich male, Gott, du merkst es kaum" ("Why do my hands stray among the brushes? When I paint you, God, you hardly notice it" [I, 263]).

23. Earlier in the cycle, we have evidence that even in technical matters, Apostol is a conservative. According to Hamilton (*Art and Architecture*, p. 69), the standard background for early Russian icons was "gold or silver, in accordance with Greek practice. But as early as the twelfth century, a ground of white or yellow ochre was substituted." Apostol was evidently working in the older tradition, for he says of his work, "Ich mal es auf Goldgrund und gross" ("I paint it on a gold background, and large" [I, 253]).
24. Hamilton, *Art and Architecture*, p. 101.
25. Ibid.
26. Ibid.
27. Ibid., p. 152. Other lines in the monk's letter reflect the Stoglav's pronouncements. The latter urged, for example, that icon painters "should be filled with humility, meekness, and piety" (H. P. Gerhard, *The World of Icons*, p. 177). These are the same qualities possessed by the Russian Saint Nicholas, by Saint Francis as he appears in the *SB*, and by the monk himself. The Stoglav of 1551 further urged the painter to "pay numerous visits to his spiritual fathers and inform them about his way of life and . . . fast and pray" (Ibid.). Although Apostol does not visit the Metropolitan, he feels a pressing need to write to him, and before going on to the problems that are really bothering him, he spends a page describing his life style: "Ich lebe fromm. . . . Ich schau ins Land, ich lausche, bete, lese" ("I live piously. I gaze into the countryside, I listen, pray, read" [III, 361]).
28. F. M. Dostoevskij, *Brat'ja Karamazovy*, I, 384.
29. The next line of this poem reads, "Mit denen dich der Heilige verschwieg" (With which the saint concealed you [I, 254]). Mövius feels this saintly painter was probably Saint Luke, patron saint of artists and purported creator of two archetypal icons in Constantinople (*Rilkes Stunden-Buch*, p. 72). She also mentions as a possibility Olympus (Alimpi, Alippi), a later Russian saint who was a monk in the Kiev Pecherskaya Lavra, and an icon painter (Hamilton, *Art and Architecture*, p. 72). Olympius was, incidentally, one of the Russian figures portrayed by Vasnetsov in Saint Vladimir's in Kiev.
30. A notable exception is the poem which begins, "Selten ist Sonne im Sobor" ("There is seldom sun in the Sobor" [I, 292]), which immediately precedes the poem about the dark peasants. We know from a prose note in "Die Gebete" that the poem was conceived by the monk while he "sich seiner Gebete im Uspenski-Sobór zu Moskau erinnerte" ("recalled his prayers in the Uspenski-Sobor in Moscow" [III, 355]). The fifteenth-century Uspenski Sobor (Cathedral of the Dormition) is one of the churches in the Moscow Kremlin. Like many Russian churches, it has little illumination from outside, with narrow windows set high in the walls. The interior, including the supporting columns, is decorated from floor to ceiling with paintings of saints. Rilke elicits all these aspects of the church: lack of sunlight, ornateness of decor, multitude of images, in the first strophe: "Selten ist Sonne im Sobór. / Die Wände wachsen aus Gestalten" ("There is seldom sun in the Sobor. The walls grow from figures" [I, 292]). Yet the mood is not gloomy or oppressive; the poem is alive with lights flickering on the golden gates of the sanctuary and on the silver and jewels surrounding the icons.
31. I have really only begun to scratch the surface of Rilke's extremely complex imagery in the *Stunden-Buch*. An example of his complicated inversion of images occurs in the last two poems of part one, in which the monk, who has been portrayed as an artist, an active and creative force, is suddenly presented in terms of passive, receptive earth-images; his soul becomes a silent steppe. On the other hand, God, seen variously as the fertile earth and a developing work of art, appears suddenly as a bard—an artist and creator. The relationship is further complicated by the fact that God-the-artist is not, like the monk, a painter, for he is blind. Once this shift of metaphoric roles has taken place, a further inversion occurs: the artist, who now envisions himself as earth, once again assumes an active role, *as* earth, by collecting and returning to the bard the latter's long-lost songs; while God, temporarily cast as an artist, is a barren one, who must take his own earlier creations back from the productive earth! In this dense cluster of images, Rilke makes the artist ultimately indistinguishable from his work of art, as well as from his source of inspiration.

32. *Tagebücher*, p. 346.
33. Ibid., p. 349.
34. For an extensive examination of this problem, see Simenauer, *Legende und Mythos*, pp. 313–80.
35. Rilke here uses one of two common Russian terms for "monastery"—*monastyr;* the other is *lavra*, which he uses elsewhere in the same poem.
36. Dmitrij Tschižewskij, *Das heilige Russland*, p. 41.
37. *Tagebücher*, p. 195.
38. Ibid., pp. 195–96.
39. It is interesting to conjecture whether Rilke knew the poem by Nietzsche entitled "Mitleid hin und her" ("Compassion To and Fro"). Rilke had read some Nietzsche, and must in addition have heard some of his ideas from Lou, who had been Nietzsche's close companion for much of the summer of 1882. Despite a very different tone (Nietzsche's poem juxtaposes bitter Romantic despair and a cold irony), there is formal similarity between the poems. Nietzsche ends his first strophe with the line, "Wohl dem, der jetzt noch—Heimat hat!" ("Happy is he who now still has a home"). He ends his fifth strophe, "Weh dem, der keine Heimat hat" ("Woe to him who has no home"). Rilke's Russian villages wait along the river "auf den, der keinen Heimat hat" ("for him who has no home"); and in a poem in the *SB* entitled "Herbsttag" ("Autumn Day" [I, 398]), the image appears again: "Wer jetzt kein Haus hat, baut sich keines mehr" ("Whoever has no house now, will build none"). It is clear that Nietzsche, despite the sneer apparent in his final stanzas, had felt deeply the position of homeless wanderer, of outcast. Indeed, the ferocity of the ending would seem possible only for someone who was determined to overcome softness and pity in himself. Rilke's tone reflects the more vague melancholy of the turn of the century, mixed with his very real conviction that he had no homeland in the conventional sense, and that he must actively search for one. It may be only coincidence that both Nietzsche and Rilke had loved, and been rejected by, Lou Andreas-Salomé.
40. Entry of 15 September 1900, *Tagebücher*, p. 234.
41. This was an unfinished painting by Kramskoy which Rilke saw in August 1900, during his visit to A. I. Kramskoy, the artist's son (Azadovskij and Čertkov, "Russkie vstreči," p. 374.
42. *Tagebücher*, p. 210.
43. Ibid.
44. See Walter Sokel, "The Devolution of Self in *The Notebooks of Malte Laurids Brigge*," in *Rilke. The Alchemy of Alienation*, ed. Frank Baron, Ernst Dick, and Warren R. Maurer, pp. 171–90. The essay is a revised and translated version of "Zwischen Existenz und Weltinnenraum: Zum Prozess der Ent-Ichung im Malte Laurids Brigge."
45. Azadovskij, "Ril'ke i Benois," p. 91.
46. Dostoevskij, *Brat'ja Karamazovy*, I, 387.
47. Rilke had at this time not yet succumbed to the seduction of Paris, a city which, almost in spite of himself, he came to love above all others, and in which part of the *Stunden-Buch* was written.
48. Hamilton, *Art and Architecture*, p. 135.
49. Ibid.

NOTES TO CHAPTER 4

1. Brutzer (*RrR*, p. 43), mentions a relationship between the *Buch der Bilder* and *Poltava*. Harald Raab, in "Rilke und die Welt der Slawen" (p. 102), mentions the *Buch der Bilder* "with its Pushkin-reflections in 'Karl der Zwölfte.'" W. L. Graff remarks, in *Rainer Maria Rilke: Creative Anguish of a Modern Poet* (p. 119), that "traces of . . . *Poltava* are found in some poems of the Book of Images." And George C. Schoolfield, in "Charles

XII Rides in Worpswede," briefly compares Rilke's poem about Charles to *Poltava*, but concentrates on Rilke's Scandinavian sources.
2. A. S. Puškin, *Poltava*, in *Polnoe sobranie sočinenij v desjati tomax*, IV, 251–305.
3. Ibid., p. 293.
4. Ibid., p. 297.
5. In his article "Charles XII," Schoolfield maintains that Rilke's Charles is a *victorious* leader in love with battle. This interpretation would seem to stem from Schoolfield's desire to show how closely Rilke adhered to the works of Verner von Heidenstam, to which Schoolfield links many details.
6. *Bylina* (plural *byliny*) is the name generally given to the oral epics of early medieval Russia; the historical songs are oral epics of late medieval Russia. The largest cycle of *byliny* has as its traditional setting the court of Prince Vladimir (978–1015) at Kiev. Most *byliny* focus on the exploits of the semilegendary Kievan heroes, and can be compared to the tales of Arthur and his knights—with the important difference that in the *byliny* the Western concept of chivalry is lacking.
7. The *byliny* have many variants, and it is not certain which ones Rilke had access to. According to Brutzer (*RrR*, p. 71), Rilke had read W. R. S. Ralston's *Songs of the Russian People*, which contains a synopsis of this particular variant on pages 59–63. But Rilke had other sources for medieval matter as well, as is obvious from his use of them in the second poem of "Die Zaren" and in several stories in the *Geschichten*.
8. Letter of 15 August 1903, *RMR-Lou*, p. 105.
9. The *bylina* variant used here is "Pervaja Poezdka Il'ja Muromca. Il'ja i Solovej-Razbojnik" ("Il'ya of Murom's First Journey. Il'ya and Nightingale the Robber") in *The Penguin Book of Russian Verse*, pp. 23–32.
10. In both works there is a symbolic emphasis on seeing. Ilya shoots out Solovey's eye so he can't see, and Rilke's monster terrifies travelers precisely because he can't *be* seen; he threatens by means of his disembodied scream. An interesting footnote to both works is found in Gogol's romantic horror tale "Vij," which Rilke had read (Brutzer, *RrR*, p. 44). There the protagonist is undone because he looks at the monster, Vij, thereby giving it power over him, and succumbing to Vij's magic. Ilya breaks Solovey's magic by destroying his vision; Rilke's heroes, unable to see the monster, are forced to take the one path that enables them to triumph: that of blind endurance.
11. The image may be based in part on the work by the Russian painter Ilya Repin, whose portrayal of Ivan clutching his dying son amid a spreading pool of blood is one of the most famous and gripping versions of the event.
12. Ronald Hingley, *The Tsars. 1533–1917*, p. 69.
13. This process of reversal occurs in several poems in the *SB*, where the monk calls God his son: "Du bist die Erbe. / Söhne sind die Erben, / denn Väter sterben. / Söhne stehn und blühn" ("You are the heir. Sons are the heirs, for fathers die. Sons stand and bloom" [I, 314]). And: "Und ich—ich soll dich Vater nennen? / Das hiesse tausendmal mich von dir trennen. / Du bist mein Sohn" ("And I—I should call you father? That would mean separating myself from you a thousand times. You are my son" [I, 312]).
14. This sympathy is nowhere to be construed as the identity of the poet with his characters. Nor, in the case of Charles XII, should Rilke's basically sympathetic attitude toward his protagonist be seen as approval of his every action. In *Karl Marx und Friedrich Engels als Literaturhistoriker* (pp. 133–34), Georg Lukács refers to the scene in Rilke's poem where Charles looses dogs on the bridegrooms of girls whom he desires for himself. Lukács condemns Rilke for not making a moral judgment against Charles's acts, and in his narrow approach to the poem, goes so far as to attempt to make Rilke the unwitting apologist for Nazi-like perversity; Lukács calls Charles's actions worthy of Goering. But Rilke was interested, not in making an ethical judgment against Charles, but in selectively utilizing the symbolic potential of this historical figure for his own aesthetic and metaphysical purposes as a poet. In any case, the dog incident was perpetrated by the old, pre-Poltava Charles, and it is possible that Rilke included it precisely as a backdrop against which to judge the transformation wrought in the course of the poem.

NOTES TO CHAPTER 5

1. Brutzer, *RrR*, p. 71.
2. E. M. Butler, *Rainer Maria Rilke*, p. 74.
3. Relatively little scholarship has been devoted to the relationship of *Geschichten* to Russia. The most important discussions occur in Butler's *Rilke*, in Eva C. Wunderlich's "Slavonic Traces in Rilke's *Geschichten vom lieben Gott*," and in Wunderlich's notes as editor of the Twayne edition of Rilke's *Geschichten*. Butler goes into some detail about Rilke's relationship to Russia in general, devoting a chapter to the topic. But she spends only a few pages on the stories, finding them "pretentious and puerile" (p. 72), and characterized by "unmitigated preciosity" (p. 75). Wunderlich in her article attempts to come to grips with Butler's harsh judgment, trying especially to demonstrate that Rilke's use of his Russian sources was artistically valid.
4. Quoted by Robert Heinz Heygrodt, "Rilke und Russland," p. 7.
5. Letter of 15 August 1903, *RMR-Lou*, p. 106.
6. See for example the discussion between the artist Braun and the Russian student Anna Mahr in Gerhart Hauptmann's play *Einsame Menschen*, written in 1891, or the basic conflict in Hauptmann's *Michael Kramer*, which Rilke saw and greatly praised in December 1900.
7. Rilke's narrator says his tale is based on a *Märchen* or *bylina*. It is not clear whether this was an oversight on Rilke's part, or whether he merely ignored the distinction between *bylina* and historical song. The historical songs, which are shorter than *byliny* and which focus on historical persons and events, often deal with Ivan the Terrible. Rilke's sources call the present story simply a *rasskaz* ("story") and a *conte populaire*.
8. Pavel Rybnikov, *Pesni sobrannye P. N. Rybnikovym*, II.
9. Rambaud, *Russie Épique*, pp. 268–72.
10. D. P. Costello and I. P. Foote, *Russian Folk Literature*, p. 151.
11. Ibid., p. 149.
12. Ibid., p. 151.
13. Rybnikov, *Pesni sobrannye*, p. 236.
14. Ibid.
15. The image of the miserly tsar with his mountain of gold may have been suggested to Rilke by his reading of Alexander Pushkin's little tragedy "The Covetous Knight" ("Skupoj rycar," in his *Polnoe sobranie*, vol. V, 331–53). The play contains a similar scene, in which an aged miser soliloquizes about his cellar full of gold, and compares himself to the tsar who

    > once ordered his troops
    > to carry earth by the handful to a pile,
    > and a proud hill arose—and the tsar
    > could from the top gaze joyfully
    > over the valley, filled with white tents,
    > and the sea, where sailing ships ran.
    > Thus I, bearing each scant handful,
    > have brought my accustomed tribute to this cellar,
    > and raised my hill—and from its height
    > I can gaze over all that's in my sway.
    >   (p. 342)

16. Rilke uses two words here to render the single Russian word *pravda* which appears in the Rybnikov text. This has been noticed by Wunderlich ("Slavonic Traces," p. 290), who points out that Rilke "seems to have followed the Russian text more closely" than had Rambaud in giving the Russian word both its primary and secondary meanings of truth and righteousness. Rambaud translates it simply as "justice." An impetus to Rilke's double translation may have come from his reading of *Le Roman Russe;* there de Vogüé says, "Truth, justice, the Russian word *pravda* has both meanings, or to put it better, it implies the two ideas in one, single and indivisible. It is a point of great consequence and

well worth our reflection: for languages disclose the philosophical conceptions of races" (p. 342).
17. Rambaud, *Russie Épique*, p. 268.
18. Rybnikov, *Pesni sobrannye*, p. 233.
19. Ibid.
20. There is in the absurd but consistent logic of this scene something reminiscent of fairy tales, where the hero's success at a task is often preceded by a long series of other people's failures. It is also related to another of Rilke's own early works, the sketch "Der Drachentöter" ("The Dragon Killer") of 1901–02 (IV, 672–87). There, a series of knights unsuccessfully try to kill a dragon and win a princess's hand. The youth who finally slays the dragon, however, rejects the princess. And to this, too, there is a parallel in the present story, in the wise peasant who alone gives the right answers, but wants no reward.
21. The image of Ivan beheading his advisers may have occurred to Rilke thanks to Rambaud, who quotes the tsar as saying that if anyone pointed out to him three boyars guilty of treason, he would boil one in a cauldron, impale the second, and "the third I would have decapitated" (*Russie Épique*, p. 268).
22. Rybnikov, *Pesni sobrannye*, p. 233.
23. Ibid.
24. Ibid., p. 234.
25. This relationship is mirrored by Ivan himself in his answer to the third riddle, "What is the sweetest thing on earth?" He expands on the peasant's simple answer—"Water, because nothing can live without it"—in a lengthy and comical digression: "If one of you felt thirsty, and they told you there was no water, and then you found out that someone had it in abundance, and your thirst was intolerable, then, it seems, you would give God knows what for a single spoonful, if only they'd give you some to drink" (Rybnikov, *Pesni sobrannye*, p. 235). Ivan unwittingly describes here his own desperate thirst for the answers and the gold.
26. Rilke makes his tsar slightly more greedy than Rybnikov's. The proportion of sand to gold in the latter is two to one, in Rilke, three to one.
27. Rybnikov, *Pesni sobrannye*, p. 235.
28. N. V. Gogol', "Nos," in *Sobranie sočinenij v šesti tomax*, III, 44–70.
29. Vsevolod Setchkarev, *Gogol. His Life and Works*, p. 157.
30. Vladimir Nabokov, *Nikolai Gogol*, pp. 3–5.
31. Eudo Mason, "Rilkes Humor," *Deutsche Weltliteratur. Von Goethe bis Ingeborg Bachmann. Festgabe für J. Alan Pfeffer*, pp. 216–44.
32. There are several likely sources for Rilke's knowledge of the waning oral tradition. These include the works of the Ukrainian poet Taras Shevchenko, especially the cycle entitled "The Kobzar"; comments by Rambaud in his chapter "The Last Kobzars" in *Russie Épique;* and various works by Gogol, especially *Taras Bulba* and the unfinished novel *The Hetman*, which contained a chapter called "The Bloody Bandurist."
33. E. M. Butler, discussing this passage, raps Rilke's knuckles for his "patronizing sneer" at the scholars who buried the songs in books, and criticizes Rilke, who, never having gone to an area remote enough to hear a *bylina* or a *skazka* recited, instead sentimentalized the very material he took from precisely such collectors and scholars as he mocks here (*Rilke*, pp. 178–79). Butler has a point, but she both misreads and underestimates Rilke. His narrator is not sad that the scholars "buried" the songs, but that the songs had "died" in the first place, and needed to be buried. In addition, Butler's question seems irrelevant. Certainly the ethnographers did a great service; Rilke, however, was a transforming and creative artist. He had no intention either of condemning the ethnographers, or of becoming one.
34. Rilke made a slip here. As Rilke's story was written in 1899, that would set the tale between 1399 and 1499, whereas the historical Ivan IV lived 1533–84. Thus the tale couldn't have been much more than 315 years old.
35. Wunderlich, "Slavonic Traces," p. 288.
36. Costello and Foote, *Folk Literature*, p. 62.

37. I. S. Turgenev, *Zapiski oxotnika* (Moscow, 1966), p. 277.
38. August Löwis von Menar, *Der Held im deutschen und russischen Märchen* (Berlin, 1912).
39. Wunderlich asserts, in "Slavonic Traces" (p. 299), that sources for this tale are "only indirectly Russian," and that its connection with Russian literature is "rather remote." I, however, do not agree with this position.
40. Butler points out the relation between Ewald and the Russian tradition of crippled bards, the *kaleki* (literally, "cripples"), who, like the usually blind singers in the Ukraine, were itinerant bards (*Rilke*, p. 77). The parallel is only partly apt, however, since Rilke emphasizes Ewald's immobility, his role as "still point," and since Ewald's primary function is that of listener and not of narrator. He does pass the tales on to the neighborhood children, but we never see him in that role. Rilke's odd and almost distasteful idealization of the cripple must be seen in the same light as his praise of poverty in the *Stunden-Buch*. Both constituted for him a kind of moral superiority based on an imagined purity, in contrast to the shallowness and corruption of the wealthy, "normal" world.
41. Taras Shevchenko, "Selected Poems, ed. Clarence A. Manning, pp. 89–108.
42. Rilke rarely made comments about political matters, except where they directly affected something dear to him. In 1907 he wrote to a friend,

> You know my opinion that the revolutionary is directly opposed to the Russian: that is, the Russian is excellently suited for it, in about the same way that a batiste handkerchief is very nice for wiping up ink—being, however, a complete misuse and ruthless misunderstanding of its actual qualities.

(Letter to Karl von der Heydt, 3 May 1907, *GB* II, 315.) In an earlier letter he had made a similar remark to Ellen Key; having just visited Maxim Gorky, who like him was wintering on Capri, Rilke writes:

> The revolutionary [seems] to me a contradiction of both the artist and the Russian.... Both have so very many intimate reasons to be against revolutions, because for both nothing is so important as patience.

(Letter of 18 April 1907, *GB* II, 312–13.) But it is important to note that Rilke made a distinction between a possible Russian revolt against the tsar, the "rightful" ruler of Russia, and a war for freedom from outside (in this case, Polish) domination, such as he depicts in "Das Lied von der Gerechtigkeit."
43. Rambaud, *Russie Épique*, p. 474.
44. Gogol', *Sobranie sočinenij*, II, 64.
45. Wunderlich, *Geschichten*, p. 140.
46. The influence of another work by Shevchenko may be found in the digression about the Ukraine. In the poetic cycle "The Kobzar," he likens the steppe full of ancient burial mounds to the "deep blue ocean." On one of the mounds sits a *kobzar*, whose thoughts rise and disappear into the sky like "a grey-winged eagle," while above the tomb "a black eagle / flies just like a sentinel" (*Poems*, p. 69; p. 65). In his description of the steppe, Rilke says the mounds (*Kurgane*) are "the graves of bygone races, which traverse the whole heath like a petrified, sleeping wave" (IV, 330). Atop the mounds one could see "figures ... crop up," and "sometimes dark birds lift off the mounds" (IV, 330). The similarity of the clustered images—ocean, man on tomb, black eagle; and wave, figures on tombs, dark birds—both in works dealing with Ukrainian unrest, both in narratives centrally involving *kobzars*, seems more than mere accident. The other possible influence on this passage, that of de Vogüé's description, was suggested in chapter 1.
47. Rilke says that no one had wanted to take Aljoscha "to the Sicz, to the Zaporozhians" (IV, 332). The Zaporozhian Sicz was a famous Cossack camp on an island in the Dniepr. The camp was located "za porohy" ("beyond the rapids"), hence, "Zaporozhian." It was the seat of the Cossack military brotherhood, and the starting point of many raids and rebellions (Aleksander Gieysztor, et al., *History of Poland*, p. 218).
48. Wunderlich, "Slavonic Traces," pp. 290–94. Both Wunderlich (p. 294) and Ernst Zinn in his notes to Rilke's story (IV, 994) give the spelling as Ostap (Mikitin) Veresai. I use the Ukrainian spelling.

49. *Russie Épique*, pp. 435–36 and 444–45.
50. Roussof and Lisenko, *Kobzar Ostap Veresáj* (Kiev, 1874), quoted in Wunderlich, "Slavonic Traces," pp. 292–93, and translated by her as "exuberant untruth."
51. From a collection by M. Dragomanoff, quoted in Wunderlich, ibid., p. 293.
52. Rambaud, *Russie Épique*, p. 436.
53. Ibid., p. 447.
54. Gogol', *Sobranie sočinenij*, II, 61.
55. Shevchenko, *Poems*, pp. 9–10.
56. Letter to Helene Voronina, 11 May 1899, Boutchik, et al., p. 152.
57. Private correspondence with Dr. Andrij Hornjatkevyč.
58. It should be noted that the formal parallels between structure and content in the poem are true only of the translation which Rilke gives in his story:

> Wie schön ist die Jugend, die uns erfreut,
> Doch wer will sie halten? Sie flieht und bereut,
> Und wenn einer fröhlich sein will, der sei's heut,
> Und für morgen ist keine Gewissheit.
> (IV, 381)

The original Italian verses have a very different form from Rilke's:

> Quant' è bella giovinezza
> Che si fugge tuttavia!
> Chi vuol' esser lieto, sia;
> Di doman non c'è certezza.

(Cecilia M. Ady, *Lorenzo dei Medici and Renaissance Italy*, p. 136.) The Italian lines are equal in length; and the refrain was not the last line, but the last two lines of each stanza (Emmy Cremer, *Lorenzo de' Medici. Staatsmann, Mäzen, Dichter*, p. 138). The Italian lacks the breathless quality which Rilke emphasizes, due to its *a b b a* rhyme scheme; Rilke's version rolls on through three identical rhymes, to culminate in a shortened line with a slant rhyme (*erfreut, bereut, heut, Gewissheit*) which does, in fact, produce the emotional effect his narrator ascribes to Lorenzo's poem. In addition, and incidentally, Rilke's narrator says that the poem was written by Lorenzo when he was "young, not yet ruler" (IV, 380), whereas Cremer points out that it is from the "Canzone de Bacco," from the later years of the Magnifico" (p. 138).
59. One wonders whether E. T. A. Hoffmann's story, "Doge und Dogaresse," which revolves around an imagined tragedy attributed by the narrator to the figures in a Venetian painting, had any influence on this image.
60. It would be pleasant to be able to ascribe the tall, sharp spires and pointed gestures to the West alone. However, this schema doesn't hold; like the Western church builders of the late Middle Ages, Russian ecclesiastical architects of the seventeenth and eighteenth centuries showed a marked liking for tall towers and pointed roofs. As to the broad gesture of prayer as opposed to the threatening one, an examination of frescoes and icons often shows supplicants with their hands open and raised; and the Znamenskaya Virgin stands with her arms raised in prayer. But Melchisedech in Venice uses the same gesture in his prayers: "He rose with outstretched arms . . . as if he were making a sacrifice" (IV, 344). Thus the symbolic dichotomy does not in this case follow East-West lines.
61. Rilke expresses a similar idea in a letter to Franz Xaver Kappus on 23 December 1903; in response to Kappus's apparent complaints about his loss of faith, Rilke says:

> If you . . . recognize that he wasn't in your childhood . . . and if you feel with horror that he also doesn't exist now, in this hour, when we are speaking of him—what gives you the right to feel his lack and seek him, who never was, as if he were lost? Why don't you think that he is the coming one, who has been forever imminent, the future one, the final fruit of the tree whose leaves we are?
> (*BjD*, p. 32)

Eudo Mason in *Rilke* (p. 21) declares that Rilke was not "troubled by the apparent contradiction between this pantheistic God who has always existed and the future God who does not yet exist. He can do this because both conceptions remain for him noncommittal, subjective hypotheses." It seems to me that there is no essential contradiction between the pantheistic God who is present, or potential, in all things, and the God who is continually in the process of being created; man and nature are constantly creating new objects, which also have the potential for containing divinity.

62. Letter of 18 October 1900, *GB* I, 108.

NOTES TO CHAPTER 6

1. As Anthony R. Stephens notes in *Rilkes Malte Laurids Brigge. Strukturanalyse des erzählerischen Bewusstseins,* the central realms of personal past and current crisis are not abandoned in the historical anecdotes of the second part, but rather, the latter allow Malte to contemplate his own situation from a distance, as it were, and to draw from the anecdotes certain conclusions about himself and his struggles (pp. 169 ff. and 203 ff.).
2. For a summary of major approaches to the novel, see Judith Ryan, " 'Hypothetisches Erzählen': Zur Funktion von Phantasie and Einbildung in Rilkes 'Malte Laurids Brigge,' " in *Materialien zu Rainer Maria Rilke: 'Die Aufzeichnungen des Malte Laurids Brigge,'* ed. H. Engelhardt, pp. 244 ff.
3. Letter to Anton Kippenberg, 25 March 1910, *GB* VI, 84.
4. Letter of 28 December, 1911, *RMR-Lou,* p. 246.
5. Letter to Lotte Hepner, 8 November 1915, *GB* VI, 86.
6. Fritz Martini, discussing the Grisha episode, notes that "it is not at all a matter of the portrayal of a gripping historical event, meaningful in itself, . . . only, rather, of the concentrated selection of narrative objects, in the accents of whose occurrences Malte discovers elements of his own life-problems, and motifs which are vital to himself" ("Die Aufzeichnungen des Malte Laurids Brigge," in *Das Wagnis der Sprache. Interpretationen deutscher Prosa von Nietzsche bis Benn,* p. 163).
7. Sonia E. Howe, *The False Dmitri. A Russian Romance and Tragedy, Described by British Eye-Witnesses. 1604–1612.*
8. For a summary of the possible historical sources of the Grisha episode, see Brigitte von Witzleben, "Zu den historischen Quellen von Rilkes 'Die Aufzeichnungen des Malte Laurids Brigge,' " in *Materialien,* ed. H. Engelhardt, pp. 281–83.
9. Rauschnik, "Dmitri, Dimitrij (Demetrier)," pp. 209–13.
10. N. Karamzin, *Istorija gosudarstva rossijskago,* p. 170.
11. Martini, *Wagnis der Sprache,* p. 172.
12. Pushkin, *Polnoe sobranie,* p. 281.
13. Ibid., p. 282.
14. Rauschnik, "Dmitri," p. 211.
15. Although Karamzin saw her as something of a victim, Marina generally does not come off well; in *byliny* and historical songs about this period, she is portrayed as "an accursed type, she is the enchantress. . . . It is in order to please her that Grisha insults the images of the saints" (Rambaud, *Russie Épique,* p. 281). There are also songs on the topic of the False Dmitry ("Griška Razstrigin"—"Grisha the Unfrocked Monk") in Rybnikov's collection.
16. Martini, *Wagnis der Sprache,* p. 171.
17. Karamzin, *Istorija,* pp. 171–72.
18. Martini, *Wagnis der Sprache,* p. 172.
19. Sokel, "Zwischen Existenz und Weltinnenraum," p. 109.
20. Letter to Arthur Hospelt, 11 February 1912, *Briefe 1907–14,* pp. 196–97.
21. That Rilke was impressed with Dostoevsky we have seen in his enthusiasm about *Poor Folk.* According to Brutzer (*RrR,* p. 46), he also owned *Diary of a Writer.* In a letter to Karl von der Heydt, from the autumn of 1906, he asks his friend to send him something good to read while he recovers from a bout of dental surgery; here he specifically

suggests "some Dostoevsky" (*Briefe 1906–07*, p. 91). And in a letter of 2 January 1914, he promises to send Eva Cassirer a copy of *The Idiot*, which he calls "perhaps the finest book by Dostoevsky" (*Briefe 1907–14*, p. 327). Thus, though his remarks about the writer are sparse, they are always positive, and it seems safe to assume that he had read widely in Dostoevsky.

22. Dmitri Chizhevsky, "The Theme of the Double in Dostoevsky," p. 126. Ethical rationalism was Dostoevsky's *bête noire*, the voice of the nineteenth-century Russian enlightenment which he battled all his life. It placed total faith in rationalism and order, and ignored the irrational, the perverse, and the individual. See, for example, the tirades directed against it by the Underground Man.
23. Ibid.
24. Ibid., p. 127.
25. Willem Laurens Graff, *Creative Anguish*, p. 219.
26. Quoted in Chizhevsky, "Double in Dostoevsky," p. 113.
27. Ibid., p. 124.
28. F. M. Dostoevskij, "Dvojnik," in *Povesti i rasskazy*, I (Moscow, 1979), 176.
29. Ibid., p. 174.
30. Gogol', *Sobranie sočinenij*, III, p. 53.
31. Graff (*Creative Anguish*, p. 218), suggests that the anecdote of the numbers probably grew out of a conversation Rilke had with his friend the philosopher Rudolf Kassner, "who admits that ever since childhood he had wondered why he never found a number instead of a pebble beside the road." One wonders whether the imagery of the anecdote may not also have been influenced by a passage in Heine's "Aus den Memoiren des Herrn von Schnabelewopski," in which the narrator describes all the passersby on a busy Hamburg street in terms of the numbers they resemble.
32. Dostoevskij, "Dvojnik," in *Povesti*, p. 157.
33. Gogol', *Sobranie sočinenij*, III, p. 142.
34. There may be an echo, too, of Ivan Gončarov's novel *Oblomov*, which begins and ends with the hero seeking the solace of his bed.
35. Dostoevskij, "Zapiski iz podpol'ja," in *Povesti*, I, 290.
36. Dostoevskij, "Dvojnik," in *Povesti*, p. 272.

NOTES TO CHAPTER 7

1. Letter of 8 November 1915, *GB* IV, 90.
2. Ibid., pp. 87–88.
3. Ibid., p. 88.
4. Ibid., p. 89.
5. Sokel, "Zwischen Existenz und Weltinnenraum," pp. 105–06.
6. Ibid., p. 106.
7. F. M. Dostoevskij, *Polnoe Sobranie Sočinenij v tridcati tomax*, III, 169.
8. Ibid.
9. Ibid., p. 172.
10. Ibid., p. 175.
11. Ibid., p. 170.
12. Ibid.
13. Ibid., p. 172.
14. Ibid., p. 169.
15. Brutzer, *RrR*, p. 48.
16. Ingeborg Schnack, *Rainer Maria Rilke, Chronik seines Lebens und seines Werkes*, I, 19.
17. Brutzer, *RrR*, p. 48.
18. Ibid., p. 49.
19. *Tagebücher*, p. 186.

20. Boutchik, et al., "Letters to Helene," p. 159.
21. Hermann Pongs, "Drei unveröffentlichte Briefe Rilkes," p. 108.
22. Ibid., p. 109.
23. L. N. Tolstoj, "Xolstomer," in *Povesti i rasskazy v dvux tomax*, II, 72. Completed in 1864, the story was first published in 1886.
24. Ibid.
25. There is even a formal link between the works. Rilke's poem is written in iambic pentameter—and Tolstoy's story begins with a perfect iambic pentameter line: "Togdà že jã nikàk ne mŏg ponjàt'."
26. *GB* IV, 92.
27. Ibid., p. 93.
28. Léon Tolstoï, *Vie et Oeuvre. Mémoires, souvenirs, lettres, extraits du journal intime, notes et documents biographiques*. See the editor's notes in Rilke, *SW* VI, 1453–54.
29. In September 1869, Tolstoy had stopped at an inn in the village of Arzamas. In the middle of the night he awoke, overcome by a feeling of inexplicable terror. He fled into the hall, hoping to escape it, but there heard the voice of Death say, "'I am here . . .' A cold shudder ran over my skin. Yes, Death, it will come, it is already here, even though it has nothing to do with me now. . . . My whole being ached with the need to live, the right to live, and at the same moment, I felt Death at work. And it was awful, being torn apart inside." After a night of hysterical prayer, Tolstoy drove off the next day somewhat calmed, "but it was always there, at the back of my mind, and it had me in its power. . . . I went on living as before, but the fear of this despair never left me again." Quotations are from the fragment "Notes of a Madman," which was written in 1880 as a fictional treatment of the portentous Arzamas experience (Henri Troyat, *Tolstoy*, pp. 319–20). It is not known whether Rilke had read the fragment; but the episode is also mentioned in a letter from Tolstoy to his wife, included in *Vie et Oeuvre*, III, 89.
30. Letter to Hepner, *GB* IV, 92.
31. Ibid.
32. Tolstoj, "Smert' Ivana Il'iča," *Povesti*, II, 141.
33. Ibid., p. 117.
34. Ibid., p. 127.
35. Ibid., p. 95.
36. Ibid., p. 124.
37. Note the oblique reference to Ivan the Terrible, an important figure for Rilke.
38. See F. D. Reeve, Introd., *Six Short Masterpieces by Tolstoy*, pp. 18–19.
39. Maurice Blanchot finds that the whole novel "circles around a hidden center, which the author didn't dare to approach. This center is Malte's death, or the instant of his collapse . . . but this fall is hidden from us" ("Rilke und das Verlangen des Todes," in *Materialien*, ed. H. Engelhardt, p. 172).
40. *GB* IV, 88.
41. Tolstoï, *Vie et Oeuvre*, I, 149.
42. Ibid., p. 151.
43. Ibid., II, 93–94.
44. Ibid., I, 83.
45. In addition to the six versions, Rilke mentions the visit in a conversation with his Polish translator Witold Hulewicz; see Hulewicz, "Rozmowa z Rainerem Marią Rilke," p. 3.
46. E. M. Butler, "Rilke and Tolstoy," p. 500.
47. *GB* I, 94 ff.
48. *Tagebücher*, pp. 234–37.
49. K. Azadovskij, "R. M. Ril'ke i L. N. Tolstoj," p. 137.
50. Maurice Betz, *Rilke Vivant. Souvenirs, Lettres, Entretiens*, pp. 153 ff.
51. Du Bos, *Extraits*, pp. 286–88.
52. Butler ("Rilke and Tolstoy," p. 496), compares in detail the two 1900 versions of Rilke's visit with that told to Betz in 1925, and points out that the latter was the least romanticized, the most realistic of the three. Her explication of the worshipful "authorized"

version—the May 1900 letter—is most revealing in terms of Rilke's later view, which was simpler, more distanced, and more ironic, and yet retained a trace of resentment at the treatment he had received.
53. *GB* I, 95.
54. *Tagebücher,* p. 234.
55. *GB* I, 96.
56. *Tagebücher,* p. 234.
57. "Taugenichts"—"Good-for-Nothing"—is the main character in a story of the same name by the Romantic Joseph von Eichendorff. There is also an echo of Lewis Carroll's Alice and her trip through the land behind the looking glass, in which, among other oddities, a whole train leaps over a brook.
58. *GB* I, 96.
59. Du Bos, *Extraits,* p. 288.
60. According to K. Azadovskij, this painting, the oldest in Tolstoy's family gallery, was of Tolstoy's great-great-grandmother, Tatyana Grigorevna Gorchakova; she took orders in 1751, so the painting was probably done in the 1750s (Azadovskij, "R. M. Ril'ke i L. N. Tolstoj," p. 140).
61. *Tagebücher,* p. 235.
62. Tolstoï, *Vie et Oeuvre,* I, 83.
63. The fragments were found in a handwritten notebook which contains the second half of the manuscript of the novel. In 1910, Rilke dictated the novel to a typist from this and another notebook, now lost. See the editor's note to *Malte Laurids Brigge, SW* VI, 1452–54.

NOTES TO CHAPTER 8

1. In this instance, as it turned out, his intended discipline and the apprenticeship of solitude were undermined not only by the distractions of travel with his family, but by his own illness and that of his small daughter.
2. *Briefe 1906–07,* p. 41.
3. Letter of 10 December 1906, *GB* II, 206.
4. Letter to Elisabeth von der Heydt, 10 February 1907, *GB* II, 261.
5. Bernhard Blume, "Jesus, der Gottesleugner: Rilkes 'Der Ölbaum-Garten' und Jean Pauls 'Rede des toten Christus,' " p. 364.
6. Werner Günther, *Weltinnenraum. Die Dichtung Rainer Maria Rilkes,* p. 63.
7. Katherina Kippenberg, *Rainer Maria Rilke. Ein Beitrag,* p. 94.
8. Blume, "Jesus der Gottesleugner," p. 336.
9. Lou Andreas-Salomé, "Jesus der Jude," p. 350.
10. Lou is writing in the tradition of secularization of the Bible which had become important during the nineteenth century. One thinks of Renan's *La Vie de Jésus* (1863) or of the works of Lou's contemporaries and fellow Russians, Sologub and Alexey Remizov.
11. Böckmann, "Der Struktruwandel der modernen Lyrik in Rilkes 'Neuen Gedichten,' " *Wirkendes Wort,* 12 (1962), p. 350.
12. Hoffmann, *Th.M. Dostojewsky,* p. 374.
13. Fedor Dostoevskij, *Brat'ja Karamazovy,* I, 177.
14. Ibid., p. 185.
15. Ibid., p. 113.
16. Ibid., p. 310. In this, his stance resembles that of de Vigny's "Le Mont des Oliviers," which doubts, not God's existence, but his goodness. See Blume, "Jesus der Gottesleugner," p. 352.
17. Dostoevskij, *Brat'ja Karamazovy,* I, 320.
18. Konstantin Mochulsky, *Dostoevsky. His Life and Work,* p. 623.

19. Böckmann, "Strukturwandel," p. 351.
20. Dostoevskij, *Brat'ja Karamazovy*, II, 347.
21. *RMR-Lou*, pp. 103–04.
22. Ibid., p. 110.
23. Ibid., pp. 104–05.
24. Pongs, *Das Bild*, p. 466.
25. Hans Berendt, *Rainer Maria Rilkes Neue Gedichte. Versuch einer Deutung*, p. 47.
26. Pongs, *Das Bild*, pp. 464–65.
27. For discussions of Rilke and Nietzsche, see Erich Heller, "Rilke und Nietzsche. Mit einem Diskurs über Denken, Glauben, and Dichten," in *Nirgends wird Welt sein als Innen*; also published in *The Disinherited Mind. Essays in Modern German Literature and Thought*. See also chapters 12 and 13 in Walter Kaufmann, *From Shakespeare to Existentialism*.
28. Heller, "Rilke und Nietzsche," p. 85.
29. Lou Andreas-Salomé, *Friedrich Nietzsche in seinen Werken*.
30. *Xorovod:* a traditional Slavic round dance.
31. Some critics who saw this coldness as a flaw include F. Kaufmann, who found the poems "without song," and Dehn, who saw them as coagulations of Rilke's many fears, "things made of fear" (both quoted in Pongs, *Das Bild*, II, 463–64).
32. *RMR-Taxis*, I, 26–27.
33. Hoffmann, *Th. M. Dostojewsky*, pp. 213–14.
34. One critic suggests that Rilke's Apollo may be a composite of his knowledge of antique sculpture; he also notes that Rilke's perceptions and observations in "Archaïscher Torso Apollos" strongly resemble Winckelmann's description of a fragmentary statue in the Belvedere in Rome (Hermann Weigand, "Rilke's Archaïscher Torso Apollos' ").
35. Wolfgang Müller, *Rainer Maria Rilkes 'Neue Gedichte'*, p. 150.
36. H. Uyttersprot, "R. M. Rilke: Nächtliche Fahrt," pp. 388–89.
37. The first letter, to Hugo Salus, is from May 1899 (*GB* I, 66). The second, addressed to Lou, is from August 1900 (*RMR-Lou*, pp. 37–39). Uyttersprot (p. 388) mistakenly dates both May 1899.
38. Uyttersprot ("Nächtliche Fahrt," p. 391) quotes Dostoevsky, the connoisseur and master of moods of St. Petersburg, who called it "the most abstract and artificial city in the whole world." But he does not pursue the literary sources of Rilke's vision of the city.
39. A work which Rilke could not have used but which reaffirms for the modern reader the malignity of the city and the powerful East-West dichotomy so strongly sensed by the Russian Symbolists, as well as by Rilke, is Andrey Bely's novel *Petersburg* (1910–13). The novel was in fact originally planned as part of a trilogy, to be called *Vostok ili Zapad—East or West* (see Dmitrij Tschižewskij, Introd., *Petersburg*, by Andrej Belyj [1928; rpt. Munich, 1967], p. 6).
40. Puškin, *Polnoe Sobranie*, V, 381.
41. Gogol', *Sobranie sočinenij*, III, 43.
42. Quoted in: Joseph Frank, *Dostoevsky. The Seeds of Revolt, 1821–1849*, p. 134.
43. Ibid., p. 135. The allusion to Pushkin is obvious.
44. Quoted in Peters, *Lou*, p. 39.
45. In 1904, Rilke's friend Benois did a series of illustrations for this poem, which were published in *Mir Iskusstva*.
46. Gogol', *Sobranie sočinenij*, III, 189.
47. *RMR-Lou*, p. 405. The Lermontov poem can be found in: M. Ju. Lermontov, *Izbrannye proizvedenija*, I, 196.
48. Brutzer, *RrR*, p. 77.
49. This interpretation contrasts to some extent with that of Brutzer, who sees Lermontov's attitude as "a tired acquiescence," an "expression of enervated decadent exhaustion," while she sees Rilke's as "an active desire, full of a sense of duty and responsibility to empathize with the primal depths of life" (*RrR*, p. 78).
50. *GB* V, 116–17. Rilke signs this letter, as he does several others to Lou at this period, with the Russian word for "farewell"—*Proščaj*.

51. *GB* V, 114.
52. Ibid., 114–15. A number of studies of the *Elegien* exist, approaching them from a wide variety of points of view. For an extensive recent bibliography of works on the *Elegien*, see Elaine Boney, *Rainer Maria Rilke. Duinesian Elegies*, pp. 141–50.
53. These encounters are described in a letter from Rilke to Doris Heidrich, July 1907, quoted in Walter A. Reichart, "Rilke's *Fifth Duino Elegy* and Picasso's *Les Saltimbanques*," p. 281.
54. A reproduction of *Tanec* can be found in V. Rakitin, *Mixail Vrubel'*, p. 30. Picasso's painting is located at the National Gallery in Washington, D.C.
55. Brutzer, *RrR*, p. 28. See also Asadowski, "Briefe nach Russland," pp. 204, 206, and 298.
56. Aleksis Rannit, "Rilke und die slawische Kunst," p. 15.
57. Ibid. Rannit suggests that there was an affinity between Rilke and Vrubel: "Had Rilke met Vrubel during the time of the *Duino Elegies*, he might perhaps have recognized *his* painter in him."
58. Elaine E. Boney, *Duinesian Elegies*, p. 97.
59. Boney points out that this section of the poem dealing with the lovers is entirely in the subjunctive, "emphasizing the unattainability of this level for the living" (*Duinesian Elegies*, p. 96).
60. See Sazonova, "Pis'ma" and Betz, *Rilke Vivant*.
61. For a discussion of their correspondence and some of the poems which grew from it on both sides, see my article, "On Daring to be a Poet: Rilke and Marina Cvetaeva."
62. *Briefe aus Muzot*, p. 363.
63. Génia Tchernosvitow, "Les derniers mois de Rainer Maria Rilke," p. 218.
64. Letter of 13 December 1926. *RMR-Lou*, p. 505.

Selected Bibliography

BIBLIOGRAPHIES AND COLLECTIONS

Brutzer, Sophie. *Rilkes russische Reisen.* Diss. Königsberg 1934; rpt. Darmstadt, 1969.

Čertkov, Leonid. *Rilke in Russland. Auf Grund neuer Materialien.* Veröffentlichungen der Kommission für Literaturwissenschaft, 2. Vienna: Verlag der Österreichischen Akadamie der Wissenschaften, 1975.
    Contains extensive materials on Rilke and Russia, particularly on his reception there.

Obermüller, Paul and Herbert Steiner, with Ernst Zinn. *Katalog der Rilke-Sammlung Richard von Mises.* Frankfurt, 1966.

Ritzer, Walter. *Rainer Maria Rilke Bibliographie.* Vienna, 1951.

ARCHIVES

A great deal of material is located in Soviet archives and collections. Items include letters sent by Rilke to Russian correspondents and materials removed from German collections at the end of World War II.

Deutsches Literaturarchiv, Schiller-Nationalmuseum, Marbach, FRG.

Henry Sagan Rilke Collection, Kenneth Spencer Research Library, Kansas University, Lawrence, Kansas.

Richard von Mises Rilke Collection, The Houghton Library, Harvard University.

Rilke-Archiv, Gernsbach, FRG.

Rilke-Archiv, Schweizerische Landesbibliothek, Bern.

Boris Pasternak Archive, Leningrad.

Gosudarstvennyj russkij Muzej, Moscow.

Institut russkoj Literatury, Moscow.

EDITIONS OF RILKE'S WORKS

German Editions

Das Igorlied. Eine Heldendichtung. Frankfurt, 1960.

Sämtliche Werke. Ed. Ruth Sieber-Rilke and Ernst Zinn. 6 vols. Frankfurt, 1955–66.
    This is the standard edition of Rilke's works.

Übertragungen. Ed. Ernst Zinn and Karin Wais. 1927; rpt. Frankfurt, 1975.
Contains Rilke's translations from English, French, Portuguese, and Italian, but not from Russian.
Worpswede. Künstler-Monographien, 64. 3rd ed. 1903; rpt. Bielefeld and Leipzig, 1910.
Contains original illustrations.

Russian Editions

Izbrannaja lirika. Ed. E. Vitkovskij. Moscow, 1974.
This small volume contains poems from Rilke's earliest period to his latest.
Izbrannoe iz Rajnera Marija Ril'ke. Ed. Alexander Bisk. 2nd ed. Paris, 1957.
"Iz Rajnera-Marij Ril'ke," Trans. Gleb Struve. *Russkaja Mysl'* (Paris), 1, 1927.
"Neskol'ko pisem Rajner Marija Ril'ke," Trans. and commentary Marina Cvetaeva. *Volja Rossii,* 2 (1929), pp. 25–45.
Includes a translation of several of the *Briefe an einen jungen Dichter.*
Novye stixotvorenija. Ed. K. P. Bogatyrev, G. I. Ratgaus, and N. I. Balašev. Moscow, 1977.
This illustrated, annotated edition of 543 pages contains parts one and two of the *Neue Gedichte,* as well as excerpts from *Larenopfer, Traumgekrönt, Advent, Frühe Gedichte,* the *SB,* the *B der B, Requiem,* the *DE,* and the *S an O.* It also includes scattered poems written in German, French, and Russian, and the *Briefe an einen jungen Dichter.*
"Vse v odnoj." Trans. S. Spielberg. *Severnyj vestnik,* No. 10 (1897), pp. 71–78.
This is a translation of the early story "Alle in Einer," *SW* IV, 77–89.
Worpswede. Auguste Rodin. Pis'ma. Stixi. Ed. I. D. Rožanskij. Moscow, 1971.
In addition to the works on Worpswede and Rodin and other essays, it contains excerpts from the *Stunden-Buch, Neue Gedichte, Elegien, Sonette,* and a number of letters unavailable elsewhere.

English Editions

Duinesian Elegies. German Text with English Translation and Commentary. Trans. Elaine E. Boney. University of North Carolina Studies in the Germanic Languages and Literatures, No. 81. Chapel Hill, 1975.
Duino Elegies. Trans. J. B. Leishman and Stephen Spender. 1939; rpt. New York, 1967.
Duino Elegies. Trans. C. F. MacIntyre. Berkeley and Los Angeles, 1961.
Duino Elegies and the Sonnets to Orpheus. Trans. A. Poulin, Jr. Boston, 1977.
Fifty Selected Poems with English Translations. Trans. C. F. MacIntyre. 2nd ed. Berkeley, 1970.
Letters of Rainer Maria Rilke. Trans. Jane Barnard Greene and M. D. Herter Norton. Vol. I., *1892–1910.* Vol. II, *1910–1926.* New York, 1964.
Nine Plays. Trans. Klaus Phillips and John Locke. New York, 1979.
The Notebooks of Malte Laurids Brigge. Trans. M. D. Herter Norton. New York, 1949.
Poems from the Book of Hours. Trans. Babette Deutsch. Norfolk, Conn., 1941.
Excerpts from the *Stunden-Buch.*
Selected Letters of Rainer Maria Rilke. Ed. Harry T. Moore. Garden City, N.Y., 1960.

Sonnets to Orpheus. Trans. C. F. MacIntyre. Berkeley and Los Angeles, 1961.
Sonnets to Orpheus. Trans. W. D. Herter Norton. New York, 1942.
Stories of God. Trans. M. D. Herter Norton. New York, 1963.
Wartime Letters of Rainer Maria Rilke. Trans. M. D. Herter Norton. New York, 1964.

Collections of Letters and Diaries

Edited by Ruth Sieber-Rilke and Carl Sieber:
  Gesammelte Briefe. 6 vols. Leipzig, 1936–40.
  This is the standard edition of the letters.
    Vol. I: *Briefe aus den Jahren 1892 bis 1904.* Leipzig, 1939.
    Vol. II: *Briefe aus den Jahren 1904 bis 1907:* Leipzig, 1939.
    Vol. III: *Briefe aus den Jahren 1907 bis 1914.* Leipzig, 1939.
    Vol. IV: *Briefe aus den Jahren 1914 bis 1921.* Leipzig, 1938.
    Vol. V: *Briefe aus Muzot. 1921 bis 1926.* Leipzig, 1940.
    Vol. VI: *Briefe an seinen Verleger. 1906 bis 1926.* Leipzig, 1936.
  Briefe und Tagebücher aus der Frühzeit. 1899 bis 1902. Leipzig, 1931, 1933.
  Briefe aus den Jahren 1902 bis 1906. Leipzig, 1929, 1930.
  Briefe aus den Jahren 1906 bis 1907. Leipzig, 1930.
  Briefe an seinen Verleger. 1906 bis 1926. Leipzig, 1934.
  Identical to *GB* VI except lacking list of correspondents.
  Briefe aus den Jahren 1907 bis 1914. Leipzig, 1933.
  Briefe aus den Jahren 1914 bis 1921. Leipzig, 1937.
  This collection contains letters not available in *GB* IV.
  Briefe aus Muzot, 1921 bis 1926. Leipzig, 1936.
  This collection contains letters not available in *GB,* V.
  Tagebücher aus der Frühzeit. Frankfurt, 1942.
  Contains no letters.
Edited by Rudolf Hirsch and Ingeborg Schnack:
  Hugo von Hofmannsthal-Rainer Maria Rilke. Briefwechsel. 1899–1925. Frankfurt, 1978.
Edited by Rätus Luck:
  Rainer Maria Rilke. Briefe an Nanny Wunderly-Volkart. 2 vols. n.p. [Frankfurt], 1978.
Edited by Ernst Pfeiffer:
  Rainer Maria Rilke—Lou Andreas-Salomé. Briefwechsel. Zurich and Wiesbaden, 1952.
Edited by Ernst Zinn:
  Rainer Maria Rilke und Marie von Thurn und Taxis. Briefwechsel. 2 vols. Zurich, 1951.
Briefe an einen jungen Dichter. Frankfurt, n.d.

Individual Letters

Asadowski, Konstantin. *See* Azadovskij, Konstantin
Azadovskij [Asadowski], Konstantin. "Briefe nach Russland. S. W. Maljutin im Briefwechsel zwischen Rilke und Ettinger." In *Rilke Studien. Zu Werk und Wirkungsgeschichte.* Berlin, Weimar, 1976, pp. 197–208.
  Contains excerpts from correspondence between Rilke and Pavel Ettinger.

SELECTED BIBLIOGRAPHY

———. "R. M. Ril'ke i A. N. Benois. Perepiska 1900–1902 gg.." In *Pamjatniki Kul'tury.* Moscow, 1976, pp. 75–105.
Contains correspondence between Rilke and Russian artist and historian Alexander Benois.
———. "Rajner Marija Ril'ke. Pis'ma v Rossiju." *Voprosy literatury,* No. 9 (1975), pp. 214–42.
Contains correspondence between Rilke and Sophie Schill, Leonid Pasternak, Drožžin, Ettinger, and V. Čertkov.
———. E. V. Pasternak and E. B. Pasternak. "Iz perepiski Ril'ke, Cvetaevoj i Pasternaka v 1926 godu." *Voprosy literatury,* No. 4 (1978), pp. 233–81.
Cvetaeva [Tsvetaeva], Marina. Unpublished letters to Rilke. Nine letters and a postcard, dated May–November 1926. Rilke Archive, Schweizerische Landes-bibliothek, Bern (several of these were published, in Russian translation, by Azadovskij, Pasternak, and Pasternak in "Iz perepiski").
Rilke's letters to Cvetaeva are located in the Boris Pasternak Archive in the Soviet Union.
Rilke, Rainer Maria. "Letters of Rainer Maria Rilke to Helene * * * [Voronina]." Ed. Vladimir Boutchik, E. L. Stahl, and Stanley Mitchell. *Oxford Slavonic Papers,* 9 (1960), 129–64.
Eighteen letters to a Russian friend between 1899 and 1925 comprise pages 146–64. The remainder of the article consists of commentary by the editors.

RILKE'S TRANSLATIONS FROM RUSSIAN

Drozhzhin, Spiridon Dmitrič. *See* Drožžin, Spiridon Dmitrič
Drožžin [Drozhzhin], Spiridon Dmitrič. "Molitva." Translated as "Gebet." In Sophie Brutzer, *Rilkes russische Reisen.* 1934; rpt. Darmstadt, 1969, p. 80.
———. "Primi menja." Translated as "Nimm mich auf." In Sophie Brutzer, *Rilkes russische Reisen.* 1934; rpt. Darmstadt, 1969, p. 79.
———. "Sila pesni." Translated as "Kraft des Liedes." In Sophie Brutzer, *Rilkes russische Reisen.* 1934; rpt. Darmstadt, 1969, p. 80.
———. "U rodnoj derevne." Translated as "Im Heimatdorf." In Sophie Brutzer, *Rilkes russische Reisen.* 1934; rpt. Darmstadt, 1969, p. 79.
Fofanov, C. M. "Vesna i noč." Translated as "Frühling und Nacht." In Sophie Brutzer, *Rilkes russische Reisen.* 1934; rpt. Darmstadt, 1969, pp. 81–82.
Gippius, Zinaida. "Ljubov' odna." In Zinaida Gippius, *Ausgewählte Werke.* Leipzig, 1948. Vol. II, 382.
Jančeveckij [Yantshevetsky], V. [Exact title of original unknown.] Translated as "Die Bittschrift." Supplement to *Bohemia,* 5 January 1902.
Lermontov, Ju. M. "Molitva" [beginning," Ja, mater Božija . . ."]. In Rilke's Anfängerheften."
———. "Molitva" [beginning, "V minutu žizni trudnuju . . ."]. In Rilke's "Anfängerheften."
———. "Vyxožu odin ja na dorogu." Translated as "Einsam tret ich auf den Weg leeren." In *Rainer Maria Rilke—Lou Andreas-Salomé. Briefwechsel.* Ed. Ernst Pfeiffer. Zurich and Wiesbaden, 1952, p. 405.
Slovo o polku Igoreve. Translated as *Das Igorlied.* In Rainer Maria Rilke, *Das Igorlied. Eine Heldendichtung.* Frankfurt, 1960.

SELECTED BIBLIOGRAPHY

Sologub, Fedor. "Esli b, serdce, ty ležalo." Translated as "Säh ich, Herz, dich vor mir liegen." In *Süsser als Gift*. Trans. Fega Frisch. Munich, 1922, pp. 67 and 369.
―――. Excerpts from "Červjak." In Rilke's "Anfängerheften."
Tjutčev [Tyutchev], Fedor. "O veščaja duša moja." Translated as "Seherische Seele mein." Item bMS Ger 58 (263), Houghton Library, Harvard University, Cambridge, Mass.
Tyutchev, Fedor. *See* Tjučev, Fedor
Yantshevetsky, V. *See* Jančeveckij, V.

Lost or Destroyed Translations

Chekhov, Anton. *See* Čexov, Anton
Čexov [Chekhov], Anton. *Čajka*.
Dostoevskij [Dostoevsky], Fedor. Excerpts from *Bednyje ljudi*.

SECONDARY SOURCES

Works Primarily on Rilke and Russia

Andelson, Robert V. "The Concept of Creativity in the Thought of Rilke and Berdyaev." *The Personalist*, 43 (1962), 226–32.
Andreas-Salomé, Lou. "Rilke in Russland." *Russische Blätter*, No. 1 (Oct. 1928), 14–17.
Asadowski, Konstantin. *See* Azadovskij, Konstantin
Azadovskij [Asadowski], Konstantin. "Briefe nach Russland. S. W. Maljutin im Briefwechsel zwischen Rilke und Ettinger," in *Rilke-Studien. Zu Werk und Wirkungsgeschichte*. Berlin and Weimar, 1976, pp. 197–208.
―――. "Rajner Marija Ril'ke: Pis'ma v Rossiju." *Voprosy literatury*, 9 (1975), 214–42.
―――. "Rilke und Russland. Zum 100. Geburtstag des Dichters." *Sowjetunion Heute*, 16 Dec. 1975, 30–31.
―――. "R. -M. Ril'ke i A. N. Benois. Perepiska 1900–1902 gg." In *Pamjatniki Kul'tury*. Moscow, 1976, pp. 75–105.
―――. "R. M. Ril'ke i L. N. Tolstoj." *Russkaja literatura*, 12, No. 1 (1969), 129–51.
―――, and L. N. Čertkov. "R. M. Ril'ke i A. M. Gor'kij." *Russkaja literatura*, No. 4 (1967), pp. 185–91.
―――, and L. N. Čertkov. "Russkie vstreči." In Rajner Marija Ril'ke. *Worpswede. Auguste Rodin. Pis'ma. Stixi*. Ed. I. D. Rožanskij. Moscow, 1971.
―――, E. V. Pasternak, and E. B. Pasternak. "Iz perepiski Ril'ke, Cvetaevoj i Pasternaka v 1926 godu." *Voprosy literatury*, No. 4 (1978), pp. 233–81.
Barnes, Christopher S. "Boris Pasternak and Rainer Maria Rilke. Some Missing Links." *Forum for Modern Language Studies*, No. 8 (1972), pp. 61–78.
Blech, Hermann. "Rilke, Russland und die slawische Melodie." In *Stimmen der Freunde*, Ed. Gerd Buchheit. Freiburg im Breisgau, 1931.

SELECTED BIBLIOGRAPHY

Böhme, Marion. *Rilke und die russische Literatur: neue Beiträge mit besonderer Berücksichtigung der Rezeption Rilkes in Russland.* Diss. Vienna 1966.

Brandenburg, Hans-Christian. "Russland—das 'Gottesland' des jungen Rilkes." *Sudetenland,* No. 3 (1961), pp. 193–98.

"Ein Brief Rilkes an einen russischen Aristokraten." *Rigasche Rundschau,* 3 (5 Jan. 1927), 2.

Brodsky, Patricia Pollock. "On Daring to be a Poet: Rilke and Marina Cvetaeva." *Germano-Slavica,* 3, No. 4 (Fall 1980), 261–69.

———. "Rilke and Russian Art." *Germano-Slavica,* 2, No. 6 (Fall 1978), 411–26.

———. "Rilke's Relation to Russian Painting." *Innsbrucker Beiträge zur Kulturwissenschaft,* Sonderheft 51. Innsbruck, 1981.

———. "Russia in Rilke's *Das Buch der Bilder.*" *Comparative Literature,* 29, No. 4 (Fall 1977), 313–27.

———. "The Russian Source of Rilke's 'Wie der Verrat nach Russland kam." *The Germanic Review,* 54, No. 2 (Spring 1979), 72–77.

Brutzer, Sophie. *Rilkes russische Reisen.* Diss. Königsberg 1934; rpt. Darmstadt, 1969.

Bušman, I. N. "Pasternak i Ril'ke," in *Sbornik Statej, posvjaščennix tvorčestvu Borisa Leonidoviča Pasternaka.* Issledovanija i materialy, 1st series, 65. Munich, 1962, pp. 233–39.

Butler, E. M. "Rilke and Tolstoy." *Modern Language Review,* 35 (1940), pp. 494–505.

Čečel'nickaja. *Russkaja literatura v tvorčestve Rajner Marija Ril'ke.* Diss. Leningrad 1949.

N. B. Included for information only; the dissertation was never published.

Crowhurst, Griseldis W. "Malte Laurids Brigge, Nikolaj Kusmitsch und die Trägheit der Materie." *Acta Germanica* (Capetown), 8 (1973), 101–16.

Drozhzhin, Spiridon D. *See* Drožžin, Spiridon D.

Drožžin [Drozhzhin], Spiridon D. "Der deutsche Dichter Rainer Maria Rilke. Erinnerungen." *Das Inselschiff* (Summer, 1929), pp. 225–33.

Emerson, Caryl. "Rilke, Russia and the Igor Tale." *German Life and Letters,* NS 33, No. 3 (April 1980), 220–33.

Franck, Marga. "Rilke und Russland." *Das Wort,* 3, No. 7 (1938), 92–100.

Frank, Semën [Simon]. "Rainer Maria Rilke und die russische Geistesart." *Germano-slavica* (Brühn), 2 (1933), 481–97.

———. "Rajner Marija Ril'ke i Rossija." *Rul'* (Berlin), 10, No. 2468 (9 Jan. 1929), 2–3.

Gronicka, André von. "Rainer Maria Rilke's Translation of the 'Igor Song' (Slovo)." *Russian Epic Studies.* Ed. Roman Jakobson and Ernest J. Simmons. Philadelphia, 1949, pp. 179–202.

Same as: "Rainer Maria Rilkes Übersetzung des 'Igor-Liedes' (Slovo)," in *Rilke Heute. Beziehungen und Wirkungen.* Ed. Ingeborg H. Solbrig and Joachim W. Storck. Frankfurt, 1975, pp. 130–54.

———. "Rilke and the Pasternaks." *The Germanic Review,* 27, No. 4 (Dec. 1952), pp. 260–71.

Heygrodt, Robert Heinz. "Rilke und Russland." *Berliner Tageblatt,* 22 Nov. 1921, p. 7.

Hkt. [pseud.]. "Boris Pasternak und R. M. Rilke." *Prager Presse,* 5 Feb. 1932, p. 8.

Ilková, Zdenka. "Rilke a Rusko." *Časopis pro moderni filologii* (Prague), 31 (1948), 94–108, and 32 (1949), 35–37.
Ingold, Felix Philipp. "Rilke, Russland und die 'russischen Dinge.'" In *Zwischen den Kulturen. Festgabe für Georg Thürer zum 70. Geburtstag dargebracht von der Kulturwissenschaftlichen Abteilung der Hochschule St. Gallen*. Ed. F. P. Ingold. Bern and Stuttgart, 1978, pp. 63–86.
———. "Rilkes Russland." *Neue Zürcher Zeitung*, No. 278 (29–30 Nov. 1975), pp. 59–60.
fpi [Felix P. Ingold]. "Sowjetische Rilke-Edition," Rev. of *Lirika. Neue Zürcher Zeitung*, No. 159 (10–11 July 1976), p. 50.
Jonas, Klaus. "Rilke und die Sacharoffs." *Frankfurter Allgemeine Zeitung*, No. 2 (28 Jan. 1966), p. 28.
———. "Rilke und die Welt des Tanzes." In *Deutsche Weltliteratur von Goethe bis Ingeborg Bachmann. Festgabe für J. Alan Pfeffer*. Tübingen, 1972.
Kopelev, Lev. "Rilke and Russia." In *Rilke. The Alchemy of Alienation*. Eds. Frank Baron, Ernst S. Dick, and Warren R. Maurer. Lawrence, Kansas, 1980, pp. 113–36.
Lavrin, Janko. "Rilke and Russia." *Russian Review*, 27 (1968), 149–60.
Legner, Wolfram K. "The Religion of Rainer Maria Rilke before His Visits to Russia." *Monatshefte für Deutschunterricht*, 30 (1938), pp. 440–53.
Lommatsch, Franz. "Rainer Maria Rilke in Russland. Begegnungen mit Tolstoi." Loose page without identification in Henry Sagan Collection, Lawrence, Kansas. Box 1, 11.3.
Magr. [pseud.]. "Rilkes russische Reisen." *Prager Presse*, 19 Nov. 1931, p. 8.
———. "Rilke und Russland." *Prager Presse*, No. 32 (9 Aug. 1931), pp. 3–4.
———. "Zu Rilkes Übertragung des Igorliedes." *Prager Presse*, No. 7 (1930), pp. 1–3.
Miller-Budnickaja, R. "O 'filosofii iskusstva' B. Pasternaka i R. M. Ril'ke." *Zvezda: literaturno-obščestvennyj i naučnopopuljarnyj žurnal* (Leningrad), No. 5 (1932), pp. 160–68.
Mühlberger, Josef. "Rilke und Russland." *Sudetenland*, 15 (1973), 161–74.
Nagy, Bela T. "Rilke und Gorki: Dokumente einer Begegnung." *Studi Germanici* (Rome), NS 14, Installment 2–3, Nos. 39–40 (June–Oct. 1976), 297–314.
Najdenowa, Ganka. *Rainer Maria Rilke und die Slavische Welt*. Diss. Berlin 1942. Typescript in Deutsches Literaturarchiv, Marbach.
Pachmuss, Temira. "Dostoevskii and Rainer Maria Rilke: The Alienated Man." *Canadian-American Slavic Studies*, 12, No. 3 (1978), 392–401.
Pasternak, Boris. Untitled pages in "Stimmen über Rilke," *Insel Almanach auf das Jahr 1967. Rainer Maria Rilke zum vierzigsten Todestag*. Frankfurt, 1966, pp. 80–82.
Pronin, V. "Ril'ke i russkaja poèzija." *V Mire Knig*, No. 12 (1975), pp. 72–73.
Raab, Harald. "Rilke und die Welt der Slawen." *Neue deutsche Literatur*, 5 (1957), 96–106.
Rakusa, Ilma. "Marina Zwetajewa und Rainer Maria Rilke. Auf Grund unveröffentlichter Briefmaterialien." *Neue Zürcher Zeitung*, No. 202 (1–2 Sept. 1979), p. 65.
Rannit, Aleksis. "Rilke und die slawische Kunst." *Das Kunstwerk; eine Monatschrift über alle Gebiete*, 5, No. 4 (1951), 13–24.
"Rilke und Marina Zwetajewa. Vortragsabend in Leningrad zu einem bisher unveröffentlichten Briefwechsel." *Neue Zürcher Zeitung*, 28 Oct. 1977, p. 37.

Rogalski, Aleksander. "Rilke i Rosja." *Zycie i myśl* (Warsaw), No. 11–12 (1959), pp. 31–44.
Röhling, Horst. "Pasternak und die russische Rilke-Rezeption." *Die Welt der Slawen*, 17, No. 1 (1972), 118–54.
———. "Gethsemane bei Rilke und Pasternak." *Die Welt der Slawen*, No. 8 (1963), pp. 388–402.
Rothe, Daria. "Rilke's Poetic Cycle 'Die Zaren.' " In *Rilke. The Alchemy of Alienation.* Ed. Frank Baron, Ernst S. Dick, and Warren R. Maurer. Lawrence, Kansas, 1980, pp. 137–50.
Rožanskij, I. D. Ed. *Worpswede. Auguste Rodin. Pis'ma. Stixi.* By Rainer Maria Rilke. Moscow, 1971.
 Includes the following essays: Azadovskij and Čertkov, "Russkie Vstreči," pp. 357–85; Rožanskij, "Rajner Marija Ril'ke. Osnovnye vexi ego tvorčeskoj èvoljucii," pp. 7–49; V. Mikuševič, "Žalobnoe Nebo," pp. 427–47; and L. O. Pasternak, "Vstreči s R. M. Ril'ke," pp. 421–26.
Rudnickij, M[ixail]. "Russkie Motivy v 'Knige Časov' Ril'ke." *Voprosy literatury*, 12, No. 7 (1968), 135–49.
Saalborn, Arn. "Rilke en Rusland. Enkele Opmerkingen." *Levende Talen* (Groningen and Batavia), (1940), pp. 318–31.
Saito, Nello. "La Russia confina con Dio: Rilke e Tolstoi." *Svizzera Italiana*, 77, No. 5 (Nov. 1949), 26–28.
Salgaller, Emanuel. "Strange Encounter—Rilke and Gorky on Capri." *Monatshefte*, 54 (1961), 11–21.
Saparov, K. "Rajner Marija Ril'ke o povesti I. A. Bunina 'Mitina Ljubov'.' " *Voprosy literatury*, No. 9 (1966), pp. 247–49.
Sazonova, Ju[lia] L. "Pis'ma Rainer M. Ril'ke." *Novyj Žurnal*, 5 (1943), pp. 281–92.
Schmidt-Ihms, Maria. "Die Zeitbank des Nikolaj Kusmitsch, Eine Analyse." *Acta Germanica*, 5 (1970), 161–75.
Schoolfield, George C. "Rilke, Gorki and Others: A Biographical Diversion." In *Views and Reviews of Modern German Literature. Festschrift for Adolf D. Klarmann.* Ed. Karl S. Weimar. Munich, 1974, pp. 105–20.
Soloveitchik, Samson, and Everett Bushnell Gladding. "Rilke's Original Russian Poems." *Modern Language Notes*, 62 (1947), pp. 514–22.
Struve, Gleb. "Iz Rajnera-Marij Ril'ke." *Russkaja Mysl'* (Paris), 1 (1927).
 Contains an essay entitled "Rajner Marija Ril'ke" and one entitled "R. M. Ril'ke po povodu Mitinoj Ljubvi."
———. "Koe-čto o Pasternake i Ril'ke." In *Boris Pasternak 1890–1960. Colloque de Cerissy-la-Salle.* Paris, 1979, pp. 441–48.
Uyttersprot, H. "Nächtliche Fahrt." *Tijdschrift voon levende Talen*, 17 (1951), 385–92.
Wunderlich, Eva C., ed. *Geschichten vom lieben Gott.* By Rainer Maria Rilke. New York, 1957.
———. "Slavonic Traces in Rilke's *Geschichten vom lieben Gott.*" *The Germanic Review*, 22 (1947), 287–97.
Zabežinskij, Georgij. "Rajner Marija Ril'ke i Rossija." *Sovremennik* (Toronto), Nos. 17–18 (1967), pp. 93–99.
Zajdenšnur, E. J. "R. M. Ril'ke u Tolstogo." *Literaturnoe nasledstvo*, Nos. 37–38 (1939), pp. 708–12.

Zarncke, Lilly. "Rilke und Dostojewski." *Theologische Blätter*, 11 (1932), 103–12.

———. "Rilkes Frömmigkeit und ihre Beziehungen zu russischem und römisch-katholischem Christentum." *Zeitschrift für systematische Theologie*, 11 (1933–34), 225–97.

Other Works

"Die Aarauer Berufs-und Geschäftsfrauen . . ." *Aargauer Tagblatt*, 11 April 1957.
  A report of visit of Rilke's Russian secretary Genja Černosvitova in Aarau, Switzerland.
Admoni, Vladimir G. "Poèzija Rajnera Marii Ril'ke." *Voprosy literatury*, No. 12 (1962), pp. 138–58.
Ady, Cecelia M. *Lorenzo dei Medici and Renaissance Italy*. London, 1955.
Afanasev, A. N. *Narodnye russkie Skazki*. 1873. rpt. Ed. V. Ja. Propp. 3 vols. Moscow, 1957.
Alpatov, M[ixail Vladimirovič]. *Aleksandr Andreevič Ivanov. Žizn' i Tvorčestvo*. 2 vols. Moscow, 1956.
———. *Russian Impact on Art*. Trans. Ivy Litvinov. 1950. Rpt. New York, 1969.
Andreas-Salomé, Lou. "Aus der Geschichte Gottes." *Neue deutsche Rundschau*, 8 (1897), 1211–20.
———. *Fenitschka. Eine Ausschweifung*. Stuttgart, 1898.
———. *Das Haus*. Berlin, 1919.
———. "Jesus der Jude." *Neue deutsche Rundschau*, 7 (April 1896).
———. *Lebensrückblick. Grundriss einiger Lebenserinnerungen*. 2nd ed. Wiesbaden, 1968.
———. "Leo Tolstoi, unser Zeitgenosse." *Neue deutsche Rundschau*, 11, No. 11 (Nov. 1898), 1145–55.
———. *Rainer Maria Rilke*. Leipzig, 1929.
———. *Rodinka. Eine russische Erinnerung*. Jena, 1923.
———. "Russische Dichtung und Kultur. I." *Cosmopolis* (London), 7 (Aug. 1897), 571–80; and II, *Cosmopolis*, (Sept. 1897), 872–85.
———. "Russische Geschichten." Rev. of *Sbornik*. Ed. Wilhelm Henckel *Die Zeit. Wiener Wochenschrift für Politik, Volkswirtschaft, Wissenschaft und Kunst*, No. 24 (9 Dec. 1899), p. 153.
———, "Das russische Heiligenbild und sein Dichter." *Vossische Zeitung*, 1 Jan. 1898.
———. "Russische Philosophie und semitischer Geist." *Die Zeit* (Vienna), No. 172 (15 Jan. 1898), p. 40.
Apollo. Dec. 1973.
  Special issue on Russian art.
Arnold, Heinz Ludwig, ed. *Rilke? Kleine Hommage zum 100. Geburtstag*. Munich, 1975.
Arseniev, Nikolaj. "O Moskovskix religiozno-filosofskix i literaturnyx kružkax i sobranijax načala XX veka." *Sovremennik*, 6, No. 30, 30–42.
Asquith, Lady Mary. *Married to Tolstoy*. London, 1960.
Aubyn, F. C. St. "Rilke, Sartre, and Sarraute." *Revue de Littérature Comparée*, 41, 275–84.
Auden, W. H. "Rilke in English." *The New Republic*, 6 Sept. 1939, pp. 135–36.

SELECTED BIBLIOGRAPHY

Bakhtin [Baxtin], Mikhail. *Problems of Dostoevsky's Poetics.* Trans. R. W. Rotsel. Ann Arbor, 1973.
Baron, Frank, ed. *The Visual Arts and Rilke's Poetry.* Lawrence, Kansas, 1975.
_____, Ernst S. Dick, and Warren R. Maurer, eds. *Rilke. The Alchemy of Alienation.* Lawrence, Kansas, 1980.
Bassermann, Dieter. *Am Rande des Unsagbaren. Neue Rilke-Aufsätze.* Berlin and Buxtehude, 1948.
_____. *Der andere Rilke. Gesammelte Schriften aus dem Nachlass.* Bad Homburg vor der Höhe, 1961.
_____. *Der Späte Rilke,* Munich, 1947.
Bauer, Arnold. *Rainer Maria Rilke.* New York, 1972.
Bauer, Edda. ed. *Rilke-Studien. Zu Werk und Wirkungsgeschichte.* Berlin, 1976.
Baxtin, Mikhail. *See* Bakhtin, Mikhail
Belmore, H. W. *Rilke's Craftsmanship. An Analysis of His Poetic Style.* Oxford, 1954.
_____. "Two Poems on a Fountain in Rome: C. F. Meyer and R. M. Rilke." *German Life and Letters,* NS 10 (1956–57), 49–53.
Bely, Andrei. *Petersburg.* Trans. Robert A. Maguire and John E. Malmstad. Bloomington, Ind., 1978.
Benda, Gisela. "The Fusion of Life and Death in Rilke's *Duino* Elegies." *The University of Dayton Review,* 10, No. 2 (1973), 65–73.
Berendt, Hans. *Rilkes Neue Gedichte. Versuch einer Deutung.* Bonn, 1957.
Bergel, Kurt. "Childhood and Love in Rilke's Fourth Duino Elegy." *Germanic Review,* 21 (1946), 48–54.
Berger, Kurt. *Rainer Maria Rilkes frühe Lyrik (Entwicklungsgeschichtliche Analyse der dichterischen Form). Beiträge zur deutschen Literaturwissenschaft,* No. 40. Marburg, 1931.
Bethge, Hans. "Das Buch der Bilder von Rainer Maria Rilke." *Das litterarische Echo,* 5, No. 10 (1903), 715.
Betz, Maurice. *Rilke à Paris et Les Cahiers de Malte Laurids Brigge.* Paris, 1941.
_____. *Rilke Vivant. Souvenirs, Lettres, Entretiens.* Paris, 1937.
Binion, Rudolph. *Frau Lou. Nietzsche's Wayward Disciple.* Princeton, 1968.
Blankenhagen, Peter H. von. "Picasso and Rilke, 'La Famille des Saltimbanques.'" *Measure. A Critical Journal,* 1 (1950), pp. 165–85.
Blei, Franz. "Rainer Maria Rilke." *Das Silberboot,* 2, No. 9 (1946), 189–90.
Blume, Bernhard. "'Allein mit aller Menschen Gram,' Eine Interpretation von Rilkes Gedicht 'Der Ölbaum-Garten.'" *Neue Zürcher Zeitung,* 29–30 Nov. 1975, p. 58.
_____. "Jesus, der Gottesleugner: Rilkes 'Der Ölbaum-Garten,' und Jean Pauls 'Rede des toten Christus.'" In *Herkommen und Erneuerung: Essays für Oskar Seidlin.* Tübingen, 1976.
Böckmann, Paul. "Der Strukturwandel der modernen Lyrik in Rilkes *Neue Gedichte.*" *Wirkendes Wort,* 12 (1962), 336–54.
Bohning, Elizabeth. "Childhood in the Works of Rainer Maria Rilke." *Canadian Modern Language Review,* 18, No. 4, 12–22.
Bollnow, Otto. *Rilke.* Stuttgart, 1951.
Boney, Elaine E. "The Concept of Being in Rilke's *Elegien.*" *Symposium,* 15 (1961), 12–21.
Borcherdt, Hans-Heinrich. "Das Problem des 'verlorenen Sohnes' bei Rilke." In *Worte und Werte.* Berlin, 1961.

Boutchik, Vladimir, E. L. Stahl, and Stanley Mitchell. "Letters of Rainer Maria Rilke to Helene * * *." *Oxford Slavonic Papers*, 9 (1960), 129–64.
Bradley, Brigitte L. "The Internal Unity of Rilke's Cathedral Poems." *The German Quarterly*, 41, No. 2 (March 1968), 207–21.
―――. *Rainer Maria Rilkes "Der neuen Gedichte Anderer Teil." Entwicklungsstufen seiner Pariser Lyrik*. Bern, Munich, 1976.
―――. *Rainer Maria Rilkes Neue Gedichte. Ihr zyklisches Gefüge*. Bern, Munich, 1967.
―――. *Zu Rilkes Malte Laurids Brigge*. Bern, Munich, 1980.
Brecht, Franz Josef. *Schicksal und Auftrag des Menschen: Philosophische Interpretationen zu Rainer Maria Rilkes Duineser Elegien*. Basel, 1949.
Brinton, Christian. *The Nicolas Roerich Exhibition*. New York, 1921.
Buchheit, Gert. *Rainer Maria Rilke*. Mengen, 1947.
Buddeberg, Else. *Rainer Maria Rilke. Eine innere Biographie*. Stuttgart, 1955.
―――. "Spiegelsymbolik und Person-Problem bei Rainer Maria Rilke." *Deutsche Vierteljahresschrift*, 24, No. 3, 360–86.
Butler, E. M. *Rainer Maria Rilke*. New York, 1941.
Camille-Schneider. "De Paris à Strasbourg et Colmar avec Rainer Maria Rilke." *Les Lettres* (Paris), 1952, pp. 184–92.
Cassirer-Solnitz, Eva. *Rainer Maria Rilke*. Heidelberg, 1957.
Castillo-Elejabeytia, Dictinio de. *La Elegia a Marina, de Rilke, Publicado en homenaje al Prof. Munoz-Cortes*. Murcia, 1977.
Černosvitova, Génia. See Tchernosvitow, Génia
Černova, A[riadna]. "Marina Cvetaeva. 'Novogodnee.' Versty No. 3 Paris 1928." *Stixotvorenie*, 1, No. 16 (1928), 16.
Rev. of Cvetaeva's poem on Rilke's death.
Čexov [Chekhov], Anton. *Anton Chekhov's Life and Thought*. Trans. Michael Heim. Berkeley, 1973.
―――. *Izbrannye proizvedenija v trex tomax*. 3 vols. Moscow, 1964.
Chadwick, N. K. *Russian Heroic Poetry*. Cambridge, Eng., 1932.
Chekhov, Anton. See Čexov, Anton
Chizhevsky, Dmitri. See Tschižewskij, Dmitrij
Čizevskij, Dmitrij. See Tschižewskij, Dmitrij
Clements, Robert J. "Rilke, Michelangelo, and the *Geschichten vom lieben Gott*." *Comparative Literature*, 6 (1954), 218–31.
Comerford, Mollie J. "Rilke in English: 1946 to 1966." *The Germanic Review*, 42, No. 4 (Nov. 1967), 301–09.
Corona Mundi International Art Center. *Roerich*. New York, 1924.
Costello, D. P., and I. P. Foote, eds. *Russian Folk Literature*. Oxford, 1967.
Cremer, Emmy. *Lorenzo de' Medici. Staatsmann, Mäzen, Dichter*. Frankfurt, 1970.
Cvetaeva [Tsvetaeva], Marina. "Novogodnee." In *Nesobrannye proizvedenija*. Munich, 1971.
Poem on Rilke's death.
―――. "Tvoja Smert'," *Volja Rossii*, Nos. 5–6 (1927), pp. 3–27.
Essay on the occasion of Rilke's death.
Davidson, Martha. "Paula Modersohn-Becker. Struggle between Life and Art." *The Feminist Art Journal* (Winter 1973–74), pp. 1–5.
Dehn, Fritz. *Rainer Maria Rilke und sein Werk. Eine Deutung*. Leipzig, 1934.

Demetz, Peter. "Man kann Rilke auch anders lesen." *Die Zeit,* No. 50 (12 Dec. 1975), pp. 11-12.
_____. *René Rilkes Prager Jahre.* Düsseldorf, 1953.
Diedrich, Anton. *Russische Volksmärchen, in den Urschriften gesammelt, und ins Deutsche übersetzt.* Foreword Jacob Grimm. Leipzig, 1831.
Donchin, Georgette. *The Influence of French Symbolism on Russian Poetry.* The Hague, 1958.
Dostoevskij [Dostoevsky], Fedor M. *Brat'ja Karamazovy.* 2 vols. Moscow, 1963.
_____. *Polnoe Sobranie Sočinenij v tridcati tomax.* 30 vols. Leningrad, 1972-79.
_____. *Povesti i rasskazy.* 2 vols. Moscow, 1979.
Dostoevsky, Fedor M. *See* Dostoevskij, Fedor M.
Drahomaniv, M. *Po voprosu malorusskoj literature.* Vienna, 1876.
Drozhzhin, Spiridon D. *See* Drožžin, Spiridon D.
Drožžin [Drozhzhin], Spiridon D. *Pamjati S. D. Drožžina.* Kalinin, 1951.
_____. *Žizn' poèta-krest'janina S. D. Drožžina (1843-1905) opisannaja im samim i izbrannye stixotvorenija.* Moscow: Tipo-Lit. Russkago tovariščestva, 1905.
Du Bos, Charles C. *Extraits d'un Journal, 1908-1928.* 2nd ed., enl. Paris, 1931.
Dudkin, V. V., and A. M. Azadovskij. "Neoromantizm. Legenda o 'russkoj duše.'" In essay "Dostoevskij v Germanii (1846-1921)" in *Literaturnoe Nasledstvo,* No. 86. *F. M. Dostoevskij. Novye materialy i issledovanija.* Moscow, 1973.
Dynnik, Valentina. "Rajner Marija Ril'ke." *Literaturnaja enciklopedija,* Vol. 9 (1936), pp. 669-71.
Eckstein-Diener, Berta. *Idiotenführer durch die russische Literatur.* Munich, 1925. Virulent attack on "Russophilism" in Germany.
Eifler, Margret. "Existentielle Verwandlung in Rilkes Aufzeichnungen des Malte Laurids Brigge." *The German Quarterly,* 45, No. 1 (Jan. 1972), 107-13. Name is erroneously listed in table of contents as *Exner.*
Eikhenbaum [Eixenbaum], Boris. *The Young Tolstoy.* Trans. Gary Kern. Ann Arbor, 1972.
Eixenbaum, Boris. *See* Eikhenbaum, Boris
Elgar, Frank. *Cézanne.* New York, n.d.
Engelhardt, Hartmut, ed. *Materialien zu Rainer Maria Rilke: "Die Aufzeichnungen des Malte Laurids Brigge."* Frankfurt, 1974.
Enslin, Morton S., and Solomon Zeitlin. *The Book of Judith.* Philadelphia, 1972.
Ettinger, Paul [Pavel]. "Erinnerungen an R. M. Rilke." *Prager Presse,* No. 215 (7 Aug. 1932), p. 10.
Fedorov-Davydov, A[leksej] A[leksandrovič]. *Mixail Aleksandrovič Vrubel'.* Moscow, 1968.
Fedotov, Georgij Petrovič. *The Russian Religious Mind: Kievan Christianity, the Tenth to the Thirteenth Centuries.* New York, 1960.
Feigel. "Rilkes 'Geschichten vom lieben Gott.'" *Die Pforte. Monatsschrift für Kultur,* 6, No. 62 (1954), 228-45.
Flekser, Akim. *See* Volynskij, A[kim] L.
Fletcher, Betty Loeffler, and Eva Schiffer. "Island and Star." *The Germanic Review,* 27, No. 4 (Dec. 1952), 280-87.
Fofanov, Konstantin. *Stixotvorenija, 1880-1887.* St. Petersburg: Hermann Gonne, 1887.

———. *Stixotvorenija i poèmy.* Moscow, Leningrad, 1962.
Forster, Leonard. "An Unpublished Letter from Rilke to Kokoschka." *German Life and Letters,* NS 15 (Oct. 1961), 21–24.
Frank, Semën. "Die Mystik von R. M. Rilke." *Neophilologus,* 20 (1934–35), 97–113.
———. "Pis′ma R. M. Ril′ke." Rev. of *Briefe aus den Jahren 1902 bis 1906. Rul′* (Berlin), 6 Nov. 1929, pp. 2–3.
Franz, Heinrich Gerhard. "Wandlungen des Menschenbildes in Rainer Maria Rilkes 'Die Aufzeichnungen des Malte Laurids Brigge'—Parallelen zur gleichzeitigen Malerei." In *Marginalien zur poetischen Welt. Festschrift für Robert Mühler zum 60. Geburtstag.* Ed. Alois Eder, Hellmuth Himmel, and Alfred Kracher. Berlin, 1971, pp. 341–68.
Franz, Michael. "Du Musst dein Leben ändern." *Weimarer Beiträge,* 25, No. 1 (1979), 150–66.
Fuerst, Norbert. *Rilke in seiner Zeit.* Frankfurt, 1976.
Fülleborn, Ulrich. *Das Strukturproblem der späten Lyrik Rilkes. Voruntersuchung zu einem historischen Rilke-Verständnis.* Heidelberg, 1960.
Fullenwider, Henry F. *Rilke and His Reviewers.* Lawrence, Kansas, 1977.
Gerhard, H. P. [Heinz Paul Skrobucha]. *The World of Icons.* New York, 1971.
Gieysztor, Aleksander, Stefan Kieniewicz, Emanuel Rostworowski, Janusz Tazbir, and Henryk Wereszycki. *History of Poland.* Warsaw, 1968.
Gnedič, Petr Petrovič. *Istorija iskusstva; zodčestvo, živopis′, vajanie.* St. Petersburg: Izd. A. F. Marksa, 1897.
Gnedovskij, B. *Zodčestvo drevnej Rusi,* Gen. ed. Mixail Capenko. Moscow, 1969.
Gogol′, Nikolaj V. [Nikolay Gogol]. *Sobranie sočinenij v šesti tomax.* 6 vols. Moscow, 1952.
Goldenweizer, A. B. *Talks with Tolstoy.* Trans. S. S. Koteliansky and Virginia Woolf. New York, 1969.
Gombrich, Ernst Hans. *Art and Illusion. A Study in the Psychology of Pictorial Representation.* 4th ed. London, 1972.
Graff, Willem Laurens. *Rainer Maria Rilke. Creative Anguish of a Modern Poet.* Princeton, 1956.
Gray, Camilla. *The Russian Experiment in Art: 1863–1922.* New York, 1962.
Gray, Ronald D. *The German Tradition in Literature, 1871–1945.* Cambridge, Eng., 1965.
Grossmann, Dietrich. *Rainer Maria Rilke und der französische Symbolismus.* Diss. Jena 1938.
Gruzinskij, A. E., ed. *Russkija narodnya skazki.* Moscow, 1913.
Guardini, Romano. *R. M. Rilkes Deutung des Daseins: Eine Interpretation der Duineser Elegien.* Munich, 1967.
Gulyga, Elena Vladimirovna. "Neskol′ko slov o proze Rilke." In *Stilistika xudožestvennoj reči,* II. Leningrad, 1975, pp. 85–93.
Günther, Werner. *Weltinnenraum; die Dichtung Rainer Maria Rilkes.* 2nd rev. ed. Berlin, 1952.
Hamburger, Käte. "Die Geschichte des verlorenen Sohnes bei Rilke." In *Fides et communicatio. Festschrift für Martin Doerne zum 70. Geburtstag.* Ed. Dietrich Rössler, Gottfried Voigt, and Friedrich Wintzer. Göttingen, 1970, pp. 126–43.
———, ed. *Rilke in neuer Sicht.* Stuttgart, 1971.
Hamilton, George Heard. *The Art and Architecture of Russia.* Baltimore, 1954.

Hartmann, Geoffrey H. *The Unmediated Vision: An Interpretation of Wordsworth, Hopkins, Rilke and Valéry.* New Haven, 1954.
Haskell, Arnold L. *Ballet Russe. The Age of Diaghilev.* London, 1968.
―――. *Diaghileff. His Artistic and Private Life.* New York, 1935.
Hatfield, Henry. *Clashing Myths in German Literature. From Heine to Rilke.* Cambridge, Mass., 1974.
Heerikhuizen, F. W. van. *Rainer Maria Rilke: His Life and Work.* Trans. Fernand G. Renier and Anne Cliff. New York, 1952.
Hell, Victor. "Tradition und Ursprünglichkeit in Rilkes Werken: Über die Beziehungen zwischen Dichtung und Malerei." In *Tradition und Ursprünglichkeit.* Akten des III. Internationalen Germanistenkongresses in Amsterdam, 1965.
Heller, Erich. *The Disinherited Mind: Essays in Modern German Literature and Thought.* 3rd ed. New York, 1971.
―――. *Nirgends wird Welt sein als Innen. Versuche über Rilke.* Frankfurt, 1975.
Henckel, Wilhelm, ed. and trans. *Sbornik. Russische Geschichten und Satiren.* Berlin, 1899.
Heresch, Elisabeth. "Oesterreichische Literatur in Russland." *Neue Zürcher Zeitung,* No. 202 (1–2 Sept. 1979), p. 66.
Herzog, Bert. "Der Gott des Jugendstils in Rilkes 'Stundenbuch.'" *Schweizerische Rundschau,* 60 (1961), 1237–41.
Hewett-Thayer, Harvey W. "Rilke and François Coppée." *The Germanic Review,* 27, No. 4 (Dec. 1952), 294–97.
Hingley, Ronald. *The Tsars. 1533–1917.* London, 1968.
Hippe, Robert. "Vier Brunnengedichte (Conrad Ferdinand Meyer, Rainer Maria Rilke, Hans Carossa, Hermann Hesse)." *Wirkendes Wort,* No. 4 (1953–54), pp. 268–74.
Hoefert, Sigfrid, ed. *Russische Literatur in Deutschland. Texte zur Rezeption von den achtziger Jahren bis zur Jahrhundertwende.* Tübingen, 1974.
Hoffmann, N[ina]. *Th. M. Dostojewsky. Eine biographische Studie.* Berlin, 1899.
Höllerer, Walter, ed. "In Sachen Rainer Maria Rilke." In *Sprache im technischen Zeitalter,* Nos. 17–18 (1966), pp. 2–48.
Holthusen, Hans Egon. "'Der Dichter und der Löwe von Toledo,' Skizze zu einer Rilke betreffenden Problemstellung." *Neue Zürcher Zietung,* 29–30 Nov. 1975, p. 60.
―――. *Portrait of Rilke: An Illustrated Biography.* New York, 1971.
―――. *Rainer Maria Rilke in Selbstzeugnissen und Bilddokumenten.* Hamburg, 1958.
―――. "Rilke nach dreissig Jahren." *Neue Zürcher Zeitung,* No. 232 (24 Aug. 1957), p. 10.
―――. *Der späte Rilke.* Zurich, 1949.
Holzamer, Wilhelm. "Allerhand Märchen." Rev. of *Vom lieben Gott und Anderes. Das Litterarische Echo,* 3, No. 24 (Sept. 1901), 1717–20.
Howe, Sonia, ed. *The False Dmitri. A Russian Romance and Tragedy Described by British Eye-Witnesses, 1604–1612.* London, 1916.
Hryńczuk, Jan. "Poglądy estetyczne młodego Rainera Marii Rilkego (1889–1903)." *Kwartalnik Neofilologiczny,* 18, No. 2 (1971), 163–69.
Hulewicz, W[itold]. "Dwa dni u autora 'Księgi obrazów.' Rozmowa z Rainerem Maria Rilke. Korespondencja własna 'Wiadomości literackich.'" *Wiadomości literackie,* 1, No. 46 (1924), 3.

———. "Potężny liryk współczesnych Niemiec. Rainer Maria Rilke. Krótka charakterystyka twórczości." *Wiadomości literackie*, 1, No. 9 (2 March 1924), 1.

———. "Romain Roland a Rilke (Na marginesie artykułu Wacława Husarskiego)." *Wiadomości literackie*, 1, No. 23 (8 June 1924), 4.

Hulewicz-Olwid, Witold. *See* Hulewicz, W[itold]

Insel Almanach auf das Jahr 1967. Rainer Maria Rilke zum vierzigsten Todestag. Frankfurt, 1966.

Insel Almanach auf das Jahr 1977. Rainer Maria Rilke, 1875 bis 1975. Frankfurt, 1976.

Iwanow, Wjatscheslaw [Vjačeslav Ivanov]. "Vom Igorlied." *Corona*, 7 (1937), pp. 661–69.

Jacobsen, Jens Peter. *Niels Lyhne*. Trans. Hanna Astrup Larsen. New York, 1930.

Jaeger, Hans. "Die Entstehung der fünften Duineser Elegie Rilkes." *Dichtung und Volkstum*, 40 (1939), 213–36.

Jaloux, Edmond. *Rainer Maria Rilke*. Paris, 1937.

Jaremič, S. *Mixail Aleksandrovič Vrubel'. Žizn' i tvorčestvo*. Moscow, n.d.

Jephcott, E. F. N. *Proust and Rilke: The Literature of Expanded Consciousness.* New York, 1972.

j. k. [pseud.]. "Powiastki Rilkego." *Wiadomości literackie*, 2, No. 47 (22 Nov. 1925), 3.

Jonas, Ilsedore. "The Shattered Image: Rilke's Reaction to the Artists of Expressionism and to Some Works of Picasso." *Michigan Germanic Studies*, 2 (1976), 121–32.

Karamzin, Nikolaj Mixailovič. *Istorija gosudarstva rossijskago*. 5th ed. Vol. 9. St. Petersburg: Izd. I. Èjnerlinga, 1843.

Karlinsky, Simon. *Marina Cvetaeva: Her Life and Art*. Berkeley and Los Angeles, 1966.

Kassner, Rudolf. *Rilke, Gesammelte Erinnerungen, 1926–1956*. Pfullingen, 1976.

Kaufmann, Fritz. "Sprache als Schöpfung." *Zeitschrift für Ästhetik und allgemeine Kunstwissenschaft*, 28 (1934), 1–54.

Kaufmann, Walter. *From Shakespeare to Existentialism*. Garden City, N.Y., 1960.

Kayser, Hans-Christoph. "Rainer Maria Rilkes Die Turnstunde. Zum Verhältnis von Dichter und Schule." *Modern Language Studies*, 2, No. 2, 44–52.

Kayser, Wolfgang. "Eine unbekannte Prosaskizze von R. M. Rilke." *Trivium*, 5, No. 5 (1947), 81–88.

Kecba, L. N. "Rečevaja realizacija èpistoljarnogo stilja v literaturnyx pis'max Tomasa Manna i Rajnera Marii Ril'ke." *Pervyj moskovskij gosudarstvennyj pedagogičeskij institut inostrannyx jazykov. Učenye zapiski*, No. 77. Moscow, 1974.

Kim, Byong-Ock. *Rilkes Militärschulerlebnis und das Problem des verlorenen Sohnes*. Bonn, 1973.

Kippenberg, Katherina. *Rainer Maria Rilke. Ein Beitrag*. 4th ed. Leipzig, 1948.

Klinger, Kurt. "Die Kunst des Fragments. Zu Rilkes verstreuten und nachgelassenen Gedichten." *Studi Germanici* (Rome), 14th ser., 2–3 Nos. 39–40 (June–Oct. 1976), 221–54.

Kohlschmidt, Werner. *Rilke-Interpretationen*. Lahr, 1948.

Kol'cov, A. V. *Polnoe sobranie sočinenij*. St. Petersburg: Izd. Razrjada izjaščnoj slovesnosti Imp. Akademii Nauk, 1909.

Kosch, Wilhelm. *Deutsches Literaturlexikon*. 2nd ed. Bern, 1963.

Kramskoj, Ivan Nikolaevič. *Pis'ma, stat'i v dvux tomax.* 2 vols. Moscow, 1965–66.
Kramsztyk, Józef. "Rainer Maria Rilke." *Wiadomości literackie,* 4, No. 3 (16 Jan. 1927), 2.
Kreid, Harald. "Rilke-Symposium in Zagreb." *Literatur und Kritik,* No. 110 (Nov. 1976), pp. 584–89.
Krummacher, Hans-Henrik. Rev. of *Rainer Maria Rilkes Neue Gedichte. Versuch einer Deutung,* by Hans Berendt. *Euphorion,* No. 53 (1959), pp. 476–80.
―――. "Rilkes 'Stunden-Buch.' Religiöse Aussage, oder Stadium der dichterischen Entwicklung?" In *Gemeinde Gottes in dieser Welt. Festgabe für Friedrich-Wilhelm Krummacher zum 60. Geburtstag.* Berlin, 1961, pp. 171–87.
Kul'ženko, S. V. *Sobor sv.kn. Vladimira v Kieve. 1862–1896.* Kiev: S. V. Kul'ženko, 1898.
Das Kunstwerk. Baden-Baden, 1951.
    Special issue, "R. M. Rilke und die Bildende Kunst."
Lasareff [Lazarev], Victor N. *Russian Icons from the Twelfth to the Fifteenth Century.* New York, 1962.
Lavrin, Janko. *Aspects of Modernism: From Wilde to Pirandello.* 1935; rpt. Freeport, N.Y., 1968.
Lazarev, Victor N. *See* Lasareff, Victor N.
Leisi, Ernst. "Rilkes Aktualität." *Neue Zürcher Zeitung,* 29–30 Nov. 1975, 57.
Leppmann, Wolfgang. *Rilke. Sein Leben, seine Welt, sein Werk.* Bern, Munich, 1981.
Lermontov, M. Ju. *Izbrannye proizvedenija v dvux tomax.* 2 vols. Moscow, 1967.
―――. *Sobranie sočinenij v četyrex tomax.* 4 vols. Moscow, 1969.
Leskov, Nikolaj S. *Sobranie sočinenij v odinnadcat' tomax.* 11 vols. Moscow, 1957.
Lipec, R[axil] S[olomonovna]. *Èpos i drevnjaja rus'.* Moscow, 1969.
Longstreth, T. Morris. "Glimpses of Strangely Moving Landscapes." Rev. of *Geschichten vom lieben Gott. The Christian Science Monitor,* 29 Dec. 1949, p. 11.
Loose, Gerhard. "Two Notes on Rainer Maria Rilke's *Duineser Elegien.*" *Modern Language Notes,* 78 (1963), 430–34.
Löwis of Menar, August von. *Der Held im deutschen und russischen Märchen.* Diss. Berlin 1912. Leipzig, 1912.
Lukács, Georg. *Karl Marx und Friedrich Engels als Literaturhistoriker.* Berlin, 1948.
Magnus, L. A. *Heroic Ballads of Russia.* 1921; rpt. Port Washington, N.Y., 1967.
Mandel, Siegfried. *Rainer Maria Rilke. The Poetic Instinct.* Crosscurrents. Gen. ed. Harry T. Moore. Carbondale and Edwardsville, 1965.
Manning, Clarence A. *Ukrainian Literature. Studies of Leading Authors.* 1944; rpt. Freeport, N.Y., 1971.
Markov, Vladimir. *Russian Futurism: A History.* Berkeley and Los Angeles, 1968.
Martini, Fritz. *Das Wagnis der Sprache: Interpretationen deutscher Prosa von Nietzsche bis Benn.* Stuttgart, 1961.
Maslenikov, Oleg A. *The Frenzied Poets. Andrey Biely and the Russian Symbolists.* New York, 1968.
Mason, Eudo C. *Rilke.* Edinburgh and London, 1963.

———. *Rilke, Europe and the English-speaking World*. Cambridge, Eng., 1961.
———. "Rilkes Humor." In *Deutsche Weltliteratur. Von Goethe bis Ingeborg Bachmann. Festgabe für J. Alan Pfeffer*. Ed. Klaus Jonas. Tübingen, 1972.
McLean, Hugh. *Nikolai Leskov. The Man and His Art*. Cambridge, Mass., 1977.
Mendels, Judy and Linus Spuler. "Zur Herkunft der Symbole für Gott und Seele in Rilkes 'Stundenbuch.' " *Literaturwissenschaftliches Jahrbuch der Görresgesellschaft*, 4 (1963), 217–31.
Metzger, Bruce M. *An Introduction to the Apocrypha*. New York, 1957.
Meyer, Herman. "Rilkes Cézanne-Erlebnis." *Zeitschrift für Aesthetik und allgemeine Kunstwissenschaft*, No. 2 (1952), pp. 69–102.
———. "Rilkes Sachlichkeit." In *Deutsche Weltliteratur. Von Goethe bis Ingeborg Bachmann. Festgabe für J. Alan Pfeffer*. Ed. Klaus Jonas. Tübingen, 1972, pp. 203–15.
———. "Die Verwandlung des Sichtbaren: Die Bedeutung der modernen bildenden Kunst für Rilkes späte Dichtung." *Deutsche Vierteljahresschrift für Literaturwissenschaft und Geistesgeschichte*, 31 (1957), 465–505.
Migner, Karl. "Karl XII. reitet in der Ukraine." In *Wege zum Gedicht*, II. Ed. Rupert Hirschenauer and Albrecht Weber. Munich, Zurich, 1964, pp. 452–62.
Miller, R. D. "Rilke's Dilemma: A Comment on the Eighth Duino Elegy." *The Gate* (Oxford), 2, No. 1 (1948), 36–41.
Minder, Robert. "Kadettenhaus, Gruppendynamik, und Stilwandel von Wildenbruch bis Rilke und Musil." In *Kultur und Literatur in Deutschland und Frankreich: Fünf Essays*. 2nd rev. ed. Frankfurt, 1962.
Modersohn-Becker, Paula. *In Briefen und Tagebüchern*. Ed. Günter Busch and Liselotte von Reinken. Frankfurt, 1979.
Morgunov, N. S. *Viktor Vasnecov. Sokrovišča mirovogo iskusstva*. Moscow, Leningrad, 1940.
Mövius, Ruth. *Rainer Maria Rilkes Stunden-Buch. Entstehung und Gehalt*. Leipzig, 1937.
Müller, Wolfgang. *Rainer Maria Rilkes "Neue Gedichte."* Deutsche Studien, Vol. 13. Meisenheim am Glan, 1971.
Münchow, Ursula. "Das 'tägliche Leben.' Die dramatischen Experimente des jungen Rilkes." In *Rilke-Studien. Zu Werk und Wirkungsgeschichte*. Berlin and Weimar, 1976, pp. 9–52.
Musil, Robert. "Discours par Rilke." *Nouvelle Nouvelle Revue Française*, March 1956, pp. 457–67.
Nalewski, Horst. *Rainer Maria Rilke*. Leipzig, 1976.
———. "Rainer Maria Rilke. Bezug und Abstand." *Weimarer Beiträge*, Dec. 1975, pp. 48–68.
Newmarch, Rosa. *The Russian Arts*. New York, 1916.
Nietzsche, Friedrich. "Mitleid hin und her." In *Gedichte*. Wiesbaden, 1956, pp. 28–29.
Nikolay Roerich. Comp. Ljudmila Vasil'evna Korotkina. Leningrad, 1976.
Novouspenskij, N. *Gosudarstvennyj Russkij Muzej. Al'bom*. 2nd ed. Moscow, Leningrad, 1964.
Novytskyi, Oleksei Petrovich. *Istorija russkago iskusstva s drevnejšix vremen*. Moscow: V. N. Lind, 1903.
Obolensky, Dimitri, ed. *Art Treasures in Russia*. New York, Toronto, 1970.
"O 'Elegjach duinezyjskich.' " *Wiadomości literackie*, 5, No. 35 (26 Aug. 1928), 2.

Olwid. *See* Hulewicz, W[itold]
Orplid, 4, No. 1–2 (1927–28).
 Special issue on Rilke.
Osann, Christiane. *Rainer Marie Rilke: der Weg eines Dichters.* Zurich, 1947.
Osokin, V. V. Vasnecov. *Zižn' zamečatel'nyx ljudej.* Moscow, 1959.
Pasternak, Boris Leonidovič. "Čudo poètičeskogo vološčenija. (Pis'ma Borisa Pasternaka)." *Voprosy literatury,* No. 9 (1972), pp. 139–71.
Pauli, Gustav. *Paula Modersohn-Becker.* Munich, 1922.
Pelenskij, Evgen Julij. *Rainer Maria Rilke i Ukraina.* Lemberg (Lviv), 1935.
Pelensky [Pelenskij], Eugen I. *R. M. Rilke in Kiev,* Lemberg, 1935.
Perry, Gillian. *Paula Modersohn-Becker: Her Life and Work.* [New York], 1979.
"Pervaja poezdka Il'ja Muromca. Il'ja i Solovej-Razbojnik." In *The Penguin Book of Russian Verse.* Rev. ed. Ed. Dmitri Obolensky. Harmondsworth, 1965, pp. 23–32.
Pervušin, N. V. "Knigopisanie i živopis' v Russkix Monastyrjax." *Sovremennik,* 17–18, No. 68, 68–77.
Peters, H[einz] F[rederick]. *Lou. Das Leben der Lou Andreas-Salomé.* Munich, 1962.
———. *Rainer Maria Rilke: Masks and the Man.* Seattle, 1960.
———. "Zum Existenz-Problem bie Rilke und Nietzsche." *Modern Language Quarterly,* 8 (1947), 472–87.
Petzet, H. W. *Das Bildnis des Dichters. Rainer Maria Rilke, Paula Modersohn-Becker. Eine Begegnung.* Frankfurt, 1976.
Philobiblon. Zeitschrift für Bücherliebhaber (Vienna), 8, No. 10 (1935).
 Special issue on Rilke.
Pickle, Linda S. "The Balance of Sound and Silence in the *Duino Elegies* and *Sonnets to Orpheus.*" *Journal of English and Germanic Philology,* 70, No. 4 (Oct. 1971), 583–99.
Politzer, Heinz. "Prague and the Origins of Rainer Maria Rilke, Franz Kafka, and Franz Werfel." *Modern Language Quarterly,* 16, No. 1 (March 1955), 49–62.
———. "Some Aspects of 'Late Art' in Rainer Maria Rilke's Fifth Duino Elegy." *The Germanic Review,* 32, No. 4 (Dec. 1957), 282–98.
Poljakov, S. A. "O Ril'ke." *Vesy,* 4, No. 9 (Sept. 1907), 96–97.
Pongs, Hermann. *Das Bild in der Dichtung.* 4 vols. Marburg, 1927–39.
———. "Drei unveröffentlichte Briefe Rilkes." *Dichtung und Volkstum,* 37, No. 1 (1936), 100–15.
Poritzky, J. E. "Die neuere russische Litteratur und ihr Einfluss auf die deutsche." *Blätter für Bücherfreunde, literarische Neuigkeiten, illustrierte periodische Übersicht über die Neuerscheinungen der Literatur,* 1 (1901), 147–51.
Prawer, Siegbert Salomon. *German Lyric Poetry: A Critical Analysis of Selected Poems from Klopstock to Rilke.* London, 1952.
———. "Rilke and the Experience of Poetry," *Germanic Review,* 27, No. 4 (Dec. 1952), 288–93.
"Przeciw Rilkemu." *Wiadomości literackie* 2, No. 44 (1 Nov. 1925), 5.
Purdie, Edna. *The Story of Judith in German and English Literature.* Paris, 1927.
Pushkin, A. S. *See* Puškin, A. S.
Puškin [Pushkin], A. S. *Polnoe sobranie sočinenij v desjati tomax.* 10 vols. Moscow, 1962.
Rakitin, V. *Mixail Vrubel'.* Moscow, 1971.
Ralston, W. R. S. *The Songs of the Russian People.* 2nd ed. London, 1872.

SELECTED BIBLIOGRAPHY

Rambaud, Alfred. *La Russie Épique. Étude sur les chançons héroïques de la Russie.* Paris, 1876.
Rappoport, P. A. *Drevnerusskaja arxitektura.* Moscow, 1970.
Rauschnik. "Dmitri, Dimitrij (Demetrier)." *Allgemeine Encyclopädie der Wissenschaften und Künste.* Ed. Ersch and Gruber. Vol. 26. Leipzig, 1847, pp. 209–13.
Rehm, Walter. *Orpheus. Der Dichter und die Toten.* Düsseldorf, 1950.
Reichart, Walter A. "Rilke's *Fifth Duino Elegy* and Picasso's *Les Saltimbanques.*" *Modern Language Notes,* 61 (April 1946), 279–81.
Remak, Henry H. H. "Rilke and Valéry on Autumn. A Comparative Explication de Textes." In *Herkommen und Erneuerung: Essays für Oskar Seidlin.* Tübingen, 1976, 365–76.
Rice, Tamara Talbot. *A Concise History of Russian Art.* New York, 1963.
Rich, Adrienne. "Paula Becker to Clara Westhoff." *Heresies,* 3 (Fall 1977). Poem.
Riha, Karl. "Naturalismus und Antinaturalismus, 1889–1900." In *Annalen der deutschen Literatur.* 2nd ed. Stuttgart, 1971.
Rilke, Rainer Maria. "Pieśniarz śpiewa przed dziecięciem-księgiem." Trans. Józef Kramsztyk. *Wiadomości literackie,* 4, No. 3 (16 Jan. 1927), 2.
Translation of "Der Sänger singt vor einem Fürstenkind," *SW* I, 437–40.
Rodenwaldt, Gerhart. *Die Kunst der Antike (Hellas und Rom).* 2nd ed. Berlin, 1927.
Rogalski, A. "Rilke i Rosja." *Zycie i myśl,* 11–12 (1959).
Roh, Franz, and Juliane Roh. *German Art in the 20th Century.* Greenwich, Conn., [1968?].
Rolleston, James. *Rilke in Transition: An Exploraion of His Earliest Poetry.* Yale Germanic Studies, 4. New Haven, 1970.
Roman, Howard. "Rilke's Dramas—an Annotated List." *The Germanic Review,* 18, No. 3 (Oct. 1943), 202–08.
―――. "Rilke's Psychodramas." *Journal of English and Germanic Philology,* 43 (1944), 402–10.
Rose, William, and G. Craig Houston, eds. *Rainer Maria Rilke: Aspects of His Mind and His Poetry.* New York, 1970.
Rottert, T. G. *I. E. Repin.* Leningrad, 1966.
Rubissow, Helen. *The Art of Russia.* New York, 1946.
Rudnickij, Mixail. "Tol'ko golos." Introd. to *Izbrannaja lirika.* Ed. E. Vitkovskij. Moscow, 1974.
Ruppel, K. H. "Literarisches Ballett in München, 'Rilke'-Uraufführung im Nationaltheater." *Neue Zürcher Zeitung,* No. 11 (21–22 May 1977), p. 35.
Russischer Realismus, 1850–1900. Baden-Baden, 1973.
Exhibition catalogue.
Rybnikov, P. N. *Pesni sobrannye P. N. Rybnikovym.* 4 vols. St. Petersburg: D. E. Kožančikov, 1861–67.
―――. *Pesni sobrannye P. N. Rybnikovym.* Ed. A. E. Gruzinskij. 2nd ed. Moscow: Sotrudnik škol, 1910.
Saalmann, Dieter. *Rainer Maria Rilkes Aufzeichnungen des Malte Laurids Brigge: Ein Würfelwurf nach dem Absoluten. Poetologische Aspeckte.* Bonn, 1975.
―――. "Symbolistische Echos in R. M. Rilkes Essay, 'Moderne Lyrik.'" *Neophilologus,* 59, No. 2 (April 1975), 277–86.

Salinger, Herman. *An Index to the Poems of Rainer Maria Rilke: Gesammelte Werke und Späte Gedichte.* Madison, 1942.
Salis, J. R. von. *Rainer Maria Rilke: The Years in Switzerland.* Trans. N. K. Cruickshank. Berkeley and Los Angeles, 1966.
Scheibel, Gertrud. *Rainer Maria Rilke und die bildende Kunst.* Diss. Giessen 1933.
Schlienger-Stähli, Hildegard. *Rainer Maria Rilke–André Gide: der verlorene Sohn. Vergleichende Betrachtung.* Zurich, 1974.
Schmidt-Pauli, Elisabeth von. *Hiersein ist Herrlich: Erläuterungen zu R. M. Rilkes Duineser Elegien.* Konstanz-Nussdorf, 1948.
Schnack, Ingeborg. *Rainer Maria Rilke. Chronik seines Lebens und seines Werkes.* 2 vols. Frankfurt, 1975.
_____. *Rilkes Leben und Werk im Bild.* Wiesbaden, 1956.
Schneditz, Wolfgang. *Rilke und die bildende Kunst. Versuch einer Deutung.* Graz, 1948.
Scholz, Albert. "Rilke's 'Marien-Leben.' " *The German Quarterly,* 33, No. 2 (March 1960), 132–46.
Scholz, Wilhelm von. "Das Buch der Bilder." *Deutsche Arbeit,* 2, No. 3 (1902), 247–49.
Schoolfield, G[eorge] C. "Charles XII Rides in Worpswede." *Modern Language Quarterly,* 16 (Sept. 1955), 258–67.
_____. "Prague and Copenhagen: Rilke's 'Aus der Kinderzeit.' " *Kentucky Foreign Language Quarterly,* 6, No. 1 (1959), 86–91.
_____. *Rilke's Last Year.* University of Kansas Publications, Library Series, 30. Lawrence, Kansas, 1969.
Schott, Rolf [Rudolf]. *Michelangelo.* Trans. Constance McNab. New York, 1962.
Schulze, Berthold. "R. M. Rilkes Werdender Gott." *Zeitschrift für deutsche Bildung,* 2 (1926), 483–87.
Schwarz, Egon. "Betrachtungen zur Rezeption Rainer Maria Rilkes." *Neue Zücher Zeitung,* 29–30 Nov. 1975, pp. 57–58.
Seifert, Walter. *Das epische Werk Rainer Maria Rilkes.* Bonn, 1969.
Setchkarev, Vsevolod. *Gogol. His Life and Works.* New York, 1965.
Seyppel, Joachim. "The 'Deadly Angel' in R. M. Rilke's Second Elegy." *Philosophical Quarterly,* 37 (1958), 18–25.
Shabliovsky, Yevhen. *Ukrainian Literature through the Ages.* Trans. Abraham Mistetsky, Andrew Marko, Anatole Bilenko, and John Weir. Kiev, 1970.
Shaw, Priscilla Washburn. *Rilke, Valéry and Yeats, the Domain of the Self.* New Brunswick, N.J., 1964.
Shevchenko, Taras. *Selected Poems.* Trans. and ed. Clarence A. Manning. Jersey City, N.J., 1945.
Sidorov, A. A. *Russkaja grafika načala XX veka.* Moscow, 1969.
Sieber, Carl. *René Rilke: Die Jugend Rainer Maria Rilkes.* Leipzig, 1932.
Simenauer, Erich. *Rainer Maria Rilke. Legende und Mythos.* Bern, 1953.
_____. *Der Traum bei R. M. Rilke.* Bern, Stuttgart, 1976.
Sinjavskij, Abram. *See* Tertz, Abram
Sir Galahad [pseud.]. *See* Eckstein-Diener, Berta
Smith, John. *The Arts Betrayed.* London, 1978.
Sokel, Walter H. "Zwischen Existenz und Weltinnenraum: Zum Prozess der Ent-Ichung im Malte Laurids Brigge." In *Rilke Heute: Beziehungen und Wirkungen.* Ed. Ingeborg H. Solbrig and Joachim W. Storck. Frankfurt, 1975, pp. 105–29.

SELECTED BIBLIOGRAPHY

Sokolov, Jurij Matveič. *Russian Folklore.* Trans. Catherine Ruth Smith. Hatboro, Pa., 1966.
Solbrig, Ingeborg H., and Joachim W. Storck, eds. *Rilke Heute. Beziehungen und Wirkungen.* 2 vols. Frankfurt, 1975 and 1976.
Sologub, Fedor Kuz'mič [pseud.]. *Süsser als Gift.* Trans. Fega Frisch. Munich, 1922.
    Translation of *Slašče jada.*
Sommerfeld, Martin, ed. *George, Hofmannsthal, Rilke.* New York, 1938.
The Song of Igor's Campaign. An Epic of the Twelfth Century. Trans. Vladimir Nabokov. New York, 1960.
Spence, Gordon William. *Tolstoy the Ascetic.* London, Edinburgh, 1967.
Spencer, Charles. *The World of Serge Diaghilev.* Chicago, 1974.
Stahl, August. *Rilke Kommentar zum lyrischen Werk.* Munich, 1978.
———. " '. . . und es war die Znamenskaja.' Rilke und die Kunst der Ikonenmaler." *Blätter der Rilke-Gesellschaft,* Nos.7–8 (1980–81), pp. 84–91.
Stahl, Ernest Ludwig. *Creativity: A Theme from "Faust" and the "Duino Elegies."* Oxford, 1961.
Stassov, Vladimir Vasilevič. *Sobranie sočinenij.* St. Petersburg, 1894.
Stein, Jack M. "The Duino Elegies." *The Germanic Review,* 27, No. 4 (Dec. 1952), 272–79.
Stephens, Anthony R. *Rainer Maria Rilke's Gedichte an die Nacht: An Essay in Interpretation.* Cambridge, Eng., 1972.
———. *Rilkes Malte Laurids Brigge. Strukturanalyse des erzählerischen Bewusstseins.* Bern, Frankfurt, 1974.
Steppuhn, Feodor [Fedor Stepun]. "Die Tragödie des mystischen Bewusstseins." *Logos,* No. 2–3 (1911–12), pp. 164–91.
Storck, Joachim W., ed. *Rainer Maria Rilke.* Ausstellung des deutschen Literaturarchivs im Schiller-Nationalmuseum. Marbach, 1975.
    Exhibition catalogue.
———. " 'René Rilkes Prager Jahre.' Zu Peter Demetz' Kritik der Ranküne." *Frankfurter Hefte,* 10 (1955), 865–70.
———. "Der sowjetische Rilkeforscher Konstantin Azadovskij (Eine Dokumentation)." *Blätter der Rilke-Gesellschaft,* 9 (1982), 79–94.
Struve, Gleb. *Russkaja Literatura v izgnanii. Opyt istoričeskogo obzora zarubežnoj literatury.* New York, 1956.
Symons, Arthur. *The Symbolist Movement in Literature.* New York, 1958.
Tarabukina, N. M. *Mixail Aleksandrovič Vrubel'.* Moscow, 1974.
Tchernosvitow [Černosvitova], Génia. "Les derniers mois de Rainer Maria Rilke." *Les Lettres* (Paris), 1952.
Telešov, Nikolaj Dmitrievič. *Zapiski pisatel'ja; vospominanija.* Moscow, 1966.
Tertz, Abram [pseud.]. *A Voice from the Chorus.* Trans. Kyril Fitzlyon and Max Hayward. New York, 1976.
Teternikov, Fedor. *See* Sologub, Fedor Kuz'mič
Thurn und Taxis, Marie von. *Erinnerungen an Rainer Maria Rilke.* Munich, Berlin, Zurich, 1933.
Tjutčev, Fedor. *See* Tyutchev, Fedor
Tolstoï, Léon. *See* Tolstoj, Lev Nikolaevič
Tolstoj, Lev Nikolaevič [Leo Tolstoy]. *Briefe, 1848–1910.* Ed. P. A. Sergeenko. Berlin, 1911.

SELECTED BIBLIOGRAPHY

――――. *Dnevniki i zapisnye knižki*. Vols. 48 and 49 of *Polnoe Sobranie Sočinenij*. Moscow, 1952.
――――. *Essays and Letters*. Trans. Aylmer Maude. New York, 1904.
――――. *Life*. Trans. Isabel F. Hapgood. New York, 1888.
――――. *Pis'ma, 1863–1872*. Vol. 61 of *Polnoe Sobranie Sočinenij*. Moscow, 1953.
――――. *Povesti i rasskazy v dvux tomax*. 2 vols. Moscow, 1960.
――――. *Six Short Masterpieces by Tolstoy*. Ed. F. D. Reeve. Trans. Margaret Wettlin. New York, 1963.
――――. *Vie et oeuvre. Mémoires, souvenirs, lettres, extraits du journal intime, notes et documents biographiques, réunis, coordonnés et annotés par P. Birukov, revisés par Léon Tolstoï*. Ed. P[avel] Birjukov. 3 vols. Paris, 1906–09.
――――. *What Is Art? And Essays on Art*. Trans. Aylmer Maude. London, 1950.
Tolstoy, Leo. *See* Tolstoj, Lev Nikolaevič
Tönsing, Ludwig. "Rainer Maria Rilke: 'Da neigt sich die Stunde.' Eine stilanalytische Interpretation." *Acta Germanica*, No. 2 (1967), pp. 55–62.
Troyat, Henri. *Tolstoy*. Trans. Nancy Amphoux. Garden City, N.Y., 1967.
Tschižewskij [Čizevskij], Dmitrij. *Das Heilige Russland. Russische Geistesgeschichte I. 10–17. Jahrhundert*. Hamburg, 1959.
――――. "The Theme of the Double in Dostoevsky." In *Dostoevsky*. Ed. René Wellek. Englewood Cliffs, N.J., 1962.
――――, introd. *Peterburg*. By Andrej Belyj. 1928; rpt. Munich, 1967.
Tsvetaeva, Marina. *See* Cvetaeva, Marina
Tucker, Henry Jr. "Zu einem Rilke-Gedicht (Ende des Herbstes)." *Monatshefte*, 43, No. 8 (1951), 391–94.
Turgenev, Ivan S. *Zapiski oxotnika*. Moscow, 1966.
Tyutchev [Tjutčev], Fedor. "Silentium." In *The Penguin Book of Russian Verse*. Ed. Dimitri Obolensky. Rev. ed. Harmondsworth, 1965, pp. 132–33.
Uitti, Karl D. *The Concept of Self in the Symbolist Novel*. The Hague, 1961.
Ullmann, Regina. *Erinnerungen an Rilke*. Sankt Gallen, 1945.
――――. "Rainer Maria Rilke." *Literaturblatt der Frankfurter Zeitung*, 66, No. 32 (1933), 13.
Uyttersprot, H. "R. M. Rilke: Nächtliche Fahrt." *Tijdschrift voon Levende Talen*, 17 (1951), 385–92.
Vernadsky, George. *A History of Russia*. 5th rev. ed. New Haven, 1961.
Vogeler, Heinrich. *Erinnerungen*. Ed. Erich Weinert. Berlin, 1952.
――――. *Heinrich Vogeler, 1872–1942. Gedenkausstellung 1972, Worpsweder Kunsthalle und Haus im Schluh. 27.5 bis 17.9.1972*. 2nd rev. ed. Bremen, 1972.
Exhibition catalogue.
Vogüé, Viscomte Melchior de. *Le roman russe*. Paris, 1886.
Volynskij [pseud.], A[kim] L. *Russkie kritiki*. St. Petersburg, 1896.
Volynsky [pseud.], Akim. *See* Volynskij, A[kim] L.
Walzel, Oskar. "Vom Beschauen zum Bekennen." In *Stimmen der Freunde*. Ed. Gerd Buchheit. Freiburg im Breisgau, 1931.
Webb, Karl Eugene. "Rainer Maria Rilke and the Art of *Jugendstil*." *Centennial Review*, 16, No. 2 (Spring 1972), 122–37.
――――. *Rainer Maria Rilke and Jugendstil. Affinities, Influences, Adaptations*.

University of North Carolina Studies in the Germanic Languages and Literatures, No. 90. Chapel Hill, 1978.

———. "Themes in Transition: Girls and Love in Rilke's *Buch der Bilder.*" *The German Quarterly*, 43, No. 3 (May 1970), 406–17.

Weigand, Elsie. "Rilke and Eliot: The Articulation of the Mystic Experience: A Discussion Centering on the *Eighth Duino Elegy* and *Burnt Norton.*" *The Germanic Review*, 30, No. 3 (Oct. 1955), 198–210.

Weigand, Hermann J. "Rilkes 'Archaïscher Torso Apollos.'" *Monatshefte*, 51, No. 2 (1959), 49–62.

Willard, Nancy. *Testimony of the Invisible Man: W. C. Williams, Francis Ponge, Rainer Maria Rilke, Pablo Neruda.* Columbia, Mo., 1970.

Wocke, Helmut. "Rilke und der Osten." *Ostdeutsche Monatshefte* (Danzig), 12, No. 10 (1932), 649.

Wolf, Ernest M. "'Ihr Erstehn ging über alles fort . . .' A Thematic Analysis of Rilke's 'Die Kathedrale.'" *The German Quarterly*, 41, No. 2 (March 1968), 196–206.

Wolfgramm, Eberhard. "Tschechow und die Deutschen." *Neue deutsche Literatur*, 2, No. 7 (July 1954), 111–20.

Wonderley, Wayne. "An Analysis of Rilke's Novella Die Turnstunde (Gym Period)." *Perspectives on Contemporary Literature*, 2, No. 1 (1976), 34–39.

Wood, Frank. *Rainer Maria Rilke: The Ring of Forms.* 1958; rpt. New York, 1970.

———. "Rilke and Eliot: Tradition and Poetry." *The Germanic Review*, 27, No. 4 (Dec. 1952), 246–59.

———. "Rilke and the Theater." *Monatshefte*, 43 (1951), 15–26.

———. "Rilke's 'Der Geist Ariel': An Interpretation." *The Germanic Review*, 32, No. 1 (Feb. 1957), 35–44.

Wosien, Maria-Gabriele. *The Russian Folk-Tale. Some Structural and Thematic Aspects.* Slavistische Beiträge, No. 41. Munich, 1969.

Wundram, Manfred. *Art of the Renaissance.* Trans. Francisca Garvie. New York, 1972.

Wydenbruck, Nora Purtscher von. *Rilke: Man and Poet.* London, 1949.

Zabel, Eugen. *Wereschtschagin.* Bielefeld and Leipzig, 1900.

Zabelin, Ivan Egorovič, *Domašnyj byt russkix carej v XVI–XVII stoletijax.* Moscow, 1872.

———. *Russkoe iskusstvo.* Moscow, 1900.

Zabežinskij, Grigorij. "Žizn', tvorčestvo i smert' poèta." In *Žizn' i Tvorčestvo Rajner Maria Ril'ke.* Paris, 1947, pp. 3–18.

Zagjanskaja, G. *Pejzaž Aleksandra Ivanova. Problema živopisnogo metoda xudožnika.* Moscow, 1976.

Zankes, Arthur. "Russlandverse im Geiste Rilkes." *Das Silberboot*, 2, No. 9 (1946), 180–82.

Poem by Zankes.

Zech, Paul. *Rainer Maria Rilke. Der Mensch und das Werk.* Dresden, 1930.

Zenkovsky, Serge A. *Medieval Russia's Epics, Chronicles, and Tales.* Rev. and enl. ed. New York, 1974.

Ziolkowski, Theodore. *Dimensions of the Modern Novel. German Texts and European Contexts.* Princeton, 1969.

Zoller, Erna. "Rainer Maria Rilke. Eine Kindheitserinnerung. Ein Betrag zu seiner Motivik." *Blätter der Rilke-Gesellschaft*, No. 3 (1974), pp. 3–19.

Zotov, Aleksej Ivanovič. *Russkoe iskusstvo XI–načala XX vekov.* Moscow, 1969.

Zweig, Stefan. *Farewell to Rilke*. Trans. Marion Sonnenfeld. Fredonia, N.Y., 1975.

Index

Accept Me (Drozhzhin), 29
After the Battle of Igor Svyatoslavich with the Polovtsians: On a Theme from the "Slovo o polku Igoreve" (V. Vasnetsov), 33–35
Alcoforado, Marianna, 170
Alexey Mikhailovich, Tsar, 174
Andreas, Karl F., 17
Andreas-Salomé, Lou: breaks with Rilke, 49, 50, 74, 194; childhood and youth, 18; as critic, 18–20, 63–64; equated with Russia, 212n. 8; and Nietzsche, 220n. 39; Rilke's last letter to, 230n. 50; and Rilke's poetry, 45, 46; as Rilke's teacher and mentor, 16–18, 20, 26; travels with Rilke in Russia, 17, 58, 204; visit to Tolstoy, 171–72, 172–73. Works: "Jesus der Jude," 182; *Lebensrückblick*, 171; "Russische Dichtung und Kultur, I," 19; "Russische Dichtung und Kultur, II," 212n. 12; "Das russische Heiligenbild," 218n. 18; "Im Zwischenland," 196
Andreev, Leonid, 214n. 30
Antokolsky, Pavel, 217n. 4
Art, Russian, 28, 60–61, 173–74, 217n. 4
—compared to Western, 60, 61–62, 66–72
—icons in, 62–64, 65, 68, 94, 95, 120, 123, 124, 219nn. 23, 27, 29; Iberian Madonna, 117; Saint Nicholas, 124; Virgin of Smolensk, 217n. 3; Virgin of Vladimir, 217n. 3; Znamenskaya, 57–58, 123, 217n. 71
—Rilke's essays on, 61–65
"At the End of the World" (Leskov), 67–68, 218n. 18
Aufzeichnungen des Malte Laurids Brigge, Die, 11, 20, 36, 48, 78–79, 130, 132–76, 226nn. 1, 6, 227n. 31, 228n. 39; Tolstoy conclusion to, 167–76, 229n. 63
Aus dem Leben eines Taugenichts (Eichendorff), 229n. 57
Aus den Memoiren des Herrn von Schnabelewopski (Heine), 227n. 31

Balmont, Konstantin, 19
Becker, Paula, 49–50, 131
Belinsky, Vissarion, 19
Bely, Andrey, 214n. 23, 30. Works: *Petersburg*, 212n. 12, 230n. 39
Benois, Alexander, 23, 27, 30, 61, 79, 213n. 31, 214n. 30, 218n. 14. Works: *History of Painting in the XIX Century: Russian Painting*, 28
Bernard, Émile, 102
Betz, Maurice, 171, 208, 228n. 52
Blok, Alexander, 212n. 12
Boris Godunov (Pushkin), 66
Brentano, Bettina, 170
"Bronze Horseman, The" (Pushkin), 195, 196
Brothers Karamazov, The (Dostoevsky), 66, 70, 80, 122, 144, 182, 183–86
Brutzer, Sophie, 33, 46, 96, 198, 216nn. 49, 62, 220n. 1
Bryusov, Valery, 19, 212n. 12
Buch der Bilder, Das, 20, 25, 84–95, 135, 221nn. 10, 14
— "Abend in Skåne," 86
— "Fortschritt," 86
— "Karl der zwölfte von Schweden reitet in der Ukraine," 85, 87–88, 221n. 14
— "Schauende, Der," 87
— "Sturm," 85–87, 88
— "Vorgefühl," 86

256

—"Zaren, Die," 82, 88–95, 221n. 10; "Das war in Tagen, da die Berge kamen," 88–89; "Der blasse Zar wird nicht am Schwerte sterben," 93–94; "Es ist die Stunde, da das Reich sich eitel," 93; "Noch drohen grosse Vögel allenthalben," 89–91, 221n. 10; "Noch immer schauen in den Silberplatten," 94; "Seine Diener füttern mit mehr und mehr," 91–93, 108–09
Bülow, Frieda von, 17, 33

Carpaccio, 100
Cathedral Folk (Leskov), 48
Charles XII (king of Sweden), 85, 87–88, 95, 221nn. 5, 14
Chekhov, Anton: *The Seagull*, 28, 36–41, 213n. 9; *Uncle Vanya*, 28, 37–38, 213n. 9
Chernyshevsky, Nikolay, 19
Children, 84, 100, 129, 136, 141; as audience for the *Geschichten vom lieben Gott*, 97, 110, 112, 119, 128, 130; disinherited, 139–40, 180–81, 182; and parents, 92, 122; and problematic role of mothers, 50–55; roles reversed, 74, 93–94, 221n. 13. See also Prodigal son
"Christ aux Oliviers, Le" (Nerval), 182
Christ in the Desert (Kramskoy), 182–83
"Coming Huns, The" (Bryusov), 212n. 12
"Compassion To and Fro" (Nietzsche), 220n. 39
Contemplation (Kramskoy), 184
"Cossack Lullaby" (Lermontov), 51–52, 54
Cossacks, The (Tolstoy), 160, 162
Covetous Knight, The (Pushkin), 222n. 15

Dance, The (Vrubel), 205–08
Death, 46, 134
—in Rilke's works: *Die Aufzeichnungen des Malte Laurids Brigge*, 133, 153–56, 166–67, 228n. 39; *Die Geschichten vom lieben Gott*, 114, 117–18, 120; *Malte Laurids Brigge* and Dostoevsky, 156–59; *Malte Laurids Brigge* and Tolstoy, 159–66; *Das Stunden-Buch*, 75–76, 80, 81
—in Tolstoy's works, 161–66, 169, 228n. 29
Death of Ivan Ilich, The (Tolstoy), 161–66, 169
"Deutsche Dichter Rainer Maria Rilke. Erinnerungen, Der" (Drozhzhin), 216nn. 51, 55
Diary of a Madman, The (Gogol), 196

Diary of a Writer (Dostoevsky), 214n. 30, 226n. 21
Dobrolyubov, Nikolay, 19
"Doge und Dogaresse" (Hoffmann), 225n. 59
Dostoevsky, Fyodor, 15, 20, 21–22, 143–44, 168, 189, 191–92, 194, 227n. 22, 230n. 38. Works: *The Brothers Karamazov*, 66, 70, 80, 122, 144, 182, 183–86; *Diary of a Writer*, 214n. 30, 226n. 21; "The Double," 146–52, 196; *The Idiot*, 226n. 21; *The Insulted and the Injured*, 156–59; *Notes from Underground*, 151, 196; *Poor Folk*, 28, 30, 226n. 21; *A Raw Youth*, 144, 195; *White Nights*, 195
"Double, The" (Dostoevsky), 146–52, 196
"Drachentöter, Der," 223n. 20
Drozhzhin, Spiridon, 23, 28, 45, 46. Works: "Accept Me," 29; "Der Deutsche Dichter Rainer Maria Rilke," 216nn. 51, 55; *In the Native Village*, 29; "The Power of Song," 29–30; "Prayer," 30
Du Bos, Charles C., 171
Duineser Elegien, 11, 53–55, 73, 85, 132, 192, 201, 204–08, 231n. 59
Dyagilev, Sergey, 61
Dyuk Stepanovich (legendary hero), 116–17

East-West dichotomy, in antipathy to Western influence, 19, 22, 60, 111; in art and religion, 61–62, 66–72; in Bely's *Petersburg*, 230n. 39; in community vs. individualism, 127; different standards applied in art, 60; Russia richer in potential, 65; spiritual conflict, 45; West misinterprets Russia, 21–22
"Ehrwürdiger Vater und Metropolit." See *Gebete, Die*
Eichendorff, Joseph von, 229n. 57
"Einsam tret ich auf den Weg den leeren," 197–201, 230n. 49
Einsame Menschen (Hauptmann), 212n. 10, 222n. 6
"Elegie an Marina Tswetajewa-Efron," 208
"Esli b, serdce, ty ležalo" (Sologub), 216n. 58
Ettinger, Paul, 23, 26

Famille des Saltimbanques, La (Picasso), 205–07
Filosofov, D. V., 61
Flekser, Akim [pseud. Akim Volynsky], 16, 19, 213n. 31

INDEX

Fofanov, Konstantin, 28, 35–36, 47
Fragment ("Brautpaar-Stoff"), 42–44
Frisch, Fega, 216n. 58
Fyodor Ivanovich, Tsar, 92, 93–95

Gauguin, Paul, 102
Gebete, Die, 30, 59, 66–70, 72, 96
Geschichten vom lieben Gott, 11, 20, 21, 25, 55, 96–131, 222n. 3, 224n. 40; "Der Bettler und das stolze Fräulein," 125–27, 225nn. 58, 59; "Der fremde Mann," 124–25; "Eine Geschichte, dem Dunkel erzählt," 103, 129–30; "Das Lied von der Gerechtigkeit," 97, 100, 117–23, 124, 125–27, 128, 224nn. 42, 46, 47; "Ein Märchen vom Tod und eine fremde Nachschrift dazu," 128–29, 225n. 60; "Das Märchen von den Händen Gottes," 99; "Eine Szene aus dem Ghetto von Venedig," 128, 225n. 60; "Ein Verein, aus einem dringenden Bedürfnis heraus," 101–02; "Von einem, der die Steine belauscht," 100; "Warum der liebe Gott will, dass es arme Leute gibt," 99; "Wie der alte Timofei singend starb," 97, 98, 99–100, 113–17, 223nn. 32, 33, 34; "Wie der Fingerhut dazu kam, der liebe Gott zu sein," 100; "Wie der Verrat nach Russland kam," 97, 98, 100, 103–09, 222n. 15, 223nn. 20, 21
Giorgione, 100
Gippius, Zinaida, 215n. 30
God: as artist, 73, 99, 100, 124, 219n. 31; and Christ, 180–86; darkness of, 23, 45, 47, 56, 180; and Dionysus, 189–91; perceptions of, in *Geschichten vom lieben Gott*, 99–100, 127–31; perceptions of, in *Stunden-Buch*, 67–83; in Russian folklore, 104–05; as Russian peasant, 72, 99, 105, 112–13; spatial metaphors for, 111, 127–31; as work of art, 59, 66, 68, 69, 71–72, 168, 219n. 31, 225n. 61
Godunov, Boris, Tsar, 134; in Pushkin's play, 137
Goering, Hermann, 221n. 14
Goethe, Johann Wolfgang von, 133–34
Gogol, Nikolay, 21, 77, 122, 145–46, 194–95, 196. Works: *The Diary of a Madman*, 196; *The Hetman*, 223n. 32; "A May Night, or the Drowned Maiden," 118; "Nevsky Prospect," 195; "The Nose," 110, 146, 148, 196; "The Overcoat," 146, 149; *Taras Bulba*, 122, 123, 223n. 32; "Vij," 221n. 10

Goncharov, Ivan, 213n. 31
Gorky, Maxim, 213n. 31, 224n. 42

Hauptmann, Gerhart, 212n. 10, 222n. 6
Hebbel, Friedrich, 135
Heine, Heinrich, 227n. 31
Hepner, Lotte, 154, 160, 161
Hetman, The (Gogol), 223n. 32
History, Russian, 224n. 42; Battle of Poltava in, 85, 87–88; False Dmitry in, 134–35; Prince Igor in, 31–32; Tsar Fyodor Ivanovich in, 93–95; Tsar Ivan IV in, 88, 91–93, 104, 134, 221n. 11, 222n. 7, 223nn. 21, 25, 26, 34; Tsar Peter I in, 85, 87; Ukraine and, 118–19, 122, 224n. 47
History of Painting in the XIX Century: Russian Painting (Benois), 28
History of the Russian State (Karamzin), 135–36, 138
Hoffmann, Ernst Theodor Amadeus, 225n. 59
Hoffmann, Nina (first German biographer of Dostoevsky), 15, 21–23, 29, 191
Hofmannsthal, Hugo von, 37

Idiot, The (Dostoevsky), 226n. 21
"I Go Out onto the Road Alone" (Lermontov), 48–49, 197–201, 230n. 49
Igorlied, Das, 28, 31–35, 164, 214nn. 21, 28
Ilya Muromets (legendary hero), 88–90, 138
"Im Zwischenland" (Andreas-Salomé), 196
"Improvisationen aus dem Capreser Winter," 180
Insulted and the Injured, The (Dostoevsky), 156–59
"In the Native Village" (Drozhzhin), 29
Ivan IV (the Terrible), Tsar, 88, 91–93, 103–09, 134, 221n. 11, 222n. 7, 223nn. 21, 25, 26
Ivanov, Alexander, 217n. 4

"Jesus der Jude" (Andreas-Salomé), 182

Kappus, Franz Xavier, 225n. 60
Karamzin, Nikolay, 118, 135–36, 138
Kassner, Rudolf, 227n. 31
"Katerina" (Shevchenko), 118
Key, Ellen, 189, 224n. 42
"Kobzar, The" (Shevchenko), 224n. 46
Koenig, Hertha, 205

258

Kramskoy, Ivan, 217n. 4. Works: *Christ in the Desert,* 182–83; *Contemplation,* 184; *Laughter,* 78, 220n. 41

Laughter (Kramskoy), 78, 220n. 41
Lay of Igor's Campaign, The. See Igorlied, Das
Lebensrückblick (Andreas-Salomé), 171
Lermontov, Mikhail, 28, 215n. 31. Works: "Cossack Lullaby," 51–52, 54; "I Go Out onto the Road Alone," 48–49, 197–201, 230n. 49; "Prayer," 30, 35
Leskov, Nikolay, 48, 63–64. Works: "At the End of the World," 67–68, 218n. 18; *Cathedral Folk,* 48
Literature, Russian: compared to Western, 19, 212n. 12; Rilke's tastes in, 20, 28, 35, 214n. 30
Living Corpse, The (Tolstoy), 28, 213n. 9
"Lucerne" (Tolstoy), 160
Lukacs, Georg, 221n. 14
Lulu (Wedekind), 212n. 10

Maeterlinck, Maurice, 37
Malczewski, Jacek, 102
Malyutin, Sergey, 213n. 31
Mann, Thomas, 42
"Marina, voici galets et coquillages," 208
"Master and Man" (Tolstoy), 162
"May Night, or the Drowned Maiden, A" (Gogol), 118
Mazeppa, 85–87, 94, 135
Medici, Lorenzo dei, 125, 225n. 58
"Meinem lieben Heinrich Vogeler mit einem russischen Heiligen," 56
Merezhkovsky, Dmitry, 19, 214n. 30
Michelangelo, 100
Mniszek, Marina, 134–35, 137, 226n. 15
"Moderne russische Kunstbestrebungen," 65
Modersohn-Becker, Paula. *See* Becker, Paula
"Mont des Oliviers, Le" (Vigny), 182, 229n. 16

"Nächtliche Fahrt. Sankt Petersburg," 192–97, 201, 230n. 39
Nagoy, Maria (wife of Ivan IV of Russia), 135, 137–39
Nerval, Gérard de, 182
Nesterov, Mikhail, 217n. 4
Neue Gedichte, 130, 132, 178–96, 230n. 31; "Archaïscher Torso Apollos," 187–92; "Früher Apollo," 187; "Der Stifter," 178–79; "Der Ülbaum-Garten," 180–86, 229n. 16
Nevsky Prospect (Gogol), 195
Nietzsche, Friedrich, 189–91, 220n. 39
Nightingale Robber. *See* Solovey Razboynik
"Nose, The" (Gogol), 110, 146, 148, 196
"Notes of a Madman" (Tolstoy), 228n. 29
Notes from Underground (Dostoevsky), 151, 196

Oblomov (Goncharov), 227n. 34
Oral literature, about Ivan IV, 103–04
—*bylina* in, 46, 85, 88–90, 96, 114–15, 116, 221nn. 7, 9, 223n. 33, 226n. 15; defined, 221n. 6; distinguished from historical song, 222n. 7
—history of, 113–14
—Rilke's knowledge of, 96, 223n. 32
Orlovsky, Grigory. *See* Schill, Sophia
Otrepev, Grigory (the False Dmitry), 134–40, 153
"Overcoat, The" (Gogol), 146, 149
"O veščaja duša moja" (Tyutchev), 216n. 58

Pan (Vrubel), 173
Pasternak, Boris, 23, 214n. 30
Pasternak, Leonid, 23, 27, 209
Paul, Jean, 182
Pauli, Gustav, 27
Perception: leads to transformation, 88, 94; loss of, 92–93; and poetry, 50, 140–41; and reality, 102; and role of viewer, 63, 86–88; as source of magic power, 221n. 10
Peter the Great, Tsar, 85, 87
Petersburg (Bely), 212n. 12, 230n. 39
"Petition, The" (Yantschevetsky), 30
Picasso, Pablo, 205–07
Polikushka (Tolstoy), 162
Poltava (Pushkin), 85, 87, 220n. 1
Pongs, Hermann, 160
Poor Folk (Dostoevsky), 28, 30, 226n. 21
"Poor Liza" (Karamzin), 118
"Power of Song, The" (Drozhzhin), 29–30
Prager Geschichten, 16
"Prayer" (Drozhzhin), 30
"Prayer" (Lermontov), 30, 35
Prodigal son, 115, 116–17, 130–31, 133, 139–40, 182
Pushkin, Alexander, 77, 146. Works: *Boris Godunov,* 66, 137; "The Bronze Horseman," 195, 196; "The Covetous

259

INDEX

Pushkin, Alexander (cont'd)—
Knight," 222n. 15; *Poltava,* 85–86, 220n. 1

"Quant' è bella giovinezza" (Medici), 125, 225n. 28

Rambaud, Alfred, 104, 119, 120–21, 121–22, 214n. 28
Rauschnik, 135
Raw Youth, A (Dostoevsky), 144, 195
"Rede des toten Christus, Die" (Paul), 182
Remizov, Alexey, 229n. 10
Repin, Ilya, 23, 217n. 4, 221n. 11
Resurrection (Tolstoy), 160
Rilke, Phia (Rilke's mother), 52–53
Rilke, Rainer Maria: trips to Russia, 17, 23, 25–26, 59–60, 96, 216nn. 51, 55, 228n. 52. Works: *Die Aufzeichnungen des Malte Laurids Brigge,* 11, 20, 36, 48, 78–79, 130, 132–76, 226nn. 1, 6, 227n. 31, 228n. 39; Tolstoy conclusion to, 167–76, 229n. 63
—*Das Buch der Bilder,* 20, 25, 84–95, 221nn. 10, 14; "Abend in Skåne," 86; "Fortschritt," 86; "Karl der zwölfte von Schweden reitet in der Ukraine," 85, 87–88, 221n. 14; "Der Schauende," 87; "Sturm," 85–87, 88; "Vorgefühl," 86; "Die Zaren," 82, 88–95, 221n. 10; "Das war in Tagen, da die Berge kamen," 88–89; "Der blasse Zar wird nicht am Schwerte sterben," 93–94; "Es ist die Stunde, da das Reich sich eitel," 93; "Noch drohen grosse Vögel allenthalben," 89–91, 221n. 10; "Noch immer schauen in den Silberplatten," 94; "Seine Diener füttern mit mehr und mehr," 91–93, 108–09
—"Drachentöter, Der," 223n. 20
—*Duineser Elegien,* 11, 53–55, 73, 85, 132, 192, 204–08, 231n. 59
—"Einsam tret ich auf dem Weg den leeren," 197–201, 230n. 49
—"Elegie an Marina Tswetajewa-Efron," 208
—*Fragment* ("Brautpaar-Stoff"), 42–44
—*Gebete, Die,* 30, 59, 66–70, 72, 96
—*Geschichten vom lieben Gott,* 11, 20, 21, 25, 55, 96–131, 222n. 3, 224n. 40; "Der Bettler und das stolze Fräulein," 125–27, 225nn. 58, 59; "Der fremde Mann," 124–25; "Eine Geschichte, dem Dunkel erzählt," 103, 129–30; "Das Lied von der Gerechtigkeit," 97, 100, 117–23, 124, 125–27, 128, 224nn. 42, 46, 47; "Ein Märchen vom Tod und eine fremde Nachschrift dazu," 128–29, 225n. 60; "Das Märchen von den Händen Gottes," 99; "Eine Szene aus dem Ghetto von Venedig," 128, 225n. 60; "Eine Verein, aus einem dringenden Bedürfnis heraus," 101–02; "Von einem, der die Steine belauscht," 100; "Warum der liebe Gott will, dass es arme Leute gibt," 99; "Wie der alte Timofei singend starb," 97, 98, 99–100, 113–17, 223nn. 32, 33, 34; "Wie der Fingerhut dazu kam, der liebe Gott zu sein," 100; "Wie der Verrat nach Russland kam," 97, 98, 100, 103–09, 222n. 15, 223nn. 20, 21
—*Igorlied, Das,* 28, 31–35, 164, 214nn. 21, 28
—"Improvisationen aus dem Capreser Winter," 180
—"Marina, voici galets et coquillages," 208
—"Meinem lieben Heinrich Vogeler mit einem russischen Heiligen," 56
—"Moderne russische Kunstbestrebungen," 65
—"Nächtliche Fahrt. Sankt Petersburg," 192–97, 201, 230n. 39
—*Neue Gedichte,* 130, 132, 178–96, 230n. 31; "Archaïscher Torso Apollos," 187–92; "Früher Apollo," 187; "Der Ülbaum-Garten," 180–86, 411n. 16; "Der Stifter," 178–79
—*Prager Geschichten,* 16
—Russian poems, 44–55, 216nn. 49, 50, 52, 62
—"Russische Kunst," 61–65
—*Sonette an Orpheus, Die,* 192, 201–04; "Da stieg ein Baum, O reine Übersteigung," 203; "Dir aber, Herr, o was weih ich dir, sag," 202–04
—*Das Stunden-Buch,* 20, 22, 23, 25, 55, 57, 59–60, 65–83, 125, 127, 140, 160–61, 168, 175, 201, 219nn. 30, 31; "Da neigt sich die Stunde und rührt mich an," 89; "Dann sah ich auch Paläste, welche leben," 81–82; "Du Gott, ich möchte viele Pilger sein," 78–79; "Du meinst die Demut," 76–77; "Du musst nicht bangen, Gott. Sie sagen: mein," 160–61; "Ein Pilgermorgen. Vor den harten Lagern," 78–79; "Herbsttag," 220n. 39; "Ich habe viele Brüder in Sutanen," 70–71; "Ich war bei den ältesten Mönchen," 72; "Ich will ihn preisen," 82; "O wo ist

260

der, der aus Besitz und Zeit," 81; "Selten ist Sonne im Sobór," 219n. 30; "Weisst du von jenen Heiligen, mein Herr?," 75–76; "Wenn ich gewachsen wäre irgendwo," 71–72; "Und du erbst das Grün," 74–75
—*Das Tägliche Leben,* 38–41, 59–60
—"Über Kunst," 218n. 10
—*Die Weise von Liebe und Tod des Cornets Christoph Rilke,* 32
—*Die Weisse Fürstin,* 37
—"Wladimir, der Wolkenmaler," 55–56
—"Die Znamenskaja. Der Madonnenmaler," 57–58
Rodin, Auguste, 39, 41, 70
Rozanov, Vasili, 214n. 30
Rublyov, Andrey, 75
Russian Critics (Volynsky), 19
Russian people: and art, 62–63, 64, 68; humility of, 20, 21, 80–81, 98, 134, 178–79; and literature, 19, 22; patience of, 14, 21, 29–30, 80, 90, 91, 117, 134, 178, 201, 204; profundity of, 21, 46, 180; and religion, 19, 58, 60, 62–64, 68, 72, 111, 183–85, 218n. 18; simplicity of, 29–30, 47, 134; slow development of, 16, 19–20, 22–23, 62, 98, 145, 187
Russian poems (Rilke), 44–55, 216nn. 49, 50, 52, 62
"Russische Dichtung und Kultur, I" (Andreas-Salomé), 19
"Russische Dichtung und Kultur, II" (Andreas-Salomé), 212n. 12
"Russische Heiligenbild, Das" (Andreas-Salomé), 218n. 18
"Russische Kunst," 61–65
Rybnikov, Pavel, 103–09

Sacharov, Alexander, 208
Sacharov, Clotilde, 208
Saints: Luke, 219n. 29; Olympius, 219n. 29; Vladimir, 64
—in Rilke's works: Charitinas, 218n. 17; Cosma, 218n. 17; Damian, 218n. 17; Francis, 81, 219n. 27; George, 56–57; Nicholas, 124, 219n. 27; Sophia, 174
Sappho, 170
Sazonova, Julia, 208
Schill, Sophia [pseud. Grigory Orlovsky], 23, 37–38, 44, 171, 172, 215n. 33, 217n. 4
Schiller, Friedrich, 135
Scythians, The (Blok), 212n. 12
Seagull, The (Chekhov), 28, 36–41, 213n. 9

Serov, Valentin, 217n. 4
Shevchenko, Taras, 118, 123, 224n. 46
Shuysky, Prince Vasili, 135, 137–38
Silence, 46, 47–48, 55–56, 73, 98
Silentium (Tyutchev), 47–48
Simenauer, Erich, 52
"Singers" (Turgenev), 115
Slavery of Our Time (Tolstoy), 160
Slovo o polku Igoreve. See Igorlied, Das
Sologub, Fyodor. *See* Teternikov, Fyodor
Solovey Razboynik (legendary figure), 90–91, 164, 221n. 10
Solovyov, Dmitry, 19
Sonette an Orpheus, Die, 192, 201–04; "Da stieg ein Baum. O reine Übersteigung," 203; "Dir aber, Herr, o was weih ich dir, sag," 202–04
Sorrows of Young Werther, The (Goethe), 118, 133–34
"Spring and Night" (Fofanov), 35–36, 47
"Steps of Life" (Tolstoy), 162
Stunden-Buch, Das, 20, 22, 23, 25, 55, 57, 59–60, 65–83, 125, 127, 160–61, 168, 175, 219nn. 30, 31; "Da neigt sich die Stunde und rührt mich an," 89; "Dann sah ich auch Paläste, welche leben," 81–82; "Du Gott, ich möchte viele Pilger sein," 78–79; "Du meinst die Demut," 76–77; "Du musst nicht bangen, Gott. Sie sagen: mein," 160–61; "Ein Pilgermorgen. Vor den harten Lagern," 78–79; "Herbsttag," 220n. 39; "Ich habe viele Brüder in Sutanen," 70–71; "Ich war bei den ältesten Mönchen," 72; "Ich will ihn preisen," 82; "O wo ist der, der aus Besitz und Zeit," 81; "Selten ist Sonne im Sobór," 219n. 30; "Weisst du von jenen Heiligen, mein Herr?," 75–76; "Wenn ich gewachsen wäre irgendwo," 71–72; "Und du erbst das Grün," 74–75
Suvorin, A. S., 27, 171
Sweeter than Poison (Sologub), 214n. 30

Tägliche Leben, Das, 38–41, 59–60
Taras Bulba (Gogol), 122, 123, 223n. 32
Teternikov, Fyodor [pseud. Fyodor Sologub], 19, 28, 229n. 10. Works: "Esli b, serdce, ty ležalo," 216n. 58; *Sweeter than Poison,* 214n. 30; "The Worm," 214n. 30
"Thoughts about God" (Tolstoy), 160
"Three Deaths" (Tolstoy), 162
Thurn und Taxis, Princess Marie von, 191, 205
Tiepolo, Giambattista, 100

Titian, 67, 70, 100
Tolstoy, Leo, 19–20, 23, 28–29, 37, 43–44, 77, 123, 156, 159–66, 167–76, 181, 213n. 31. Works: *The Cossacks,* 160, 162; *The Death of Ivan Ilich,* 161–66, 169; *The Living Corpse,* 28–29, 213n. 9; "Lucerne," 160; "Master and Man," 162; "Notes of a Madman," 228n. 29; "Polikushka," 162; *Resurrection,* 160; "Slavery of Our Time," 160; "Steps of Life," 162; "Thoughts about God," 160; "Three Deaths," 162; *War and Peace,* 160; "What Is Art?," 160, 218n. 10; "Work for the Night Is Coming," 162; "Yardstick," 160–61, 228n. 25
Tolstoy, Nikolay (Leo's father), 169–70, 175
Tolstoy, Nikolay A. (Rilke's host), 27, 46
Tolstoy, Nikolay N. (Leo's brother), 169
Tonio Kröger (Mann), 42
Trubetskoy, Pavel, 23, 213n. 31
Tsar Ivan IV with the Body of His Son (Repin), 221n. 11
Tsvetaeva, Marina, 42, 208, 215n. 30
Turgenev, Ivan, 30, 115, 209
Tyutchev, Fyodor, 47–48, 216n. 58

"Über Kunst," 218n. 10
Uncle Vanya (Chekhov), 28, 37–38, 213n. 9

Vasnetsov, Apollinary, 217n. 4
Vasnetsov, Viktor, 33–35, 64, 217n. 4; and the Cathedral of Saint Vladimir in Kiev, 64
Vega, Lope de, 135
Veresaj, Ostap Mykytovyč, 120–22

Vie de Jesus, La (Renan), 229n. 10
Vigny, Alfred de, 182, 229n. 16
"Vij" (Gogol), 221n. 10
Vladimir the Great, Prince of Kiev, 88, 116, 221n. 6; Cathedral of, 64
Vogeler, Heinrich, 5, 56
Vogüé, Viscomte Melchior de, 15, 21–22, 224n. 46
Volkonsky, Prince, 209
Volynsky, Akim. *See* Flekser, Akim
Voronin, Helene, 218n. 16
Vrubel, Mikhail, 217n. 4, 231n. 57. Works: *The Dance,* 205–08; *Pan,* 173

War and Peace (Tolstoy), 160
Wedekind, Frank, 212n. 10
Weise von Liebe und Tod des Cornets Christoph Rilke, Die, 32
Weisse Fürstin, Die, 37
Westhoff, Clara (Mrs. Rainer Maria Rilke), 26, 41, 49–50, 177–78, 179
"What Is Art?" (Tolstoy), 160, 218n. 10
White Nights (Dostoevsky), 195
"Wladimir, der Wolkenmaler," 55–56
"Work for the Night Is Coming" (Tolstoy), 162
"Worm, The" (Sologub), 214n. 30
Wunderlich, Eva, 224n. 39
Wyspiański, Stanisław, 102

Yantschevetsky, V., 23, 28, 30, 214n. 16
"Yardstick" (Tolstoy), 160–61, 228n. 25
Yergolskaya, Tatyana Alexandrovna, 168, 169–70, 175, 176

"Znamenskaja. Der Madonnenmaler, Die," 57–58

Patricia Pollock Brodsky is associate professor of German at the University of Missouri, Kansas City. She previously taught at Cleveland State University and California State College, Long Beach. She received her Ph.D. and M.A. degrees from the University of California, Berkeley.

The manuscript was edited by Julia Fitzgerald. The book was designed by Jim Billingsley. The typeface for the text and display type is Times Roman, based on a design by Stanley Morison about 1932. The text is printed on 55-lb. Booktext Natural finish paper, and the book is bound in Holliston Mills' Roxite Linen finish cloth over binder's boards.

Manufactured in the United States of America.